Voyages with John

Voyages with John

Charting the Fourth Gospel

Robert Kysar

Baylor University Press
Waco, Texas

Scripture quotations are from the New Revised Standard Version Bible, © 1989, Division of Christian Education of the National Council of the Churches of Christ in the United States of America. Used by permission. All rights reserved.

Book Design by Diane Smith
Cover Design by Joan Osth

Library of Congress Cataloging-in-Publication Data

Kysar, Robert.
  Voyages with John : charting the Fourth Gospel / Robert Kysar.
    p. cm.
  Includes bibliographical references and index.
  ISBN 1-932792-43-0 (pbk. : alk. paper)
  1. Bible. N.T. John--Criticism, interpretation, etc. I. Title.

  BS2615.52.K97 2006
  226.5'06--dc22

                                2005032261

Printed in the United States of America on acid-free paper

Dedicated to
The Reverend Mr. Donald Sower,
Longtime Friend and Colleague

Contents

Acknowledgments

We gratefully acknowledge the permission to reprint previously published material in this volume. The following include the sources of that permission.

Chapter 1: "Rudolph Bultmann's Interpretation of the Concept of Creation in John 1, 3-4." *Catholic Biblical Quarterly* 32, no. 1 (January 1970): 77–85. Revised from the original publication. Used by permission.

Chapter 2: "The Eschatology of the Fourth Gospel—A Correction of Bultmann's Redactional Hypothesis." *Perspective* 12, no. 1 (Winter 1972): 22–33. Revised from the original publication.

Chapter 3: "Christology and Controversy in the Prologue of the Gospel of John." *Currents in Theology and Mission* 5, no. 6 (1978): 348–64. Published as "Christology and Controversy: The Contributions of the Prologue of the Gospel of John to New Testament Christology and Their Historical Setting." Revised.

Chapter 4: "Pursuing the Paradoxes of Johannine Thought: Conceptual Tensions in John 6. A Redaction-Critical Proposal." Pages 189–206 in *The Living Text: Essays in Honor of Ernest W. Saunders*. Edited by Dennis E. Groh and Robert Jewett. Lanham, Md.: University Press of America, 1985. Revised from the original publication. Used by permission.

Chapters 5, 6, 7, 8: "The Fourth Gospel: A Report on Recent Research." Pages 2389–2480 in *Aufstieg und Niedergang der Römishen Welt: Geschichte und Kultur Roms im Spiegel der neueren Forschung*. Herausgegeben von Hildegard

Temporini und Wolfgang Haase. Part 2, 25.3. Berlin and New York, Walter de Gruyter, 1985. Revised.

Chapter 9: "Anti-Semitism and the Gospel of John." Pages 113–27 in *Anti-Semitism and Early Christianity: Issues of Polemic and Faith.* Edited by Craig A. Evans and Donald A. Hagner. Minneapolis: Augsburg Fortress, 1993. Adapted and used by permission.

Chapter 10: "Johannine Metaphor—Meaning and Function: A Case Study." Pages 81–112 in *The Fourth Gospel from a Literary Perspective.* Edited by R. Alan Culpepper and Fernando F. Segovia. Semeia 53. Atlanta: Society of Biblical Literature, 1991. Revised from the original publication. Used by permission.

Chapter 11: "The Making of Metaphor: Another Reading of John 3:1-15." Pages 161–81 in *"What is John?" Readers and Readings of the Fourth Gospel.* Edited by Fernando F. Segovia. Society of Biblical Literature Symposium Series. Edited by Gail R. O'Day. Atlanta: Scholars Press, 1996. Revised from the original publication. Used by permission.

Chapter 12: "The Dismantling of Decisional Faith: A Reading of John 6:25-71." Pages 161–81 in *Critical Readings of John 6.* Edited by R. Alan Culpepper. Leiden: Brill, 1997.

Chapter 13: "The Gospel of John in the Twenty-first Century." Panel Presentation on "The Gospel of John at the Close of the Twentieth Century" for Johannine Literature Section of Society of Biblical Literature Conference, November 22, 1994. Published as "Coming Hermeneutical Earthquake in Johannine Interpretation." Pages 185–98 in *"What is John?" Readers and Readings of the Fourth Gospel.* Edited by Fernando F. Segovia. Society of Biblical Literature Symposium Series. Edited by Gail R. O'Day. Atlanta: Scholars Press, 1996. Revised from the original publication. Used by permission.

Chapter 14: "The 'Other' in Johannine Literature." Paper presented at the Southeast Region of the Society of Biblical Literature Conference, March 11, 2000. Revised.

Chapter 15: "Expulsion from the Synagogue: The Tale of a Theory." Paper presented for the Johannine Literature Section of Society of Biblical Literature Conference, November 25, 2002. Revised.

Chapter 16: "The Sacraments of Johannine Ambiguity." Paper presented for the Johannine Literature Section of Society of Biblical Literature Conference, November 21, 2004. Revised.

Charting the Voyages:
An Autobiographical Introduction

Looking back over my career as a student/scholar, I realize that I have been on voyages with the Gospel of John for many years. The first voyage was in the years of my theological and graduate education, ranging from my first course on the fourth gospel through the preparation and defense of my dissertation on Bultmann's and Dodd's interpretations of the prologue of the gospel. My voyages with John continued then into my teaching and publishing, focusing more and more on this one gospel.

A perusal of a list of my articles on the Fourth Gospel demonstrates the variety of methods of interpretation I employed over the course of some forty years. In retrospect, however, I can now discern four particular voyages that together constitute my adventures with this gospel. The first journey entails the years when I studied and interpreted John with the tools I received in my education, namely, the historical-critical method. Alongside the historical-critical method was theological criticism, which often used historical techniques to discern the teachings of a biblical document. Then, for reasons I will describe later, I began to study and practice some kinds of the so-called new literary criticism which eventually came to influence the study of John in significant ways. Finally, in the years near and after my retirement in 1999 I became increasingly interested in the challenges to biblical criticism originating in what some call postmodernism. In writing my portion of a book on biblical interpretation (coauthored with Joseph Webb between 2000 and 2004), I discovered the extent to which I was attracted to postmodernist thought (cf. Kysar and Webb, *Postmoderns*). To date, I think, there is too little evidence to speak of a clearly defined "postmodern critical method," so I regard my papers and publications of the last few years as efforts to anticipate what might emerge in the future.

The movement among these types of criticism, however, is not so simple. In each of the four voyages my interest in theology was prominent. From the beginning of my career I had an interest in the search of the beliefs of the early Christian community. One might say that the reason for my use of any of the critical methods was to discern what fundamental convictions were expressed in the New Testament. Therefore, readers will doubtless see in many of the articles gathered here at least an implicit preoccupation with theology. For that reason, the second division of this book is devoted to what we will call "theological criticism." That section comprises one of four pieces devoted to a survey of scholarship in Johannine studies. The theological section, along with the last two articles in the historical-critical section constitute the substance of my survey of Johannine scholars roughly between the years 1960 and 1980. Since a good deal of my scholarly interest has been interpreting contemporary scholarship, it is appropriate that this collection should include samples of those interpretations.

This collection of essays, which represents some of my voyages with John, includes my very first publications on the gospel in 1970 through two previously unpublished papers prepared and read for the Johannine section of the Society of Biblical Literature in 2000–2004. The interpretative methods have gradually changed through the years but in every case they have been applied (almost exclusively) to the Gospel of John.

Moreover, taken together the essays in this collection form maps of the ocean of the human search to understand not only the fourth of the gospels but also the whole of Scripture. My own story of shifts in interpretative methods would not be important except for the fact that the main features of these voyage are characteristic of shifts in biblical interpretation in general in North America and even beyond. It seems worthwhile, therefore, to select a number of my articles from over the years and lay them out in what is roughly a chronological order. That order proves to be the same sequence of the main elements of interpretation in the last half of the twentieth and the first half of the decade of the twenty-first centuries.

The articles I have chosen for inclusion in this collection, therefore, represent the phases of my own understanding of biblical interpretation and of some of the major issues with which Johannine scholars had to deal in the thirty-five years between 1970 and 2005. I invite readers to look both to the content of the articles with regard to Johannine scholarship and to the method of interpretation evidenced in the four divisions of the book: historical, theological, literary, and postmodern. To bind the individual articles into separate itineraries of sorts, I have offered introductions to the four types of methods used. In these introductions I try to describe the setting out of which the essays in the section arise. In large part, these are little more than some historical observations about New Testament interpretation in the years I wrote and first published the articles.

My use of the historical-critical method of biblical interpretation entails saying something personal about my journey in research. These autobiographical notes, I hope, will allow readers to see how the person of the interpreter and her or his method are related. I entered seminary in 1956 in the midst of the spread of neo-orthodox (or neo-reformation) theology in North America. The faculty of my seminary was seriously divided in their assessments of this new movement. There were a good many of my seminary teachers who continued to think in terms of the liberal theology of the beginning of the century. Many of them were trained in that sort of theological thought and were committed to it both in terms of their intellectual stand but also in terms of their personal investments. On the other hand, those who had made the turn (or were in the process of making the turn) toward a more European neo-orthodoxy were for the most part very exciting teachers, because their views were changing even as they continued their courses. Notwithstanding this theological split in my seminary, the biblical courses were still taught from the perspective of a classical liberal historical-critical method. The new theological wave in our nation had little impact on my basic training in biblical studies. You need not bother to read Barth's commentary on Romans, we were told, because *it is not a commentary at all.* I cannot remember any biblical instructor suggesting that a new approach to biblical interpretation came along with the neo-orthodox theology, even though that was clearly evident in Barth's work. By the time I began my Ph.D. work, the atmosphere had changed very little, and the historical-critical methods of interpretation prevailed. My own theological thought, however, was in flux. During my graduate years, I became enthralled with the work of Rudolf Bultmann. Actually, two years as a college chaplain before returning to do my residency for a doctorate had taught me that neo-orthodoxy was not an effective framework within which to do ministry. Early in my Ph.D. work, the philosophy faculty of Northwestern University introduced me to existentialism. Several members of the graduate philosophy department were themselves major contributors to existentialist thought.[1] Existential theology immediately became an attractive and exciting alternative for me, and I was becoming bored with the subdisciplines of biblical historical criticism (most especially, background studies).

I chose to do my dissertation on a comparison of the exegetical methods of C. H. Dodd and Rudolf Bultmann as they are reflected in the work of these two scholarly giants on the prologue of John. The dissertation got me a Ph.D. and a handful of articles, but it was not publishable and in many ways was a clumsy and unwieldy study. Although what it did for me includes at least two things: It focused my interest on methodology, an interest that I have to this day, and demonstrated one way existentialist theology might handle exegesis. Most important, it helped me to understand how an interpreter's own views shape her or his readings of a text.

Yet in my early scholarly efforts I remained committed to the historical-critical methods, as the essays in the first section of this collection show. My first important contribution to Johannine studies, *Fourth Evangelist* was the survey of scholarship on the Fourth Gospel, which I wrote while on a sabbatical leave at Yale University (1973–1974) and published in 1975 by Augsburg Publishing House. For all its weaknesses, that book labeled me a chronicler and critic of scholarly research on John. Most of my early invitations to publish involved reports on scholarly trends and consequently four of the articles in this collection comprise one of my reviews of scholarship.

It may be that my efforts to understand and report on Johannine research planted seeds which were later to sprout in my sharp turn away from the historical-critical methods and toward literary studies. On the other hand, it could be that shift was due simply to my going with the flow among some scholars who were friends as well as colleagues. At first, I did literary studies in conjunction with historical-critical efforts. I was not interested in dumping the whole load of historical-critical methods to devote myself strictly to literary pursuits—or maybe I simply did not have the courage to abandon the investments I had in the older methods. All my books were written primarily from the historical-critical perspective, and I only slowly began to publish articles on the newer methodology (see part 3 of this collection). My earliest attempt at a kind of narrative criticism in *John's Story of Jesus* (1984) was only partially successful (even though it remained in print until 2003). I later chose to issue a revised edition of *John, the Maverick Gospel* (1993) in large part because I wanted to strengthen the literary content of the book without entirely abandoning the substance of the historical criticism of the first edition.

In only the past decade have I become increasingly suspicious of the historical-critical enterprise. I began to realize how fragile our historical reconstructions are and yet how they often become elevated in our discipline as in some way "proven." My efforts to understand some of the more recent research intensified my uneasiness with the prevailing historical-critical research. My first venture into this rather vague field (which was really a kind of ideological criticism) involved a study of the "other" in Johannine thought, first done for a regional meeting of the Society for Biblical Literature and which is included in this volume in a revised form.

Nevertheless the papers I prepared for the 2002 annual meeting of the Society for Biblical Literature and a conference honoring Raymond E. Brown (2003) are what defined my new position. A consultation group of the society asked me to present a survey about how Johannine research reflected the Fourth Gospel's representation of the historical Jesus. Much to the dismay of some of the leaders of the consultation (all personal friends of mine), in that paper I again and again concluded that our historical inquiries got us nowhere in trying to find clues of an early Christian tradition in the Fourth Gospel. In another paper for the Johannine section of the society that same year, I chose to trace what seems to me to be the gradually increasing doubt about the theory that the Johannine Christians were expelled from the Jewish synagogue and that this experience shaped much of the gospel (in part 4 of this volume, "The Expulsion from the Synagogue: The Tale of a Theory"). Needless to say, my "tale" of this theory did not please the established scholarly circles of the society. Later for a conference honoring Raymond Brown, the conference organizers asked me to do something on the concept of the Johannine community. My discussion of "The Whence and the Whither of the Johannine Community" criticized the whole scholarly process behind the supposition of such a community. On that occasion, I fully realized that I had stepped into a new and controversial phase in my scholarship.

Having traced the movement in my methodological commitments over the past forty years or so, I need to point out that all of these voyages with John have been efforts to serve the church. After all, the development of my biblical studies career began in seminary and was a result of my intention to become a parish pastor. Consequently, my scholarly efforts were and are always a part of my commitment to the interpretation of the Bible for the church. Without the assumption that I was in some way enriching the use of the Bible by Christians, I would never have had the motivation for what has turned out to be my scholarly career. In some of my publications that Christian commitment is clearer than in others, but in every case it is important to what I have tried to do. I intended even those articles which are critical of the church and its teachings (e.g., "The 'Other' in Johannine Literature" in part 4 of this book) to enrich the lives of Christians. Moreover, I have become increasingly worried by the standard and "official" interpretative methods employed within the church for the sake of doctrine and ethics.

This collection of articles brings me up to the place I now stand in the voyage into the future with the Gospel of John. At seventy-plus years of age, I doubt that I will make many more contributions to the story of Johannine scholarship in this new century, even though I am not yet quite ready to throw in the towel. Whatever I may do in the next years, I am honored to have been a part of a community of scholars devoted to the study of the Gospel of John. My efforts to chart the voyages of Johannine scholarship reflect a long and somewhat meandering trek, but it has held many satisfactions along the way.

None of the articles gathered here holds the magic key to the ever-puzzling Fourth Gospel, but each is an honest attempt to shed some light—however dim—on that document. I hope, therefore, that they will contribute in a helpful way to the readers' own voyages with biblical material.

PART I

Historical Criticism

The historical-critical method of interpretation dominated biblical studies through the nineteenth and most of the twentieth centuries. While these critical approaches began to be questioned in Europe after World War I, in North America their dominance was well entrenched until the middle of the twentieth century. Since then, however, an increasing number of biblical scholars have grown skeptical of some of the assumptions of historical methods and sought either to strengthen or replace them.

What all of the historical-critical methods have in common is that they depend almost exclusively on the assumption that the meaning of any passage can be discerned only by understanding the historical context and reference of the passage. Historical critics usually contend that the "true meaning" of any biblical passage is the one the author intended in its composition. Therefore, the task of historical critics is to get "behind" the text to its origin or to see "through" the text to the matters to which it refers. History plays a key role, then, because meaning is always historically shaped and determined by the text's origin. From this basic assumption grew an abundance of more specialized critical endeavors that have profoundly enriched biblical studies.

The articles included in part 1 are all efforts to discover something about the meaning of the Gospel of John by probes into what lies behind it. In the first essay, Rudolf Bultmann is the central figure: "Rudolf Bultmann's Interpretation of the Concept of Creation in John 1." Bultmann figures prominently in these early essays in this collection because

throughout the 1970s in North America critics were struggling with the
influential German New Testament scholar and theologian. They were in
many cases trying either to move behind his work or "around it." What
is most valuable, I believe, in this first article is Bultmann's view of the
importance of self-understanding in theology and biblical interpretation. My analysis of his interpretation seeks to show how certain of the
interpreter's theological and philosophical presuppositions influence the
way he reads John 1:3-4 and calls into question the possibility of "neutral" or "purely scientific" interpretation. Furthermore, Bultmann insists
that when we read and interpret a text we are at the same time reading
and interpreting ourselves. With that view, he anticipates some of what
emerged after him in literary investigations and lays a foundation of some
of the themes even in postmodern thought. Today I would call some of
what I say in this article "ideological criticism," a contemporary movement in biblical investigation (cf. Yee, and the article, "The 'Other' in
Johannine Literature," in part 4 of this collection). This article on Bultmann was originally a part of my dissertation, so that its essential content
goes back as far as the 1960s. As I reread samples of my early work, I realized that my suspicion of historical inquiry was present even in the years
I wrote my dissertation.

Historical criticism was concerned to discover the original setting and
meaning of a text but also to reconstruct (insofar as possible) the development of the document itself through the history of its transmission.
Hence, the historical method gave birth to source and redaction criticism
as efforts to understand how biblical documents evolved. The second essay
in this section examines how Bultmann sought to understand Johannine
eschatology by reference to the document's peculiar history. "The Eschatology of the Fourth Gospel" reviews the issues in the eschatology of the
Fourth Gospel and Bultmann's proposed solution to those issues, as well
as my counter proposal. It is linked with the fourth of the articles in the
section that also deals with anomalies in the Johannine text—in this case
its paradoxes.

"Christology and Controversy in the Prologue of the Gospel of John"
is of a similar kind with the exception that the focus shifts to views of
Christ expressed in the prologue and from them proposes a historical
setting for the passage, namely, controversy between Jewish and Christian
communities. While the investigation of the background of the prologue
might be the basis on which its christological statements are understood,
the third essay begins with what the passage teaches about Christ and
then draws some conclusions about its concrete setting in life. It is a good
example of how the reconstruction of the setting for the gospel contrib-

utes to its interpretation. Moreover, in this discussion the role of comparison of theological ideas in the Fourth Gospel and other New Testament
documents is important.

The fourth chapter returns to Bultmann and the supposed editing
of the gospel document early in its history. "Pursuing the Paradoxes of
Johannine Thought" is an effort to understand the tension between what
we often call the present and the future eschatologies expressed in John
6. Bultmann claimed that the Fourth Evangelist "demythologized" early
futurist eschatology to formulate the emphasis on the presence of eschatological phenomena in the Christian's life. That is, Bultmann proposed
that the Fourth Evangelist stripped the idea of God's promises for the
future of their formulation in what seems to have been apocalyptic con-
ceptuality. My argument is that the difference between apparently contradictory ideas in the gospel's view of eschatology are deliberate and part of
the evangelist's understanding of the Christian hope for both the present
and the future. The proposed tension became the taproot for what I would
later call the ambiguity of the Fourth Gospel. (See "The Sacraments and
Johannine Ambiguity" in part 4.) At this stage, however, contradictions
in a document often constituted one kind of evidence for postulating the
evangelist's incorporation of a source whose ideas were not consistent
with those that came from the evangelist.

The last two essays of this section are portions of a review of current
scholarship published in 1985. "Literary Probes in the Gospel of John"
and "Historical Puzzles in John" explore what scholars were saying in the
effort to resolve some of the difficulties of the Gospel of John. The first
of these does not deal with the literary criticism that emerged later and is
the topic of the third section. Rather it explores how scholars sought new
ways of dealing with the text to reveal its historical condition.

Our first voyage will keep us thinking about historical circumstances
and the needs of the community responsible for this enigmatic gospel.

Chapter One

The Concept of Creation in John 1

Heinrich Ott has written, "Understanding . . . is a function of [humans] in the wholeness of [their] existence; it extends to the whole of the human situation" ("Language and Understanding," 132). Biblical interpretation has not always grasped and articulated with sufficient clarity the fact that exegetical understanding is a function of the exegete in the wholeness of her or his existence. Exegesis has too often been set in isolation from the larger framework of the exegete's self-understanding in general, or more specifically his or her theological and philosophical postures. This isolation resulted in what often has been shallowness in the discipline. It is to the credit of Rudolf Bultmann that he awakened the theological world as a whole and biblical interpretation in specific to the problem of preunderstanding and its function in the hermeneutical task (Bultmann, *Existence* 289–96).

The purpose of this paper is to attempt a simple demonstration of the manner in which an interpretation of a passage reflects and relies upon the larger realm of the understanding of the exegete. More specifically, this paper is an effort to illumine the manner in which Bultmann's theological motifs have shaped his interpretation of John 1:3-4. I will endeavor to penetrate what might be called the "logic" of Bultmann's exegetical method so as to see more clearly precisely how his theological understandings are operative in determining his interpretation. I suggest that one may see in Bultmann the influence of theological presuppositions upon biblical interpretation and therefore the inescapable unity of exegesis and theology. My procedure will be, first, to summarize briefly what Bultmann has to say about John 1:3-4 and in particular his interpretation of the concept of creation in those verses. Second, I will attempt an analysis of Bultmann's exegesis in light of the theological motifs which have most obviously influenced his interpretation. Finally, the paper attempts to draw some general conclusions from this study of an exegete's method.

A Summary of Bultmann's Interpretation of the Concept of Creation in John 1:3-4

In his commentary on John, Bultmann argues that we should not understand the prologue to the gospel as theological or cosmological speculation. The concern of the prologue as a whole, he argues, is with the experience of revelation; it is a liturgical hymn, which articulates the experience of the Christian community with its Lord. It arises then not out of philosophical or even theological reflection but out of the self-understanding of the worshiping community.

Bultmann believes that the evangelist's use of *egeneto* ("came into being") in verse 3 is intended to exclude any speculation about the origin of the world. What the evangelist seeks to affirm, Bultmann says, is the self-understanding of the worshiper, which is the human's proper being. What is said of creation in 1:3-4 bears upon an individual's proper self-understanding; it has to do with the reader's proper sense of creatureliness. Hence, it is liturgical and confessional in nature rather than speculative.

Still, Bultmann asserts verse 3 affirms a concept of *creatio ex nihilo* ("creation out of nothing"), and he points out that this doctrine is also found in the Fourth Gospel at 17:24 in the expression *katabolēs zōē kosmou* ("the foundation of the world"). In interpreting John 1:3 Bultmann emphasizes its liturgical and nonspeculative meaning and at the same time insists that the verse teaches *creatio ex nihilo* (*Gospel* 37–38).[1]

Verse 3 affirms, moreover, that in the role of the logos in creation no separation of the logos and God is implied. Hence there is a unity here of creation and revelation: "The world is God's creation and as such God's revelation" (*Gospel* 20; cf. Brown, *Commentary–Gospel* 1:25).

Bultmann thinks verse 4a is a statement of the continuous creative process under the power of the logos *ho genonen en autō zōē ēn* ("that which came into being was life"). "The life of the whole of creation has its origin in the logos." The punctuation of 3b-4a does not change the point of the passage: that which is created does not have its life from itself but has it bestowed. So the logos, Bultmann maintains, is *zōē* ("life") in that logos is the life-giving power and has life in the sense that he "makes alive" (*lebendig macht*). That this is the meaning of Christ as *zōē* ("life") is evident from the affirmation of the gospel as a whole, e.g. 5:21, 26; 6:33; 10:28 (*Gospel* 21).[2]

Since the logos is *zōē* ("life"), he/she can be *phōs* ("light"). That the logos is Creator (making alive) allows that the logos be Revealer as well. Creation is preparation for redemption. *Phōs* ("light") is that which makes clear and gives the possibility of seeing. However, "to see" is to understand oneself properly in the world. So the *phōs* ("light") is

> the brightness in which I can find myself and find my way about and in which I have no anxiety and am not at my "wit's end." The brightness therefore is not an external phenomenon, but it is the illumination of being (*Erhelltsein des Daseins*). (*Gospel* 22)[3]

If the logos is the light of humanity, one may suppose that there is the possibility of enlightened existence given in the very origin of life; that is, one is given the possibility of salvation. So creation is revelation, since that which is created has been given the possibility of knowing its Creator, and hence knowing itself.[4] What is disclosed in the saving revelation is the human's proper self-understanding in the light of creation. Humanity's authenticity involves the knowledge of their creatureliness and the demands of the Creator. Still, Bultmann is careful to say that this content of revelation is neither a theory of creation nor a feeling of creatureliness (*a la* Schleiermacher) but an existential self-understanding (*existentielles Selbstverständnis*) (*Gospel* 44).[5] As a consequence of all of this, Bultmann can say that the coming of the logos as the light of the world means that Jesus gives the world the "realized possibility" latent within creation. "The saving revelation restores the lost possibility of the revelation in creation" (*Gospel* 26).

Theological Motifs in Bultmann's Interpretation of John 1:3-4

The logic of Bultmann's interpretation of these verses is only evident after one has recognized the role played by four of his theological presuppositions: 1) the anthropocentric understanding of all Christian doctrine, 2) the theme of human dependence, 3) the unity of the concepts of creation and redemption in Christian thought, and 4) the character of natural revelation as self-understanding. I will attempt to demonstrate how each of these is operative in Bultmann's exegetical method.

Bultmann's theological method is notably characterized by its *anthropocentric feature*. He has affirmed that Christian theology is always to be understood in terms of what doctrine says about humans. His famous declaration of the anthropocentric nature of Christian theology is found in the "Preliminary Remarks" to his exposition of Pauline theology: "Every assertion about God is, simultaneously, an assertion about [humanity] and vice versa. For this reason and in this sense Paul's theology is, at the same time, anthropology" (*Theology* 1:191). On this basis, he declares that one cannot speak of God except as one speaks of God's relation to humans (*Jesus* 69). Therefore what we might know about God is primarily what we know about ourselves and our finitude (*Essays* 98).[6]

Pursuant of this anthropocentric method, Bultmann has undertaken to interpret the Christian doctrine of creation as a statement about humanity. The doctrine is not a theory about the past, he says, but speaks of humanity's present situation. "It grows out of the wonder at the riddle of the world that encompasses [humans] as the uncanny." Therefore, the purpose of the doctrine of creation is not to understand humanity in terms of the world about us, but to comprehend the world in terms of our fundamental concerns. "[F]aith in creation is the expression of a specific understanding of human existence" (*Existence* 175–76; cf. *Theology* 1:227–28).

Still another theological motif betrayed in Bultmann's exegesis of John 1:3-4 is that of *humanity's utter dependence upon God*. If there is any one theme that finds continual expression in Bultmann's thought, it is the theme of our dependence upon God. The radical reliance upon God for human existence is explicated by Bultmann's use of the concept of "nothingness." "[W]e are suspended in nothing," he writes, and "to be God's creature means to be constantly encompassed and threatened by nothingness." The concept of creation is humanity's recognition that except for the creative will of God, we fall back into the nothingness from which God has created us (*Existence* 175–76). Our existence is unconditionally derived from God's free creative will. For Bultmann that utter dependence is the very core of the Christian affirmation concerning creation.

The same theme of the utter dependence of humanity is very much evident in Bultmann's exposition of the doctrine of Christian redemption. Correlated with human dependence upon God in creation is the conviction that salvation means, above all else, our final and unreserved surrender to God. The end of humanity's ill-founded efforts to be independent and our acceptance of dependence upon the grace of God in Christ is, for Bultmann, the essence of Pauline soteriology (*Theology* 1:134–46; *Existence* 80–83 and 149–57; cf. *Theology* 1:228–29).[7]

It is, therefore, abundantly clear that a pervasive motif of human dependence upon the divine runs throughout Bultmann's theology. Along with the theme of anthropocentricity, that motif is very much evident in the Bultmannian interpretation of John 1:3-4. The references in the passage to creation are read essentially as references to humanity's self-understanding in the world (i.e., anthropocentrically), and those references are understood to mean humanity's primordial dependence upon God for existence. So it seems evident just how Bultmann's interpretation of this Johannine passage is premised upon his strongest theological commitments.

Bultmann's allegation that John 1:3 expresses a Johannine affirmation of *creatio ex nihilo* is a striking illustration of the further influence of his theology upon his exegesis. That Bultmann should find this traditional doctrine of creation in verse 3 at all is remarkable. No less remarkable is his assertion that *creatio ex nihilo* is the meaning of the expression *kataboles kosmou* ("the foundation of the world") at John 17:24 (*Gospel* 38). On the surface, creation out of absolute nothingness would seem to be rather far removed from the meaning of either John 1:3 or 17:24. Moreover, *creatio ex nihilo* would seem to be speculation of the kind Bultmann would seek to avoid. How is it that he is able to claim that such a doctrine is referred to in John 1:3?

Bultmann's exegesis surely betrays again his theological predispositions. Actually, that he is able to find *creatio ex nihilo* in 1:3 and 17:24 is directly the result again of the two theological motifs mentioned above, namely, an anthropocentric interpretation of doctrine and an emphasis upon the theme of human dependence. Combined here with these two motifs is still another theological tendency in the Bultmannian system, namely, his inclination to emphasize *the unity of the doctrines of creation and redemption*. We must now consider how these three theological presuppositions combined to account for his interpretation of 1:3 and 17:24.

In the essay entitled, "Faith in God the Creator," Bultmann discusses the doctrine of creation from nothing as an existential appraisal of the human situation.

> God's creation is a creation out of nothing; and to be God's creature means absolutely and in every present to have one's source in [God], in such a way that were [God] to withhold [the] creative will the creature would fall back into nothing. . . . We understand the world as God's creation only when we know about this nothingness that encompasses every created thing. (*Existence* 175)

Here *creatio ex nihilo* is not a speculative doctrine of the origin of the world but a statement of the total reliance of all humans upon God for their very being. In other words, the traditional doctrine is interpreted anthropocentrically and in terms of a radical understanding of human dependence. Bultmann's article then goes on to explore the relation of Christology to faith in God as Creator. He suggests that *creatio ex nihilo* has its equivalent in Christian redemption.

16

To have faith in the cross of Christ means to be prepared to let God work as the Creator. God *creates out of nothing, and whoever becomes nothing before [God] is made alive.* Whenever the cross really leads me to the knowledge of my own nothingness and to the confession of my sin, I am open for God's rule as the Creator who forgives me my sin and takes from me nothingness, death. (*Existence* 181; italics mine)

The link between creation and redemption is just at the point of humanity's utter dependence!

Here, then, are the ingredients which have led Bultmann to read *creatio ex nihilo* out of John 1:3 and *kataboles kosmou* ("the foundation of the world") in 17:24. He has given the traditional doctrine a new existential interpretation in terms of the central motifs of his own theological thought. He has read John 1:3 in terms of his concern for our radical dependence upon God. He was able, next, to assert that the doctrine which most vividly expresses that dependence in creation, namely, *creatio ex nihilo*, is present in the meaning of the text. Hence behind the simple flat assertion that the creation thought in John 1:3 is *creatio ex nihilo* lies a distinctive and complex method of interpretation.

Bultmann's explication of *creatio ex nihilo* has introduced still another feature of his theological thought which has had significant influence upon his exegesis of John 1:3-4. Bultmann's interpretation of these two verses of the prologue clearly affirms that *creation and redemption are an inseparable unity* in Christian thought. Moreover, his understanding of the words *zōē* ("life") and *phōs* ("light") pivots around the unity of Christ's creative and redemptive work (*Gospel* 38, 43-45). I contend that Bultmann's interpretation is seriously shaped by the radical significance he attaches to the continuity between creation and redemption.

This continuity is important to the whole theological system proposed by Bultmann. It appears that the Heideggerian concepts of authenticity and inauthenticity were instrumental in Bultmann's development of the doctrine of creation. If he were to adopt the concepts of authentic-inauthentic into the Christian framework, it meant that he had to stress anew a concept of creation which made possible both of these modes of existence (Heidegger, *Being* 312-13).[8] Authentic and inauthentic existence logically imply an original intention or direction for existence, i.e., the essence of authentic life. In Christian thought that original intention is a part of the doctrine of creation. Bultmann's theological thought, therefore, necessitates a strong doctrine of creation which sets the stage for redemption, or to use Bultmannian language, makes authenticity possible. Redemption, then, makes actual what has been possible in creation.

It is understandable, therefore, that the German exegete should find in the prologue of John an affirmation of the radical unity of creation and redemption. A clear continuity must be affirmed, if Christian thought, as Bultmann conceives it, is to hold together in any cogent manner.

The suggestion that creation and redemption are a single revelation leads us to a final consideration of Bultmann's theological orientation. In his exposition of John 1:3-4 he stresses that in creation there is a revelation essential to our proper self-understanding. This statement is typical of his exegesis: "Creation is at the same time revelation, inasmuch as it was possible for the creature to know of [the] Creator, and thus to understand [her or] himself " (*Gospel* 44). Furthermore, Bultmann's interpretation of the logos as *zōē* ("life") and *phōs* ("light") takes for granted the revelation inherent in creation.

Bultmann's insistence upon a *legitimate "natural revelation"* persists in his theological writings. However, it is shaped by the two controlling motifs of his theology, which have been discussed here, namely, the emphasis upon anthropocentricity and the utter dependence of humanity as creatures. Natural revelation is not a means of comprehending God through the natural process, but of correctly comprehending humanity as a creature and of honoring God (*Existence* 83). The revelation inherent in creation is a thoroughly "negative" revelation, which informs us humans of our decisive limitations and our inescapable dependence. When nature and history are combined, they shatter all human ambitions and self-assurance (*Existence* 118). Consequently, this natural revelation refers us away from self-reliance to a dependence upon the forgiving grace of God in Christ. Viewed from the perspective of God's act in Christ, nature and general history are illuminated as God's revelation of human limitation. So Bultmann denies that there is anything like a "natural theology" which serves as a foundation for Christian theology (*Faith and Understanding* 313–31). He is able, first, to assert that there is revelation in creation and at the same time preserve the uniqueness of the Christian revelation and, second, to affirm that the revelation in Christ is the key to the revelation in creation. Again, he emphasizes the unity of revelation.

Bultmann's theological stance with regard to the matter of revelation in creation clearly affects his interpretation of John 1:3-4. Since he can affirm a "natural revelation," he has no hesitancy about interpreting the creative work of the logos as revelation. Both in creative and redemptive functions logos is revelation. Bultmann, however, seriously qualifies the nature of that revelation with the other dominant theological themes of his thought.

To summarize, Bultmann's interpretation of the concept of creation in the passage under consideration is most obviously a reflection of at least these four theological motifs which seem to function as presuppositions for his exegesis: 1) his anthropocentric posture, 2) his emphasis upon the theme of human dependence, 3) his radical affirmation of the unity of creation and redemption, and 4) his view of natural revelation.

Some General Conclusions

If the exposition of Bultmann's interpretation of the concept of creation in John 1:3-4 has succeeded in laying bare the internal logic of his exegetical method, then it would appear that we are safe in venturing two conclusions:

First, the interpreter of a text is a major contributor to the total hermeneutical task. If Bultmann's theological presuppositions are instrumental in controlling his interpretation of the text, then it seems clear that the text and the interpreter are equal constituents of the hermeneutical procedure. We exegetes bring to our task a "framework of meaning" or a "complex of categories" which includes among other things our own theological presuppositions and preferences (cf. Kysar and Webb, *Postmoderns*, ch. 6). The meaning we assign to a passage is the result of our effort to understand the words of the text in terms of our own world of meaning. It is then impossible for us to understand a text without contributing our own theological presuppositions to that understanding (cf. e.g., Heidegger, *Being* 312–13).

This means that interpreters cannot in any way "neutralize" their own interests and commitments for the sake of "objective" exegesis. To insist upon this would be to deny exegetes their humanity; it would be asking us to function not as humans but as machines. The answer is not that interpreters should lay aside their presuppositions, commitments, and preferences, but rather that they should understand them. When we understand them, we are then in a better position to define their impact upon how we read a text.

The second conclusion suggested by this study is, therefore, that exegetical method must become more self-critical. In the fullest self-consciousness, we exegetes need to examine our own method in terms of its presuppositions. Insofar as exegesis may ever become a disciplined "science" (and, perhaps, the term is not appropriate at all), it must be radically self-critical. To do exegesis means, in addition to the interpretative task itself, to do preliminary and periodic analysis of our methods. Only when we are fully aware of our exegetical methods, their presuppositions and internal logic, are we capable of anything approaching faithful interpretation of the text.

Chapter Two

The Eschatology of the Fourth Gospel

The long-awaited publication of the English translation of Rudolf Bultmann's monumental commentary on the Fourth Gospel, *Das Evangelium
des Johannes*, in 1970 occasioned a revival of the discussion of some of the
important contributions of that commentary to the field of Johannine
theology. Not least among these contributions was Bultmann's rather radical proposal regarding the eschatology of the Fourth Gospel. The present
study proposes to review that proposal and then offer a revision of what
otherwise seems a viable reading of the gospel. In brief, I will defend the
thesis that, while Bultmann correctly understood the Fourth Evangelist
as one of the first and most radical of the demythologizers, he misunder-
stood the nature of the demythologization process which the primitive
Christian tradition underwent at the hands of the evangelist.

A Brief Review of the Problem of Johannine Eschatology and Bultmann's Proposed Solution

The discussion need not be detained by a lengthy review of the problem
posed by Johannine eschatology itself, for that problem is generally understood as one of the several difficulties the interpreter of John must face.
Suffice it to say here, the problem of Johannine eschatology consists of
the presence and even the juxtaposition of passages which express, on
the one hand, some of the primitive eschatology and, on the other hand,
clear declarations of present and immediate eschatological phenomena.
Whereas the eschatological judgment can be spoken of as occurring in
the immediate encounter of humans with the logos (e.g., 3:19 and 9:39),

a judgment in the future—at *to eschatē hēmera* ("the last day")—is promised elsewhere in the gospel (12:48). "Eternal life" is an immediate experience of the believer (3:36; 5:24; and 8:51 for instance) and a future hope (12:25). The same is true for resurrection (5:21, 24, and 26 as opposed to 6:39-40, 44, and 54). Other of the apocalyptic events appear to be part of the believer's immediate present (e.g., the defeat of "the ruler of this age," 12:31), while still others continue to maintain their futuristic quality (e.g., the parousia in 14:3, 18, and 28 and the messianic tribulations discussed in chapters 15 and 16).[1]

Obviously, the most immediate solution to this problem would seem to be that the evangelist purposely intended the statement of the present and future characters of eschatology in a kind of paradoxical manner, and there are many who would maintain that this is precisely the case.[2] Bultmann, however, proposed a radically different solution which has now become the context for any consideration of the eschatology of John. His contention is that only the passages which express the presence of the eschaton are representative of the mind of the evangelist.

For our purposes, Bultmann's position can be summarized in three of his conclusions regarding the Fourth Gospel and its theology. First, he believes the gospel as it stands is a rather elaborate composite work. It consists, on the one hand, of the work of the evangelist and a number of sources used in the composition of the gospel and, on the other, the result of a process of redaction by a later group(s). Furthermore, the work of the evangelist suffered serious disarrangement which later redactors attempted (without success, Bultmann believes) to correct. Bultmann contends that with his careful application of style and content criticism, he is able for the most part to distinguish the main lines among the three strata of the gospel, namely, the evangelist's sources, the work of the evangelist, and the work of the redactor(s).[3] His method of criticism for the gospel first developed in connection with the similar problem posed by the Johannine epistles and was carefully conceived and applied with the result that Bultmann seems to have absolute confidence in it ("Analyse").[4]

The second major conclusion of his study, insofar as it concerns us, is his view of the evangelist. The author of John was, Bultmann believes, a Jew in all probability, but not one who came out of an orthodox stream of Judaism. To the contrary, the evangelist embraced a gnosticized brand of Judaism (*Theology* 2:13). More important, the evangelist proved to be the first who radically undertook the task of demythologizing the primitive Christian tradition.[5] Where Paul began this process somewhat modestly, the Fourth Evangelist thoroughly reread the tradition, particularly at the point of its eschatological beliefs (*Christ and Mythology* 32–34).

The historizing of eschatology already introduced by Paul is radically carried through by John in his understanding of *krisis* and *krima* as both having the double sense "judgment" and "sunderance." The judgment takes place in the fact that upon the encounter with Jesus the sunderance between faith and unfaith, between the sighted and the blind, is accomplished (3:19; 9:39) (*Theology* 2:38).

Consequently, the eschatological passages in the present gospel which originated from the hand of the evangelist are those which express an "existential eschatology," i.e., the eschatological themes understood in terms of the immediate present of the person of faith. Myth, and no less eschatological myth, when interpreted existentially, "speaks of the power or the powers which [a human] supposes he [or she] experiences as the ground and limit of [her or] his world and of his [or her] own activity and suffering" (*New Testament and Mythology* 10). The eschatology of the Fourth Gospel is, then, a "historical" eschatology in which the eschatological event is the encounter of a person with the Christ-event in the proclamation of the church, and all the primitive apocalyptic eschatology (i.e., the mythology) of the Christian tradition has been abandoned (*Christ and Mythology* 81–83).[6]

Finally, Bultmann concluded that the redactor(s) was an early second century Christian most concerned with restoring an orthodox flavor to the gospel, which would make it palatable to the church of his day. The "ecclesiastical redactor" went about making additions to the gospel which fall into five categories:

> (1) the sacramental, (2) the futuristic eschatological, (3) those which attempt at some point to harmonize the gospel with synoptic tradition, (4) those which lay claim to apostolic and eyewitness authority for the evangelist and therefore for [the] gospel, (5) and a miscellaneous group which are assigned to the redactor for a variety of textual and theological reasons. (D. M. Smith, *Composition* 214–15)

The additions of the second type—the futuristic eschatological—succeeded in restoring to the gospel an eschatological message which speaks both of the present fulfilled phenomena associated with the "last day" as well as future and yet unfulfilled themes. Bultmann contends the original evangelist never intended this futuristic dimension, and its presence in the gospel can only be regarded as the unfortunate intrusion of a primitive mythology in an otherwise far more sophisticated, demythologized message.

A Proposed Corrective to Bultmann's Hypothesis

It seems Bultmann has not taken seriously enough his own proposal that the evangelist was a demythologizer of the older Christian eschatological tradition. What the master Marburger himself finally does with his observation that John was one of the first radical demythologizers of the Christian tradition is to suggest that the evangelist *eliminated* from the gospel all the mythological eschatology in preference to an existential, present eschatology. It seems to me that Bultmann has failed to apply his own understanding of the method of demythologizing to the evangelist, for he claims in his programmatic essay on demythologizing "whereas the older liberals used criticism to *eliminate* the mythology of the New Testament, our task to-day is to use criticism to interpret it" (*New Testament and Mythology* 2). It appears that Bultmann has really understood the evangelist as an *eliminator* rather than an *interpreter* of myth.

The difference can be illustrated by looking further at the description of Bultmann's demythologizing hermeneutic and his applications of it. In his original essay, "The New Testament and Mythology," he proposes that the crucifixion-resurrection is a mythic account which carries kerygmatic meaning. "[M]ythological language is only a medium for conveying the significance of the historical (*historisch*) event." (*New Testament and Mythology* 37). According to Bultmann, the New Testament demythologizers (Paul and John) do not eliminate the mythological language of crucifixion-resurrection, but rather they utilize it for their purposes of proclamation (*Theology*, e.g., 1:292–306). Moreover, a cursory examination of Bultmann's own sermons will intimate that he himself, as a preacher, has not tried to eliminate myth but retain and interpret it (*Word and Beyond*). Yet in spite of this professed and even applied method, he insists that the Fourth Evangelist thoroughly purged the tradition of the mythological eschatology. Bultmann is found here, I believe, in a serious contradiction.

Yet what of the stylistic differences by which he claims we can distinguish the alleged work of the redactor(s) from that of the original evangelist? Even if one were to grant (as I believe I would, at least tentatively) that there are stylistic characteristics found uniquely in those passages which Bultmann attributes to the redactor(s),[7] the redaction hypothesis is not the only alternative by which to account for those stylistic differences. Those variations may be explained by the simple fact that the evangelist has utilized the language and style of the Christian tradition passed on to the "Johannine" community alongside the community's own style and language. As Bultmann has utilized style criticism to isolate what he believes to be the sources at the disposal of the evangelist (*Gospel*, passim), one could argue that the style of the alleged redactional passages isolates them only as one portion of pre-Johannine tradition. In other words, this distinctive style Bultmann believes he has isolated does not necessitate the conclusion that the passages are later than the evangelist.

Nor does Bultmann's content criticism necessitate a redaction hypothesis. It is obvious that the eschatological passages assigned to the redactor have precedent in a pre-Johannine Christian tradition. It is less easily shown that the same is true of the rest of the passages Bultmann assigns to the ecclesiastical redactor—especially the sacramental passages; however, it is nonetheless defensible (W. F. Howard, 143–59). Moreover, I do not find it convincing to argue that, when taken as a whole, these allegedly redactional passages constitute a point of view far too ecclesiastical for any but the post-Johannine church.

I propose that the evangelist may have been in immediate contact with a form of Christian tradition that was similar to the oral tradition utilized by the Synoptic Gospels, and that that tradition had a content and style distinctively enough its own. When placed alongside the evangelist's work, the difference is vaguely discernible (but not nearly as clear as Bultmann finds it). It is, of course, also implicit in this argument that the evangelist made use of that tradition in a sometimes exact form. That this may be true has been, I believe, increasingly demonstrated by studies done on the relationship between the Fourth Gospel and the synoptic tradition. Most notable of these studies is the careful and exhaustive work of C. H. Dodd published in *Historical Tradition*. Dodd's work demonstrates to a high degree of satisfaction that behind the Fourth Gospel there lies an ancient oral tradition which by means of form criticism can be distinguished in its general outline. Dodd's concern to demonstrate further that this pre-Johannine tradition merits "serious consideration as a contribution to *our knowledge of the historical facts concerning Jesus Christ*" (243) seems an unnecessary and unwarranted intrusion into his study. (Cf. Teeple, "Oral Tradition," esp. 59–61.) Still, his basic project to illuminate the tradition that John used seems successful and continues to stimulate study. Dodd's project has received considerable support in its general thrust from a number of other sources[8] until it is safe to venture the conclusion that such a tradition did indeed contribute to the formation of the gospel in spite of the widely and correctly held insistence that John did not know or utilize the Synoptic Gospels themselves.[9]

The general understanding of the gospel offered here is supported by some of the recent ventures into the application of form criticism of the Fourth Gospel, especially the work of J. Louis Martyn. Martyn has argued that John is an intricate blending of the historical tradition (which he calls *einmalig*) and commentary on the situation of the Christian missionary in the evangelist's own time. The latter, Martyn suggests, is particularly concerned with the dialogue between a Christian church and a synagogue. The result is a "two-level" drama. Martyn specifically proposes that Johannine eschatology is then primarily the effort to make the traditional Jesus speak to the evangelist's present situation (*History and Theology* 139, and passim).[10] It is the contention of the present argument that John's eschatology has this double level characteristic and that the two levels consist of the primitive Christian eschatology in its unadulterated mythical form, on the one hand, and the demythologized, existential eschatology, on the other. This dual character can be explained in view of the effort of the evangelist to interpret the mythology of the tradition for the sake of the task of the contemporaneous missionaries.

That the evangelist willfully left myth and existential meaning side by side in what I believe to be good demythologizing method is suggested by the proximity of the two kinds of passages in the gospel. Examples of the close proximity include the following: (1) On the subject of judgment, 12:31 and 12:47 both speak of the judgment that is taking place in the immediate encounter with Jesus, but 12:48 declares, "on the last day the word that I have spoken will serve as judge." (2) On the subject of resurrection, 5:24 declares the believer "has passed from death to life," but only a few verses later we find the assurance that the "hour is coming" when the resurrection will occur (5:28-29). Or again on the theme of resurrection, in the midst of the affirmation of the traditional apocalyptic resurrection in 6:39-46 (in which the refrain *anastēsō auto en tē eschatē hēmera* ["I will raise him on the last day"] appears no less than four times) comes the word of Jesus, "Very truly, I tell you, whoever believes *has* eternal life" (6:47).

Now Bultmann would understand this proximity as evidence of the work of the redactor(s). The redactor has, Bultmann would argue, inserted emendations precisely at those points at which the evangelist's present eschatology has been most clearly expressed. It is my proposal that the proximity suggests the manner in which the mythical statement and its interpretation are placed side by side. Moreover, the proximity of the passages suggests the teaching technique of the evangelist. Readers will come to understand the mythical, apocalyptic themes in this immediate and existential manner. Consequently, we have what appears to be either contradictory or paradoxical allusions to the eschatological phenomena.[11]

Conclusion

What then is the character of the Johannine eschatology? This study affirms that Bultmann's theological interpretation (although not his literary-historical judgments) of the gospel is essentially correct. The evangelist seems to have undertaken an interpretation of the primitive Christian eschatology in the direction of what—for the lack of better terminology—has been called "existential eschatology." That is, the evangelist appears generally to have demythologized the primitive eschatology, which means that the author detemporalized it. The hope which was inherent in the futuristic eschatology of the primitive church became understood as a hope which was realizable in the present, in one's encounter with the kerygmatic Christ. The future was made present, and the present became impregnated with the hope that was previously assigned to the future. John is so bold as to declare that we need not look to the future for the ground and sustenance of faith; we need only look to the potential of the kerygma which is proclaimed in the present of our lives. For the *eschaton* is today; "the hour has come and now is."

Chapter Three

Christology and Controversy in the Prologue of the Gospel of John

The startling introduction to the Gospel of John, which we have come to call its prologue, has often been noted. It strikes one with the same force as an abrupt change of mood or form in a piece of art, say an unusual movement in a symphony or a touch of color in an otherwise subdued painting. It is not the purpose of this article to say anything profoundly new about those eighteen verses. So much has already been said that one wonders if there is any more to say. What this article attempts to do is to ask what exactly the unique contributions of the Christology of the prologue are when compared to other New Testament expressions. I will seek to isolate just where it is that the prologue surges ahead of other christological passages in the New Testament, not where it only states, in its peculiar language, affirmations which we can see were emerging elsewhere in the early Christian communities. If we can succeed in isolating those peculiarities of the prologue's Christology, we can then suggest possible reasons for these unique contributions. My concern is with the prologue as it stands. I assume the passage makes sense as a unit in relationship to the gospel as a whole, and I am interested in that segment. Hence, questions of the use of the prologue before its combination with the gospel, of the authorship of the passage, of its component parts, and of its original relationship to the gospel will not directly be part of the purview of this piece.[1]

The Unique Contributions of the Prologue
to New Testament Christology

Themes Shared with Other Christological Passages

Actually, there is much in the prologue that touches upon common themes in other New Testament christological expressions. To be sure, those common themes stand out forcefully as a result both of the peculiar way the prologue expresses them and of the context of the passage. Anyone can tell another, "love you," but some can add particular force to the common expression by choice of words (and metaphors) and the context of the conversation in which the expression is set. We must look first at those points in the prologue which share a common theme with other New Testament statements about Christ (J. T. Sanders, 29–57).

It was ingenious of the author of the prologue to employ the category of the *logos* ("Word"), given its rich and varied meaning in both the Hellenistic and Jewish traditions.[2] Still, one finds the employment of this term throughout the prologue to be a Johannine expression of a common theme in New Testament Christology. That theme is the identification of Christ with God stated in such a way as to affirm the singleness of God. (i.e., to preserve monotheism). The statements of the prologue in verse 1, especially, are of a piece with other kinds of New Testament expressions used with the same intent. There are at least three that come immediately to mind: "The form of God (*morphē theou*)" of Philippians 2:6; "the image of God (*eikōn tou theou*)" of Colossians 1:15; and that enigmatic statement in Hebrews 1:3, "the reflection of God's glory and the exact imprint (*charaktēr*) of his very being (*hypostaseōs*)." All are concerned to state the nature of the person of Christ within the confines of monotheism. We cannot deny that the prologue does so even more provocatively and imaginatively. We must also recognize, however, its agreement with the sense of these other passages.

Furthermore, the delicate relationship of the logos with God affirmed in verse 1 seems a more sophisticated thinking-through of the kind of idea given expression in Philippians 2:6b which might be translated, "did not grasp at (or cling to) equality with God" (*ouch harpagmon hēgēsato to einai isa theō*). The Philippian passage raises so many of its own exegetical problems that we dare not tarry over the comparison any further (Beare 73–88). It does seem, however, that both passages make admittedly feeble efforts to suggest the relationship between God and the preexistent Christ.

The assertion of the role of the logos in creation gives readers pause: "All things (*panta*) came into being through him" (v. 3) and "the world came into being through him" (v. 10). The affirmation of the role of

Christ in creation, however, is not solely the property of the prologue, for we find the New Testament making that confession elsewhere. Compare these verses in the prologue with Colossians 1:16, Hebrews 1:2c, and 1 Corinthians 8:6 (although, admittedly, the last of these is difficult to interpret; see Conzelmann, *1 Corinthians* 144–45). Even the use of the *panta* ("all things") is common in one of its forms in all these passages.

In verses 9 through 13 the prologue declares logos came into the world and there had powerful soteriological results. The mode of expression is peculiar to this passage. The Johannine preference for the expressions "world (*kosmos*)," "true (*alēthinon*)" and "truth (*alētheia*)," "light (*phōs*)," and "his own (*hoi idioi*)" is not surprising given the occurrences of these words elsewhere in John. However, the central confession of the real worldly appearance of the Christ is, of course, not peculiarly Johannine, as Philippians 2:7-8 shows. Nor is the prologue alone in stressing the soteriological importance of that worldly venture. What the prologue says in a universal metaphor, Hebrews 1:3b expresses through a cultic metaphor—"making purification of sins." That expression in the Hebrews hymn says much the same thing as the prologue suggests when it speaks of the "enlightenment" produced by Christ's coming (v. 4) and its subsequent empowering of persons to become children of God (v. 12). I might press the comparison further to suggest that "children of God" in verse 12 parallels the Colossians expression, "the head of the body (*hē kephalē tou sōmatos*)," at 1:18. (This Colossians expression may have originally meant that Christ was head of the cosmos, but with the addition of the words, "of the church," it refers to the body of Christian believers [Lohse, *Commentary* 42–43]). The prologue claims that it is belief in "his name" which appropriates the saving results of the worldly appearance of the logos (v. 13; cf. Untergassmair). Such an idea is not uncommon throughout the New Testament (e.g., 1 Cor 6:11), but the role of the name is especially highlighted in the Philippian hymn (2:9-10).

The portion of the prologue most often emphasized as a unique contribution is verse 14, and I would not minimize the incarnational thrust of the passage. It is necessary, however, to see this declaration in the larger context of New Testament christologies. John's famous statement, "the word became flesh and dwelt among us," is a way of articulating that this divine, preexistent logos, through whom creation was accomplished, became a human being.[3] The hymn found in Paul's epistle to the Philippians (2:5-11) likewise claims that the one who was in the form of God and shared some sort of divinity became human. Listen once again to the statements made in that hymn: "he emptied (*heauton ekenōsen*) himself," exchanged the form of God for the "form of a servant (*morphēn doulou*)," "born in the likeness of a human and being found in the figure (*schēmati heuretheis*) of a human." The intent of the Philippian hymn here seems clearly to be the affirmation of the genuine humanity of Christ, and it is, I suggest, another way of saying that he "became flesh." Nor is the fleshliness of Christ unique in itself to the prologue. We find tucked away in two other brief christological passages the same expression: "Having been put to death in the flesh (*thanatōtheis men sarki*)" begins a hymn found in 1 Peter 3:18f. and "was manifested in the flesh (*hos ephanerōthē en sarki*)" similarly introduces the hymn at 1 Timothy 3:16. While not denying the power of John 1:14, we can recognize that the humanity of Christ, and even that humanity understood as fleshly existence, is not the unique contribution of the prologue. Does the prologue not suggest a unique incarnation? Yes, in a way it does, to be sure, but so also does Colossians 1:19: "in him all the fullness (*plērōma*) was pleased to dwell." The *plērōma* must surely mean the realm of the divine (Lohse, *Colossians and Philemon*, 59). The prologue touches the common theme of the *plērōma* in Christ when in verse 16 it refers explicitly to "his fullness (*tou plērōmatos autou*)." The result is that 1:14 is not alone in claiming that Christ became human, that humanity in this case meant fleshly existence, and that that existence was the "humanization" of God.

What I have attempted in this discussion is to demonstrate some of the common ground the Christology of the prologue shares with other affirmations, most especially other christological hymns. With its companions, it affirms the divine character of Christ within the sharp limitations of monotheism, the role of the preexistent Christ in creation, the soteriological appearance of Christ in the human world, and the genuine humanness of his sojourn in the world as one who was the embodiment of the divine. On these points, we must say that the Christology of the prologue explicates, however forcefully and memorably, what others in the early Christian communities were saying of their Christ. Where then do its unique christological affirmations lie?

The Unique Christological Themes in the Prologue

Christ's Preexistence. There is a sense in which one can say that the prologue affirms Christ's preexistence in an absolute way. With overtones of Genesis 1, the prologue begins, "In the beginning (*en archē*)." Although commentators do not agree on the meaning of the word, we may compare this expression with Philippians 2:6a, "existing (*hyparchōn*) in the form of God." Does the Pauline (or pre-Pauline) hymn mean a preexistence like that which we find in our prologue? Several things lead one to think that the prologue affirms more. The absence of the idea that Christ is the agent of creation does not force the meaning of "existing (*hyparchōn*)" in Philippians back to pre-creation, in contrast to the prologue. [4] Moreover, the clear echo of Genesis 1:1 in the prologue seems to mean that the author wants the reader to think of nothing short of that mysterious and supra-temporal "first." If one is able to read Philippians 2:6a without pre-conceived dogmatic blinders, one may see the possibility that the passage means only that Christ existed before his incarnation.

The uniqueness of the *archē* ("beginning") of the prologue also stands out sharply when contrasted with Colossians 1:15b and 18. In the Colossians expressions of the creation motif, Christ is not spoken of as existing before all creation, but as the *first born of all creation* (*prōtotokos pasēs ktiseōs*), the beginning (*archē*) of the church, and of the resurrection. (In this Colossians passage Christ is the "first" [*prōtotokos*] of both the creation and the second creation—the resurrection.) We can safely conclude that, in all probability, the author(s) of the prologue asserts Christ's preexistence in a more radical fashion than other New Testament writers. The prologue pushes the existence of Christ, the logos, beyond the reaches of human imagination.[5]

Exaltation in Incarnation. Another unique feature of the prologue is a bit more puzzling. When we compare the christological hymns of the New Testament we are struck by a pattern of exaltation/humiliation/exaltation (Fuller, *Foundations* 245–47). The Philippian hymn is perhaps the best example of this pattern, but the lesser known hymns in 1 Peter 3:18-22 and 1 Timothy 3:16 express that same general form without reference to a preexistent exaltation. The Hebrews hymn (1:2-4) stresses the exaltation with only a passing reference to Christ's purification of sin. The Colossian hymn (1:15-20) moves directly from what we might call preexistent exaltation (vs. 15-17) to post-resurrection exaltation (vs. 18-20) without mention of a humiliation. The prologue, however, presents us with an entirely different pattern. It speaks of the exalted station of the logos before creation and in creation (vs. 1-3) and then shifts to what I would term "exaltation in incarnation" (vs. 9-18). Regardless of the question of whether the hymn as it now stands represents the merger of two independent hymns or of whether verses 9-13 are intended to speak of the historical appearance of the logos,[6] we are left with a christological hymn which is silent with regard to the post-resurrection status of Christ. There is, unlike the other hymns, no concern here to affirm the continuing status of Christ following his historical-fleshly appearance. We are faced with a hymn that concludes on the salvific impact of Christ's earthly life (v. 18).

Two related questions arise. First, why would a christological hymn omit reference to the post-resurrection exaltation? Second, what meaning does such an omission have for christological thought? I can only make suggestions for the resolution of each of these questions.

First, could it be that the hymn, standing as it does as the prelude of the gospel, intended only to prepare the reader for the subsequent narration of Jesus? Did the evangelist want the hymn to leave unanswered the question of the destiny of this enfleshed logos? In Johannine theology as a whole it is the exaltation of the crucifixion which, paradoxically, informs the reader of Christ's status—a status which he has held all along during his earthly sojourn.[7] Hence, all of the formulations of a post-resurrection exaltation would seem at least only partially appropriate. If this is so, then we have some reason to think that the hymn as it stands in the gospel was never intended to be complete without the remainder of the gospel—a view which does not auger well for the theory that the prologue represents a hymn composed and used independently of the gospel.[8]

To the second question, what meaning does the omission of a post-resurrection exaltation have, I again offer only a suggestion. It means perhaps that the evangelist never saw the incarnation itself as a humiliation from which Christ was rescued in a post-resurrection exaltation. Unlike the Christology of the Philippian hymn, the prologue does not suppose that the entrance of the logos into the human realm was a "self-emptying."[9] The incarnate logos is not devoid of the majesty of his preexistent status. For the author of the prologue (and the Fourth Evangelist) Christ's earthly ministry is the presence of the full divine being—the presence of glory (*doxa*).[10] Indeed, this understanding of the incarnation of the logos is consistent with the picture of Jesus one finds in the Fourth Gospel as a whole. The Johannine Jesus is one who walks among humans as a human yet with the majesty and power of the divine (e.g., 1:47; 2:25; 7:30; and 8:20). Even his passion is not the humiliation of the death of a victim. The gospel's passion narrative presents Jesus not as a victim, but as Lord of the situation. Pilate has no authority over him (19:11; see Forestell).

This is not to say that the Christology of the prologue and the gospel as a whole is docetic—that Christ's humanity is pure pretense. Unlike Ernst Käsemann (*Testament*), I take 1:14a seriously. The incarnation is real, but so is the glory perceptible in the incarnate one. The implications of the suggestion that the humanity of Christ is not a humiliation but a continued exaltation does not necessarily challenge the authenticity of the humanization of the logos. What does seem implicit is that the author of the prologue did not understand humanity and divinity as incompatible opposites! Rather the passage seems not to suppose that the humanization of the logos meant that divine glory was thereby discarded, but that humanity could contain the divine nature of Christ without compromise. If these suggestions are to any degree accurate, it means that the author of the prologue brought to the conception of the incarnation a different understanding of humanity than did the author of the Philippian hymn. Whatever the case may be, it is clear that the prologue presents us with a strikingly different concept of the earthly Jesus—one in which there is no humiliation, no loss of exaltation.[11]

The Theme of Resistance to Christ. The third unique contribution of the Christology of the prologue has to do with the persistent theme of resistance to Christ. This theme runs throughout the eighteen verses. Immediately in verse 5, we hear of the effort of the "darkness" to overcome the light of the logos. The world did not know the logos; even his own people (*idia*) did not receive him (vs. 10 and 11). While the fact of Jesus' crucifixion may mean to other New Testament writers the rejection of Christ (e.g., Phil 2:8 and 1 Pet 3:18c), the prologue understands the cross differently and prefers to present the rejection of Jesus in a more general way. For this author the rejection was far more than the plot to put him to death.[12] It was a more fundamental resistance to the truth and light which confronted humanity in the incarnate logos. Again, we have in the prologue a theme that finds prominence in the gospel as a whole, namely the dramatically dualistic presentation of the realm of unbelief and faith. It may be that dualism which is responsible for the prologue's radical emphasis upon the rejection of Christ. For that reason the christological statement of the prologue is framed within a dualism—light/darkness, (perhaps) God/flesh-blood-human, and (by implication) true/false. Fundamental to the prologue and to the gospel as a whole is the author's perception of a schism among humanity, one that may be schematically symbolized as two opposite realms.

The Polemic Tone of the Prologue. If we read the other christological hymns alongside of the prologue, one thing that stands out is the sense in which the latter seems on the attack or on the defense against an attack. Notice each of these features of the prologue: (1) the use of the adjective "true (*alēthinon*)" at verse 9; (2) the disclaimer regarding John the Baptist stated not once, but twice (vs. 6-8 and 15); (3) the care taken to insist that the life given to those who believe in Christ is not of human origin but divine (v. 13); (4) the contrast of grace and truth through Christ to the Law through Moses (v. 17); (5) and finally the use of the important modifier, "only" or "unique (*monogenous* and *monogenēs*)" appearing in verses 14 and 18. The gospel elsewhere uses this term twice (3:16 and 18; but see also 1 John 4:9). It appears that the author of the prologue (and the evangelist) wants to insist that Christ's sonship is of a peculiar sort, possibly against the charge (I suggest) that his sonship is of a kind with others who may honorifically be called "sons of God" (Marsh, 110; cf. *Theological Dictionary* 4:737–41).

Why this polemic tone, especially in a confessional hymn? In the second part of this essay I will propose a possible explanation. Suffice it for now to say that while the prologue is a confessional hymn, as it stands in the text it is confession for a specific occasion. That is, it seems to be intended as the affirmation of a view of Christ within a situation that challenges such a view. It does not necessitate much reading between the lines to see that this hymn reflects an occasion that called for Christian confession over against other views. It is not necessarily unique that Christians should affirm their faith in Christ over against other views; the epistle to the Hebrews appears to be another good example of this. But that a christological hymn should reflect so clearly a believing community under attack is particularly striking in the case of the prologue.

The Intimacy of the Father and Logos. The polemic, however, goes further. A unique feature of the Christology of the prologue appears in the final verse, "the unique God (or Son) who is in the bosom of the Father has exposed (*exēgēsato*) him." This striking statement is set within the Jewish conviction that God cannot be seen without fatal consequences (Exod 33:18 and Isa 6:5), and must be read as a continuation of verse 17 which asserts the superiority of Christ over Moses. Therefore, in a sense we see here another instance of the polemic character of the prologue. Still more, however, is found here than the assertion that Christ has revealed God in a more intimate fashion than even Moses. Christ is the "exegesis" of the very being of God! As the prologue stands, it begins with the declaration of the intimacy of the logos and the Father (vs. 1 and 2) and in verse 18 concludes with the functional results of that intimacy. The effects of the incarnation are that one may now know God in a new way. The delicate exposition of the relationship between the logos and God in the early verses of the prologue has its point in verse 18. What is evident from this last verse is that the prologue is less concerned with the ontological status of Christ in relationship to God than with the claim that Christ is the unfolding of the divine nature for humanity. This dramatic conclusion of the prologue makes clear that the functional (revelatory) dimension of the logos is what primarily interests Christians. The early part of the prologue affirms the preexistent, exalted status of the logos, not for its own sake, I think, but in order to drive home its practical results for the human being. The exposition of the Father for humans is the heart of this christological statement! If we have been suspicious from the start that the prologue was not chiefly interested in ontological speculation about the nature of Christ, verse 18 confirms our suspicions. It is the soteriological results, the effect of the presence of the logos among humans, which is the principal theme of this hymn (cf. J. A. T. Robinson, *Human Face*).

The unique contributions of the prologue to New Testament Christology have been narrowed to at least these: the radical and absolute pre-existence of the logos, the pattern of continuing exaltation even through humanization, the persistent emphasis upon the resistance to the revelation in Christ, the pervasively polemic tone of the passage, and the functional effects of the relationship of the Father and the Son. However, there is still one final and more general feature of this passage worthy of our attention.

A Hymn. The Gospel of John begins with a hymn. Let us not fail to note the uniqueness of that simple observation (Brown, *Commentary–Gospel* 1:18). We could classify the major christological passages generally into three categories: the hymns (those which we have mentioned above), the titles used of Christ (e.g., "Lord" in the epistles of Paul), and the legendary materials (most especially the birth narratives of Matthew and Luke). What is interesting is the fact that, while the Synoptic Gospels employ the second and third categories, the Fourth Gospel is the only canonical gospel to use the first. Why does the Fourth Evangelist choose to begin this gospel with a hymnic affirmation? The legendary materials utilized by Matthew and Luke seem far more appropriate for the gospel genre than does a hymn. We can say, as does Charles Talbert, that both forms employ mythic materials. Furthermore, we might even concede Talbert's point that the miraculous birth stories imply preexistence and assert something of the ontic nature of Christ (*What Is* 52ff.). Still, how odd that a gospel which narrates a story from a historical perspective should begin not with historical or narrative materials (indeed not even with the historical invaded by the activity of God) but with the hymnic affirmation of Christ's preexistence.

There are at least two possible implications of this fact. These implications go two ways, if you will: a hymn set within the structure of a gospel and a gospel initiated with a hymn. To explore the first, perhaps it is the case that the hymn is conditioned by its gospel setting. That is to say, one only understands the hymn in the context of the life and ministry of Jesus. The thrust of the hymn is therefore once again functional. It is not concerned primarily with the ontic nature of Christ but with the existential impact of the life and ministry of that one person. The mythology of the logos with God, of the logos incarnated, and of the logos revealing God to humanity is all concerned to say that in the work of Christ one encounters truth which is of such importance one can only ascribe it to "*the beginning.*" This is not to say that the prologue alone among christological hymns of the New Testament focuses on the functional impact of Christ. (Contrast Fuller, *Foundations* 247ff. with Cullmann, *Christology* 3–4, 326.)

The prologue expresses, however, that functional salvific emphasis in a unique way, namely, by introducing a document that professes to be a narrative proclamation of the good news.

How about the implications in the opposite direction: what does it mean for the gospel that it is introduced with a christological hymn? It has long been held that the Fourth Gospel is a literary piece that does not neatly fit the genre known to us through the Synoptics. As a narrative proclamation, it is of a somewhat different kind from its colleagues in the canon. (One might even label it "the maverick" among the gospels.) At least we can say that the Fourth Evangelist seems to have wanted a hymnic assertion concerning the nature and effect of the one who is the subject of the document to foreshadow the document.[13] It would appear, then, that the Fourth Evangelist is the least concerned with historical narrative, that the prologue signals the reader that the Christ story about to be narrated is one that continues beyond the resurrection right up to the reader's own time, and that the Christ of faith affirmed in the prologue is no different from the Jesus of history. Again, we could say much the same of the Synoptic Gospels except that this theme is more evident and seems to be more self-consciously employed in the Fourth Gospel. The results are that, because the author has tipped the reader off in the prologue, the narrative can move easily and with rapidity back and forth between bits of history about Jesus and the life of the community lived under the lordship of Christ (Martyn, *History and Theology*).

This discussion in no way exhausts the implications of the presence of a hymn introducing a gospel narrative, but perhaps it indicates some features, each of which merit further investigation.

A Proposed Setting for the Unique Christology of the Prologue

Christological thought never develops within a vacuum. Like all human reflection, it is trapped within historical situations and shaped by those situations. This is most assuredly true of the Christology of the prologue. It is not primarily the result of a purely logical pursuit, which sets out to unfold the implications of a new discovery. Rather, the prologue seeks to respond to real, concrete, historical situations. This is not, I hope, a raw historicism, but a hard realism. It is a realistic appraisal of the way in which early Christian thought emerged. The earliest Christians were to a great degree pragmatists who were interested in the protection and growth of their faith against formidable odds. If there is such a person as a pure theologian capsulated from the historical realities of the world, the early Christian (and most especially the author of the prologue) was not such a creature. For this reason, we look for historical explanations for the emergence of the peculiar christological affirmations of the prologue. Indeed, we think they are best enlightened by an understanding of the situation to which they were intended to speak. To suggest such a situation does not "explain them away," in any sense neutralize their importance, or compromise their truthfulness. To suggest such a situation does, however, bring them to life as confessions of real Christians entangled within the throes of a real-life condition.

A Response to Jewish Arguments

It appears that those features which have been isolated as the unique con-tributions of the Christology of the prologue are best illumined by refer-ences to a historical situation which many students of the Fourth Gospel are proposing as the setting of the document. These features reflect the controversy that may have been waging between the Christians of the Fourth Evangelist's community and the Jews of the local synagogue. How do the traits of the Christology of the prologue imply some such Jewish-Christian dialogue? How might this help us understand the christological thrust of our passage?

The implication of a Jewish-Christian dialogue is clearest in the polemic features of the prologue. We have already suggested that the Christology of the prologue is Christology on the attack or on the defense. The hypothesis that the polemic quality of the prologue is directed toward a Jewish-Christian dialogue finds its clearest evidence, of course, in verses 17 and 18. In those verses it appears quite clear that the author intends to say that the revelation found in Christ is superior to the revelation found in the Torah (Barrett, *Gospel According to St. John* 141; Lindars, *Gospel of John* 97–98). (Note, however, that there is no denial of the conviction that the Torah is genuine revelation; Pancaro, *Law*.) Against Jewish claims that God discloses the divine will exclusively in the Law of Moses, the author of the prologue asserts that it is Christ from the bosom of the Father who leads one to grace and truth. Verse 11, too, may imply a response to the Jewish rejection of Christ, especially if *idioi* means "his own people and tradition" (Brown, *Commentary–Gospel* 1:10). The author's insistence that Christ is the "unique son" may be directed towards claims that Jesus is only one among many in the Jewish tradition whose faithfulness earned them the title, "sons of God."

Given the relatively clear inference of these passages, we are justified in suggesting that the other polemic features of the Christology of the prologue are occasioned by a Jewish-Christian discussion. Christ is the true light over against other claims that the Torah is the light of God (v. 9).[14] Could it be that the Jewish opponents were arguing that Jesus was the equal of John the Baptist but no more (vs. 6-8 and 15)?[15] The insistence that Christ empowered persons to become children of God born of the divine and not human will (v. 13) may imply the superior status once again of the salvific potency of Christ's revelation as opposed to the Torah.

The emphasis upon the rejection of Christ that we found in the prologue may also have been rooted in a Jewish-Christian dialogue. The community out of which and for which the author of the prologue writes was perhaps acutely aware of the failure of the kerygma to reach Jewish hearers (Nicol, *Sēmeia* 146–47). In response to that kind of refusal to believe, the author confesses the community's conviction in Christ. Such a resistance to belief may also have been one of the components which made the dualistic scheme of the prologue (and the gospel as a whole) relevant to readers. Both the evangelist and the Johannine community were, perhaps, keenly sensitive to the gulf dividing them from their opponents, probably in the synagogue. It is the tension of that relationship, caused by the intensity of the controversy, which enabled them to think in such simple divisions as light and darkness. All of this suggests that the prologue was written for a confessing church caught in a situation in which they were both under attack and smarting from the failure of their message among their neighbors. They were, then, understandably determined to respond to that attack and to explain the failure of their opponents "to see the light." The nature of that explanation is presented in cosmic proportions—"the light shines in the darkness, and the darkness has not engulfed it" (v. 5; cf. Kysar, *Maverick Gospel* [1993], 65–70).

J. Louis Martyn has made much of the thesis that one of the issues at stake in the Jewish-Christian dialogue was the Christians' view of Jesus (*Jesus* 1:247–73). Against that background, it is perhaps clear why the author of the prologue would want to explicate the ontic nature of Christ in the early verses and to make the claim for the absolute preexistence of Christ. If the opponents of the Johannine church had leveled charges against the claims that Christ was the divine revelation, it is only natural that the response would be a more radical assertion of that claim. One defensive posture is to overemphasize one's contention. Christ was not simply a human, but the incarnate logos who existed with God from "the beginning." Furthermore, such a radicalized claim would have most force if placed within the aura of the Torah (Gen 1:1). Hence, on the opponents' own grounds, the author tries to say that Christ was with God even before the creation of the universe. However, our author also had to defend the functional, salvific effect of Christ, and we find that defense in the concluding verses of the prologue. Against all Jewish claims of revelation, the author sets the Christian claim that Christ has exposed the true nature of God, lifting the human above the will of God known in the Torah.

Perhaps the most devastating argument against the Christians of the Johannine community was that they believed in a Messiah, a preexistent unique Son of God who had suffered and died. This was doubtless the jugular vein of the Christian position, approaching at times even embarrassment for the believer. (See 12:34 as an example.) The response of the prologue and of the whole gospel is in terms of a denial that the life and ministry of the incarnate logos was a humiliation. While others (e.g., the Philippian hymn) attempted to turn that humiliation into a triumph of obedience, the prologue suggests that it is no humiliation at all. By modifying the exaltation-humiliation-exaltation pattern in this hymn, the author seems to be saying that Christ lived his earthly life with a continued divine splendor. Even in his incarnation (and by implication in his human death) his glory was continuously beheld by those with eyes of faith. To the charge, "How can you believe in a Messiah who died humiliated on a cross?" the author of the prologue responds, "There was no humiliation but only glory!"[16] Now this response may have been less than satisfying for some, but it was one way of attempting to defuse the power of the opponents' argument.

There is some reason, therefore, to believe that the unique Christology of the prologue was occasioned by a lively Jewish-Christian controversy. Its polemic tone, its radical assertion of preexistence, its preoccupation with the rejection of Christ, its defense of the revelatory effect of Christ's life, and its refusal to see incarnation as humiliation all may be understood as responses to attacks directed toward the Christian community, possibly by members of the local synagogue. To be sure, all of this is by way of inference from the most explicit (vs. 17 and 18) to the most implicit (the absence of humiliation). Nevertheless, the unique Christology of the prologue may reflect Christology amid controversy. There is still another question.

Why Preface a Gospel with a Christological Hymn?

Does this proposed occasion for the prologue offer any answer for why a christological hymn opens our Fourth Gospel? It may be asking too much to insist that any proposal totally resolve the question of the hymn-gospel combination we find in the Gospel of John. After all, one cannot think that a proposed historical setting illuminates every nook and cranny of a document. Still, there are some intriguing possibilities that may help clarify the role of the hymnic prologue, and I want to do no more than a preliminary probing of some of those possibilities.

The hymn might have been an appropriate way to launch an important motif of the gospel, namely, an emphasis upon the impact of Jesus upon persons. I think the gospel is primarily interested in the functional, existential effects of the ministry of Jesus. In this person—his words and deeds—one finds the manifestation of God. We have already seen that one of the clearest contributions of the prologue to New Testament Christology may be its stress upon the salvific effects of Christ. The dramatic conclusion of the hymn (v. 18) appropriately ushers the reader into the narrative with ample preparation for what the gospel wants to say. Is it possible that this functional concern of the prologue and the entire gospel offers the antithesis of Jewish charges against Christian belief? The charges might have taken a form like this: "You Christians place too much importance upon Jesus. You attribute too much to him!" The response of the prologue is a resounding, "No, this is who we must say he is in the light of what he has done for us!" The prologue makes that kind of response. The gospel goes on to invite readers to hear Jesus' words and see his deeds and conclude if the prologue is not correct in its lofty claims for Christ.[17] The hymnic preparation for the gospel is an appropriate and forceful way to demonstrate that the claims made for Christ are rooted in the genuine experience of the Christians.[18]

Second, we have argued that the absence of the humiliation theme in the Christology of the prologue might, in part, be a rebuttal of the charges of the Jewish opponents. Could that possibly be one of the reasons a hymn introduces the gospel? Let us suppose that the evangelist wanted to present a narrative proclamation of the kerygma that stressed the incarnate glory of Christ to the exclusion (or near exclusion) of a humiliation theme. Perhaps the author's purpose was to do this in order to ward off the threatening charge that Christians believed in a spineless, humiliated Messiah. What better way to introduce a gospel concentrated upon incarnate glory than with a hymn that extolled the glory of Christ both in his preexistent and in his incarnate states? The hymn sets the stage for a "glorious ministry." This is not to say that hymnic confession is the only means by which the exaltation tone of the gospel could be set; but surely the majestic style of the hymnic genre is more effective in setting that tone than, say, historical legend.

This is all very speculative, to be sure, and should be taken only as a hypothesis that requires further testing. It is possible that the evangelist attached the hymn to the gospel for a number of reasons. The combination was an effective way of demonstrating how the statements made of the person of Christ are rooted in the experience of the effects of Christ. Moreover, the hymnic preface was also an effective way of setting the stage for a narrative of glory and not of humiliation. Furthermore, this unique introduction to the gospel was an effort to counter attacks upon Christian belief: an attack upon the appropriateness of Christian affirmations about the person of Christ and an attack upon the Christian belief in a humiliated Messiah. In sum, it seems possible to understand the Christology of the prologue as a reflection of a crisis of faith in the Johannine community, a crisis brought on by a debate between the Christians and the Jews of the locale.[19]

Conclusion

The Christology of the prologue shares a good deal with christological affirmations found in other strata of New Testament literature. It is not, then, an entirely new "high Christology" unrelated to the general tendencies of reflections about Christ ranging from the mid-50s C.E. to the end of the first century.[20] Still, it sounds some new chords in the medley of early Christian affirmations. It has some unique motifs, some different emphases, and some peculiar themes that set it apart from other christological statements. If these probes into the historical setting of the prologue are at least reaching in the right direction, it may be clear also that we can understand the unique contributions of the prologue in terms of a Jewish-Christian controversy. We perceive the issues in that controversy only by means of risky deductions, and the danger of a historical reductionism lurks nearby (i.e., that we reduce every theme in the prologue to a consequence of the proposed setting). Still, there may be enough evidence (some hard, some soft) to make the proposal a viable option.

I offer one final conclusion to our joint efforts, and it is a very general one. The Christology of the prologue is one which developed (or emerged) only as the Johannine Christians confronted real and difficult experiences in the life of their church.[21] The style of such christological reflection suggested to us in the case of the prologue is instructive. The Johannine Christians seemed inclined to respond to the crisis in their church by searching for new and more relevant ways of expressing and understanding their faith in Christ. They apparently did not choose to respond by clinging to what might have been older christological understandings. They viewed christological reflection as an ongoing process by which believers are forced again and again to reevaluate affirmations and again and again reformulate what it is they wish to say. I suggest that this mode of theological reflection is appropriate not alone for the Johannine church of the first century and not alone for the crisis of that Jewish-Christian confrontation, but for the Christian community of any age, and most especially our own.

Chapter Four

Pursuing the Paradoxes of Johannine Thought

Ernest W. Saunders has suggested that the work of the Fourth Evangelist "reflects the mental and artistic qualities of a theological poet . . . (who) delights in the use of antitheses" (20). Indeed, the paradoxical nature of much of the thought of the Gospel of John is well known and widely recognized. One may call it poetry, contradiction, paradox, or dialectic, in accord with how generous one would like to be, but its presence is hardly deniable. Many of the motifs of the gospel are presented in a perplexingly paradoxical manner which is puzzling at best. It is this feature of the gospel that led C. K. Barrett to label Johannine thought "dialectical" (*Essays* 54, 55, 68). To be sure, this recognition that the evangelist thought in such a dialectical fashion helps one deal with the contradictions of the thought of his work. But perhaps there is more involved.[1]

The question is whether or not redaction criticism of the gospel casts any light on the dialectical method of the evangelist. That is, is it possible to find in the poles of that dialectical thought the distinction between tradition and redaction? If such a discovery were possible, we might better understand the paradoxes of the thought of the gospel and the nature of the evangelist's dialectical method. We might then provide historical and communal dimensions within which the dialectical method was developed and employed.

The thesis of this article is that such a discovery is possible in a provisional way. It is feasible to say that the dialectical manner of thought and expression which we attribute to the evangelist arose out of the dialogue between the author's own views and those of the contemporary community, and traditional positions. Hence, the dialectical method of the Fourth Evangelist is really the theological method of the community, as it dealt with its own experience in light of the thought which was passed on to it from earlier times.[2]

Is it possible to demonstrate this to be the case? I propose that one can understand the gospel in this manner when equipped with two essential tools and procedures.

The first is the ideological or content criteria for source and redaction distinction. Contradictions of thought in the text may be indications of the collision of tradition and redaction.[3] Therefore, one must attend to the ideological tensions, expose them, and explicate them as fully as possible. These tensions must be allowed to stand for what they are, and all tendencies to harmonize them must for the moment be suspended.

The second tool required for exploring the paradoxes is simply the findings of other tradition-redaction studies and related constructions of the history of the Johannine community. I refer here specifically to the findings of Robert Fortna in his quest for the isolation of the "Signs gospel" and the Fourth Evangelist's redaction of it (Kysar, *Fourth Evangelist* 13–82)[4] and the proposals of J. Louis Martyn along with Raymond E. Brown and others regarding the history of the Johannine community (Martyn, *History and Theology*; Brown, *Commentary–Gospel* and *Community*).[5] With some modifications I suggest that we can use the work of scholars in these two areas to help us understand the emergence of the contradictions in Johannine thought. After we have isolated and clarified the tensions in a given passage, we can view the poles of that paradox in the light of what we know of the tradition of the community and its history.[6] When we do so, the possibilities of a tradition-redaction distinction may become clearer. That is, in some cases we may find that one pole or the other would seem to have been more compatible with the *Sitz im Leben* of the earlier Johannine community as Fortna, Martyn, or others have described it. This is not, of course, to say that we can *prove* certain passages or ideas to have been part of the evangelist's tradition in distinction from others. At best what we are able to do is to find certain passages or ideas which would seem to have been more at home in *what we think we know* about the pre-gospel tradition than in that setting in which we understand the gospel to have been written. I suggest that what we are trying to do here is to define the contours, the general shape of the tradition as it appears in the gospel. What I will attempt is the description of a *feasible* view of tradition and redaction. It is necessary to understand that we can do no more than this—no more than a general description (a silhouette, if you will) of the tradition which seems coherent, albeit most speculative.

With this general description of the proposal before us, I will suggest the way it might work in the analysis of the themes of faith and eschatology in chapter 6.

Human and Divine Responsibility in the Act of Faith

We are confronted in chapter 6 with certain passages which seem to presuppose an act of will for which one is responsible in believing or not believing in Christ, on the one hand, and certain other passages which seem to suggest that a divine act alone is responsible for faith. We want to be careful not to impose upon the text the modern issue of free will and determinism. Still, in the text there seems to be present a tension between human and divine responsibility for faith, and it is that tension we want to examine and reflect upon.[7]

The most striking of the passages which appear to stress the divine cause of belief in humans is verse 44. There Jesus is made to say, "No one can come to me unless drawn (*helkysē*) by the Father who sent me." (cf. 12:32). The point is made equally clear in those passages in which Jesus refers to believers as those whom the Father has given him (*didōmi*); there are three such passages in chapter 6—verse 37, 39, and 65. In verse 64 we learn that Jesus knew who would *not* believe, as if the matter had been determined by divine choice. If this emphasis on the divine role in the faith act is a kind of election of some sort, the fact that Jesus claims that he chose the Twelve may be another bit of evidence (v. 70).

The evidence in the chapter for an emphasis on the human responsibility in the act of faith is less dramatic but nonetheless real. In verse 29 the "work" (*ergon*) God wants of persons is that they believe. By themselves the use of "whoever comes to me" (*ho erchomenos pros eme*) in verse 35 and its variant in verse 37b would seem to imply human volition. In verse 36 we are told that some see but do not believe, which presupposes that believing is an act of the will after having "seen" the Son. Verse 40 claims that all who see and believe are given eternal life. The most interesting assertion of the human role in believing and failing to believe is found, however, in the closing verses of the chapter. Some disciples (*mathētai*, i.e., those who had believed) find Jesus' words too difficult and leave him. They will not follow him further (v. 66). And then Jesus asks the "Twelve" (*dōdeka*) if they too will leave him, implying that they are free to do so (v. 67). This powerful conclusion of the chapter makes little sense if we do not suppose that one is responsible, to some degree at least, for his/her own belief and unbelief.[8] Verse 30 likewise may presuppose the willful act of believing as a response to a sign. Verses 40 and 45b might also evidence the importance of human action in faith.[9]

In this chapter, then, we find the evangelist caught between two conflicting points of view with regard to responsibility for faith. The tension is heightened by the fact that the two poles of the paradox appear side by side (cf. the chart below). While verse 36 seems to make the most sense if we suppose some importance attributed to the human will in believing, verse 37 clearly asserts that those who believe are those whom the Father has given the Son. Likewise, the Father gives some the possibility of coming to Jesus (v. 65), but those who believe are free to cease believing and turn away from Jesus (v. 66). While John seems to want readers to know there is a human dimension to the act of faith, one must stress equally that faith is possible only among those whom the Father has "drawn" or "given" to the Son. The evangelist appears to intend the paradoxical truth of these two positions; hence he or she affirms both views side by side.[10]

It may be enough to say that the Fourth Evangelist thought dialectically about the responsibility for the faith-act (and that would indeed put him or her in some good company). Perhaps all we can say is that the author was convinced that faith was a dual responsibility. But is it possible to view this paradoxical tension as a result of tradition and redaction? Is it possible that John is a dialectical thinker on this issue precisely because of a dialogue between the present community and their tradition? There is no way to demonstrate that this is the case. We can, however, suggest a feasible way in which this dialectic grew out of the relationship between John and a pre-gospel tradition.

Fortna proposed that the evangelist utilized a simple "Signs gospel" in constructing a gospel that was essentially a missionary tract designed to win converts (*Gospel of Signs* 225).[11] If Fortna is correct, the view advocated in the early form of the gospel was a rather naïve one: if you could read a straightforward account of the wonders done by this man, Jesus, you would soon come to believe in him as Messiah. The wonders are narrated in order to arouse faith. The conclusion of the Signs Gospel, Fortna suggests, is found now at 20:31 and reflects the original purpose of the source: "These are written so that you may come to believe that Jesus is the Messiah, the Son of God."[12]

Is it possible that the basic tradition passed on to the evangelist emphasized the human responsibility for faith and unbelief? We could perhaps reconstruct one thread of the Johannine community along these lines: The community early in its history held to a simple voluntaristic point of view when it came to the question of responsibility for faith. In their missionary efforts, they maintained that the individual was free to respond in faith to the story of Jesus. Yet conceivably with the passage of time and with increasing difficulties in winning converts to their faith (especially, perhaps, from the synagogue), the position of the community

began to shift. They were again and again confronted with the unwill-
ingness of persons to be persuaded that Jesus was the Messiah; indeed,
there may have been mounting hostility among their Jewish colleagues in
the synagogue to their missionary efforts (cf. Martyn, *Gospel* 102–3). The
idealism which characterized the earlier period of their history became
tempered with a hard realism: some people are not going to embrace the
gospel message when they encounter it. With this experience, the Johannine community had to begin to rethink its earlier optimistic and rather
naïve point of view, namely, that humans are totally responsible for belief
and unbelief.

By the time the Fourth Evangelist wrote there was a sober recognition
that people did not so readily respond in faith to the kerygma. It was in
the context of this realization that the author introduced into the gospel
a second layer or stratum of material.[13] In that layer of material faith is
understood as more than the simple, free response of persons to the narration of Jesus' wonders. There is a sense in which faith is God's gift to
some and not to others. That motif which credits divine action as responsible for faith was the effort to explain the reality of unbelief—to account
for the failure of the gospel message to evoke faith from so many persons.
John could not simply repeat the point of view of the community's tradition, because their experience proved that point of view inadequate by
itself.[14]

The experience of the Johannine community, however, probably
involved more than the simple frustration of their evangelistic enterprise.
Rather than succeeding in winning many of the residents of the city to
their faith, as they had hoped to do, there were those in their city who had
turned on them and were opposing their efforts (e.g., 16:1-4). The Johannine community was in the throes of a heated battle with its brothers and
sisters of the local synagogue. Out of this environment of disillusionment
and struggle arose the view that belief and unbelief are the results of God's
activity (and even that the cosmos was divided dualistically along the lines
of "light" and "darkness"). The earlier view which stressed human responsibility for faith was now set in opposition to a newer emphasis on the
divine responsibility for faith. The paradoxical understanding of this matter which we find in chapter 6 (as well as elsewhere in the gospel, e.g., 17:6
and 20:27b) may therefore be the result of a dialectical tension arising
from the relationship of tradition and redaction.

Realized and Futuristic Eschatology

If we grant the possibility that the conceptual tension regarding the responsibility for faith arose in the relationship between tradition and redaction,
we can view another such tension as further evidence of that relationship,

specifically the commonly recognized polarity of realized and futuristic eschatology in the gospel. My thesis is simply that we can see the likelihood that the future eschatology of the gospel is rooted in the Johannine tradition, while the present or realized eschatological view is the theological reflection of the community in dialogue with that tradition. (On the eschatology of John, cf. Kysar, *Fourth Evangelist* 207–14.)

The futuristic emphasis is visible in chapter 6 in the refrain, "that I should raise him on the last day," or some form of that statement. It is found in verses 39b, 40b, 44b, and 54b.[15] Over against this promise of the future work of Christ is the affirmation of the presence of an eschatological blessing. In some form or another, the assertion that the believer already *has* eternal life is to be found in verses 40a, 47, 50b, 51, 54a, and 58b. (Verses 50b, 51 and 58 contain the promise that those who eat the heavenly bread will not die.) So here we are suspended again on the poles of the Johannine dialectic, again made worse by the close proximity of the affirmations. Notice they are found back to back in verse 40 and again in verse 54. The apparent *intentionally* contradictory relationship here may be inescapable, as it is elsewhere in the gospel (e.g., 5:24-29).

Elsewhere I have argued against Bultmann's thesis that the future eschatology is the addition of the ecclesiastical redactor.[16] It seems more feasible that the evangelist is intentionally revising (demythologizing, if you like) futuristic eschatology with a realized eschatology. Pressing that argument one step further suggests that the tension between those two modes of eschatological thought is the result of changes in the conditions of the community and hence in its theological reflection. It is not hard to imagine that the futuristic eschatology was part of the tradition John inherited and that the earliest community embraced such a view. Indeed, it may have been an only slightly Christianized form of an apocalyptic view embraced by the synagogue of which the Johannine community had been a part. Can we, then, conceive of the present eschatology emerging out of the experiences of the community in the time between its comfortable life in the synagogue and its troubled existence expelled from its religious home?

If it is the case that the Johannine Christians were locked in controversy with the Jews of their former synagogue (and not all would agree), we may imagine that it was natural for Johannine theology to begin to move away from a futuristic eschatology which was only an adaptation of a Jewish view. Granted that the synagogue had come under the influence of Jewish apocalyptic thought, the members of the synagogue in John's city may have embraced an eschatology very much like those of the Johannine Christians among them. As a result of the dialogue with the Jews, the Christians may have sought a more distinctive view of eschatology, and their search may have led them naturally to an eschatology which stressed more the present than the future. The search involved a quest for a peculiar self-identity by which the community could understand itself apart from its roots in the synagogue. Certainly some realized eschatological themes may have been present already in tradition, for those themes appear to have been a part of the earliest Christian thought. It was left to the evangelist only to revive, strengthen, and elaborate them.[17]

Furthermore, if the trauma of the expulsion from the synagogue was as severe as some think it was and if the life of the Johannine Christian was threatened in a controversy with their former colleagues, realized eschatology may have been an attempt to respond to a need for a more meaningful present for the believers. I suggest that the trauma of expulsion and persecution was perhaps answered in Johannine thought with a view that affirmed the immediate blessings of God in spite of the difficulty of the present. The gospel addresses the need of the present, not by a further emphasis upon a future hope, but by a new emphasis upon the present reality—the believer already has eternal life.[18] If this proposal is at all feasible, combine it with a suggestion that Johannine Christians, not unlike their brothers and sisters of other churches, were in need of a revision of eschatology in light of the delay of the parousia, and you have a reasonable view of the emergence of the present eschatology of the Fourth Gospel (cf. 14:1ff. and 16:18-19).[19]

A Further Complication

The attempt here has been to sketch a picture of the development of Johannine theology which is consistent with our knowledge of the tradition and the history of the community and which adds historical and communal depth to our view of the paradoxical thought of the gospel. There is, however, one further and complicating note on these themes in chapter 6 which must be added. I have suggested that the close proximity of the poles of the paradox is a result of the deliberate effort of the evangelist to relate tradition and redaction in a dialogical manner. That point is further highlighted by the juxtaposing of futuristic eschatology and the view that faith is the responsibility of God's action. At verses 39 and 44 we find the proposed *later* view of responsibility for faith linked with the proposed *earlier* view of eschatology. Then, in verse 40 both types of eschatology are yoked with an emphasis on the proposed traditional view of the human responsibility for faith (cf. the chart below).

What are we to make of this? It appears that the further we probe the paradoxes of the Fourth Gospel the more aware we become of the (apparently) deliberate tension the evangelist creates between the theology of the tradition and the views of the current community. The Fourth Evangelist may have wanted to affirm the views of the tradition, while at the same time claiming the necessity of rethinking those views. The result is the paradoxical position of the gospel, which suggests that truth is always multisided. To understand faith, one must see both the divine and human dimensions. To articulate the way in which God has made the realities of the last days available to the Christian, one must speak both of the fulfilled and the unfulfilled, yet promised, sides of the issue. To understand those two themes in relationship with one another one could only think of the two interlaced with each other. Hearing the theological message of the Fourth Gospel, then, is like listening to stereophonic music. Countervailing sounds come at you from both the right and the left simultaneously, and they are so closely related that separating one from the other deprives you of the full impact of the music. This was all part of the "theological poetry" he wrote.

John's dialectical method is, therefore, the result of the way in which the gospel seems to preserve and affirm the theological positions of the Johannine tradition, while at the same time offering revisions and correctives out of the community's contemporaneous experience and thought. John is affirming, again and again, throughout much of the thought of this gospel, that theological reflection proceeds within the lively dialogue between traditional and contemporary positions. Through its paradoxes, we hear the gospel saying that religious thought always emerges in a context shaped at once by historical tradition and the contemporary experience of the community of faith. For the evangelist, tradition was a "living text" to be reread, under the guidance of the Spirit-Paraclete, in the light of the needs of the church. In this way, the dialectical thought of the evangelist is more than the brilliance of a single mind. It is the continuous conversation of a community with its own past and its own present experience.[20]

Conclusions

We are left now only with the task of briefly assessing the perils and promises of the proposal here sketched. There are at least three dangers which need to be mentioned. First, the method for seeking distinctions between tradition and redaction is a perilous one because it depends on our own logic of contradiction. That is, what we view as ideological tension, paradox, or contradiction is necessarily defined by our own concept of what is opposite in thought. Are we safe in assuming the evangelist (and/or the early Christians) embraced a similar concept of logical opposition, or is the problem of paradox in the gospel only *our* problem and not one that the evangelist or Johannine community would have recognized? We must cautiously assume, I think, that John was as sensitive to logical contradiction as we are, until we can know otherwise.[21]

Another peril of the enterprise taken up in this article lurks in the dependence upon the recent work of source criticism and reconstructions of the history of the Johannine community. If they are wrong, so are we! Still, I wonder if our understanding of the gospel is going to grow if we sit cautiously by, awaiting the day when we have a proven thesis upon which to proceed.

Still another peril that must be faced is the fact that our approach of presupposed religious thought emerges out of historical conditions and reflects those conditions. The redactional views we propose to find in the gospel are accountable on the basis of the concrete social and historical setting of the community, which we suppose to have been the case. To say that religious thought is a reflection of historical and social conditions, however, is not necessarily a reductionism; it is but a suggestion of one of the several influences which may account for religious thought.[22] Such a view as this does not minimize the creativity of the evangelist or the religious community; it only recognizes the context within which that creativity took place.

On the other hand, the proposal outlined here promises several things. First, it promises to provide a way of sketching the broad perimeters of tradition and redaction in the thought of the Fourth Evangelist—a method greatly needed in contemporary theological interpretation of the gospel. At least in a general and provisional way, then, we may be able to outline the shape of the history of Johannine religious thought. However general and tentative the results may be, at least it affords us an opportunity to grasp some sense of the flow of ideas in the history of the Johannine community.[23]

Second, our proposal may provide us a glance into the theological method of one of the most perplexing writers of first-century Christianity. As a result of this hazardous and speculative experiment, we may be able more clearly to see how the poetic mind of the Fourth Evangelist worked—indeed, how the evangelist and the early Johannine community conceived of the theological task itself. That, in turn, has implications for the way in which theological reflection in the church of the twentieth and twenty-first centuries might be done. This promise is surely worth the perils of the proposal!

Appendix: Summary Charts

Faith—Divine Responsibility	Faith—Human Responsibility
v. 37 Those who come to Son are those to the Son are those *given* (*didōmi*) by God.	v. 29 The *work* (*ergon*) of persons is to believe (*pisteuō*)
v. 39 Son should not lose those *given* (*didōmi*) to him by God.	v. 30 A *sign* (*sēmeion*) occasions faith
v. 44 No one comes to Son unless *drawn* (*helkō*) by the Father	v. 36 Persons see but do not believe.
v. 64b Son knew from the *beginning* (*ex archēs*) who would not believe.	v. 40 God wants *all* (*pas*) who see and believe to have eternal life. +
v. 65 Those who have possibility of coming to Son are those God has given (*didōmi*) him.	v. 64a Some do not believe even though Son has spoken words of *spirit and life* (cf. 63b: *pneuma estin kai zōē estin*)
(cf. v. 70)	v. 66 Disciples left Jesus because of his words.
	v. 67 The 12 are asked if they will leave Jesus.
	(cf. vs. 35, 37b, 40, 45b)
Present Eschatology	**Future Eschatology**
"The believer has eternal life." (E.g. v. 40a: *echē zōēn ainion*)	Son will raise believers on the last day. (E.g., v. 39b: *anastēsō auto [en] tē eschat hēmera*)
	v. 39b *
v. 40a +	v. 40b +
	v. 44b *
v. 47 v. 51 v. 54a	v. 54b
v. 58 (cf. v. 50b)	

*Proximity with future eschatology

+Proximity with human responsibility and both present and future eschatology

Chapter Five

Literary Probes into the Gospel of John

At the center of those efforts to do studies of the literary character of the Fourth Gospel stands a complex of problems. We can summarize them briefly in terms of the question of the literary unity of the document. Many have seen evidence that the gospel as it stands does not constitute a unified piece of work. There are numerous *aporias* ("difficulties") in the narrative that raise the question of whether or not we are dealing with a document which is whole or which reflects its original order. A few examples will suffice to illustrate the point: The order of chapters 5 and 6 seems disrupted. In chapter 5 we are told that Jesus is in Jerusalem, but as we begin chapter 6 we are suddenly told without any transition that he is back in Galilee. In 14:31 Jesus seems to conclude his final discourse with his disciples only to continue for three more chapters! In 7:3-5 it sounds as if Jesus has not worked his signs in Jerusalem in apparent contradiction to narratives in chapters 2 and 5. The prologue (1:1-14) employs terms not used elsewhere in the gospel (e.g., logos); and chapter 21 presents a narrative, which seems strange after the conclusion of the gospel in 20:30-31.

The list could go on, but these examples suggest one of the problems with which the literary critic of the document is concerned. Can we understand the gospel as an integral whole and interpret it as such? Do the difficulties in the narrative result from the history of the composition of the gospel? Has the order of the gospel been disrupted in other ways? In summary, it may be said that there are two major directions taken in contemporary research to deal with the difficulties posed by the Fourth Gospel as a purely literary document.[1] Some have investigated the structure of the gospel and concluded that it has suffered serious disarrangement and others insist that it makes sense in its present order. Still others have taken the aporias, along with additional evidence, as a basis from which to construct histories of the composition of the document and have proposed that literary difficulties result from the process of its composition.

Structural Analysis and Literary Methods

The basic question is simply whether John as it stands comprises a logical whole or whether it does not. Among the most influential of those who argue that it cannot be interpreted as it stands is Rudolf Bultmann, whose famous theory of rearrangement has been widely debated. Bultmann, for instance, resolves the conflict between chapters 5 and 6 by linking chapter 6 with 4, showing how the former follows naturally after the narrative of the latter. Chapter 5 would more naturally lead then into the narrative at the beginning of chapter 7 (*Gospel* 209). Bultmann's rearrangement is much more complicated, as a perusal of the table of contents of his commentary will show.

Bultmann is neither the first nor the only modern scholar to propose some kind rearrangement of the Fourth Gospel. The theories are numerous, ranging from the simplest reversal of chapters to elaborate reconstructions of the original text. However, for the most part, theories of this kind were more prominent in the years of scholarship prior to the period with which we are here concerned. Since Bultmann, to my knowledge only two significant proposals for rearrangement have been advanced: T. Cottam and H. Edwards. However, M. Làconi has more recently revived the notion of disarrangement by suggesting that the Fourth Evangelist was not able to complete the gospel and a disciple later discovered additional writings of the evangelist and inserted them freely into the incomplete gospel.[2]

On the whole, theories of displacement and rearrangement have not been embraced by a majority of contemporary scholars. Representative of the response to such theories is the critique of Brown who quite rightly poses three objections to these efforts. First, he points out that endeavors to rearrange the contents of John invariably express more of the mind of the commentator than the mind of the evangelist. In rearranging the text, the scholar imposes modern concepts of logic and narrative flow upon the text of the first-century writer. Second, explanations for how the displacement occurred seem less than adequate. Brown points out how suspiciously convenient it is that in Bultmann's theory we are always dealing with misplaced complete sentences. Is it realistic to suppose that a damaged scroll (Bultmann's proposed explanation for the supposed disorder of the Fourth Gospel) would be broken *only* at the point of the pauses between sentences? Finally, it is a matter of judgment whether or not the gospel as it now stands makes sense to the reader. Many commentators have shown to the satisfaction of others how the structure of the present gospel presents a logical narrative and discourse flow (Brown, *Commentary-Gospel* 1:xxvi–xxviii). It is a fair judgment to say that theories of displacement and reordering of the gospel have little support in contemporary research.

Much more vigorous is that school of research that has worked on the structural unity of the gospel. Included in this group are those who approach the gospel in different ways. Some commentators simply defend the thesis that there is a logical development in the structure of the document as it stands. Exemplary of such scholars is J. Schneider who rejects all theories of displacement, claiming that they try to impose a modern logic upon the meditative thought of the gospel. He also rejects all source and theories involving a "foundational gospel" or theories of multiple redaction (which, we will see below, are also ways of dealing with the literary problems of John). Instead of these, Schneider simply treats the gospel as a logical, coherent whole (*Evangelium* 24–25; cf. Girard, "La structure").

Our attention, however, will focus here upon another direction in showing the unity of the gospel, namely, the efforts of some to do structural analysis of the text. Within the wider range of biblical criticism, various forms of structural, phenomenological, and text-linguistic approaches are flourishing, and it is obvious that such methods are to be reckoned with as one of the waves of future criticism. It is not surprising, therefore, that scholars have expended so much effort on the study of the Fourth Gospel. Perhaps most important is the work of B. Olsson, whose method is that of text-linguistic interpretation. It is his task to find within the text itself the key for determining its meaning. This method is markedly holistic which sets it apart from both the rearrangement theories we have mentioned and the more prominent theories of tradition, source, redaction, and composition we shall examine below. The semantic structure of the passage is the decisive feature. Olsson's methodological procedure involves establishing the *Text-konstitution* by analyzing elements of the information units of the passage and then establishing "the connection between '*die Textkonstitution*' and '*die Text-rezeption*' with an 'ideal receiver' in mind." Finally, the method describes the linguistic and literary character (or text-type) of the passage. This method, Olsson observes, stands under the influence of French structuralism, *Text-linguistik*, and American discourse analysis. With his method Olsson studies two passages from John—a narrative (2:1-11) and a dialogue text (4:1-42). The message of these two texts is essentially the same—how Jesus' works create a new people of God. They are "typological texts" that use "screens" (Jesus' works in 2:1-11 and Scripture in 4:1-42) through which to filter meaning (1–17, 275–82, quote 17).

The conclusion to which Olsson comes—relevant to our discussion at this point—is merely that we can justifiably interpret the Fourth Gospel as it stands without recourse to its prehistory or disarrangement. In the author's words, "a textual analysis of the type I have here performed is necessary, and is perhaps the best way to find answers to many problems concerning John which are not yet solved" (289–90, quote 290.)[3]

In some quarters the new forms of structuralism are presented in opposition to more established types of historical-critical studies. H. Lona, however, uses the methods in a complementary fashion. In a study of Abraham in John 8, Lona has explored the passage with a number of different methods and shows how they can be integrated. Our interest at this point is with his application of literary semiotics to this passage. Literary semiotics views the text as a whole and presumes that there is no difference in sorts of literature, that is, between the so-called world literature and minor literature. The task is to isolate the "universals of narrative" by which the formulation of a particular narrative of any kind is recognizable; therefore, all literature is a concretizing of general narrative structures. The semiotics approach shows that the historical-critical methods are often one-sided and that critics must supplement them with more holistic studies. On the topic of the function of Abraham in chapter 8, the semiotics approach is not interested in the preliterary history of the themes and traditions in the passage, e.g., views of Abraham in Judaism. Its concerns are with the form of the text and the synchronized role of signification. The "meta-narrative elements" in the passage reveal how the author intended to present Abraham as part of the witness to Christ. The Fourth Gospel attempts to articulate the essential nature of faith as a new kind of presence of the divine. Hence, the role of Abraham is reversed in the progress of the narrative (compare v. 56 with the previous discussion of Abraham).[4] Lona's efforts are to demonstrate the productiveness of the use of a holistic (in this case semiotic) method alongside of the more traditional methods of criticism.

Another kind of holistic method that is intended to supplement and correct more traditional methods is advocated by J. Breuss. Breuss designed his study of 2:1-12 to exemplify a method that he contends is more rewarding both in terms of deciphering the text and in terms of unearthing the contemporary relevance of the gospel. His method is "phenomenological structuralism." It attempts to supplement the work of the historical-critical methods, especially form and redaction criticism (see below), with a more descriptive characterization of the text. It approaches the Fourth Gospel as a linguistic form and seeks the "intentionality" of the text. He stresses that all of the New Testament documents are intended to awaken faith—they are kerygma—and as such they have a peculiar character as literary works. Furthermore, Breuss's study attempts to find some happy, middle ground between the allegorical-typological interpretations of the church fathers and the modern historical-critical studies. The text as it stands produces a "horizon" of meaning by which it must be interpreted. Breuss argues that the Cana sign is narrated in order to evoke faith. The resurrection of Christ is intentionally brought into view by the reference to the third day (v. 1), and Jesus is centralized in the narrative as the bridegroom. As a linguistic form, the Cana story uses space and time in a unique and theological way, all in order to announce Jesus as Son of God. It has a series of interrelated implications which the phenomenological method describes. "*Phänomenologischer Strukturalismus*" views the text as one not simply out of the past but intended for proclamation.[5]

There is a certain reactionary element detectable in these efforts to find meaning in the holistic approach to the Fourth Gospel. Some of these newer critics think the traditional critical inquiries have segmented and stratified the gospel and have thereby veiled the meaning present in a consciously constructed literary unit. To be sure, some corrective direction away from the efforts of other types of literary criticism may be needed. One cannot but be impressed, for example, with Lona's analysis of the narrative progress through chapter 8 as compared with Bultmann's fragmentation of the same passage. Furthermore, one may with some confidence claim that the present gospel and its sections as they stand surely must have made sense to someone in the history of its origin, whether it be the original author or a redactor. Hence, attention to the structural unity of the Fourth Gospel seems justifiable.

On the other hand, such holistic approaches to the gospel are not without their difficulties. When they ignore the historical questions involved in the composition of the gospel, they err in a parochial direction to the same degree as a traditional historical-critical method errs when it refuses to consider the possibility of unity in a passage. Lona's method has the virtue of seeing such structural analysis as a supplement rather than a replacement of concern for the history of the text and its composition. Moreover, some of the elaborate structural analyses seem to find nuances and literary techniques that are perhaps more at home in the mind of the modern critic than in the mind of the ancient writer (e.g., Escande). Finally, one cannot escape the feeling that such analyses tend at times to belabor the obvious (and Olsson's work is occasionally of this type). In my judgment, the attention to the literary structure of the Fourth Gospel is a productive and promising venture although it is seriously limited, especially when used in isolation from the other more traditional methods.

While it does not of itself offer the solution of all of the literary problems of the gospel, it is useful at some points.

Source and Tradition Analysis

Our discussion turns now to those efforts to resolve the literary difficulties of the Gospel of John by proposing some form of the history of its composition. Under this rubric, we must examine a wide variety of proposals, but they have one thing in common. In every case, they present a thesis for the process by which the Fourth Gospel was composed and brought to its present form. The result of these proposals is to offer among other things a solution to the literary difficulties that this document poses. However, we must hasten to point out that the criteria used for developing these theories are not alone literary. Content criticisms, as well as literary concerns, have converged to make the proposals we are about to survey tenable at least to their authors. Out of the maze of differing hypotheses we may construct three major types which, with variations, may be used to summarize research on the history of the composition of the gospel: 1) form and tradition, 2) source (both single and multiple) and 3) developmental theories. In advance of our survey of these three types, however, we must mention in passing the question of the methods involved in the reconstruction of the history of the composition of John.

Methods Used in Theories of Composition

The efforts to reconstruct the history of the composition of the Fourth Gospel have not only produced a significant variety of results but have employed a veritable array of methods. It is necessary to review the major types of methods employed in discerning stages in the history of the composition before proceeding to look at the reconstructions themselves.

Prominent among the criteria used in order to isolate stages in the history of composition are *stylistic differences*. Where investigators find what appear to be stylistic variations within the gospel, they may posit the existence of different levels or sources. Bultmann employed stylistic differences as one of the bases for his source theory of the Fourth Gospel. It appears that these differences were the major criterion by which he was able to separate the presence of any one of his three proposed sources, as well as the work of the evangelist, and the additions of the later redactor (*Gospel*, passim). H. Teeple's elaborate source proposal also employs stylistic differences. He denies that any one of the criteria used in his analysis is of more importance than the others, but his initial separation of sources relies heavily upon the variations in style he finds within John (*Literary* 118-19, 145-46). Using stylistic differences in a less significant way is common to the source theories of Temple (50-62), Fortna (*Gospel of Signs* 212), and Nicol (*Sēmeia* 7, 25, 30–40). However, these proposals use the stylistic criterion to support a source separation that is premised primarily upon other methodological criteria. Fortna, for instance, argues that stylistic differences of themselves are inconclusive and are not an adequate means of detecting sources within the gospel. Nonetheless, once a source has been separated by a more reliable method (in Fortna's case the presence of aporias), the isolated source may be *confirmed* by demonstrating that it reflects a style different from that material supposed to come from the hand of the evangelist (*Gospel of Signs* 212). Stylistic differences are also employed by Brown in his effort to distinguish the stages in the composition of the Fourth Gospel in his developmental theory (*Commentary–Gospel* 1:xxiv–xxv).

Bultmann also argued that *aporias in the gospel*—incongruities between passages following upon one another—were indications of the author's employment of sources or the additions of a redactor (*Gospel*, passim). Fortna has made such difficulties in the flow of the text the foundation of his isolation of a "Signs Gospel" (*Gospel of Signs* 19–20). Nicol's proposal appeals to the aporias not as the major means of demarcating between source and redaction but as a supportive bit of evidence once the content of the source has been isolated by other means (*Sēmeia* 14–16). Brown (*Commentary–Gospel* 1:xxiv–xxv) and Lindars (*Behind* 14–18) have each made extensive use of this criterion in designating the different stages in the composition of the Fourth Gospel. G. Reim proposes that the evangelist employed a "fourth synoptic gospel." His theory claims that, when there are disturbances in the order of the gospel, at those points one most often finds synoptic materials inserted. Reim insists that such insertions have produced the disturbances (*Studien* 238–39).

The discernment of peculiar forms of material as contrasted with the rest of the gospel is still a third method of detecting source material. Nicol's basic criterion for his source theory utilizes just such a form analysis. He argues that one finds a number of wonder stories among the more ordinary long, dramatic narratives of John. The form of these wonder stories is more typically synoptic than Johannine (*Sēmeia* 14–16). Temple, too, professes a methodology which is form-critical in nature (68–251). Schnackenburg, less confident of form distinction as a means of source separation, nonetheless employs it in a supportive role (*Gospel* 1:64–67). Yet the most significant use of form criticism as a basis for understanding the history of the composition of the Fourth Gospel is found among those who hold that the evangelist utilized some oral tradition which was related to the Synoptic Gospels. C. H. Dodd's work is the most thorough application of this method (*Historical Tradition*).

Tensions within the content of the passage are another means used by some to argue for evidence of source and redaction or distinctions among stages in composition. Again Bultmann stressed this factor. "Content criticism" led him to find the distinctive theological ideas of the contributors to the composition of John (*Gospel*, passim).[6] Such ideological differences between passages seem also to be what Schnackenburg means by the "tensions" between tradition and redaction which he finds in the gospel (*Gospel* 1:59, 64-67). J. Becker, following the work of Bultmann, also employs this method ("Wunder" 132-34). Rather than using such ideological tensions as the primary detection device in the search for the history of composition, Fortna (*Gospel of Signs* 17, 19, 212) and Nicol (*Sēmeia* 7, 25, 30-40) exercise this method in a secondary and confirming manner. Lindars is also wedded to this criterion, along with form analysis, in order to support his theory of stages in the development of the Fourth Gospel (*Behind* 14-18.). G. Richter's proposal depends exclusively upon theological tensions within the thought of the gospel ("Präsentische").

Finally, we might mention what could be called *literary structure*. Teeple has variations in the structure of the narratives and discourses as part of his arsenal of methodological devices to build his source theory. For him this criterion is a broad one which encompasses the aporias we mentioned above, the use of catchwords, and other such structural variations (*Literary* 118). W. Wilkens's developmental theory depends almost exclusively upon the disturbances of the structural unity in the Fourth Gospel. His thesis of a *Grundevangelium* behind John is founded upon the isolation of what he calls a Passover framework in the gospel. This framework, which is a latter addition, signals the shadow of the earlier gospel lurking within the structure of the present document (*Entstehungsgeschichte* 92-93).

In summary, these five criteria for detecting moments in the history of the composition of the Fourth Gospel are employed in varying degrees by the scholars and with widely differing results. Most notable, perhaps, is the fact that no single method by which one proceeds to look behind the gospel at its history is unanimously accepted. The methods vary as widely as do the results of the methods. With so little consensus on method, there can be little agreement as to the results of this sort of inquiry. Perhaps a case in point is the issue of stylistic differences. Bultmann's theory depended heavily upon the use of stylistic criteria. Then the works of E. Schweizer (*Ego*) and E. Ruckstuhl (*Einheit*, and "Johannine Language") endeavored to show that John is distinguished by its unity of style. On the other hand, Fortna has made a vigorous defense of his source theory by showing that, even with the use of the style characteristics offered by Ruckstuhl, his proposed source has "stylistic integrity" (Fortna, *Gospel of*

Signs 302–18). The jury can hardly proceed with a verdict until the court has ruled on what kind of evidence is admissible. Neither can the history of the composition of the Gospel of John be written until there emerges some greater degree of consensus on the kind of method that may be validly used. Still, the area of the history of the composition of the Fourth Gospel is rich with hope for the resolution of some Johannine puzzles, even though its methodological base remains structurally weakened by scholarly disagreements.

With this brief overview of the methods completed, we may turn now to the survey of the three basic kinds of hypotheses for the history of the composition. In each case, with these theories investigators have attempted to respond to the perplexing question of the literary unity of John. Each suggests through his or her theory that the unity of the composition was marred (perhaps ever so slightly) when earlier materials were incorporated and/or later materials inserted into the document. In both cases, the critic can detect the presence of the source or redaction by the telltale marks of their inclusion.

Source Theories

Many scholars of John today take for granted that the author employed a source or sources for the composition of the gospel. In this case, critics propose that the source(s) was a written document with some degree of unique literary identity before being incorporated into John. The following discussion will examine those theories in terms of the proposed content and character of the source, moving from the simplest of the proposals to the most complicated.

Surely, the simplest of the source theories endorsed today is the "signs source"—a single source that contained a number of wonder stories about Jesus. The enumeration of the "signs" of Jesus in the gospel (2:11 and 4:54) plus the allusion to various other signs (12:37 and 20:30) have been taken as hints of the order and language of the proposed "signs source." In its barest and most conservative form, this theory holds that the Fourth Evangelist drew two or more accounts of these wonders from a source, alluded to others with references to "other signs," and perhaps at 20:30-31 utilized the conclusion of the source as the conclusion of the gospel (e.g., Schulz, *Evangelium*).

Of greater interest are those who have attempted to outline the shape of a signs source by detecting what the evangelist might have drawn from that source. Four scholars in particular have proposed that the source was comprised of seven or eight wonder stories that were incorporated into the gospel. Schnackenburg, Nicol, Bultmann, and Becker all agree that the following narratives were drawn into John from the source: the wedding at Cana (2:1-11), the healing of the nobleman's son (4:46-54), the feeding of the crowd (6:1-5), the healing at Bethesda (5:2-9), the walking on the water (6:16-21), the healing of the man born blind (9:1ff.), and the raising of Lazarus (11:1-44). (We should note that there is not full agreement on exactly which verses and portions thereof in every case came from the source and which constitute redactional additions.) In addition, all four regard 20:30-31 as containing a conclusion most probably incorporated from the signs source. Nicol further suggests that the source may have contained not only a narrative concerning the first disciples but also the discussion of Jesus with the Samaritan woman. Becker thinks it is likely the source, in addition to the wonder stories, also contained an account of the Baptist (1:19ff.) and the calling of the disciples (1:35ff.) (Schnackenburg, *Gospel* 1:64-67; Nicol, *Sēmeia* 30-40; Becker, "Wunder" 35; cf. Kysar, *Fourth Evangelist* 26-27). Bultmann's often debated *sēmeia* source supposes a considerably enlarged collection beyond the wonder stories themselves. In addition to the call of the disciples (1:35-49) and the discussion with the Samaritan woman (4:4-7 and scattered verses through 40), he claimed that these materials were also constructed out of the source: 7:2-10, 19, 21-23, the discussion of the Law in 7:19, 21-23, and the discussion of signs at 10:40-42 and 12:37-38 (*Gospel* 97-108, 113-21, 175-202, 204-9, 210-18, 237-47, 287-95, 329-39, 393-409, 452-53, 698).[7]

Teeple and Fortna, while differing radically in most other ways, share the conviction that this source comprised more than narratives of wonder stories and related accounts. Both argue that the source entailed, beyond these narratives, an account of the passion. Hence, Fortna hypothesizes the existence of a "Signs Gospel" employed by the evangelist. It was a kind of "rudimentary gospel" essentially devoid of discourse material. Teeple's proposed source also has the features of such a simple gospel but lacks any resurrection material (Fortna, *Gospel of Signs* 235-45; Teeple, *Literary* 166-248). These two picture a source that was more than a collection of wonder stories; it was a conscious gospel genre.

The views of the character of this proposed source also vary considerably. Bultmann conjectured that the *sēmeia* source was written in Greek but with strong Semitic influences. It was based upon a rather naive concept of the wonders as the means of eliciting faith and pictured Jesus as a divine man. Bultmann seems to have found extensive Hellenistic influence in the features of the source (*Gospel* 113-21, 211). Becker follows Bultmann in many respects. The distinctive thing we can say about this source is its Christology. Jesus was portrayed as one of the Hellenistic wonder workers—a *theios anēr*.[8] The wonders are epiphanies of the identity of Jesus and intended to evoke faith. Such a Christology was quite different from that of the Fourth Evangelist, and the two views result in christological confusion in the Fourth Gospel as a whole (Becker, "Wunder" 136-43; Bultmann, *Gospel* 180). Nicol understands that the source was a chris-tocentric collection, but insists that it reflects more influence from the Jewish thought world than the Hellenistic. The purpose of the signs was to demonstrate that Jesus was the expected Jewish Messiah in order to win converts from among Jewish readers. Its origin is, then, more than likely from among a Jewish Christian congregation. The wonders attributed to Jesus portray him as the mosaic prophet of Jewish expectation. The Jewish characteristics of the isolated source materials confirm, for Nicol, the Jew-ish Christian origin and the Jewish audience of the document (*Sēmeia* 44).

Schnackenburg ventures much less in the way of conjecture concern-ing the character of the source. The wonder stories are simple and direct with little or no theological expansion; they are manifestations of the glory of the incarnate one. He seems to lean in the direction of stressing the Jewish rather than Hellenistic features of the document (*Gospel* 1:67, 526-27). Teeple, too, finds indications of an acquaintance with Jewish Christianity in the source (which he labels S). It is written in semitized Greek. However, he doubts that it came from the pen of a Jewish Chris-tian and argues that the gospels of Mark and Matthew influenced the source. He believes that it reflects a late date (after 75 C.E.) and the Chris-tian tendency to "deify" Jesus. It presented Jesus as a worker of wonders to which there are responses of both faith and hostility (*Literary* 143-47). It is obvious that Teeple's larger source reconstruction results in a quite different characterization of the document. Finally, Fortna proposes that his "Signs Gospel" originated in a Jewish Christian milieu at an unknown date as part of a missionary enterprise among Jews. It was designed to show that Jesus was indeed the Messiah and grew out of a tradition that had close contacts with the synoptic tradition. Above all, the whole of the representation of Jesus, including his passion and resurrection, focuses upon his messianic character (*Gospel of Signs* 221-34).

At this point it is appropriate to look at those theories that propose more than one source. Some of those who detect a signs source behind the Fourth Gospel believe either that it was the only source utilized by the evangelist or that it is the only source that can be isolated. We should dis-tinguish these single source theories from the multiple source proposals, some of which include a signs source and some of which do not.

Leading the way among the multiple source theories of the recent period is, of course, Bultmann's proposal. In addition to the *sēmeia* source, described above, Bultmann argues that the evangelist used two other detectable sources—the *Offenbarungsreden* ("revelatory speeches") and a passion narrative source. (He also alludes to other sources and traditions that were likely employed by the author of John, particularly a source that paralleled the synoptic tradition.) The *Offenbarungsreden* was a collection of speech materials with a distinctly gnostic flavor. These speeches are always found on the lips of Jesus with the sole exception of the prologue of the gospel. They are characteristically poetic and liturgical in their style. The passion narrative utilized by John was not one or all of the Synoptic Gospels but another document. In some cases, the source paralleled the synoptic accounts, but in other cases it gave the evangelist unique passion materials. These three sources—*sēmeia*, speech, and passion—were incorporated by the evangelist along with other additions and revisions. Bultmann, however, sees still another hand in the formation of the gospel—a later "ecclesiastical redactor." The redactor added significantly to the gospel in an attempt to shape it into a more "orthodox" statement. For example, this proposed redactor is responsible, in Bultmann's opinion, for the sacramental passages and the apocalyptic eschatology of the gospel (*Gospel* 13–83, 131–67, 218–34, 247–324, 342–87, 419–43, 490–518, 523–631, 637–717).[9]

Two more recent multiple source theories are important: Teeple's "S source" has already been described, since it roughly parallels other signs source proposals. His "G source" is comparable to Bultmann's *Offenbarungsreden*. G was largely a collection of speech material, originating in a milieu Teeple labels "semi-gnostic." It reflects a Hellenistic and mystical form of thought. The work of the Fourth Evangelist enhanced the somewhat gnostic tendency of the "G source." A second-century redactor further supplemented the gospel (*Literary* 143–47).

Another and somewhat different multiple source theory later came from the pen of S. Temple. His proposal has many affinities to the foundation gospel (or *Grundevangelium*) ideas we will discuss under the developmental theories, but since he postulates other sources as well, we treat it in relation to the multiple source theories. In brief, Temple finds a narrative-discourse source which became the core of the Fourth Gospel. The distinctive feature of this core gospel was the wedding of discourses to narrations. He isolates occurrences of this pattern (e.g., 6:1-35, 41-51, 60 and 66-70) and attributes them to his proposed core gospel. Temple contends John added enlargements upon this narrative-discourse pattern (e.g., in 6:36-40 and 61-65). The evangelist performed midrashim of a sort on this material as it was woven into the gospel. While the style of the enlargements is quite distinct from the narrative-discourse materials, there is no discernible difference in style between the narratives and the discourses themselves—a view which sets Temple apart from so many investigators who have argued that the narratives and discourses of John are different in style (Kysar, "Source Analysis"). The gospel's author also employed other sources, according to Temple: A liturgical hymn used in the prologue, a "two signs source" (consisting of 2:1-11 and 4:46-54), and a "euchartistic homily" (6:52-59), to mention only three of the additional ten sources Temple finds in the Fourth Gospel (37f., 50-62, 68-251, 285-96).

These source proposals, from the simplest signs source to the complex multiple source theories, are fascinating and in some cases promising. What they offer which is most rewarding is a basic hypothesis upon which the student of John can study the redactional work of the evangelist and construct a history of the Johannine tradition (see below). By far the current source proposal which seems to attract the most attention and, at the same time, criticism is that of Fortna.[10] It is fair to say that his theory is one around which much future discussion will center. This is not to say, however, that source criticism is well established in the circles of Fourth Gospel scholarship.[11] Unlike the two (or four) source hypotheses for the Synoptic Gospels, none of these theories approaches the status of widespread acceptance. And perhaps this is for good reason. First, as we have seen, there are still serious methodological problems eroding the competence of Fourth Gospel source criticism. Second, nothing like a consensus has emerged from among the source critics themselves. While a signs source of some kind seems to have considerable acceptance, there are still major differences among different reconstructions of this hypothetical source. For example, did the signs source have the form of a collection of wonder stories as Becker, Nicol, and Schnackenburg maintain, or did it fall roughly into the gospel genre with passion material as a part of its contents as Fortna, Teeple, and Temple would have us believe? Finally, we may simply ask if, given the formidable problems of source criticism of John, it is even possible to isolate with any precision the source materials. We need still further debate among the source critics themselves and confirmation from others before sufficient consensus is within reach.

Developmental Theories

A second major option in understanding the history of the composition of the Gospel of John is a view which envisions the evolution of the gospel through different stages. Instead of proposing that John used one or more written documents in the construction of the gospel, a number of scholars believe that in some form a fundamental piece of literature was expanded by successive editions or that a tradition was translated into literary form at a number of stages. For the most part, too, these theories understand the history of the composition of the gospel within a single school or tradition. That is, the source theories sometimes propose that the source(s) came from a milieu and community discernibly distinct from that of the Fourth Evangelist. However, the developmental proponents most often understand that the gospel grew up through stages within one community that, although it changed through the passage of time, was nonetheless continuous with the community that originated the first stage of the gospel. Hence, the source theorists speak of a "pre-Johannine" tradition in the source(s), while the developmentalists frequently prefer to speak even of the earliest level of the gospel materials as Johannine. Generally, we may separate two subclasses of hypotheses within what we are calling the developmental theories: the first are patterns of oral-written-redacted; the second are patterns of basic gospel-redaction. Both subtypes stress a kind of maturational scheme in the history of the composition of the Fourth Gospel.

The modern-day precursor of the developmental theories of our first subtype is M.-E. Boismard, who resolves the tensions between futuristic and realized eschatology in John by supposing the gospel went through two major additions. The first edition of the gospel, he proposed, included the futuristic eschatology. The second stratum of the gospel, including the realized or present eschatology, is the result of a second edition. Both of these editions were dependent upon the work of John, son of Zebedee. Finally, the evangelist Luke was responsible for redactional additions to the second edition of John as is evident by the Lukan characteristics of chapter 21 and the prologue ("L'evolution," and "Saint Luc"; cf. Parker, "Two Editions").

Boismard's proposal is relatively simple when compared to the more elaborate theory of the influential American scholar, R. E. Brown. Brown finds five different stages of development in the history of the composition of John: 1) The original source of the gospel was a body of oral tradition which may have had its roots in the memories of John, the son of Zebedee. 2) At the next stage the materials were developed into "Johannine patterns"—dramatic narratives, long discourses, sign narratives linked with sayings materials, and the development of peculiarly Johannine features, such as misunderstanding and irony. All of this transpired within a single community, a Johannine "school." The principal figure was at first, perhaps, John, son of Zebedee, but during the second stage one of his prominent disciples emerged. 3) This disciple of John was responsible for the organization of the oral materials into a coherent gospel. This initial structuring of the gospel gave the materials a fundamental pattern, which exists right down to the present document. Not all of the oral materials known within the community were incorporated into the written gospel at this stage, however. 4) This same disciple produced a second edition of the gospel, possibly as a result of a new situation faced by his community, more specifically perhaps by the exclusion of the Johannine church from the synagogue (as suggested by 9:22-23. 5) Finally, another figure still further edited the gospel. Brown proposes that this figure was a pupil of the evangelist (called a "friendly redactor" to distinguish this figure from Bultmann's "ecclesiastic redactor"), and his or her work was an effort to preserve other traditional materials which were not included in the gospel in either of its previous editings. At this final stage, for instance, much of the farewell discourse materials were added and eucharistic words were transposed from their last supper setting to their new home in chapter 6. Thus, with this elaborate reconstruction, Brown is able to account for the literary puzzles of John. Moreover, so far as Brown is concerned, it solves the problem of the relationship of John to the Synoptics: at stage one many of the materials had common ground with the synoptic tradition, but there was no literary dependence on the Synoptics (*Commentary–Gospel* 1:xxxiv–xxxix).[12]

Another English-language author, B. Lindars, offers a similar reconstruction of the compositional process behind the Fourth Gospel. For convenience, we have reduced his theory to a number of stages to make comparison with others easier. 1) At the first stage, Lindars speculates, there were a number of unrelated traditions and perhaps short collections of materials. Among these might have been a collection, which contained the two numbered signs (2:22 and 4:54), and possibly more. However, any reconstruction of these small collections is impossible. 2) Homilies were produced out of this traditional material. These written, separate homilies were addressed to a community immersed in dialogue with the synagogue. 3) The first form of the Fourth Gospel was little more than an effort to publish a collection of these sermons, but the evangelist did so in the gospel genre under the influence of the form but not necessarily the content of the Gospel of Mark. This first form comprised a section on the ministry of Jesus introduced by the witness of the Baptist (1:6-7a) and concluded with the same (10:40-42) along with a narration of the passion and resurrection. 4) The threat of persecution from the Jewish sector evoked a second edition. Here a number of sections were added (e.g., chapter 11) and some of the portions of the gospel rearranged, e.g., the transposition of the temple cleansing story from the passion narrative to chapter 2. 5) A number of "post-Johannine additions" (e.g., chapter 21) were made to the revised gospel (*Behind* 38-41, 43-60, 62-78; *Gospel of John*, 47-48, 51-54).

These three schemes for the emergence of the Fourth Gospel through a compositional process represent the first subtype of developmental theories. Brown and Lindars both propose a process beginning with Johannine oral tradition and involving a number of editions and a redaction before the gospel reached its present form. Our second subtype is different, for it posits a "foundation gospel" which subsequently underwent revision. The first instance of this kind of theory is the proposal of Wilkens. He postulates a three-step process of development. 1) A "foundation gospel" ("*Grundevangelium*") was written which was in effect a kind of Signs Gospel containing a Galilean signs ministry, a Judean signs ministry, and a passion narrative. Its author was the "beloved disciple." 2) At the first redaction of the foundation gospel, this disciple added discourse materials rather extensively, leaving unaffected the framework of the original gospel. The redactors, however, added these materials with care so that they cohered well with the narratives (e.g., the bread discourse in chapter 6). 3) The second editing of the gospel was again the work of the beloved disciple, but, in this case, involved a rather drastic rearrangement of the original pattern of the gospel. The beloved disciple reworked the entire document into a Passover gospel, inserting allusions to the Passover (2:13; 6:4; and 11:55). The additional materials worked into the gospel at this stage had strong paschal themes (e.g., the Nicodemus conversation). This rearrangement brought the relocating of the temple cleansing in its present position. Hence, the composition of John was a process over two or three decades and represented the changes in the thinking of the one author, the beloved disciple (Wilkens, *Entstehungsgeschichte* 92–122, 127–64, 171–74).

More recently Richter produced a proposal that should be discussed, and again we have summarized his hypothesis in terms of stages. 1) Soon after its expulsion from the synagogue, a Johannine Jewish Christian community produced a *Grundschrift*. This foundational writing took a form similar to the gospel genre. It probably incorporated a signs source along with passion and resurrection narratives different from those of the Synoptics. Its eschatology was futuristic and apocalyptic, and its Christology was Jewish-messianic. 2) Later in the Johannine community a new Son of God Christology emerged and caused a schism between those who embraced this view and the older Jewish Christian group. The one we call the Fourth Evangelist edited and expanded the foundational writing to give expression to this newer Christology. The evangelist represents the conflict between the two schools of Johannine Christianity in the conflict between the historical Jesus and the "Jews." Among the additions made in this reworking of the *Grundschrift* were the prologue, along with other christological passages, and sections giving expression to the new, realized eschatology. 3) An anti-docetic redactor made considerable additions to the gospel. Between stages 2 and 3 Richter posits the emergence of a Johannine docetism which still further fragmented the community, but which produced no docetic redaction of the gospel. The redactor responding to the conflict with the docetic Johannine Christians attempted to reshape the gospel slightly in order to address this issue. That editor added passages which stressed the humanity and physical reality of Jesus, e.g., 1:14-18 and 20:24-29. It is probably from this same author or circle that the Fourth Evangelist came. Richter obviously understands that the process of composition is most clearly detectable in the theological themes of the Fourth Gospel, most especially in its Christology and eschatology; and he sees the development of the gospel resulting from intracommunity conflicts and schisms ("Präsentische"; cf. Mattill).

Boismard (along with Lamouille) revised and expanded his original proposal in what is part of a massive study of the interrelationship of the four gospels. Boismard and Lamouille propose that the Fourth Gospel developed in four distinct stages, beginning with a kind of "foundation gospel." 1) The first stage was the composition of a gospel account leading from John the Baptist through the resurrection stories. It was a simple gospel which professed an early Prophet-New Moses Christology and a futuristic eschatology. The authors structured it simply around Jesus' ministry in Samaria, Galilee, Jerusalem, and Bethany, followed by the passion-resurrection narratives. One whom the two interpreters call "John 1" wrote this first form of the gospel in Aramaic. They suggest but do not argue that John 1 may have been the disciple, John, son of Zebedee. His work was influential in the writing of two of the primary sources behind the gospels of Mark and Luke. Lamouille and Boismard call this first Gospel of John, "Document C," and date it about 50. 2) The second stage in the writing of the Fourth Gospel is the amplification of "Document C" by another figure designated "John 2" (probably, John the Elder). Under the influence of other sources for the Synoptic Gospels, this second edition of John retained the order of "Document C" but included additional discourse and narrative materials. Writing about 60–65 C.E. John II introduced a Davidic view of Christ along with basic elements of a word and wisdom Christology. It is at this stage that the gospel took on its pejorative use of "the Jews" and "the world" and its present or realized eschatology. 3) Some thirty-five to forty years later, this same author, John 2, produced a second gospel, soon after the writing of the first of the Fourth Evangelist. The second gospel by John 2, however, followed a different structure from that dating back to "Document C." The author introduced a pattern of feasts as the basic outline of his second gospel account (an order preserved in the present form of John). Changes included the addition of the prologue and chapter 21, the integration of elaborate numerical symbolism in some narratives, and the transformation of the gospel's view of Christ with the insertion of the Son of God and Son Christologies. In this case, John 2 stressed the mysterious origins of the Son of Man, gave prominence to the Spirit, and added sacramental interpretations of traditional materials. 4) The fourth and final stage is the work of still another figure, who is called "John 3." Boismard and Lamouille propose that the primary role of this figure was to integrate the two gospels written by John 2. However, while fusing the two previous editions of the gospel, he added some *logia*, inserted an apocalyptic eschatology, and (strangely) inverted chapters 5 and 6. The result of his fusion is the present form of the Gospel of John (Boismard and Lamouille 11, 16–70).

This brief overview of six developmental theories certainly does not do justice to them and runs the danger of suggesting that there are more points of consensus among them than is actually the case. The intent here, however, is to give the reader a sampling of the kind of history of composition typical of these hypotheses. As a whole, they are both intriguing and satisfying, if sometimes terribly complex and very speculative. While supposing a rather complex history of development, they sometimes may appeal as simple explanations of complex Johannine problems. They are also sweeping in their coverage, proposing solutions at once for literary and theological difficulties in the Fourth Gospel, resolving the question of the relationship of this gospel to the Synoptics, and outlining a community history. They have the further appeal that they do not presume to delineate precisely among the materials incorporated at each stage (with the exception of Boismard and Lamouille, who propose detailed reconstructions of each document at each of their four stages). Hence, in a way they are less ambitious than source-critical theories. Yet I still hold some reservations about these developmental proposals, since it appears that the method of discerning the different stages or levels in the Fourth Gospel is no freer from difficulties than the source theories. Furthermore, like the source theories, we are left with a nagging problem: if the redactor in each case left such contradictions and aporias as to make the distinction of stages (or sources for that matter) evident to the investigator, how are we to account for the editor's less than polished work? Does the redactor's willingness to expand the document at hand with additional and sometimes contradictory materials suggest that this person was less than sophisticated as a writer and theologian (not to mention as an editor), and that he or she was exceedingly tolerant of a variety of views? Or, was it the case that the proposed redactors were so respectful of the community's earlier traditions that they could not abort them? In the opinion of this writer, however, the signs source theories and the developmental proposals of Brown, Lindars, and Richter, Boismard and Lamouille provide an arena within which the Johannine literary puzzle may eventually work out.

Form and Tradition Criticism—The Relationship of the Fourth Gospel and the Synoptics

There is still another avenue open to those who would pursue the resolution of the literary questions of the Fourth Gospel, and its taproot is the classical question of the relationship of the Fourth Gospel and the Synoptics. Through form and tradition criticism it is possible, say some, to discover the literary dependence of John on one or more of the Synoptics and to find then close at hand the fact that in the process of incorporating synoptic materials the Fourth Evangelist produced a document which has the appearance of some disunity or, at least, disruption. Because of similar form and tradition analysis, others would say that no literary dependence upon the Synoptics is evident, but that there is evidence of the Fourth Evangelist's use of oral tradition which had contacts with synoptic traditions. The incorporation of the preliterary materials into the gospel left the document marred by its well-known problems.

Those who argue for the literary dependence of the Fourth Gospel upon one or more of the Synoptics are fewer in number than prior to the publication of the seminal works of P. Gardner-Smith (*Saint John* and "St. John's Knowledge").[13] In the minds of many, that study demolished the grounds for explaining the similarities between John and the Synoptics on the basis of literary dependence and pointed in the direction of a preliterary contact between the two traditions. B. Noack emphasized that Gardner-Smith pointed contemporary scholarship away from the idea that the Fourth Evangelist knew and used one or more of the Synoptics.

Still biblical scholarship is never homogeneous, and the debate continues. Among those who have forcefully retained a position advocating literary dependence of John upon a synoptic is J. A. Bailey. His method is to isolate passages in either Luke or John where there appears to be an intrusion in the narrative or discourse movement. If there is a parallel to the material in which the intrusion occurs in another gospel, he maintains that some borrowing has taken place. His conclusion is that passages in which the gospels of John and Luke disagree with Mark and Matthew indicate literary dependence between John and Luke. He finds eleven such passages and concludes that they constitute evidence that John did know and use the third gospel (e.g., the anointing of Jesus in John 12:1-8 and Luke 7:36-50). Other passages indicate a less direct literary contact, however, and so he concludes that, in addition to some degree of literary dependence of the Fourth Gospel upon Luke, the two must have occasionally used common traditions (e.g., the words of the risen Christ to Peter, John 21:1ff. and Luke 24:34). Bailey's thesis is then that there existed essentially two kinds of relationships between the Fourth Gospel and the third: at some points a direct literary dependence of the former upon the latter and at other points their mutual use, each in its own way, of a common, related tradition (Bailey 115; cf. Richter, "Gefangennahme").

Barrett built his illustrious commentary on John on his conclusion that the Fourth Evangelist knew and employed Mark and to a lesser degree Luke. In 1955, he expressed the opinion, for instance, that "the Johannine passion story is an edited version of the Marcan, into which John has introduced some fresh material." In the revised edition of his commentary, he defends his position. He surveys the views of those who deny literary dependence and counters with the evidence that John either knew the Gospel of Mark or some document very similar. He contends that the simpler solution is that John presupposed the existence of Mark and perhaps at points Luke (*John and Judaism* 14–18, quote 18, and *Gospel According to St. John*).

F. Neirynck also champions the thesis that chapter 20 is the Fourth Evangelist's construction on the basis of direct knowledge of the Synoptic Gospels. Still, Boismard hypothesizes that John did not know the Synoptic Gospels themselves but used sources that were subsequently employed by the synoptic evangelists. Therefore, for instance, proto-Luke was the main source used by the Fourth Evangelist in the passion narrative, just as other hypothetical synoptic sources were influential in shaping the Gospel of John (Boismard and Lamouille).

J. Blinzler has suggested along different lines that John had knowledge of Mark and perhaps also of Luke but employed them only from memory of their content. In other words, there was no direct "copying" of a synoptic by the Fourth Evangelist, but the influence of Mark and Luke through the memory of the evangelist (59). G. Reim offers a still more ingenious proposal. The original edition of John ended at chapter 17, but was drastically transformed when the Fourth Evangelist incorporated large portions of a now lost "fourth synoptic gospel." The incorporation of this synoptic material is obvious in the passion narrative, Reim contends, and elsewhere in passages where its inclusion has caused disturbances in the Johannine narrative (*Studien* 214–16, 233–46; cf. "John IV," and "Probleme"). The passion narrative is the focus of H. Klein's study that compares Luke and John and proposes, as a resolution to the similarities and differences between the two, a common written source employed by both. A document was constructed out of the sources employed by Mark and Luke and that document became the basis for the construction of the passion and resurrection stories in the Fourth Gospel.

It is noteworthy that there is more evidence in contemporary scholarship for theories of a "mediated knowledge" of one or more of the Synoptics than for direct literary dependence.[14] With the exception of Barrett and a part of J. A. Bailey's thesis, those who are seeking indications of the Fourth Gospel's use of the Synoptics resort to intermediate phenomena, such as human memory, a fourth synoptic gospel, sources used by the Synoptics, or a source constructed out of synoptic sources. Another proposed mediating link between the Synoptics and John is oral tradition. Dodd's carefully constructed position was that the contact of John with the Synoptics was through an oral tradition, which was independent of the Synoptic Gospels but was comprised of some materials similar to those that found their way into the first three gospels. Dodd came to this conclusion by studying those passages in the Fourth Gospel where some synoptic contact seems apparent and then moving through those where synoptic features are less and less clear. His method throughout is form critical, and he finds that the Johannine material can be analyzed in terms of forms in much the same way form criticism has analyzed the synoptic materials. His conclusion that the synoptic and Johannine gospels emerged out of a common oral tradition is buttressed not only by his study of the relationship between Johannine and synoptic passages but also by his success in showing that the forms characteristic of the Johannine material are like those believed to exist in the synoptic tradition. A further part of the agenda of Dodd's enterprise is to argue, based on the existence of a preliterary tradition employed in John, the likelihood that there is historically reliable information about Jesus in the Fourth Gospel (*Historical Tradition* 349, 366–87, 423; cf. Higgins).

Dauer's study of the Johannine passion narrative confirms Dodd's general thesis. Dauer finds that the Johannine passion account depends upon an independent oral tradition. The written Synoptic Gospels influenced the oral Johannine tradition, and the influence might possibly have gone the other direction as well. Dauer does hedge a bit, however, when he recognizes the possibility that, by the time the Fourth Evangelist drew on the tradition, it had taken on a written form (335–36; cf. Sable, and Boismard, "Precédé"). Dauer's inconclusiveness on the question of whether this independent and distinctively Johannine tradition was still oral or had been written by the time of its incorporation in the Fourth Gospel is exemplary of others who take a similar view. They in effect conclude that we cannot be sure whether this tradition was oral or written in its last stages before the Fourth Gospel. E. Haenchen compares a number of passages with their synoptic parallels, eliminates the possibility of literary dependence, and concludes that the contact between the two is explainable by positing a common tradition. However, he does not declare himself on whether the Fourth Evangelist used this tradition in its oral or written forms ("Johanneische"). E. Siegman and R. Schnackenburg both studied 4:46-54 with much the same result (Schnackenburg, "Traditionsgeschichte"). F. Hahn finds form-tradition analysis the best way to understand 1:35-51. Finally, we mention in passing the enticing and careful work of F. L. Cribbs, who not only argues for a common oral tradition upon which the evangelist drew but also that Luke was influenced by portions of the early Johannine tradition and attempted through his gospel to reconcile certain features of the Markan-Matthean traditions with the Johannine tradition ("Study").

It seems clear that it is much easier to explain the similarities and differences between the Synoptics and John by reference to preliterary contacts than by postulating some type of literary dependence. It is hard to understand the variety of resemblances between John and the Synoptics and still explain the vast differences as the result of the Fourth Evangelist's use of a literary form of the Synoptics. At least one may conclude that those who would argue for a literary dependence have yet to produce evidence that will sway the majority of scholars. On the other hand, appeal to oral tradition may be too easy. The category of "oral tradition" is nebulous, to say the least. What has been established, it seems, especially by the careful work of Dodd fortified by less inclusive studies, is that the Johannine materials manifest characteristics of narratives and discourses that had been preserved orally before their commitment to writing. Hence, the existence of a long and perhaps complex history of tradition behind the Fourth Gospel is likely. That it had contacts with the synoptic traditions seems equally reasonable. The pivotal question is whether the Fourth Evangelist was responsible for translating that oral tradition into written form or whether such a translation occurred before the evangelist used the material and whether it was even available as a written source(s). The answer to that question hinges upon the degree of success the source critics have in demonstrating that the traditional materials in John have literary features apart from those picked up in the process of the Fourth Evangelist's redaction. Doubtless Fortna has taken us the furthest in trying to establish that those literary features are precisely the character of the signs source materials in John. If we pose the question in terms of which situation seems the more likely to have allowed for the aporias of the Gospel of John—the evangelist's use of a written source or oral tradition—reason would seem to dictate a decision in favor of the former. We may reasonably assume that the author of John was more inhibited in incorporating a fixed, written tradition than a pliable, oral one. The process, however, of multiple redactions advocated by the developmental theorists seems equally believable: translation from oral to written gospel in stages leaves ample opportunity for the production of a less than polished literary whole.

Conclusion

In concluding the discussion of efforts to probe the literary problems of the Fourth Gospel, we must be careful with our generalizations. Theories of disarrangement have given way in contemporary research to two movements that are vastly different in their goals. On the one hand, there are those who attempt to do structural analysis of John (or portions thereof) as it stands. They assume as they embark upon their ventures that the gospel makes some sense as a literary whole without recourse to either rearrangement or investigation of its history. In some cases, the results of their work have shown some validity to their presupposition. On the other hand, there are those who maintain that we will not understand the appearances of disunity and brokenness in the Fourth Gospel until we understand its history of composition. They have offered us significant evidence that John stands upon the shoulders of a rather developed tradition. That tradition reached the Fourth Evangelist in either written or oral form and was incorporated by the evangelist into the gospel either in one or a series of stages.[15] These two general alternatives (structural analysis and history of composition) are, of course, not exclusive of one another, as I have said. Those responsible for the production of the Fourth Gospel embedded tradition in the gospel in an imperfect way with the consequence that John as we have it is marred with breaks, contradictions, and repetition. Yet to the logic of the redactor-evangelist (or even a series of redactors) the completed work constituted a literary whole which is entitled to analysis as such. While structural analysis and history of composition are strikingly different methodologies, their cooperation is called for, since neither one without the other seems capable of telling us all that the most curious of us would like to know about the Gospel of John.

Chapter Six

Historical Puzzles in John

The literary problems of the Gospel of John are only one fraction of the dilemma posed by that document for interpreters. Equally perplexing are a series of puzzles that we may roughly call historical in nature. The problems and their proposed solutions do not neatly subdivide themselves into such categories as literary, historical, and ideological; but the differences these three categories pose for us are sufficiently sound to allow one to grasp some handles on the interpretive problems of John. In the main, the questions and proposals that we are about to survey in this section root in inquiries that are fundamentally historical. For each of the subdivisions of this section we will find basic puzzles in the Fourth Gospel, the solutions of which seem to lie in a proper understanding of the history surrounding the document.

History of Religions Analysis

First in importance among these historical problems is the question of the historical context of thought out of which John comes. This is the question of the lines of philosophical and religious thought in the Roman world which might have influenced the thought of the evangelist and hence constitute the framework within which we can properly understand the gospel's ideas. A classical illustration of this difficulty is the dualistic language and symbolism of the Fourth Gospel, e.g., light and darkness, the world above and the world below.

If interpreters are to understand this dualistic thought properly, it is necessary that they have some grasp of the intellectual milieu that influenced the author of the gospel and in the light of which they may justifiably interpret their thought. For instance, was Hellenistic philosophy highly influential on the evangelist's thought? If so, then we would be wise to view the Johannine dualism in terms of philosophical, perhaps neoplatonic, categories. We could then properly assume that John intended to speak with symbols of a cosmic, ontological dualism. On the other hand, if the Judaism of the time influenced the evangelist more crucially, then our reading of the dualistic symbols must be considerably different. For example, if that form of Jewish thought prevalent at Qumran and expressed in the so-called Dead Sea Scrolls was instrumental in forming the evangelist's thought, we might understand the gospel's dualistic language in an eschatological and even apocalyptic framework rather than a cosmological one. The historical inquiry concerning the intellectual milieu of the Fourth Gospel is not a question of pure curiosity, then, for it has determinative effects upon the interpretation of the thought of the evangelist.

The search for the intellectual milieu, however, is fraught with difficulties. History of religions research is far from simple, for we know that the rudimentary task of seeking and analyzing parallels between the Fourth Gospel and other extant literature of the Roman world of the first century does not constitute the isolation of the thought world of the gospel. The method has become much more complex than that. We seek not just parallels but must probe behind those parallels to find the intent of their language. Two authors may use very similar language and symbols and mean entirely different things by them. Therefore, we cannot assume that parallel language and literary form mean that one influenced the other. Another fact plagues the whole method of history of religions research, namely, that the Fourth Evangelist has surely "christianized" contemporary thought. Therefore, it is sometimes difficult to know to what degree a Hellenistic or Jewish concept has shaped the Christian concept of the Fourth Evangelist (Kysar, "Background").

Still another development in history of religions research has further complicated the process of isolating John's intellectual world: what was once thought to be a sharp and easy distinction between Hellenistic and Jewish in the first century seems no longer tenable. Perhaps such a distinction was cultivated only for the sake of the convenience of interpreters. However, the growing consensus is that the cultural intercourse of the Roman world was so thorough and so rich that to isolate insulated pockets of this or that form of thought does violence to the historical reality. Specifically, this means that there was probably no Judaism which we can confidently claim was pure of influence from the Hellenistic culture of the time. Nor is it safe to assume that a Hellenistic movement untouched by Jewish colorations might have influenced the Fourth Evangelist (M. Smith). The result of this is that the task is made much more difficult. We must attempt to mark off some general intellectual framework that influenced the author of John, and within a christianized form of which the gospel can be justifiably interpreted, without at the same time ignoring what a rich and syncretistic cultural phenomenon the Roman world of the first century of the common era was.

Finally, we need to recognize that the Gospel of John has persistently presented history of religions research with one of its most formidable tasks. Scholars have proposed nearly every conceivable religious and/or philosophical movement in the Roman world as the intellectual setting of the Fourth Gospel (cf. Dodd, *Interpretation*). In recent years, there has never been anything like a consensus of scholars on the history of religions background of the gospel, and the major trends have shifted rather dramatically. What follows is only suggestive of the vast research on this question.

Gnosticism

We must begin with Gnosticism as the first alternative for the thought world of the Fourth Evangelist because of its mighty proponent, R. Bultmann. His thesis, boldly and consistently worked out, created a tidal wave throughout the scholarly world that still has not entirely subsided. Many were swept along with the force of that wave, persuaded by Bultmann's evidence and its results. Others have persistently swum in different directions. In brief, Bultmann's thesis is this: the intellectual home of the Fourth Evangelist was in the context of an oriental Gnosticism which is best expressed in gnostic literature of an admittedly post-Christian date but which existed in preliterary form before the advent of Christianity. The Gospel of John thus became the storm center for the debate over a pre-Christian Gnosticism. Bultmann claimed that this pre-Christian gnosis had already influenced Judaism before the beginnings of the Christian movement, (e.g., Qumran) and that it was in the gnostic modes of thought that Christianity took its definitive form (Bultmann, *Gospel*, passim; *Theology* 2: pt. 3; and *Primitive Christianity*).

Among more recent scholars, the gnostic thesis is still very much alive, but we can perhaps vaguely distinguish two degrees in which Gnosticism is understood to have been influential upon the thought of the Fourth Evangelist. Some propose a strong degree of Gnosticism embraced by the evangelist, while others argue that a lesser degree was perhaps not embraced as much as used by the author. Among the leading proponents of the former position is S. Schulz whose commentary on John persistently argues for the gnostic setting. Schulz maintains that the logos concept of the prologue, for instance, may have been structured in part out of Hellenistic Jewish speculation concerning wisdom (e.g., Wis 9:9-12; Sir 24:5- 31), but the decisive concept of the personification of the logos stems without doubt from a Hellenistic Gnosticism. Similarly, the Son of Man title in the Fourth Gospel had been thoroughly "gnosticized" by the time the evangelist utilized it; this is evident by the concept of preexistence and the "sending" motif in Johannine Christology. Schulz speaks of a "gnostic speech tradition" which influenced the author of John at such points as 8:28; 12:23f.; and 13:31f. The Johannine envoy Christology with its conception of Christ as one sent by the Father into the world is thoroughly gnostic in its presuppositions; and the incarnational thought of the gospel also roots in gnostic categories. The paraclete idea is similarly a mixture of Jewish thought with Gnosticism, since it is connected in Schulz's analysis with the Son of Man motif. The dualism of the thought of the Gospel of John reflects how the Old Testament and Jewish dualism of an ethical and eschatological kind was transformed into a cosmic and even physical enmity. Johannine Christology is then one of pure exaltation in which the historical man Jesus is real (not just an appearance) but in no sense compromised in his divinity by this world and in no sense humiliated by it. The humanity of this heavenly being is but a "disguise" or "veil" through which his glory is perceptible (Schulz, *Evangelium* 27-29, 63-64, 70, 211, 189).[1]

Schulz's view is perhaps the clearest perpetuation and defense of the Bultmannian thesis in the literature of the last several decades. L. Schottroff also reflects the influence of Bultmann but perhaps has radicalized his view. Schottroff's position builds upon what she takes to be a proper understanding of Johannine dualism. The thought of the gospel begins with and is everywhere defined by an antithesis—the presence of salvation and its absence. These two poles define the individual. The distance from one or the other of these two poles defines everything. Their distance from the evil world determines the nature of "life" and "love," and other such terms for salvation. Consequently, none of the dualistic features of Johannine thought are temporal but strictly salvational, that is, expressions of the two antithetical poles of acceptance or rejection of salvation. The dualism is not cosmological, or ethical; nor is it a "demythologized" mythology, as Bultmann maintained. What appears as the ethical dimension of the dualism is nothing more than another way of expressing the decisional options of acceptance or rejection. Johannine Christology is also to be understood in the context of this radically dualistic conception. The evangelist places the tradition of the fleshly existence of Christ, the revealer, within a gnostic dualism. Christ is the otherworldly revealer whose earthly appearance is preserved in the Christian language of his flesh (incarnation) but whose heavenly reality is alone important for faith. Schottroff speaks of the fleshly reality of Jesus as the "irrelevant given" with which the evangelist had to deal, since it was part of the tradition. However, the evangelist drastically transformed the tradition by an exclusive focus upon the glory of the revealer, visible even in his earthly sojourn (Schottroff, *Glaubende* 228–34, 237–38, 268–79, 289–90, 293–94; "Johannes"; "Heil").

Both Schulz and Schotroff remind one of the view of E. Käsemann who also stresses that the predominant motif in Johannine Christology is upon the glory of Christ at the expense of his earthly reality. Käsemann speaks of that view as a "naive docetism." Yet while he emphasizes the docetic quality of the Johannine Christ, he does not attempt a history of religions explanation for that peculiar quality (Käsemann, *Testament* 7–13, 21–26, 32–35; cf. "Aufbau").

J. Becker has tried to understand John's dualism and has proposed a kind of history of its development. For the moment our interest is only in what Becker designates the "third phase" of that development, namely a gnostic dualism. While the earlier phases have roots in early Christianity and Qumran, the evangelist was primarily active in developing the gnostic dimensions of the dualism ("Beobachtungen"). K. Fischer has found gnostic influences elsewhere, claiming that 10:1-18 roots in a gnostic myth. The speech of Jesus in that passage is most certainly drawn directly from the gnostic view of the redeemer. Still, the author of John has broken with the pattern of gnostic speeches at a number of points to give this passage a distinctive feature, e.g., the fact that a sharp distinction is made between the identities of the redeemer and the redeemed.

These studies propose an extensive contact with Gnosticism on the part of the Fourth Evangelist. Others more cautiously propose that this religious phenomenon may have significantly influenced the evangelist. An eminent Johannine scholar, R. Schnackenburg, is a good example. While he does not wish to deny the influence of Gnosticism on the evangelist, Schnackenburg does not believe that that influence was isolated from the other religious conceptualities of the period. He believes, for instance, that the one clearly gnostic feature of Johannine Christology is the persistent concern for the origin and destiny of the redeemer. Yet this feature expresses more of a negative influence from Gnosticism than a positive one. This is to say that the Fourth Evangelist intended by this emphasis to respond to the gnostic insistence upon origin and destiny. Likewise, the evangelist "took into consideration the gnostic manner of speaking of the Son (of God) and thereby bound it with his view of the

Son Christology." Therefore, while there are clear contacts between the gnostic redeemer mythology and Johannine Christology, the author of John is not borrowing so much as preempting the gnostic view in order to answer the concerns of those who share that persuasion. Gnostic concepts are also influential in the dualism of the Fourth Gospel, particularly in the notion of "life." A certain form of Syrian Gnosticism influenced the evangelist but that influence was significantly conditioned by other influences (Schnackenburg, *Johannesevangelium* 2:162–66, 273–79, 440–43, quote 166; cf. "Menschensohn" 135–37).

G. Stemberger argues along similar lines that John's purpose in part was to respond to gnostic concerns. He argues that the Johannine community lived in a world deeply influenced by Jewish Gnosticism, and that the evangelist usurped the core of gnostic thought. This is particularly evident in the fact that the gospel has no interest in a history of Jesus' childhood. Moreover, Johannine eschatology is a response to the gnostic preoccupation with the relationship of the individual with space and time ("Er kam"). F. G. Untergassmair's monograph includes a study of the history of religions setting for the concept of name in the gospel. He concludes that a contact with a gnostic milieu similar to the one expressed in the "Gospel of Truth" cannot be denied. There are still, however, other contacts with the Old Testament exhibited in the name concept, and when it is all said and done we must conclude that, while the evangelist was in touch with a number of different intellectual spheres, the concept is on the whole the evangelist's own creation (Untergassmair, esp. 363–64). G. MacRae goes one step further in suggesting that John's author deliberately drew from a syncretistic milieu which includes gnostic elements in order to articulate a view of Jesus with universal appeal ("Ego-Proclamation," and "Jewish Background").

In general it must be said that the arguments for a gnostic influence upon the Fourth Evangelist are significantly diminished as compared with the years just prior to and after the publication of Bultmann's commentary. It will become evident that I believe the majority of scholars are now looking in different directions for the intellectual foundations of Johannine thought. More important, there are increasing indications that the so-called gnostic elements in the thought of the gospel are traceable to features of heterodox Judaism in the first century. Hence, rather than speaking of a pre-Christian Gnosticism with some sort of discernible identity of its own, scholars are pointing to gnosis within the structures of other religious movements of the time (E. Yamauchi). The suggestion is that we cannot legitimately speak of Gnosticism as a separable religious entity before the advent of Christianity and must instead seek the gnostic influence upon John in the other intellectual settings. There was, we believe, a syncretistic tendency in Judaism, for instance, which included, perhaps, pregnostic ideas and concepts. Yet the evidence is not all in as yet on this debated issue. The publication of the documents from Nag Hammadi makes available a rich depository of direct, gnostic thought; and its importance for the study of the Gospel of John must be established before a further verdict on the gnostic question can be reached (Facsimile Edition, and J. M. Robinson, *Nag Hammadi*; cf. Janssens)

The Old Testament and Rabbinical Judaism

The prominence of Bultmann's theory of the gnostic setting for John should not blind us to the continued efforts to show that the gospel is rooted most firmly in Old Testament and rabbinic thought. If anything, the shift of scholarship in recent decades has been toward the elucidation of Old Testament and rabbinic thought in the gospel. It is instructive that when W. F. Howard wrote his survey of then recent criticism of the Fourth Gospel in 1931 the chapter devoted to the background of the thought of the gospel was devoid of any discussion of Old Testament and rabbinic thought. Today our attention must in contrast give extensive attention to this alternative.

The question of the Old Testament citations in the Fourth Gospel is often debated.[2] Yet there is greater consensus on the fact that a good deal of the thought of the gospel roots in Old Testament thought itself.[3] The logos concept in the prologue is often thought to have been constructed out of Old Testament and rabbinic materials.[4] Brown presents a strong case for the parallels between the logos in the prologue and statements concerning wisdom in the Old Testament and intertestamental materials, e.g., wisdom was active in creation and came into the world only to experience rejection (Wis 9:9-10 and Sir 15:7; Brown, *Commentary–Gospel* 1:520-23). H. Moeller, F.-M. Braun, and A. Feuillet all suggest that the combination of the Old Testament concept of word and the Jewish speculation regarding wisdom produced a rabbinic myth which the Fourth Evangelist used as a model for describing Christ as the logos (Braun, *Jean le théologien II*, 137; Feuillet, *Prologue*, 224-25, 239-42; cf. De Pinto). Others, however, have found different rabbinic patterns behind that Johannine concept. J. Ackermann thinks rabbinic mythology centered around the Sinai event was instrumental in shaping the logos idea. P. Borgen points to a midrashic interpretation of Genesis 1:1ff. similar to the kind found in the Jerusalem Targum on Genesis 3:21 ("Observations," and "Logos;" cf. Hambly). M. McNamara also finds the targumic materials crucial for the setting of the logos, particularly the Palestinian Targum (*Neofiti*) on Exodus 15:18 in which the word of God is identified with light ("Logos," *Targum* 101-6, and "New Testament" 255f., 145-49).

Johannine Christology as a whole, too, may be significantly indebted to the Old Testament and rabbinic thought. Brown summarizes his position, "the Fourth Evangelist saw in Jesus the culmination of a tradition that runs through the Wisdom literature of the Old Testament" (*Commentary–Gospel* 1:cxxii). On the other hand, F.-M. Braun argues at length for the prophetic as well as the wisdom motifs as formative precursors of the Johannine Christ (*Jean le théologien II* 49-152; cf. Reim, *Studien* 247-60, and Richter, "Bist"). One aspect of that Christology which has received lengthy and numerous investigations is the envoy motif (the sending of the son). P. Borgen finds Johannine agency similar to the rabbinic principles of the official agent, although he believes that the Fourth Evangelist has combined those rabbinic principles with a concept of the heavenly agent found in Hellenistic Judaism (especially, Philo; Borgen, "God"; cf. Ford). J. P. Miranda's studies of the envoy motif conclude that the prophetic literature was most determinative for the Fourth Evangelist's thought, although he finds certain gnostic elements combined with it. However, in later work on the question, he holds that the Jewish concepts of the messenger and the legal envoy in the prophetic form were more influential (*Vater* 130-307, and *Sendung* 90). J.-A. Buhner argues that there are two levels in this Johannine motif—the first reflecting Jewish apocalyptic thought and the second rabbinic understandings of the representative figure (262-67, 422-33; cf. O. Michel).

The descending-ascending theme in Johannine Christology is most often the focus of efforts to find gnostic influence, but here too there have been attempts to discover Old Testament-rabbinic thought patterns. B. Vawter makes a case for the use of the Ezekiel passages concerning primeval man by the evangelist. Moeller is content to see sapiential ideas once again at work (94-95; cf. MacRae, "Jewish Background"), while McNamara believes the Targum on Psalm 68:18 shaped the Johannine idea of the death of Christ as ascension ("Ascension," *New Testament* 145-49). J. Coppens's study of the Son of Man sayings in the Fourth Gospel concludes with the suggestion that the sayings are a kind of *pesher* or *midrash* of the Daniel Son of Man, with the evangelist borrowing from the Isaiah *Ebed Yahweh* ("Servant of the Lord") passages his ideas of glorification and exaltation. From the Old Testament and intertestamental thought the sayings have drawn the ideas of exaltation and humiliation, the glorification of God, and the descent-ascent motifs ("Fils").

It is not surprising that the famous "I Am" (*egō eimi*) sayings in John have evoked a great deal of history of religions study, in particular the so-called absolute form of those sayings (those without predicates, e.g. 8:24, 28, 58; 13:19). The hypothesis that the Greek translation of passages in "Deutero-Isaiah" forms the backdrop for these sayings has been advanced by two American scholars, R. E. Brown and P. Harner. Those Isaiah passages in which absolute monotheism is asserted (plus Gen 28:13 and Ezek 20:5, according to Brown) formed the basis of a rabbinic use of "I am He" as a surrogate for the name of God. It was used especially in the liturgy for the Feast of Tabernacles (e.g., *Mishnah, Sukkah* 4:5). This usage, in turn, led the author to employ the expression on the lips of Jesus (Brown, *Commentary–Gospel* 1:535–37; Harner 15–36, 56–57; cf. Feuillet, *"Ego eimi"*; Reim, *Studien* 261. I). De La Potterie stresses that the literary form of these sayings reflects a Jewish style ("Je suis").

The so-called allegorical speeches, closely associated with the absolute "I Am" sayings (chapters 4, 6, 10, and 15), have likewise been understood out of Old Testament-rabbinic settings. Brown finds the wisdom ideology of Sirach 24:21 influential in 4:10-14, and Brown and Feuillet agree that a similar background for chapter 6 is feasible (Brown, *Commentary–Gospel* 1:178–79, 272–74). Feuillet sees in chapter 6 a delicate interweaving of a number of Old Testament themes: the manna of the Sinai desert and Jesus as the Mosaic-type Messiah, the messianic banquet, and sapiential overtones (*Johannine* 58–87). T. Preiss insists that the exodus motif is strongly influential in the chapter, evident both in its Passover setting and in the portrayal of Jesus as the Moses-like Messiah. He stresses that manna is linked with Torah in rabbinic thought; hence the discourse of the chapter asserts that Jesus is superior to both the Sinai manna and the Torah ("Étude sur le chapitre 6"). Borgen's provocative and lengthy study of chapter 6 proposes that the evangelist has employed there a midrashic interpretation of manna, weaving a homily out of the material. Borgen also finds influences of Philonic-like midrashim and a Jewish "judicial mysticism" reflected in the passage (*Bread from Heaven* 148).[5] J. A. Simonis vigorously defends the tenet that chapter 10 is rooted in the biblical images of the shepherd rather than in Mandaean gnostic thought. R. Borig has argued much the same with regard to chapter 15 and insists that what we see there is the radicalization of the Old Testament images (e.g., the true vine—Simonis, 320–22; Borig 106–7, 135–87, 192; cf. Derrett). Feuillet, however, finds more contacts with the sapiential literature (especially Sirach 24:17-20) than does Simonis (Feuillet, *Johannine* 87). R. Brown demurs before the attempt to attribute too much of the shepherd and vine speeches to the Old Testament, and prefers to credit more to the evangelist's own creativity (*Commentary–Gospel* 2:672).

The tantalizing paraclete passages of the Fourth Gospel (14:15-17, 26; 15:26-27; 16:7-11, 12-14) have evoked a number of investigations which propose an Old Testament-rabbinic background for the evangelist's thought. The influence of the book of Ezekiel stimulated the Fourth Evangelist's creation of the notion of the paraclete, thinks. B. Vawter (455–58). Brown agrees that the prophetic themes of the Old Testament loom large in the paraclete passages. In addition to these, the "tandem relationships" of the Old Testament (e.g., Moses-Joshua and Elijah-Elisha), personified wisdom, and Jewish angelology have converged in the paraclete theology (*Commentary–Gospel* 2:1137–39; cf. Riesenfeld, "Probable"; Bornkamm, "Paraklet"). U. Müller insists that the history of religions question concerning the paraclete passage is solved only as one investigates the history of the forms in which the sayings are found. Doing this, he finds that the paraclete is rooted in the notions surrounding the departing hero and his authentication of his testimony in the Jewish intertestamental literature (e.g., "Testament of the 12 Patriarchs"; see Müller, "Parakletenvorstellung").

The proponents of the gnostic hypothesis make much of John's dualism, but advocates of an Old Testament-rabbinic background, too, have argued their case in this connection. G. Stemberger holds that the dualism of the Fourth Gospel is of an ethical kind and roots not in Gnosticism but in Old Testament and Jewish thought, although he sees significant signs of Hellenistic influence as well as rabbinic. The light-darkness imagery is, however, founded in Isaiah, as well as Jewish wisdom and apocalyptic literature (*Symbolique* 44–144). O. Böcher sees less Hellenistic influence in the dualism. It arises, he proposes, out of Old Testament thought as it was interpreted in the centuries just prior to the advent of Christianity. Hence, it is a dualism of an ethical and eschatological kind. Still, Böcher believes that sectarian, not rabbinic, Judaism before the Fourth Evangelist shaped the Old Testament motifs we find in Johannine dualism (11–16; cf. Achtemeier).

Passover motifs in the gospel are further grounds for arguing that its intellectual setting is in Old Testament and rabbinic thought. J. K. Howard understands that the Passover themes in the gospel are intended to present Jesus as the perfect Passover lamb and the "antitype of the old order." L. Morris agrees that the Passover imagery is present in the temple cleansing and in chapter 6, as well as in the farewell discourses and the passion narrative (*New Testament* 64–72). A. Jaubert's argument that the calendar followed by Jews in Palestine at the time of Jesus was the one in use at Qumran has important implications for the Passover motif in John. With this calendar it is clear that the Fourth Gospel's representation of the last meal is a Passover meal ("Calendar").[6]

Likewise mosaic motifs in the Fourth Gospel are grounds for the case that this gospel is rooted in Old Testament-rabbinic thought. F. Glasson contends that the evangelist shaped the Christology of the gospel around the mosaic figure. W. Meeks agrees, but finds the background of Johannine mosaic imagery far more complex than simple Old Testament-rabbinic thought (*Prophet-King*; cf. idem, "Moses"). A. Lacomara's study is of different kind. He attempts to unearth a deuteronomic typology in the gospel. M. Girard departs from the mosaic theme but, like Lacomara, finds a pattern in the structure of John derived from an Old Testament book, in this case the seven day structure of Genesis 1:1–2:4a (cf. Barrosse, and Trudinger, "Seven").

Finally, we must note two additional studies that have demonstrated indirectly the basis of Johannine thought in the Old Testament and rabbinic concepts. A. E. Harvey tries to show that the entire gospel is a legal trial of Jesus argued in typical rabbinic fashion, and shows how such an understanding elucidates the meaning of the gospel. Harvey's work is associated in a way with the thorough and persuasive work of S. Pancaro. The latter explores the concept of Law in the gospel and demonstrates how thoroughly central the concern for the relationship of Jesus to the Torah is for the Fourth Evangelist. Pancaro convinces many of us that the evangelist understood belief in the revelation of God in Christ as obedience to the Law. However, it is obedience in contrast to the resistance to belief offered by the opponents of Jesus in the gospel in their attempts to be faithful to the Law. In the process of his investigations (which we will mention again in another context below) the author shows how consciously interested the Fourth Evangelist was to be faithful to Old Testament Law (*Law*).[7]

Hellenism and Hellenistic Judaism

C. H. Dodd's influential work published in 1953, *Interpretation*, made a strong case for the influence of Hellenistic modes of thought (especially Philonic and Hermetic) upon John (e.g., 133). Since Dodd, however, there has been a discernible decline of interest in the elucidation of the Fourth Gospel by reference to Hellenistic thought. The reasons for this may be found in what could be called a rediscovery of the Jewish character of the Fourth Gospel, but more exactly the rediscovery spurred by the importance of the scrolls found at Qumran. Yet, the interest in the Hellenistic contacts with the Johannine tradition is still very much alive, however diminished from the level of importance to which Dodd assigned them.

We mentioned above that Miranda detects Hellenistic influences in the Johannine christological motifs of the descending and ascending redeemer along with the parallel concern for the questions of the origin and destiny of that figure (*Vater* 130–307). Likewise, C. H. Talbert believes that the descending-ascending mythology employed in John was drawn from Hellenistic Jewish thought, where it was used in reference to a savior described with various names and may have been associated in its Jewish stream with angelology ("Myth"; cf. Talbert, *Gospel*). E. Schweizer found that the preexistence theme in Johannine christological thought originated in Jewish wisdom speculations in the Hellenistic world (*Ego eimi*, and "Religionsgeschichtlichen"). J. Beutler attempted to trace the roots of the gospel's use of witness argumentation to a syncretistic setting in the Hellenistic world. Witness terminology in John, he suggested, parallels most closely Jewish Hellenistic apologetics of the kind we know in Philo and Josephus. Nevertheless, other aspects of this Johannine theme are clearly more at home in Jewish apocalyptic thought, and so Beutler posits its home in the Jewish dispersion (esp. 363-64).

R. Schnackenburg has similarly found the motivation for the "I Am" sayings in the evangelist's concern for the Hellenistic world. The formal structure of the speeches is similar to the soteriological type of speech one finds in oriental Hellenism (*Johannesevangelium* 2:64-67). Just as Schnackenburg understands that the evangelist used a Hellenistic form in order to communicate with the wider Roman world, so E. Linnemann has defended the Dionysian background of the sign at Cana (2:1-12). In responding to the criticisms of Bultmann's proposal, Linnemann argues that the pericope is a piece of dialogue material between the Christian community and the Dionysian mystery; it is a counter proposal to the Dionysian cult.

G. Stemberger is not content to root the whole of the dualism of the gospel in Old Testament-rabbinic thought, for he finds that aspects of that dualism (e.g., servitude and freedom) are evidently expressions of a Stoic contact. Such Hellenistic influences enter the complex of the dualistic symbols both in their pre-Johannine form and through the mind of the evangelist (*Symbolique* 44-144; cf. Whittaker).

Heterodox Judaism

Less seems to have been done in the way of investigations of Hellenistic influences on the thought of John. This is probably due to a new sensitivity to the syncretistic nature of first-century Palestinian Judaism itself. One need not look beyond the confines of the homeland of Judaism to find a religious movement that appears to have absorbed into itself a number of seemingly contradictory features. It is, of course, the Qumran discoveries which have alerted scholars to this possibility with the result that we no longer think of Hellenistic Judaism as the only syncretistic form of the Mosaic faith during the first century C.E. In fact, it has become less and less clear just what should properly be called rabbinic and what heterodox Judaism. Putting that issue aside, there are a number of studies which suggest that John was most at home in a Judaism quite Palestinian in nature yet quite different from what we know as rabbinic Judaism.

Some suggest that Johannine Christology has been influenced by the kind of view which the Qumran community held of its "teacher of righteous," especially in the "Psalms of Thanksgiving." J. Price has drawn out an impressive list of the parallels between the two. For instance, both Jesus and the teacher of the "Thanksgiving Psalms" claim to have a special knowledge from God and a special commission to teach it to a select group of persons. W. Brownlee thinks John 1:29 may express the Qumran notion of the messianic "man." He claims that the Johannine view of Christ is clearly linked with the language of the Qumran community.

O. Betz has done the definitive comparison of the Johannine paraclete concept and the Qumran materials. He focuses on the forensic quality of the paraclete figure and finds impressive contacts with the various intercessory agents in Qumran thought, most especially the angel, Michael. He believes that the figure of Michael served as a model for the gospel's portrayal of the paraclete. It was in Qumran that the angel Michael was identified with the spirit of truth, and the evangelist has given the attributes of both to the paraclete (Betz 56–72, 113–66, 206–12, 293–336; cf. Price 24; contrast Leaney, "Johannine" 43–53, 57, and "Historical" 146–59). While G. Johnston dissents from Betz's study at a number of points, he too agrees that the Qumran literature provides the most helpful parallels to the paraclete (Johnston, *Spirit-Paraclete* 83, 99, 106, 116–17, 120–21, and "Spirit-Paraclete").

The most obvious contact between John and the Essene community of Qumran, however, is at the point of dualism. A number of scholars have investigated the similarities between the two dualisms with the result that they posit an indirect rather than a direct relationship between the two. They maintain that one cannot suppose a literary dependence of the evangelist upon Qumran literature. Brown reaches this conclusion by insisting that the only parallels which are admissible as evidence of a direct relationship are those which cannot be explained on the basis of a common background in the Old Testament (*Commentary–Gospel* 1:lxii–lxiii). L. Morris stresses the important differences between the two concepts, but admits that the similarities are too numerous and important to be dismissed as accidental or as arising from a common background. Morris suggests that Qumranian thought was transmitted to the Johannine community through followers of John the Baptist who at one time had been adherents of the Essene sect (*Studies* 329–33, 353–54). J. Price concludes that the dualism we find in both John and Qumran documents was a common notion in Jewish circles of the first century C.E. (19–25).

J. Charlesworth's examination of the materials is perhaps the most exhaustive. He concludes that the comparisons demand a link between the two. He thinks, however, it is unwarranted to posit a literary dependence. John's author did not borrow dualism from Qumran, but employed the language of that sect group to articulate the community's images which arose out of Christian views. Charlesworth and R. Culpepper go on to examine the parallels between the Gospel of John and the "Odes of Solomon." Their examination definitively establishes that the odes are not the source of the gnostic-like thought of the gospel. Instead, they show that the odes and the gospel have a common background and both were affected by the kind of thought we see exemplified in the Qumran materials (Charlesworth, "Critical," and "Qumran"; Charlesworth and Culpepper).[8]

A. Hanson has analyzed the relationship between John 17 and *Hodayoth* column XV. He concluded that the Qumran psalm is the nearest thing in pre-Christian literature to the form of chapter 17. He asserts that there was undoubtedly a link between the thought of the Fourth Evangelist and Qumran, most especially on the matter of predestination ("*Hodayoth*"; cf. Coetzee; Fensham).

The Qumran studies, however, do not constitute the only investigations of the gospel's roots in a non-rabbinical, heterodox Judaism. A number of studies have posited the existence and the influence of a kind of Judaism not necessarily equated with the Qumranian community. W. A. Meeks's definitive study of Moses in John proposes the Judaism that shaped the image of Moses in the gospel was a fascinating mixture of phenomena. The traditions that were instrumental in the Fourth Gospel show evidence of some interaction between Jews and Samaritans (*Prophet-King* 317). P. Borgen likewise posits the existence of a syncretistic Judaism. The kind of interpretation that is evident in chapter 6 was at home in the milieu in which Jewish exegesis was infected by a kind of non-rabbinic mysticism (*Bread from Heaven* 147). O. Böcher's proposal apropos the dualism of John is that the Jewish sectarian thought of the kind known at Qumran radically affected Old Testament imagery before it was transmitted to the Fourth Evangelist. Johannine theology is at home, he concludes, not in pharisaic-rabbinic thought but in an apocalyptic-sectarian Judaism (16).

O. Cullmann advanced a theory that John was the product of a community that originated in the conversions of persons from a heterodox, marginal Judaism. The background of thought and form of the Johannine community was a syncretistic, borderline Judaism. Acts 6 identifies the converts from that form of Judaism as "Hellenists," and Acts 8 represents them with Stephen. These so-called Hellenists shaped early Johannine thought. Qumran Judaism, the Baptist sect, and Samaritanism all colored the development of the tradition embedded in the Fourth Gospel. Cullmann further traces this link with syncretistic forms of Judaism beyond the Johannine community and to Jesus himself (*Johannine*; cf. "Jesus"; F.-M. Braun, "Cercle").

This terse overview of the search for the intellectual background of John has both a negative and a positive implication. First, the implication of the variety of the results of the history of religions analyses of the Fourth Gospel is the fact that there is nothing like a clear consensus of scholarship on the question. The differing results show that researchers do not yet have anything approaching a confident proposal upon which work may continue. Second, however, the positive implication of our survey is that there are trends indicative of the mood of contemporary scholarship. We propose that those trends are two. The first is more efforts are now being expended with more promising results in the area of the Jewish background of the Fourth Gospel than in the areas of Hellenism and/or Gnosticism. Second, scholars have achieved noticeable degrees of success in the effort to show that the particular form of Judaism behind John is syncretistic in nature. The first trend, we think, is clear simply in terms of the vast amount of work and the number of scholars who find Johannine roots in Old Testament and rabbinic thoughts forms, while the efforts to effect the reconstruction of a Hellenistic or gnostic backdrop for the gospel are failing to win wide adherence. Still, the second trend is less obvious from what we have discussed thus far. In addition to those works that clearly allude to a sectarian form of Judaism as the gospel's roots, it is important to take note of the fact that many who would find the Old Testament-rabbinic background plausible also find indications of the influence of apocalyptic Judaism or Hellenistically colored Judaism in their investigations. This points, it seems to me, to the fact that it is a Jewish milieu that best accounts for the thought of the Gospel of John, but that we cannot understand that Judaism in terms of simple Old Testament-rabbinic motifs. Much more likely is that the Judaism we are seeking to unearth behind the gospel was rooted in the Old Testament and related to the rabbinic movement, but was also swayed by "sectarian" features which might have included apocalyptic, mystical, and Qumranian characteristics.

No history of religions proposal is adequate, however, that does not in the last analysis take account of the creativity of the evangelist and the Johannine community. In this way, the study of G. Fischer is perhaps exemplary of the trend which we see in contemporary scholarship. He undertook to understand 14:2f and concludes that we must admit to the convergence of a number of motifs from differing backgrounds, which have then been significantly transformed by the creative thought of the evangelist. There are indications of resemblances to concepts in Jewish Hellenism and in Jewish apocalypticism, both rooted in a fundamental

Old Testament idea (the hope of God's dwelling with the people of Israel and the temple). However, the combination of the metaphors of "house" and "rooms" is the evangelist's creation of a peculiar theology (Fischer, esp. 290-98; cf. Barrett, *John and Judaism*, esp. 58). Fischer pointed toward a syncretistic kind of Judaism which has been shaped by a number of different movements including Hellenism, and which has been taken up by the evangelist and stamped with that author's own unique form of thought. It may well be that this kind of history of religions hypothesis for the Fourth Gospel proves to be the most elucidating and rewarding working basis for further progress toward the solution of the enigma of the document.

Sitz im Leben Analysis (The Purpose of the Gospel of John)

What was the specific purpose of the gospel? Whatever its intellectual background may have been, the reader wants to know what the evangelist intended it to do. Furthermore, what was the special situation in the Christian community that motivated the publication of a document of this kind? Around these questions (which interpreters ask of any piece of literature) there are peculiar features of John that exasperate the urgency to have some answers. There are, for instance, the curiously negative uses of the expression "the Jews," scattered throughout the gospel (e.g., 6:41, 52). The usual opponents of Jesus in the Synoptic Gospels (the "scribes and Pharisees") are much less prominent in the Johannine account than this generalized group labeled "Jews." Moreover, at the conclusion of the gospel (20:30-31) the author tells the reader that the book is intended to produce faith. Still, the ambiguity of the Greek mars this significant passage. Does it mean the gospel was written to evoke new faith or to nurture further faith on the part of the believer? One is impressed that the Gospel of John as a whole is certainly more than a missionary tract with only conversion in mind. Finally, could the concrete setting for this document illuminate some of the gospel's other puzzling characteristics, say, the defensive quality of the discourses of Jesus throughout the first twelve chapters, or the exclusive overtones of the farewell discourses?

For years (even centuries) the hopes of portraying the concrete, real-life setting of John have motivated a great deal of scholarly research. Moreover, the success of much of the redactional criticism of the Synoptic Gospels has perhaps encouraged Johannine scholars to "go and do likewise." In the early 1960s there was some interest in arguing that the purpose and the setting of the book centered in a missionary enterprise among Jews living in dispersion (e.g., T. C. Smith, *Jesus*; van Unnik; J. A. T. Robinson, "Destination"; and Wind). Then the pendulum swung in the direction of regarding it as a document intended to nurture faith within a community of Christians and attention was focused on the conditions experienced by that community. It is fair, I think, to summarize the major thrusts of research on the *Sitz im Leben* of the community around four foci, while not disregarding the obvious differences among views within each of them.

A *Dialogue with the Synagogue*

An important option for understanding the concrete setting in life of the Fourth Gospel has been given clear and forceful articulation in the work of J. L. Martyn. Martyn's major thesis is that John is in effect a drama taking place on two historically different levels at the same time. On the one level is the conflict of Jesus with his opponents; on the other level is the conflict of the Christians of the Johannine community with members of a local synagogue. The drama represents both Jesus and the Christians of the evangelist's own day as well as the Jewish leaders of Jesus' day and the Jewish leaders of the evangelist's day—in both cases the latter members of the pairs only thinly disguised. Christians of the Johannine church were suffering conflict with members of the local synagogue. Jews were leaving the synagogue to embrace the Christian faith, while others were holding the new faith but trying to maintain their allegiance to the Jewish community. According to Martyn, the use of the expression "excluded from the synagogue" (9:22; 12:42; and 16:2) refers to the fact that in the evangelist's own time the Johannine Jewish Christians are being forced out of their Jewish community by virtue of the enforcement of the "Benediction Against Heretics." The result was that the two religious communities—Jewish and Christian—were locked in a struggle which made them both defensive. The Christians in particular were being challenged to respond to a number of questions posed by Jewish leaders: Who is Jesus? (Are Christians not ditheists?) Can one follow both Moses and Jesus? What is the significance of Jesus' death? (Martyn, *History and Theology*, "Source Criticism," and "Glimpses").[9]

Martyn's hypothesis has received extensive support from a number of studies, many of which are independent of his work and approach the question from a variety of different directions. Our summaries of those studies here indicate briefly their confirmation of the notion that the gospel's *Sitz im Leben* involved a dialogue with the synagogue, but we do not intend thereby to diminish their contributions in other ways. The work of W. Meeks has solidified Martyn's thesis in a number of ways. Meeks's history of religions investigation of the Moses motif in John concludes with the suggestion that "Johannine traditions were shaped, at least in part, by interaction between a Christian community and a hostile Jewish community." Later his comparison of the agent theme in John and Philo points creatively in the same direction. The qualities of the Johannine polemic are, he believed, due to the failure of the Johannine community to win Jews over to their convictions. Finally his "sociological analysis" of the functional role of the descending-ascending symbol in John offers the proposal that the Johannine community was a sectarian group for whom the ingroup-outgroup distinction loomed very large. That sectarian character of the community was the result, Meeks proposed, of its exclusion from the synagogue and its search for a new "social location" (*Prophet-King* 318, "Divine," *"Am I a Jew?"* and "Man"). Among other studies that support the thesis in general are the following: H. Leroy's form critical study of the misunderstanding theme in John (191-93); R. Fortna's redactional critical work on the basis of his proposed "Signs Gospel" ("Source" 159); J. Beutler's history of tradition analysis of the gospel's witness argumentation (339-64); H. Mulder's probe of the relationships of Gentiles and Jews in the book (however, Mulder's article is known to me only through Wind, 40-47); F. Manns's exegetical study of the theme of freedom in 8:31-59 (102-5); and E. Grässer's examination of the polemic quality of the gospel's treatment of the Jews (cf. Hickling).[10]

Grässer's work found ample reason for the negative treatment of those labeled "the Jews" in this gospel. R. Leistner, too, attempted to understand the gospel's apparent anti-Jewish character. Although he did not posit the same kind of church-synagogue conflict as does Grässer, his study demonstrated the evangelist's dominant concern for Christian-Jewish relationships (142-50). R. Fuller's redactional study of "the Jews" in the gospel more explicitly establishes the way this expression arose from the church-synagogue conflict ("Jews").[11]

A number of others have affirmed the anti-Jewish polemic or apologetic as well. Schnackenburg and Brown both understand that the "Jews" referred to in a derogatory way in John are contemporaries of the evangelist who have rejected the Christian faith. Like Meeks, Brown proposes that by the time of the writing of the gospel the period of missionary work among the Jews had ended, and Christians and Jews are "locked in struggle" with one another. Schnackenburg adduces equally impressive evidence that the anti-Jewish tone reflects the evangelist's own day and believes that the synagogue ban of Christians had affected the Christians of the Johannine community. Thus, it is fairly certain that this polemic tone was occasioned by the *Sitz im Leben* of the writing. Brown maintains that the Fourth Evangelist holds out hope for winning over those "hidden Christians" still within the folds of the synagogue, and Schnackenburg agrees that there is still some element of evangelistic purpose in the gospel

vis-a-vis the Jews but alleges that the attitude of the evangelist is fundamentally hostile (*Commentary–Gospel* 1:lxx–lxxv; Schnackenburg, *Gospel*
1:165–67).[12]

Some have uncovered a similar kind of setting by means of investigat-
ing the way in which the Gospel employs Jewish ideas. Meeks's contention
is that the evangelist forces the Jewish ideas to their extreme in a kind of
reductio ad absurdum ("Am I a Jew?"). This has been ascertained most clearly
by the work of M. De Jonge on the messianic-christological notions. His
conclusion is that Johannine Christology is developed for the purpose
of assisting Christians reply to the objections of Jewish protagonists. De
Jonge explicitly endorses Martyn's thesis in the process of showing how
the figure of Nicodemus represents the Jewish Christians who are trying
to cling to their Jewish affiliation (De Jonge, "Jewish" 262–63, "Jesus,"
"Use" 71–73, and "Nicodemus").

Nevertheless, perhaps the most impressive research on a Jewish
theme in John, which has the effect of confirming the hypothesis of a
church-synagogue dialogue, is the examination of Law in the gospel by S.
Pancaro. A persistent conflict posed by the document is the relationship
of the authority of Jesus and the authority of the Torah. While the latter
is never denied, the former is made to supersede the Law. The evangelist's
concern is to defend the legitimacy of Jesus' messiahship in response to
those attacks from Jewish opponents of the evangelist's own day. The gospel further drives home the point that faithfulness to the Law means the
acceptance of the claims of Jesus, and those who refuse to accept those
claims in the name of faithfulness to the Law are, in fact, abrogating the
Law. Judaism was, Pancaro suggests, trying to sustain itself in the wake of
the destruction of the temple and the crisis of faith that followed. In self-
defense, it condemned the Christians as heretics and banned them from
the synagogue. It is precisely in this real-life situation that the evangelist
wrote the gospel to bolster the Christian community (*Law* 489–546; cf.
"Relationship"). Pancaro vividly lays out a situation that both stems from
the evidence of the gospel itself and in turn illuminates the thought of
that document.

An Anti-Docetic Polemic

Another kind of polemic which has more traditionally been ascribed to
John is an attack upon docetic Christology. Irenaeus (*Against Heresies*
3.11.7) claimed that John was directed against the gnostic distortion of
the faith. E. Hoskyns wrote his neo-orthodox interpretation of John with
a strong emphasis upon the anti-docetic flavor of its thought. Bultmann's
contention that the gospel was sympathetic toward Gnosticism is perhaps

responsible for the fact that the anti-docetic theme has not been pursued vigorously by contemporary scholars, but it is still not devoid of its supporters.

Dunn combines anti-docetic and anti-sacramental themes to fashion a hypothesis for one of the gospel's major thrusts. Chapter 6 is the evangelist's carefully constructed response to both a docetic Christology and a countermovement among Christians to stress the literal character of the Eucharist—the bread and wine as actual body and blood. Dunn's approach is to claim that chapter 6 is not eucharistic at all but a declaration that Jesus was indeed flesh and blood humanity. The evangelist thus strikes out with both hands—one against the docetic understanding of Christ and the other against a literalistic sacramentalism. Others find what they regard as an anti-docetic polemic in a less prominent place in the gospel—a subtheme or purpose. Schnackenburg finds evidence of this kind of an attack only in 1:14 and 19:34f (*Gospel* 1:169–72). Brown agrees but includes 8:38-39 and 6:51-58 as further indications of an anti-docetic concern (*Commentary–Gospel* 1:lxxvi–lxxvii; cf. Borgen, *Bread of Heaven* 148). J. N. Sanders and B. A. Mastin support a comparable view (Mastin, 52). Lindars is more cautious and, along with Brown, relegates the anti-docetic stratum of the gospel to a later stage in the history of composition (Lindars, *Gospel of John* 61–63; cf. Wilkens, *Zeichen* 167–68). Richter more radically stresses the proposal that the Fourth Gospel underwent an anti-docetic redaction. For instance, 1:14 and 5:15b-58 as well as 19:34b-35, 39-40; 20:2-10 and 24-29 are redactional, anti-docetic additions. The so-called anti-docetic redactor, who plays an important role in Richter's scheme for the history of the composition of the gospel, was concerned to correct Johannine Christology and sacramentalism in order to respond to a docetic movement which had developed in the community ("Fleischwerdung," *Strukturbildendes*, and "Präsentische").[13]

A Samaritan Mission

Some Johannine researchers have been intrigued with the possibility that the Fourth Evangelist and the Johannine community had a special relationship with the Samaritan region and its people. That intrigue has brought the announcement of a number of theories that claim John had some missional intention regarding the Samaritans. H. Odeberg offered such a thesis as early as 1929 as an explanation of chapter 4. J. Bowman followed in the late 1950s, and the task was advanced on several fronts ("The Fourth Gospel and the Samaritans"; cf. Scobie).

W. Meeks concluded that the Johannine community had drawn a segment of its members from among the Samaritans who shared a common tradition regarding Moses with others in that community. More recently, however, he has qualified his earlier proposition with the caution that the Samaritans were hardly a dominant factor in the Johannine community and that the Fourth Evangelist demonstrates little sensitivity to the motifs and concerns of the Samaritan thought (*Prophet-King* 216–57, 313–19; "Galilee"; and "Am I a Jew?"). G. W. Buchanan is more radical in his appraisal of the evidence. His view is that the Fourth Evangelist came from a Samaritan church in which there was a strong anti-Jewish prejudice. He understands the anti-Jewish themes in the Gospel of John as indications of Samaritan leanings. Other evidence of Samaritan influence bolstered proposal, e.g., the prominence of the northern prophets of Israel's history, Elijah and Elisha (cf. B. P. Robinson and Reim, *Studien* 207–9). E. D. Freed builds his case for a similar view on a culmination of evidence and shows how this hypothesis enlightens Johannine eschatology. The evangelist was trying to appeal to Samaritans ("Samaritan," and "Did John").

M.-E. Boismard's study of 3:23 leads him to find more prominence for the mission to the Samaritans than chapter 4 alone would suggest. But he does not propose a Samaritan mission as a goal for the gospel as a whole ("Aenon"). J. Purvis has scrutinized these theses for a Samaritan mission in the gospel and from his examination of the evidence concludes that, rather than a Samaritan mission, the evangelist was concerned with an anti-Samaritan polemic against a northern, sectarian prophet, a kind of Samaritan magus figure ("Fourth Gospel").[14]

A Universal Appeal to Christians

Finally, we must note in passing those who affirm the popular point of view that John was intended primarily to appeal to Christians out of a multitude of different backgrounds. This view has received the endorsement of the noted scholar C. K. Barrett, who understands the many contradictory views of the Fourth Evangelist as an attempt to speak meaningfully to all Christians. Barrett describes the evangelist's theological method as dialectical; truth is not singular but paradoxical. To eliminate any one aspect of the evangelist's tenets, contradictory though it may seem, is to miss the whole truth of his view (*John and Judaism* 70–76). G. MacRae has articulated a similar view: the evangelist wanted to say that Christ transcended all of the things which could be said of him. Under the influence of a Hellenistic syncretism the evangelist used a multitude of forms and expressions out of various milieus. The author of John did for Christianity what Philo attempted for Judaism ("Fourth Gospel"). J. Schneider's commentary is premised on the assumption that John wanted to appeal

not only to persons out of a Jewish but also a Hellenistic background. The
synthesis which the evangelist affected was for the purpose of wide appeal
(*Evangelium* 36–37).

This kind of a view is supported by P. Lamarche's understanding
of the prologue of the gospel. The purpose of this introduction, thinks
Lamarche, is to demonstrate the relevance of Christ for all persons—verses
1-9 are intended for the Gentile nations, while 14-18 for the Jewish nation.
R. Longenecker likewise believes that the evangelist employed the logos
concept deliberately to provide a "terminological bridge" between persons
of Hellenistic and Jewish origins (47). Brown refutes the proposals that
the Fourth Evangelist was interested in conversions only among Jews of
the dispersion by citing passages such as 1:9, 29, and 12:35. John is interested not just in Jews, but in Christian believers of all heritages (*Commentary–Gospel* 1:lxxvii–lxxviii).

Of these options for the gospel's *Sitz im Leben* it is clear that the proposal of a synagogue dialogue attracts to itself the greatest support. Not
only has Martyn's hypothesis received persuasive confirmation from many
different corners of Johannine criticism, but it also has been the focus of
some of the most enlightening scholarship at least in the years 1970–2000.
This proposal that the Johannine community was locked in a struggle
with the local synagogue(s) with both factions fighting for their own identity seems most convincing. It lights up many aspects of the gospel, e.g.,
the apparent anti-Jewish character of the document. The impressive thing
about this proposal is that it explains for us both sides of the puzzling
Jewish question in the book. While the gospel is openly anti-Jewish at any
number of points, it is obvious that its roots are clearly Jewish. Martyn's
thesis elucidates both sides of this coin in a way none of the other proposals do. The implications and refinements of this proposed setting for the
gospel must be further worked out, but it will be at the center of Johannine *Sitz im Leben* research for some time.

On the other hand, the gospel's anti-docetic features cannot be
denied and cannot easily be explained at present on the basis of Martyn's
proposal. Yet if the preponderance of Johannine research is correct in
contending that the document went through a process of composition
before reaching its present form, it may well be that those anti-docetic features are best attributed to a later stage of composition. Brown and others,
I believe, are correct in assessing the minor role played by this anti-docetic
corrective. Therefore, we can at least tentatively hold that those features
came into our gospel by a means of a redactional process later in its life,
perhaps at a stage which brings us close to the *Sitz im Leben* of the gospel.
Regarding the universal appeal and the Samaritan mission proposals, we

suggest that the evidence which elicits these hypotheses is better explained as part of the syncretistic intellectual setting of the gospel. That is to say, the reason it appears to have concern for a Samaritan mission and for an appeal to persons of various backgrounds is that the thought of the gospel rests in a Judaism which was not homogeneous and exclusively rabbinic in nature. There were doubtless features of this syncretistic Judaism which were from a northern, Samaritan influence. Similarly, Johannine Judaism was not pure of Hellenistic influences; hence, the Gospel of John seems to reflect an interest in the Greeks because of the Hellenistic colorings of the Judaism that affected it.

Such a view of the intellectual and the real-life settings of John lock together to form a comprehensive and elucidating whole, the results of which give us some significant handles on the historical problems surrounding this puzzling gospel. Yet they also open up still another question upon which we must touch briefly, namely, the history of the Johannine community.

History of the Johannine Community

The efforts to resolve the history of the composition along with the analysis of the *Sitz im Leben* of the Fourth Gospel pose the question of the history of that community responsible for the document. A reconstruction of that history seeks to shed light upon a number of other issues. For instance, how is it that John articulates such an unusual Christology—the Son of God from above? Or, how is it that it teaches side by side the dogma of the presence of the eschatological blessings in the life of the believer and the hope of the realization of those blessings yet in the future? An outline of the history of this community may, it is hoped by some, resolve a few of the questions of the peculiarities of the Gospel of John. Scholars posit such outlines in each case upon other proposals concerning both the history of the composition of the gospel and its setting—both intellectual and concrete. Consequently, each outline of the history of the community is a structure founded in the not yet quite dry concrete of other hypotheses.

Before we examine those proposed histories of the community, however, it is important to notice a study that attempts to define the nature of that community. R. A. Culpepper proposed that it was essentially a "school." He examines the characteristics of the ancient schools in the Greco-Roman world, and then demonstrates that many of those characteristics are discernible in the community behind the Fourth Gospel. The ancient schools, for instance, held in reverence a figure of the past who was responsible for founding the school. In the Fourth Gospel there is indication that the beloved disciple was regarded in just such a way. On the basis of a series of characteristics such as this, Culpepper believes we are justified in saying that the community behind John's gospel was a school in this ancient sense. Hence, with such an understanding we are able to discern the peculiar role of this allusive figure, the beloved disciple, and to comprehend how it might have been possible for the community to preserve tradition through the years before the production of the gospel.

Efforts to reconstruct a history of the Johannine community include three major proposals, all within about one decade of one another. Two of these may be summarized by means of describing the pivotal stages through which the community went. The first is the effort of Martyn to flesh out his proposal for the *Sitz im Leben* of John with the meat of history. Martyn finds three distinct stages in the history of the community:

The Early Period (ca. 40–85). The beginnings of the Johannine community were among Christian Jews living in the synagogue, harmonious with their Jewish traditions. Jesus was understood simply in terms of Jewish expectations. The Johannine materials were shaped into homilies during this period and eventually into a kind of rudimentary gospel, perhaps similar to the "Signs Gospel" proposed by R. Fortna. That the beloved disciple was a historical figure in this period is mentioned as a possibility.

The Middle Period. Tensions developed between this group of Christian Jews and the synagogue as a whole. Two traumas occurred: First, the benediction against the *Minim* ("heretics") was introduced with the result that some of the Christian Jews retreated from their overt confessions of the Christian faith in order to preserve their place in the synagogue, while others who were persistent in their profession were alienated from the synagogue, becoming what Martyn calls Jewish Christians. Second, some of the Johannine Christians may have been tried and even executed. The consequence of this tragedy was the emergence of the gospel's radical Christology—Christ as one from above, the stranger in this world—and the sharp division of the community from the "world" and the "Jews."

The Late Period. This was the period of the refinement of the identity of the community in relation to other Christian communities. In effect, Martyn thinks there was concern for "crypto-Christians" (those still abiding within the synagogue). The Johannine community developed its sharp either/or position toward them and identified these hidden believers with the world and the Jews. Still, there were also "other sheep"—other Christians scattered by the expulsion from the synagogue and persecution ("Glimpses").

Richter's reconstruction isolates four stages in the history of the community:

1. *Jewish Christianity.* A group of Jewish Christians was expelled from the synagogue. They understood Jesus as a prophet-Messiah like Moses and embraced a futuristic eschatology. A *Grundschrift* was written to give expression to their faith.

2. *The Johannine Faith.* The Son of God Christology arose within this group of Jewish Christians, resulting in a split between those who embraced this new Christology and those who clung conservatively to a Messiah Christology. The Fourth Evangelist edited the *Grundschrift* in accord with the newer Christology of one group and with the present realized eschatology which this group embraced.

3. *Johannine Docetism.* The Christology of the Fourth Gospel was interpreted by a part of the community in a docetic manner, although they made no additions to the gospel.

4. *Johannine Anti-Docetism.* An anti-docetic movement within the community developed in response to the docetists among them. They grouped around a redactor who significantly edited the gospel to comport with the response of this new subgroup to the docetism. They embraced both the present and the future eschatologies of the gospel ("Präsentische"; cf. Mattill).

Brown has commented on these two reconstructions, proposed his variations in relationship to them, and outlined a history of the community of his own. First, he agrees with Martyn and Richter that the Johannine community took its beginnings among Jews who viewed Jesus as one who fulfilled the messianic expectations. He believes, however, that some of these early Johannine Jewish Christians may have come from among the followers of the Baptist and that the beloved disciple was a historical figure of this early period—a follower of the Baptist and the unnamed disciple in 1:35-40. To this group were added still others who radically reshaped the Christology of the early community. Samaritan Christians and others converted from among Jews of an anti-temple view brought into the community a new Christology which departed significantly from the simpler messianic views of the primary group. The result of this merger was that the Johannine Christians became suspect by the synagogue authorities. Brown thinks the actual expulsion from the synagogue antedates the formal benediction against the *Minim*. At this stage, significant numbers of Gentiles aligned themselves with the enlarged community now separated from the synagogue. All of this took place, Brown believes, before the writing of the first edition of the gospel.

Beyond this Brown discusses the relationship of the community with five other groups. With the "Jews" the Johannine Christians debated the oneness of Christ with the Father and the relegation of the temple and feasts to minor importance by the presence of God in Christ. The Johan-nine Christians disputed the loyalty of the "crypto-Christians"—those who embraced the Christian faith within the bosom of the synagogue—and equated them with the "Jews." The Johannine Christians also regarded other Jewish Christians as inadequate in their faith, for they did not accept the divinity of Christ. "Christians of Apostolic Churches" were regarded as confused in that they did not understand that Christ was preexistent. Finally, the Johannine Christians eventually criticized the "Secessionist Johannine Christians" for not regarding Jesus as fully human ("Johan-nine Ecclesiology," and, "'Other' Sheep"). (Cf. the discussion of Brown's reconstruction of the history of the composition of the Fourth Gospel on pp. 65–71 in the previous chapter).

In general, we may observe a number of things about these attempts to speak of the history of the Johannine: First, all understand that the community roots are in Jewish Christianity. Second, all understand that the community suffered expulsion from the synagogue, although there is considerable difference as to just when in the history of the community this alienation took place and the degree of its effect. All recognize, third, that in the community there developed a radically different Christology, departing from a simpler messianic view, although again there is no agree-ment as to the cause of this new Christology. (Brown is clearest in pro-posing the reason for this mutation of Christology.) Fourth, Richter and Brown see a docetism arising to play a significant role in the life of the community. (Martyn does not attempt to trace the history beyond the origins of the community.) Fifth, Brown and Martyn understand that the relationship of the Johannine Christians expelled from the synagogue to their former colleagues, the "crypto-Christians" still in the synagogue, was important for the community. Likewise, these two interpreters see sugges-tions in the gospel that the relationship of the church to other Christian groups was equally important to the developing community.

It is clear that with each of these three proposals we have suggestions that are yet tentative and provisional. It is difficult to issue verdicts of their success when they have still such skeletal form. Yet the tracing out of the history of the community promises to be one of the future concerns of Johannine research as scholars test and expand upon these first offerings. It is also clear from what we have said that as the work of the history of the composition progresses, along with redaction criticism, the refinements of the history of the community may be within our reach. Nonetheless, these proposals offer us considerable insight into the kind of community resid-ing behind the Gospel of John (but cf. Kysar, "Whence and Whither").

Date and Authorship

What of the questions of date and authorship? We have avoided these matters until now, for they are determined in large part by the stands taken on the other issues we have reviewed thus far. The date of John has persistently plagued scholarship, and researchers were often inclined to date it very late, even into the middle of the second century C.E., until the discovery in 1935 of the "Roberts Fragment" (P[52]). That discovery pushes the date of our document back to the first century, for it seems clear that the gospel (or some portion of it) was known in Egypt as early as 125. The Johannine "high Christology" has caused many to think that the composition of the gospel is late, but now we see that it cannot be as late as some would suppose. How do we account for the seemingly late character of Johannine thought (e.g., its Christology), on the one hand, and on the other hand, the seemingly Jewish Christian features which augur for an earlier date? We can no more easily solve the matter of authorship. Was the author an eyewitness of the historical Jesus as 21:24, among other passages, would seem to suggest? What is the relationship between the authorship of the book and the mysterious beloved disciple? What about the mentions of another anonymous disciple(s)? The determinations of the date and authorship are fraught with difficulties and hence have evoked numerous kinds of solutions.

Date

The most widely accepted date for the Fourth Gospel among scholars today is 90–100 C.E. By far the majority of scholars understand that it was at this date completed or completed except for minor redaction. We need mention here only the exceptions to this consensus. The only significant exception is a movement toward dating the gospel earlier. (Cf., however, the argument for a later date offered by Teeple, *Literary* 150, 152.) Within the last several decades an increasing number of scholars have joined what had been only a handful of proponents for an earlier date, and the consequence is what might be called, without exaggeration, a significant movement. We cannot recount here all of the evidence employed on behalf of their cause, except to list a few. Some see clear evidence of the hand of an eyewitness in the writing of the gospel. The author of the document refers to geographical sites in the present tense (e.g., 5:2), and certain place-names used have received modern archaeological confirmation. The Palestinian character of John suggests an early date, as do certain so-called primitive Christian traits (e.g., the word *christos* is not used as a name). Sometimes the argument for an early date is coupled with other proposals: the evangelist did not know and use the Synoptic Gospels and therefore must have written before they were in existence; or, the anti-Jewish polemic witnessed in the Fourth Gospel more likely reflects a pre-70 situation when Christianity was still part of the Jewish faith.

This kind of evidence is employed to make the case for a pre-70 dating of the gospel by such persons as L. Morris (*Studies* 288, 291; *Gospel* 33–34), G. A. Turner, L. Cribbs ("Reassessment"), and Cullmann (*Johannine* 97), and J. A. T. Robinson (*Redating* 290–311).[15] While this movement is still very much a minority force within contemporary scholarship, it must be acknowledged that many of the reasons for dating the gospel late in the first century have recently been weakened. For instance, the older assumption that the higher Johannine Christology could not have developed earlier than the last decade of the century has been successfully challenged by J. A. T. Robinson. Those who assume such a view premised their conclusion on an evolutionary ideology, which is no longer tenable. On the other hand, the older dating of the gospel often appealed to the theory that the Fourth Evangelist knew and used the Synoptic Gospels—a theory that we have seen has fallen into increasing disfavor. The issue of the date remains an open question, and we need to reevaluate it in the light of the more recent understandings of the gospel.

Authorship

Admittedly, the question of the identity of the Fourth Evangelist has not evoked a great deal of speculation recently, but still there is enough discussion of the matter for it to merit our brief inclusion here. We can summarize the stands of the contemporary investigators under four types of efforts to establish the identity of the evangelist:

First, some propose that the Fourth Evangelist is none other than the disciple, John, son of Zebedee. By virtue of the fact that Irenaeus (*Against Heresies* III,1) declared himself to be of the opinion that John, son of Zebedee, was the author of John that view has become the traditional position. Furthermore, the alleged eyewitness quality of the gospel supports the view that the evangelist was John, son of Zebedee. Today at least four notable scholars champion this view. Morris argues at length in favor of this answer to the authorship question, believing that the claims for eyewitness testimony at 1:14, 19:35, and 21:24 are to be taken at face value (*Studies* 139–213, 128–276; *Gospel* 9–15, 29–30; contrast Parker, "John the Son"). Among others, B. De Solaces uses the argument that the Fourth Gospel is strangely silent about the sons of Zebedee, while at the same time giving extensive attention to the beloved disciple who is closely aligned with Peter (as the sons of Zebedee are in the Synoptic Gospels). W. De Boor is representative of the efforts of scholars of this persuasion to dismiss the theory of the early martyrdom of John, son of Zebedee (a theory that, of course, eliminates him from contention as the author of the gospel). De Boor does this by arguing that Mark 10:39 refers not to the martyrdom of John but to Jesus' disciples in general. Finally, in a monograph, J. Colson reasons that John (the beloved disciple) was a priest and reports the ministry of Jesus from that perspective (De Boor, 1:15–20; cf. Clergeon and contrast Kilpatrick).

The second option for consideration is that John, son of Zebedee, was not the author of the Fourth Gospel itself but the originator of the tradition which was written in the gospel by another—possibly a disciple of John. The eyewitness quality of the book impresses those who maintain this position but find it hard to conclude that the author was John, son of Zebedee. Connected with this discussion again is the identity of the beloved disciple. Like those scholars mentioned above, proponents of this second view are inclined to identify the beloved disciple with John, son of Zebedee. Perhaps the most carefully argued of the presentations of this position is that of F.-M. Braun (*Jean le théologien* 396ff.). John passed on his memoirs in tiny bits to secretaries who used considerable freedom in writing them up, and then another figure served to write from these materials the gospel itself on behalf of John. However, John died before the task could be completed. It is the author who completes the writing who identifies John with the beloved disciple. Schnackenburg in some of his writings generally adopts this position (*Gospel* 1:85–91, 94, 101–2). Brown understands that the beloved disciple, John, son of Zebedee, was responsible for the first stage of the composition of the gospel and one of his disciples for stages two through four (*Commentary–Gospel* 1:xcii–xcviii, 1:xxvii–xcviii). N. E. Johnson proposes that John (the beloved disciple) collected his experiences with Jesus into a document that was later incorporated into the gospel by a friend and disciple of John. A. M. Hunter's position is similar (*Gospel* 12–14, and *According to John* 104–6, 118).

The third alternative is somewhat different. J. N. Sanders proposed that John Mark, not John, son of Zebedee, is responsible for the Gospel of John. The whole association of the gospel with John, son of Zebedee, is ill-founded, originating among gnostic Christians looking desperately for apostolic grounds for their faith. The beloved disciple is Lazarus, as 11:5 clearly tells us. It was rumored Lazarus would never die, having been raised by Jesus (21:22). Lazarus left his memoirs behind, and they fell into the hands of another eyewitness, John Mark, who composed the Fourth Gospel out of them ("St. John"; Sanders and Mastin 29–52).[16]

Finally, the greatest number of scholars is content to say simply that we can never know the identity of the Fourth Evangelist. The evidence is simply not conclusive, and the question must be left open (e.g., Marsh, 21–25). Many also concede that the beloved disciple is an anonymous figure whose identity our historical inquiries cannot establish. Lindars, for example, along with T. Lorenzen and R. Schnackenburg (in a later writing) conclude that we cannot identify the beloved disciple (Lindars, *Gospel of John* 29, 33; cf. Schulz, *Evangelium* 2). Lindars thinks that it is likely the beloved disciple was one of the original twelve, but Schnackenburg and Lorenzen place him within the Johannine community and not among the original disciples (Schnackenburg, "Origin" 239-41; Lorenzen 76, 79, 82). Brown likewise announced that he has changed his position from that expressed in his commentary, and he no longer thinks the beloved disciple was one of the Twelve ("Johannine Ecclesiology" 388). Cullmann, too, holds this position, but thinks nonetheless that this anonymous figure was author of the Fourth Gospel (*Johannine* 77-78; cf. Schneider, *Evangelium* 41-42). While the beloved disciple is a concrete historical figure, he is used in the gospel in a paradigmatic way, thinks Schnackenburg ("Origin" 234), Lorenzen (80-81; cf. Agourides), A. Kragerud, P. Minear ("Beloved"; cf. Thyen, "Entwicklungen"), and D. Hawkin. They do not agree, however, on precisely what the relationship of Peter and the beloved disciple in the Fourth Gospel was intended to suggest. (For an interesting comparison of the beloved disciple and the Qumran teacher of righteousness cf. Roloff.) On the other hand, R. Mahoney argues that the Fourth Evangelist uses the beloved disciple in a way a historical figure known to readers could not be used (303-4). (For the view that the beloved disciple was purely a symbolic figure without historical reality cf. Loisy 220; Dibelius; and Bultmann, *Gospel* 484.)

The evidence, both internal and external, is far too flimsy for the historian of the Johannine literature to claim to know the identity of the author of that document. All efforts to do so waver under the winds of criticism. Wisdom and scholarly honesty are served best by the admission of our ignorance. That the beloved disciple was a figure in the history of the community seems a tenable position, although to say much more than that is to venture too far. It does seem likely that he was instrumental in the preservation of a tradition incorporated in the Fourth Gospel, and for that reason we may assume that he claimed some authority—whether as a disciple of Jesus or not. That he or she serves the evangelist as a paradigmatic figure, too, seems fairly certain as the redactional studies show. This means we cannot identify this person with the Fourth Evangelist.

We conclude our section on the historical puzzles in the Gospel of John with a few observations. First, it seems clear that the intellectual setting of the gospel was somewhere in the morass of syncretistic first-century Judaism before the effects of the Council of Jamnia (ca. 90-100 C.E.). Second, it was the dialogue with that Judaism out of which it came that occasioned the writing of this gospel. Third, the history of the community, while visible only in its essentials, indicates that the Johannine school was once at home in the Jewish synagogue and that its expulsion occasioned (along with other factors?) a radical reshaping of its thought. That the community underwent still other strains and changes is likely, given the probability that the gospel was the subject of later redactionary work at least of a minor kind. The gospel emerged in somewhat the form we know it in all likelihood, but not necessarily, after 70, but no later than 90. It was written by an anonymous figure in the community who preserved the traditions of the group centered in a distant figure of the past known in the gospel as the beloved disciple.

PART II

Theological Criticism

The critical approach to a biblical text that seeks to discover and systematically articulate its religious teachings is by definition "theological." Theology is the concern of the Christian and Jewish communities of faith.[1] Therefore, theological critics are most often people of faith whose work is intended to enrich a community of faith. This is a viable distinction, I believe, even though the precise nature of biblical theology and its relationship to historical criticism remains complex and unclear. What I will call theological criticism is simply the investigation of the biblical texts for constructing a statement of the text's views of faith and life for the sake of the church or synagogue.

In the case of the Fourth Gospel, theological criticism has sought to unearth the fundamental teachings of the gospel on matters of God, Christ, the Holy Spirit, the church, the sacraments, and so forth. In part, a sense that the teachings of this New Testament document are not simply the reiteration of those of the rest of the second Testament drives the theological quest. The concern for the distinction between John and Paul or John and the Synoptics arose early in the history of the church. Eusebius recorded that in the second century Clement of Alexandria declared the first three gospels were historical, while John composed "a spiritual Gospel" (*Ecclesiastical History* 6:xiv, 7). Whatever Clement meant by "spiritual," John was thought to be of special value beyond the historical records of Jesus.

Theological critics are inherently systematic, it seems, even if they do not attempt to construct complete systems of thought (as systematic or dogmatic theologians might). Consequently, New Testament theology is interested in the relationship among the various themes related to the teachings of the Bible. For instance, how does the Johannine dualist world view link up with the gospel's Christology? How do the present and futuristic eschatology relate? This is not so much to test the author's consistency, as it is to flesh out as fully as possible the meaning of any single theme.

The gnostic Christians were apparently the first to interpret John "theologically," as Heracleon's commentary witnesses (cf. Schnackenburg, *Gospel* 1:195). Their interpretation may even have been the cause of the schism that became the primary cause for the composition of 1 John (Brown, *Commentary–Epistles* 49–68). The body of believers that was to become the "orthodox church" had to interpret John in such as way as to free it from gnostic ownership. Hence, the theological interpretation of the gospel was an issue even before the document was regarded canonical. In the following centuries, John became the source for a number of what evolved into central affirmations of Christian faith, and the church used it to define the nature of orthodoxy. (Cf. Kysar, *Maverick Gospel* [1993].) The interpretation of John for theological purposes continued through the twentieth century.

The methods of theological interpretation vary among critics, and I think it is impossible to describe a single method by which the church discerns the doctrinal teaching of the Fourth Gospel. For that reason, among others, the theological interpretations of John have produced a vast variety of positions. For some, it is the foundation on which an orthodox and conservative theology is constructed (e.g., Carson); for others John is the "mystical" gospel (Countryman); and for still others the drastic "Gentile" gospel that was responsible for the split between Judaism and Christianity (Casey). The text itself is ambiguous enough to make all these views possible and rule out the possibility of one theological method.

The theological criticism of John was and remains a primary reason for my attraction and life-time preoccupation with it. My own preference has always been to give first attention to the theology of the New Testament, and John has provided endless theological fields to be plowed. What has intrigued me about this document is its potential richness for theological analysis. The peculiar combination of a puzzling Christology and an idiosyncratic worldview have, along with other features, continued to entice me. The articles included in this collection demonstrate my persistent interest in theology (especially early in my career).

There are few theological themes on which the gospel presents a consistent and unequivocal perspective, but the best candidate for such a theme would seem to be Christology. It is not, however, so much that there is nothing ambiguous about the Johannine view of Christ, for there surely are seemingly contradictory perspectives on Christ (e.g., the expression of the incarnation in 1:14). Still, the one persistent theme is the gospel's christocentricity. Everything seems to pivot around the strange Christ figure. Its view of Christ is the anchor of all of its theological themes, and all are determined to some degree by that view. The central role of Christ, however, includes utter mystery. No presentation of the Christ figure in the New Testament remains as impenetrable as that found in John. It is that mystery, along with its centrality, that makes the Johannine view so unique.

The two articles that comprise this second section of this collection are part of a review of Johannine scholarship written in the mid-1980s. In many ways, however, they still remain relevant to the theological criticism of this gospel and have proven to be helpful to students. The first article attempts to suggest how theological critics do their work through redaction criticism and theories of the history of the composition of the Gospel of John. The second and longer article summarizes scholarly research on seven particular theological topics.

Chapter Seven

Seeing Johannine Theology
through Temporal Lens

The puzzles of John include more than its literary characteristics or the many historical questions surrounding its origin and development. To the contrary, as we enter the thought of the gospel we come face-to-face with what surely seems even more insurmountable problems. If readers open John expecting to find a consistent, logical articulation of the Christian message, they are soon disappointed. On the one hand, it is rich with provocative ideas, but, on the other hand, it is replete with contradictions. We have already alluded briefly to what appears to be a contradictory eschatology within the gospel: passages which advocate a futuristic eschatology (e.g., 12:48) and those which teach a realized, present eschatology (e.g., 3:18; 9:39). There has also been mention of some of the christological perplexities—the logos concept (1:1ff.), the descending-ascending motif, and the envoy symbolism. We have already discussed the intellectual background of the dualism of the gospel, but we are still left with the task of determining the meaning of these polarities that seem to control the thought of the evangelist (e.g., 1:5). These problems are sufficiently disturbing in themselves, but there are still others. For example, we may ask what the relationship of knowing and believing is (e.g., 8:31 and 17:8). What is the role of the *signs* (compare 2:11 and 6:26)? What does the Fourth Evangelist mean by the use of the term *paraclete* for the Spirit? What is the author's view of the sacraments, given the glaring omission of any account of the institution of the Lord's Supper but in the light of the discourse in chapter 6?

Johannine thought represents a fertile field for the theological critic (e.g., J. Giblet). This is so especially since we find as we attempt to isolate a theme in the gospel that each individual theme of its thought is inseparably intertwined with others. The result is that we can hardly examine one of the individual members of the body of the theology of the Fourth Gospel without examining the entire body, and what begins as a monograph on a single Johannine theological motif ends up as a survey of the entire thought of the gospel! Notwithstanding this fact, the last several decades of research on John have witnessed the nearly endless writing of theological analyses. Our survey must be both selective and abbreviated. In the literature on the subject, there are two fundamental kinds of theological criticism. The first is what we are calling "Seeing Johannine Theology through Temporal Lens." This type of theological inquiry is concerned to trace the themes in the Fourth Gospel through a route of development or emergence and is very much involved with the history of the community, which we have examined in the article on "Historical Puzzles." This theological method of studying Johannine thought encompasses the results of redactional criticism as it pertains to the thought of the evangelist. The second major type is simply the more traditional analysis of theological ideas without attempts to suggest the history of the theme in the Johannine community. The following article discusses that type of theological analysis.

Christology

As we have mentioned before, U. Müller speaks of his method as "community theology" (*Gemeindetheologie*). He presents evidence that 1:14 and 16 are statements of a christological tradition which the Johannine community received within the context of a hymn, which was a part of the community's tradition. He asserts that these statements are marked by a Christology of glory which in effect ignores any possibility that in the death of Jesus that glory might somehow have been compromised. (Cf. the article "Christology and Controversy" in the present book.) There is no sense of the offense of the cross evident in this traditional material. The revelation of glory transmits grace to the believer, and, in that way, humans grasp divine life through the divinity of the revealer. On the other hand, the Fourth Evangelist was concerned with the possible offense of the death of Jesus and with the tendency of his community to ignore that death. Consequently, the gospel is an effort to assert the facticity of the death of Jesus, while still honoring the traditional Christology of glory. We see further evidence of that tradition and the efforts to revise it in 1 John (Müller, *Geschichte*, esp. 69–72; cf. idem., "Bedeutung," and J. Becker, "Beobachtungen"). Müller's study of the paraclete passages also reveals two levels of theological understanding. He believes that 15:18–16:15 presupposes a different Christology and eschatology than do the passages in chapter 14. In the former an older apocalyptic view of the judgment of the world is operative, and the paraclete, it is said, does nothing new. Müller contends that the evangelist received the materials of chapter 14 and revised them into the view expressed in 15:18–16:15. The paraclete is given a function in judgment only after the community has experienced the rejection of the world and exclusion from the synagogue. On the other hand, the view in chapter 14 assigns the paraclete only an intra-community function. Consequently, the paraclete materials must be read in terms of the changing situation of the community and the way in which those changes effected revisions of earlier views (Müller, "Parakletenvorstellung"; contrast Boyle).

Müller's efforts have much in common with the work of the redactional-critical studies of John. Four theological themes have received attention in those studies, the first of which is Christology. W. Nicol, like Müller, has been interested in the concept of glory in Johannine Christology; but, unlike Müller, Nicol finds that the redactional work of the evangelist deepened the concept of glory. Nicol believes that the signs source employed by the evangelist stressed the fleshly history of the revealer, and the evangelist reworked that material to stress that the divine glory was present in that fleshly history (*Sēmeia* 125–27). W. Wilkens believes the Fourth Evangelist wanted to make clear that Jesus was more than a miracle worker, more than a divine man, and hence connected the signs with the "I Am" sayings in order to stress the divine glory present in the works of Jesus. As a result of the evangelist's work, the passion of Jesus—the supreme expression of his glory—is foreshadowed in the signs (*Zeichen* 49–57; cf. idem., "Abendmahlszeugnis," "Evangelist," and "Erkweckung").

J. Becker, too, believes the evangelist assayed to deepen the epiphany character of the signs material, and hence shifted attention away from Jesus' wonders to his cross and resurrection ("Wunder," 144–47). For Schottroff the Fourth Evangelist accomplishes the redactional transformation incorporating the signs material into the context of Johannine dualism. This had the effect of making Jesus appear no longer as a divine man but as the heavenly revealer (*Glaubende* 267, 274–76). R. Fortna sees less evidence that the Fourth Evangelist drastically transformed the Christology of his proposed "Signs Gospel." The evangelist's redactional work, however, makes the signs point more clearly to Jesus' glory; but whereas the "Signs Gospel" climaxed with the resurrection as the sign par excellence, the Fourth Evangelist stresses the crucifixion as the life-giving event for believers. In general, the evangelist attempted to shift attention away from the

wondrous act itself to the theological significance of the act. Indeed, the
Fourth Evangelist preserved some of the aspects of the divine man Christology found in the "Signs Gospel," but moved away from that christological category ("Source" 152–55, 164–66, and "Christology" 490–94).

Miracle Faith

Closely related to Christology is the second theme about which redactional studies have been concerned, namely, miracle faith. Redaction critics tend to believe that the Fourth Evangelist was uncomfortable with the
view of the kind of faith evoked by wondrous acts. Still, their understandings of how the evangelist revised the view of source materials are by no
means in accord. Some understand that the Fourth Evangelist wanted
to distinguish between two levels or stages of faith—the level evoked in
response to a wondrous act and a higher level of "pure faith." Both Nicol
and Fortna believe that the evangelist reworked the source material in
order to clarify this difference (Nicol, *Sēmeia* 99–106; Fortna, "Source"
156–66; cf. Brown, *Commentary–Gospel* 1:196; Lindars, *Gospel of John*
203). To others, however, it appears that the evangelist intended much
more to discredit faith entirely that was based solely on wonders.
Becker contends that the evangelist believed the only authentic faith
was faith in Jesus' words ("Wunder" 145–46), and Wilkens stresses
that true faith is a response not to a wonder itself but to the glory of
Christ expressed in the wonder. Moreover, the evangelist holds word-
faith in highest regard (*Zeichen* 44, 59).

Still another understanding of the Fourth Evangelist's redactional
view of the signs faith is that of F. Schnider and W. Stenger. They
propose the "Signs Source" emphasized that one believed because
one saw the sign, while the Fourth Evangelist stressed that one saw
the sign because one believed. In other words, the evangelist inverted
the relationship between signs and faith (83). L. Schottroff offers the
view that the Fourth Gospel contains a contradictory view of this
matter. The evangelist has combined two traditions—one containing
the concept of signs as legitimating acts on the part of Jesus, the other
preserving the account of Jesus' refusal to use signs as a means of
arousing faith. The evangelist combines these traditions, and seems
to have believed that it is how one perceives signs that accounts for
either true or false faith. The object of true faith is the heavenly reality; false faith has as its object only an inner-worldly phenomenon
(*Glaubende* 247–57, 355).

Soteriology and Geography

R. Fortna alone has pursued the other two topics with the redactional technique. He has compared the materials in the gospel from his proposed source and those of the Fourth Evangelist and found a significant shift of soteriology. The proposed "Signs Gospel" maintains that salvation is simply a matter of believing in Jesus, and the signs point to an abundance of health and life because of Jesus. The author has in effect "spiritualized" the meaning of the signs and greatly enhanced the soteriological dimension of the "Signs Gospel." At the hand of the evangelist the physical focus of the signs gives way to symbols of the spiritual life ("Christiology to Soteriology"; cf. Brown, *Commentary–Gospel* 1:530).

Fortna has also examined the theological meaning of place-names in the Fourth Gospel, again contrasting the source and the work of the Fourth Evangelist. In the "Signs Gospel" geography does not appear to have had any special significance. However, in John Samaria and Perea function for the evangelist as contrasts to the lack of faith among the Judeans. The author of the gospel also uses Galilee in the symbolic sense of the place of faith and discipleship. In contrast, Judea is the locale that represents the rejection of Jesus, or at best his ambiguous acceptance. Hence, Fortna shows that the evangelist enriched the source material by using geography in a theological manner ("Christiology to Soteriology").[1]

Using temporal lens to see Johannine theology tries to show how the Fourth Evangelist used tradition or sources and is a promising but still fledgling method (von Wahlde). It is, of course, dependent upon a competent source or tradition analysis, and perhaps the fact that such theories are not widely accepted weakens the enterprise. Still, if it is true that the Fourth Gospel incorporated a body of material which was in some way part of the tradition prior to the evangelist, it is clear that we will never fully understand the theology of the gospel until we can grasp the theological perspectives of the different levels of material in the document (i.e., source and redactor). In some ways, it is appropriate to say that the future of Johannine theological analysis lies with the sort of methods we have just examined. To understand the dialogue (if you will) between the evangelist and tradition is to grasp what may be the key to a good number of the theological puzzles of John (cf. Kysar, *Maverick Gospel* [1993]). Finally, redactional-critical studies of this kind are ways of adding further credence to the theories of the history of composition upon which they are based. The ability to show that redactional studies enlighten the gospel demonstrates that a source proposal is at least close to the target.

Chapter Eight

The Framework of Johnannine Theology

This article moves from historical analysis of Johannine theology to the more traditional treatments of theological themes in the Fourth Gospel. The thematic approach does not usually purport, at least directly, to bear upon the history of the theme. By far thematic studies outnumber those we have just reviewed. They attempt to find clarity in the thought of the gospel without recourse to differences between the views of the evangelist and the traditions incorporated in the composition. There is an enormous amount of literature devoted to this enterprise, and this article can do no more than suggest the issues with which scholars have been concerned and cite some of the major contributions.

Christology

No one seriously doubts that the foundation of Johannine theology is found in its Christology. The issue is how we are to understand the view or views of Christ that pulsate there. The discussions of the last several decades have centered in three more specific areas of the Christology of the gospel. The first of those areas is the relationship between history and faith in the presentation of Jesus; that is, what is the relationship between the historical tradition regarding Jesus of Galilee and the experience of the Johannine community with the living Christ. The second is the relationship between flesh and glory, or if you prefer between the humanity and the divinity of the Johannine Christ. The third area is still another relationship, in this case between the function and the person of Christ.

Around these three areas are clusters of scholarly work, each of which deserves attention.

The relationship of history and faith. F. Mussner has most clearly and insightfully pursued this question in the Johannine presentation of Christ. Proceeding from an understanding of history informed by the existentialist thinkers (M. Heidegger; W. Dilthey; H.-G. Gadamer), Mussner seeks to comprehend the "historical understanding" of the Fourth Evangelist. Through a study of the verbs used in the gospel to designate one's means of knowing Jesus (e.g., "to see," "to hear"), Mussner claims to have found something of the way in which the evangelist spanned the temporal distance between the present and the historical Jesus. The author of the gospel knows the historical figure in such a way as to apprehend the true identity—the "hidden mystery"—of Jesus. This is so, argues Mussner, by virtue of the eyewitness testimony upon which the Gospel of John is based, the inspiration of the paraclete, and the Fourth Evangelist's own capacity to articulate a vision with a certain language (Mussner, *Historical Jesus* 709, 17-90; cf. Traets 194-97; and Gnilka).

For a similar view, we might compare H. Schlier, who likewise credits the evangelist with penetrating the essential meaning of the historical facts of Jesus. The meaning behind the history or under the empirical reality of Jesus is the nature of his person. The nature of the person of Jesus stands beyond the historical realm itself ("Christologie" 85-88, 98-100). In this connection, D. M. Smith has spoken of the evangelist's "metahistorical presentation of Jesus," that is, of the multidimensional character of the Christ of the Fourth Gospel—the historical Jesus and his spiritual presence in the community (*Johannine Christianity* 374-77).

The *heilsgeschichtliche* ("salvation history") school of interpretation understands the issue somewhat differently. O. Cullmann claims that John viewed Christ as the central figure in three separable periods of saving history—the history of Israel, the life of Jesus himself, and the life of the church. Because of his "salvation history" perspective, the evangelist chose the genre of the gospel in order to express the soteriological meaning of the history. The link between the evangelist and the Johannine community, on the one hand, and the historical Jesus, on the other, is precisely that the former is in some sense continuous with the work of Christ in history. So, for Cullmann, the Fourth Evangelist deals with historical materials in such a way as to highlight their meaning for the life of the church (*Salvation* 270-78, 285; cf. "Évangile").[1] J. C. Fenton's suggestion should not be confused with Cullmann's, but the two are related. Fenton proposes that the framer of the gospel was concerned to explain through historical references to Jesus the reality of the evangelist's own day. For instance, that the Christian is born from above (3:3) is understandable in reference to Christ's birth from above (3:16; cf. Carnegie; Morris, *Studies* 65–138).

The relationship between the fleshly existence of Jesus and the divine glory. The second major area of christological investigation is even more complex. What is revealed in Christ? Or, what is the relationship between the two halves of 1:14? R. Bultmann formulated that relationship in terms of a radical paradox. God manifested the divine glory in a hidden or disguised way within the fleshly reality of the revealer (*Theology* 2:50, and *Gospel* 63; cf. Thussing; and Barrett, *John and Judaism* 149–70). On the other hand, E. Käsemann has taken Bultmann's position further. Contending that chapter 17 is the key to Johannine Christology, Käsemann suggests that the Fourth Evangelist intended the symbols of the gospel to be taken quite literally. If we take them literally, it is clear (at least to Käsemann) that the evangelist embraced a "naive docetism." There is no humiliation of the Johannine Christ. Jesus never lays the divine glory aside, and his radical obedience, far from being an emptying of divine glory, is the form in which the divine glory is manifested. We should not misunderstand the incarnation of 1:14 to be the entry of the divine glory fully into human life, but as the encounter of the heavenly and earthly realms. The evangelist is interested only in bombarding the reader with the one dogma of the unity of the Father and the Son. This unconscious docetism naturally gave rise to later Gnosticism in the Johannine community (*Testament* 7–13, 21–26, 34–35, 65; cf. "Aufbau"). This view receives indirect support from B. A. Mastin. Mastin insists that the evangelist wanted to stress that the title "God" was applicable to Jesus and that this title was intended not merely functionally but in terms of essence. For the Fourth Evangelist Jesus was by nature God.

Two others have argued a position similar to Käsemann's, while carefully distinguishing their views from his. First, S. Schulz argues that the Fourth Gospel has no real interest in the humanity of Jesus. For the evangelist, he is the divine revealer, "God striding upon the earth." However, this view is not docetic, for Jesus is a common person whose earthly existence is quite real. It is, nonetheless, a "Christology of exaltation" in which the humanity of the revealer consists of nothing more than a transparent "disguise and veil" of the divine glory. The humanity of Jesus is combined with a powerful preexistent, incarnational theology in John to produce this Christology of glory (Schulz, *Evangelium* 64, 209, 211–12; and *Stunde* 323, 331, 352).

Second, Schottroff views the human, earthly reality of Jesus in a less positive way. For the Fourth Evangelist, Jesus' humanity was the baggage of the tradition, which was reluctantly stored within the more influential framework of the gospel's dualism. The Christology of John is not docetic, for the humanity of Jesus is never denied. However, it is essentially irrelevant. The flesh of the revealer is an inner-wordly reality that is always of little interest to believers. Their only interest is in the otherworldly, heavenly reality. Hence, while Jesus was a human, this is not an object of faith. Schottroff claims that to fail to understand the omnipotent role of the dualism of the Fourth Gospel is to miss the true understanding of Johannine Christology. Hence, for the evangelist it is alone the glory of Christ that is of interest to the Christian (*Glaubende* 268–70, 289–90).

These views of the prominence of the divine nature of Christ in John have been the subject of a great deal of debate[2] and have in recent years been balanced with what we might call a new emphasis upon the reality of the humanity of the Johannine Christ. W. H. Cadman anticipated this view in a little known position. In contrast to Käsemann, Cadman understands the christological symbols of John as metaphors for the close relationship of the human Jesus with God. The Fourth Gospel describes the human quality of Jesus with the titles "Son" and "Son of Man," each of which refers to the perfect humanity expressed in Jesus of Nazareth. That perfect humanity is one of the major thrusts of the gospel, and, according to Cadman's interpretation of 17:24, Christ extended that humanity to all people. The incarnation is the unifying of the perfect humanity of Jesus with the logos (13, 29–30, 59, 40–42, 74).

Cadman's emphasis upon the human dimension of the Johannine Christ is akin to two studies of the Son of Man motif in the Fourth Gospel which argue the proposition that for the evangelist this title denoted the genuine humanity of Christ. F. J. Moloney finds that the Son of Man sayings are the evangelist's way of alluding to the incarnational mode of Christ and are correctives of other messianic notions. In contrast to the Son of God title, the Fourth Evangelist used the Son of Man title only of the human Jesus and his earthly ministry. "There is a concentration on the human figure of Jesus in the use of the title 'Son of Man.' . . . The Son of Man reveals the truth to [humans] because he is [human]—because of the incarnation" (*Johannine Son of Man* 208–13, quote 213; cf. idem., "Johannine Son of Man"). J. Coppens's study of the same theme independently comes to some similar conclusions. He finds a possible anti-docetic polemic in the Johannine Son of Man Christology. Unlike Moloney, however, he discovers that the Son of Man sayings comprise a quite distinct stratum of material in the gospel, possessing a distinctive style and content from the other christological themes of the document.

According to Coppens, the evangelist reshaped and combined them with a theme of glorification after death ("Fils," and "Logia").[3] Both Moloney and Coppens, however, find in the Son of Man materials a clear affirmation of the Fourth Evangelist's commitment to the humanity of

Christ.[4] To this direction in understanding the Christology of the Fourth Gospel we add K. Berger's contention that 1:14 means the entrance of the logos into the human Jesus and not the preexistence or the full identity of Jesus and the logos (cf. Minear, "We Don't Know" 136).

Much more common in the circles of Johannine theological criticism is the proposal that throughout the presentation of Christ the author wanted to insist upon the indivisibility of the flesh and glory, the humanity and divinity, of the revealer. Some understand the "envoy Christology" of the Fourth Gospel to be a compendium of this synthesis. E. Haenchen and J. Kuhl have both attempted expositions of the christological sending motif, which stress the synthesis of the human and divine. Both articulate the characteristics of this divine envoy in a representative of God. Haenchen finds the gospel text wanting to say that through the words of the envoy, Jesus, the Father becomes word. Therefore, as one hears the words of the envoy, one is hearing the word of God, especially in the "I Am" sayings ("Vater"). Kuhl sets Jesus apart from any strictly human, prophetic representative of God by speaking of him as the "absolute envoy" of God enjoying a unique relationship with the Father. For the Fourth Evangelist the humanity of Jesus is the station along the way in the total journey of the divine messenger (65–88, 94–128, 130–38).

Other critics have tried to understand Johannine Christology in a similar way. F.-M Braun contends that the Johannine Christ is continuous with the Holy Spirit and that the writer presents Christ in two stages. In the first stage, Christ is incarnate in real human form to draw persons to himself. In this stage he is visible and constrained by the limitations of time and space as a preparation for the second stage. In the second stage he is freed of those constraints, is invisible, and completes the work of the visible stage by extending his presence to all humanity. Hence, the Johannine Christ is "indivisible"—both human and divine at once (*Jean le theologien III. Sa theologie 1* 224, 243–46, and *Jean le theologien III. Sa theologie 2* 288–89). A. Feuillet invokes the orthodox understanding of the trinity and finds the Johannine Christ consistent with that dogma. The relationship between Jesus and God is supremely a mystery, Feuillet says, in which Jesus is equal to God even throughout his incarnate mode. His dependence is to be understood as a dependent relationship in the context of full equality. He is genuinely human, and his humanity is no mere vestment. Still, it is a temporary humanity in which, in a mysterious and incomprehensible way, the equality with God is retained (*Mystère* 69–77, 239–40). Barrett's article on the gospel's subordinationist Christology is relevant here, for he stresses that the passages of the gospel subordinating Christ to the Father are to be taken seriously (e.g., 5:19 and 10:22-39). Taken in context, this means that the Fourth Evangelist leaves us

with a paradox—a mystery. "John—may we not say?—simplifies the theme
of the relation of Jesus to God by presenting him in a somewhat inhuman
humanity, and as both claiming and denying equality with the Father"
("Father" 148-59, quote, 159).[5]

   The relationship between the person and function of Christ. Our third and
final area of christological investigation probes this delicate relationship
and is for some the means by which Johannine Christology becomes clear.
A number of scholars find the Fourth Gospel much more interested in
affirming the functional effects of Christ than in stating the nature of
his person. J. A. T. Robinson was the most radical of those to formulate
this view of Johannine Christology. He does not reduce the whole of the
Christology to function, for he acknowledges that the evangelist is interested in metaphysical unity (10:30) as well as functional meaning. The
Fourth Evangelist was able to bind function and nature together. Still,
the primary thrust of the gospel is to present Jesus as one who, amid his
humanity, lived in complete dependence upon the Father. The language
of the Fourth Gospel is parabolic and points to the functional relationship of Christ and God. *How* Jesus was rather than *what* he was is the
cutting edge of this gospel (Robinson, "Use").

   Like Robinson, J. Riedl maintains that the Fourth Evangelist held
together a function-nature view of Christ but stresses that the gospel seems
to say that the clue to the person of Christ is in his works. Hence, what
Jesus does implies who he is. What his works imply is that Christ is a free,
independent individual who is one with the Father by virtue of both will
and nature. Therefore, for Riedl, the Johannine Christ is binary (24-26,
40, 414, 420-23; cf. Schnackenburg, *Gospel* 1:154-56). Schlier's view is
only slightly different. For him what Jesus does is actually the revelation
of his person. When Jesus reveals himself, he reveals God. Therefore, one
might say that in Schlier's understanding of the Christology of John, in a
real sense *function is person* ("Offenbarer" 254-60; cf. Wennemer).

   J. T. Forestell's work is really a study of the soteriology of the gospel,
but it has importance in this connection as well. Forestell rather effectively demonstrates that the dominant understanding of the function of
Christ in John is in terms of revelation. The gospel presents a process of
revelation that climaxes in the cross. Revelation is not communication
of knowledge but of life; in other words, it is event. All cultic concepts
of sacrifice are missing, because the gospel understands revelation itself
as salvific. The revelation is, however, nothing other than the manifestation of the person of Christ and his relationship with the Father (19-57,
191-92).

   K. Haacker's study takes a different approach to the question of the
identity of Jesus in John and of the relationship of that identity to Christ's

function. A phenomenology of religion methodology forms Haacker's view. He thinks the handle we seek on Johannine Christology is accessible through understanding that the author wanted to present this figure as the historical founder and original authority of the Christian movement in comparison with the function of Moses in Judaism (John 1:17). The evangelist employs symbols (e.g., spatial symbols such as descending and ascending) in order to claim the divine origin of the founder. He therefore stresses the historical Jesus and the work of that historical man as the continuing basis for the life of faith in the community of Christians (25–173).

In summary of these efforts to elucidate the Christology of the Fourth Gospel we wish only to offer some observations and a warning. First, the warning: contemporary interpreters are too often inclined, it seems to me, to analyze the Christology of this early Christian document by means of categories which are in all probability not those of the evangelist. Did the evangelist operate within the conceptual framework of such polarities as faith and history, human and divine, or person and function? In all likelihood, the evangelist did not consciously use such categories. The understanding of the evangelist's view of Christ will gain ground when we are able to grasp those modes of thought in which the evangelist, and not necessarily the interpreter, is at home. Hence, I think that an enterprise such as that of Schottroff has a great deal more promise (although I cannot agree with many of the conclusions she reached) than say, for example, that of Feuillet. Still, the hermeneutical circle necessitates that at some point the questions of the contemporary interpreter intersect with those of the evangelist, and for that reason, none of these efforts is to be dismissed.

Nonetheless, we can observe that, with the christological criticisms of the last several decades, the questions with which we must deal have emerged in better focus. More specifically, the results of our survey show that much of the investigation of Johannine Christology has been done within what appears to be a dialectical framework, and that hint is a valuable one for future probing of the gospel (cf. the article, "Pursuing the Paradoxes" in this volume). The Fourth Evangelist seems to have formulated a view of Christ within a tension between several poles—whether we know precisely what those poles of thought were remains yet doubtful. Retreating to our earlier discussion, it may well be that the tensions, within which the evangelist molded the views we find in the Fourth Gospel, are better understood within a reconstructed history of Johannine thought (i.e., tradition analysis).

Eschatology

As with most features of his proposal concerning John, Bultmann caused extensive debate as a result of his understanding of the eschatology of the document. It was his contention that the gospel's author embraced a strictly realized or present eschatology. Bultmann thought the evangelist held that all the blessings associated with the final days were already present in the life of the believer. Therefore, those eschatological passages that stress the presence of these phenomena in the lives of believers were from the hand of the evangelist (e.g., 3:18; 5:24, 25). Those passages which affirm the older, apocalyptic and futuristic eschatology, he thought, were the work not of the evangelist but of the later ecclesiastical redactor (e.g., 5:28; 6:39-40, 54; 12:48; *Theology* 2:39-40, and *Gospel* 155-57, 247-62, 233-37, 345-47). With his proposal, Bultmann was thus able to account for the seemingly contradictory nature of the eschatology of the Fourth Gospel, but he was not able to win a great deal of support for his position. The search for a better understanding of this dimension of the gospel continues. (For a summary of some of the positions and a revision of Bultmann's, cf. Kysar, "The Eschatology of the Fourth Gospel," reprinted in part 1 of this collection.)

It is instructive that none of the five major contemporary contributors to this subject employs Bultmann's thesis. J. Blank contends that John's eschatology is correctly understood only as an extension of its Christology. His investigation focuses on the issue of judgment, and he finds that the evangelist has employed the word *krisis* to mean both judgment and decision. According to Blank's analysis, the individual's decision brings either judgment or freedom from judgment. The decision not to believe brings with it the experience of judgment, which is to say that judgment is the consequence of a negative human response to revelation. In this sense, then, the eschatological reality of judgment is present already in the human experience. Yet Blank does not believe that the evangelist intended in any way to deny the future dimension of eschatology. There is for the believer a future hope for resurrection. Verses 28-29 of chapter 5 mean that Christians entombed until the last day will experience resurrection at that time. Therefore, Blank argues that there are aspects of the eschatological realities that are present and aspects that are yet in the future (*Krisis* 42, 65, 94-99, 124-39, 179, 196, 282, 345).

Blank's analysis has a good deal in common with the work of P. Ricca. The latter, too, thinks that the key to Johannine eschatology is its symbiotic relationship with Christology. He calls the evangelist's eschatology a "personalized eschatology," meaning that it is grounded in the person of Christ. The eschatology of the Gospel of John contains three spheres—the event of Christ's appearance, the experience of believers, and the eschatological realities yet to be experienced in the future. Judgment and eternal life are present realities. The unbeliever is without hope and hence already judged. The believer, on the other hand, embraces a future hope and has thereby transcended judgment. Eternal life is not identical with resurrection in the Fourth Gospel, Ricca says. The Christian already has eternal life but anticipates resurrection in the last day. Both Ricca and Blank understand the eschatology of the gospel in the context of a scheme of saving history. For Ricca, it is because of the Fourth Evangelist's salvation history perspective that he does not dissolve the future sphere entirely into the present (63–180; cf. Cullmann, *Salvation* 289–90).

Riedl joins his colleagues in affirming the christocentricity of Johannine eschatology. Eschatology in the Fourth Gospel is a function, he says, of Christology. According to his proposal, the relationship of the present and future dimensions is relatively simple. The present contains the eschatological blessings, but they are concealed and visible only to the eyes of faith. The future fulfillment will bring the removal of their concealment and reveal clearly what is as yet known only in faith. Riedl thus holds tightly to the temporal distinctions but does not employ a salvation history scheme in order to do so (18–23, 34–36, 39; cf. Martin).

Schnackenburg understands the eschatology of the gospel to center in the conviction that the evangelist abandoned all such temporal distinctions. John did not reject the futuristic dimension of the eschatological hope but reshaped it in nontemporal categories. Schnackenburg comprehends the view of the gospel's creator in terms of ontological, not temporal categories. He agrees, however, that Johannine Christology is the controlling thought of its eschatology (*Gospel* 1:159–60, and *Johannesevangelium* 2:532–40).

It is in the work of Käsemann that we find evidence of the influence of Bultmann's position. While it is true that the Christology of the gospel influences its view of the eschatological blessings, Käsemann's understanding of the former subject is radically different, and therefore his grasp of eschatology, too, differs. He contends that the Fourth Evangelist rejected the older apocalyptic future expectations entirely, but introduces another kind of future eschatology in chapter 17. The hope for a heavenly perfection and unity we find in that chapter constitutes the evangelist's remolding of the older eschatology. Similar to Schnackenburg, Käsemann believes the evangelist detemporalized and spiritualized the traditional Christian apocalyptic hopes (*Testament* 13–21, 70–73; cf. Gundry, "My Father's House"; and Fischer, "Die himmlicheWohnungen," esp. 295).

Again, I believe that we would do better if we sought the resolution of this feature of the Fourth Gospel in the history of the thought of the community than in the sort of analyses we have just reviewed. It seems likely that the Fourth Evangelist did radically rethink the eschatology of the tradition, as especially Schnackenburg and Käsemann suggest. It would be much easier to understand that rethinking in the light of an analysis of the distinction among the strata of Johannine eschatological thought, perhaps in a manner similar to that offered by Richter ("Präsentische"; cf. Brown, *Commentary–Gospel* 1:cxviii). I believe that efforts to impose a history of salvation framework upon the mind of the evangelist are doomed to failure, and almost equally unpromising are those proposals for *the manner* in which the author understood some aspects of the eschatological hope realized (e.g., eternal life) and others still hoped for (e.g., resurrection).

Dualism

How shall we understand Johannine dualistic language? To begin our discussion we return to L. Schottroff's studies of the gospel's dualism. As we have said, she proposes that the poles of the Johannine dualism are simply salvation and the deprivation of salvation. All of the language of the gospel bears upon the existential matter of accepting or rejecting salvation. The language varies, but the point is persistently the same—all of the negative mythology points to the rejection of salvation, while the positive symbols indicate one reality, salvation. Hence, the dualism is not ethical, cosmic, apocalyptic, anthropological, or even demythologized. It is the forceful use of language and symbol to drive home the choice of salvation or deprivation (*Glaubende* 228–34, 237–38, 293–94; cf. "Johannes," and Schulz, *Evangelium* 67–71).

G. Stemberger proposes that the dualism of the gospel is a moral distinction. Hence his understanding of the same material is the direct opposite of Schottroff's. What is involved in the gospel's dualistic options is the moral discernment between good, rooted in God, and evil, rooted in Satan. Ultimately then, the dualism of the gospel, like the fundamental Jewish dualism, is really a monism—good is the only reality, and evil is unreality. This moral dualism is set within a concept of the saving history of God's work and hinges in the last analysis upon the person of Christ. Hence, the dualism of the Fourth Gospel is (like other features of the theology of the document) christocentric (*Symbolique* 239–44; cf. N. Lazure). As different as Schottroff's and Stemberger's proposals are, they agree that the dualism solicits human choice and describes the results of that choice (cf. Bultmann, *Theology* 2:15–21).

We must mention only in passing here a number of studies that treat the individual members of the dualistic language of the gospel, in particular, studies of the concepts of the "world" and "truth." Most of the investigations of the notion of the world in John conclude in effect that this term points to the phenomenon of human rebellion or distortion of existence. H. Schlier proposes that the world represents the human effort to exist independent of the Creator and thus obscures the real nature of human existence ("Word" 161–64). T. H. Olbricht arrives essentially at the same point: "The world" symbolizes the failure to maintain a relationship with God and open rebellion against God (242–44; cf. Bultmann, *Theology* 2:26–32; Cassem; Morris, *Gospel* 126–28; and Heinz). "Truth" (or "true"), on the other hand, is understood by most scholars as the saving reality of the Christ event. Y. Ibuki insists that truth in the Fourth Gospel is an event—the event of the word and the event of love. It refers ultimately to the unity of being and love in the unity of the Father and the Son (355–57). J. Blank contends that truth has to do with revelation that centers in the person of Christ ("Wahrheits-Begriff" 167, 170). S. Aalen similarly stressed the salvific quality of truth. L. J. Kuyper reads the Johannine concept out of the Old Testament background and concludes that truth has to do with the redemptive faithfulness of God. (Contrast Dodd, *Interpretation* 170–78; cf. de La Potteries, "Verità"; Schlier, "Meditationen"; Schnackenburg, *Johannesevangelium* 2:279–80; and Morris, *Gospel* 293–96.)

This brief summary of the research on Johannine dualism is obviously inadequate, but it indicates some of the issues that are at stake in this discussion. Stemberger's thesis seems to stop short of the heart of Johannine thought and proposes a view that is not congenial to the thought of the gospel as a whole. On the other hand, the individual studies of the concepts of the world and truth point rather consistently toward something like the understanding proposed by Schottroff. Without necessarily accepting all of the baggage that accompanies Schottroff's analysis, it is certain that her notion of Johannine dualism resonates clearly with the thought of the Fourth Evangelist. The elaborate mythology of Johannine dualism seems to point simply in one direction—the acceptance of the saving revelation in Christ. This means that in the Fourth Gospel dualism functions not so much to describe the cosmos as it does to call persons to decision regarding their two options.

Witness, Signs, and Faith

There is a sheaf of questions surrounding the nature of faith in the Fourth Gospel. This bundle of issues centers in the question of what faith is and what evokes it, but also involves the relationship of seeing and knowing to believing. Attached in a way that is almost impossible to separate are the issues of the role of witness and of signs in relation to faith. A reading of John shows that these issues are closely interrelated, so we will try to epitomize as a whole the mood of contemporary research on these matters.

In the course of his treatment of signs, S. Hofbeck deals with the question of faith in John. He finds that signs have a double function: for those who believe the signs are revelation, while for those who refuse to believe they function to conceal the true identity of Jesus. Yet, there are two "believing" ways of responding to the signs. The interest in the wonders of Jesus for their own sake is not truly faith; but a believing response which leads on to a personal encounter with Christ is also possible as a result of the signs. Hence, the signs have a witness character about them (177–78). J. M. Boice agrees with this witness role of the signs and argues that they have evidential value, for they give verification of the identity of Christ and that verification is the basis of faith (99). W. Inch stressed the same point: The signs are the evidence faith needs, and they are then apologetic in nature. The signs, however, are not direct evidence for faith. They are better understood as faith giving evidence of itself rather than evidence that demands the faith response (35–38; cf. Dennison).

J. C. Hindley is satisfied that he can find two values in the signs. One value is in terms of the evidence they supply for faith. They are the grounds for inference. Still, their "sign value" is more than the basis for inference. It points to some divine power in the act to the perception of God in Christ (330–31). Schnackenburg disagrees with much of this when he argues that the signs, like all of the witness motifs in John, do not authenticate faith or "prove" it. The signs "enlighten" the reason of the observers but in no sense persuade or convince them (*Gospel* 1:519–20, and "Revelation" 135–36).

J. Gaffney addresses the question of why some persons believe and some do not, and he finds three different reasons given for this. In some cases, moral disposition is the determinative factor (e.g., 3:20-21); but in others a divine influence or its absence is the reason for belief or unbelief (e.g., 5:44). Finally, other passages claim that it is the effectiveness of witness, which causes faith (233–36; cf. Grelot, 61; Morris, *Gospel* 335–37; and Heer). A. Vanhoye puts emphasis upon the role of "an interior invitation" to believe (e.g., 6:45). The combination of the external witness and the internal witness of the Father seem at times to produce faith (e.g., 6:36-37, 43-45, 64-65; Vanhoye, "*Notre foi*" 339–48). H. Schneider claims that the Fourth Gospel gives two reasons for the failure to believe. One is the inability of the human mind to perceive God through the ambiguity of the revelation in flesh. The other is the hiddenness or incompleteness of the revelation itself until after the crucifixion. Finally, he recognizes the gospel sometimes speaks of faith as a gift from God (6:37, 29). L. Walter's little study of belief and unbelief in the gospel contends that the evangelist followed an early tradition which understood that unbelief was a result of divine intention. By means of this tradition, the gospel's author in effect refuses to be scandalized by unbelief. This does not mean, however, the evangelist embraced a predestinarianism. Those who refuse to obey play a significant role in the history of salvation, but they too are responsible for their condition and not excused of their failure. F. Manns comparably stresses that the author built the concept of faith on human freedom. John 8:31-59 presents two models—Abraham and the Devil—and the choice between the two is a free one (Walter, 127; Manns, 199; cf. articles on paradox in John and "Dismantling Decisional Faith" in part 3 of this volume).

C. Traets pursues the role of seeing in relationship to believing and finds that the sensual perception of the man Jesus is the starting point of faith. Yet, a deeper insight, in which it is no longer the man Jesus but the Father in Jesus who is the object of perception, follows that sensual perception. The gospel presents, therefore, a dynamic relationship between sensual seeing and the vision of faith.

The role of knowing in relationship to believing is more complicated (Traets, 51-52, 120-21, 197, 244; cf. Mussner, *Historical Jesus* 18-23, 82-88). J. Gaffney maintains that knowing and believing are not synonymous, for the former is used with a distinctively intellectual flavor and the latter with a stronger volitional flavor. Schnackenburg seems to agree when he suggests that revelation leads to a deeper knowledge but only after one experiences being grasped through a personal and total submission ("Revelation" 131, 136-38). Schlier finds more evidence that the two verbs are used interchangeably, and the kind of distinctions, which Gaffney and Schnackenburg make between them, is not evident (*Glauben*).

How, then, is this faith evoked? What is the role of witness in the birth of faith? This is the subject of a monograph by Boice in which he argues that witness constitutes the whole concept of revelation in Johannine thought. Jesus' self-witness is revelation, for it betrays the consciousness of his relationship with the Father. Furthermore, it is a self-authenticating witness just because it arises from that relationship. The revelation is one that contains the words of Jesus and propositions arising from those words, and hence is not without content. Moreover, the witness to Jesus by others is also revelatory, continues Boice. In other words, witness to revelation is itself revelation. This includes the divine witness given by the Fourth Gospel through the witness of the Baptist, the signs, and the witness of Scripture—as well as the human witness, e.g., that of the disciples. The latter is revelation because the Spirit inspires it. The signs are one more form of divine witness. They are symbols that point toward the reality symbolized, but, at the same time, they participate in that reality toward which they point. Boice claimed, therefore, that there is an organic concept of revelation in the Gospel of John growing out of the function of witness (Boice 14–130).

Others, however, give us a different picture of the gospel. J. C. Hindley argues that the self-witness of Jesus has no obvious self-authenticating value. Moreover, the witness is without content except for the bare assertion that Jesus and the Father are one. Hindley finds that the passages, which speak of the "internal witness" of the Father (3:27; 6:37, 44; 18:37), supplement the self-witness of Jesus (Hindley 321, 324–28; cf. Bultmann, *Theology* 2:66; and Walker).

The signs function in the phenomenon of faith as a sort of theory of cognition, claims S. Hofbeck. The signs are used to stress that, in contradistinction to the Synoptic Gospels, in the Fourth Gospel there is no difference between Jesus himself and the kingdom. The whole message of revelation is Jesus, who is synonymous with the kingdom (158–60). Schnackenburg's view is comparable, for he believes the signs declare the complete eschatological salvation present in Christ (*Gospel* 1:521–25; cf. Wilkinson, "Study"). P. Riga holds, however, that the signs authenticate the message of Christ and by doing so create a situation, which demands decision. In the latter function, they are comparable to the parables in the synoptic traditions, and indeed have a certain parabolic quality as well as function (402–10). Feuillet has argued that the concept of sign is connected with the christophanies in both the mighty works of Christ in his earthly ministry and in the post-resurrection presence of Christ in the life of the church ("Christophanies"; cf. Smalley, "Sign").

It is obvious that there is either a very profound concept of faith and its evocation in the Fourth Gospel or else a very muddled and confused one. A third alternative is that the gospel represents the culmination of the thinking of the Johannine community about this subject over an extended period of time with several significant revisions in that thinking occurring because of new experiences in the community. In my opinion, this last alternative best accounts for the views expressed in John. Hence, the efforts to find a profound "theory of cognition" and a tightly woven concept of witness and sign may be fruitless. Surely, however, Traets is correct in observing in the Fourth Gospel a provocative understanding of the relation of sensual perception and faith perception. The multiple functions of signs is better explained by the critiques of the history of the theology of the gospel (see above) than by those offered in this section.

Finally, we see evidence in the gospel that the community struggled over a period of years with the question of why some believe and others do not. The result is that there are a number of differing proposals within the Gospel of John. Perhaps at one stage, freedom of choice was the dominant position of the community and, at a later stage, a less optimistic mood prevailed. This later mood resulted in what appears now to be the predestination motif and/or the motif of the divine initiative in the birth of faith (cf. Kysar, *Maverick Gospel* [1976], 65–83).

The Spirit-Paraclete

The fascinating concepts of the Spirit and the paraclete have provoked much concern among those interested in the religious thought of the Fourth Gospel (cf. e.g., Brown, *Commentary–Gospel* 2:1135–36, "Paraclete in the Fourth" 113–14, and "Paraclete in the Light" 158ff.). What we might summarize as two contexts enables us to comprehend the general concept of the Spirit. First, for some Johannine pneumatology is primarily a function of the Christology and of the testimony themes of the gospel. In this case, the Spirit is closely associated with the question of the birth of faith just discussed. Second, for others, however, the pneumatology is primarily a function of the eschatology of the gospel.

Johannine pneumatology as primarily a function of Christology. The recent work of F. Porsch contributes significantly to the efforts of those who hold this position. He discovers through his study that the notion of the Spirit is "christologically concentrated." The Spirit enables one to recognize Jesus as the God-sent revealer, to execute an awakening, and to deepen and strengthen faith. Characteristic of Johannine pneumatology is that the concept of Spirit is associated with word. The word of Jesus is Spirit (6:63); and hence the "word-event" is pneumatic event, and pneumatic event is word event. The *pneuma* is the peculiar power by which the word becomes the words of eternal life. The Fourth Gospel is supremely, then, a "pneumatic gospel." It always presents the Spirit as another "form of appearance" ("*Erscheinungsform*") or designation for the presence of Christ. The Spirit is above all the power of the word (Porsch, 405–7).

J. M. Boice seems to agree with much of Porsch's analysis, because he understands that, throughout John, it is the Spirit that makes possible the witness of the apostles to revelation. The Spirit also supplies the "internal witness" that, in turn, makes the embracing of revelation an option. The Spirit is part of the Fourth Evangelist's understanding of how the kerygma is received and affirmed (120–22, 143–45). H. Schlier, too, believes John's author holds that the truth of revelation is grasped and affirmed by persons only by means of the Spirit ("Heilige"). In a comparable manner, de La Potterie thinks the Spirit is a necessary ingredient in the Johannine scheme of salvation. It is the Spirit who interprets the revelation which otherwise remains obscure and mysterious ("Paraclet" 96, and "Parole et Esprit").

Pneumatology as primarily a function of the eschatology. Those who connect pneumatology with Johannine eschatology stress more the role it plays in the gospel's system of present eschatology. G. Locher argues that the Spirit makes the past as well as the future present for the believers (578). J. Blank maintains that Johannine realized eschatology is possible only because of a peculiar and strong view of the Spirit (*Krisis* 215).

Yet, why does the evangelist give the Spirit this specific designation, "Paraclete"? G. Johnston proposes it was for two reasons. The first is to repress a movement that gave undue prominence to certain angelic intercessors (especially Michael) and asserted the superiority of Jesus to all such intercessors. The second reason for the use of the title paraclete is to identify the power displayed among certain leaders in the church with the Spirit and thus explain their power by reference to the continuing presence of Christ in the life of the community (*Spirit-Paraclete* 119–46). De La Potterie offers a less complicated proposal. The evangelist simply wanted to separate and label two periods in the history of God's salvific work—the work of Christ and the work of the Spirit. This separation demonstrated decisively the dependence of the Spirit upon Christ ("Paraclet" 90–96). Brown suggests a similar proposal, namely, that the author of the gospel wanted clearly to distinguish the role of the Spirit in the community following the resurrection (*Commentary–Gospel* 2:1139–41; cf. Morris, *Gospel* 662; and Kuhl, 135). For Porsch, the paraclete is simply the Johannine way of speaking of the Spirit in a forensic setting (406). There seems to be much agreement that the title paraclete was a way by which the Spirit could be related to Christ and its work made dependent upon Christ's (e.g., Locher, 578; Schulz, *Stunde* 359; Blank, *Krisis* 329; Bammel; Leaney, "Historical" 158).

The attribution of the title, "Spirit of truth," to the paraclete constitutes another problem. What did the Fourth Evangelist intend by this title? Boice understands that the title identifies the Spirit-Paraclete with God and Christ, as well as denoting the function of this figure as the one who delivers the truth to humans (152). Porsch thinks that the unity of word and Spirit enlightens this title. "The Spirit of truth" is the forensic description of the word empowered by the Spirit (324, 406). For Müller, the title gives expression to the peculiarly Johannine notion of the Spirit arising as it does from the dualism and Christology of John's gospel ("Parakletenvorstellung" 43–48). Locher contends that it is simply a functional designation for the work of the Spirit. The Spirit leads people from ignorance to truth (577).

About the function of the Spirit-Paraclete there is little significant disagreement. Most often it is said that the paraclete functions in two realms—among the disciples and in the world. In the first realm, the para-clete is the interpreter of the revelation in Christ and the one who enables persons to appropriate the revelation (Blank, *Krisis* 330-31; Brown, "Para-clete in the Fourth" 114; Boice, 153). De La Potterie speaks of this func-tion as the "interiorization and spiritualization" of the witness of Christ ("Paraclet" 92, 99; cf. Woodhouse), and Schlier holds that the Spirit is the continuation of the revelatory work begun in Christ ("Heilige" 101-3). In the second realm, Brown and de La Potterie understand the function in a negative way—the indictment of the opponents of Christ and the revela-tion. Schlier, however, suggests a more positive function for the paraclete, namely, the illumination of the situation of the world and its alienation from its Creator (de La Potterie, "Paraclet" 97-103; Brown, *Commentary-Gospel* 2:1136; Schlier, "Heilige" 104-5; cf. Locher, 577).

The paraclete works through the disciples of the church and is tied with the tradition of the community, says Schlier, and the sending of the Spirit is parallel to the sending of the disciples. These two (the sending of the disciples and the Spirit) are the primary constituents of the church (Schlier, "Heilige" 106-7; cf. Kuhl, 130; Locher, 574-76; and Patrick, 337-39). Brown proposes that the paraclete concept enabled the Johan-nine community to understand and trust the continuance of the tradition reaching back to the historical Jesus, even though an increasing number of apostolic eyewitnesses were dying. Moreover, the paraclete concept was the Johannine response to the crisis caused by the delay of the Parousia (*Commentary-Gospel* 2:1142-43; cf. Schlier, "Begriff" 268). Müller, too, sees that the concept of the paraclete functioned to add legitimacy and authority to the tradition. Along with this function, it provided the con-tinuity between the work of Christ and the ongoing work of God in the church ("Parakletenvorstellung" 48ff.).

At this point, the differences among the interpreters are not glaring. It appears that Johnston's thesis of an anti-angelic polemic in the para-clete materials is unnecessary and improvable. Likewise, I feel some dis-comfort with Porsch's extensive efforts to find a contemporary theology of the word associated with the Johannine paraclete concept. My own understanding of the paraclete title is simply that the evangelist wanted to christianize a notion which was indirectly influenced by Qumran, particu-larly to use it in a forensic setting. Brown is surely correct that Johannine pneumatology attempted to meet the problems of the increasing num-ber of deaths among the eyewitnesses and the delay of the Parousia. The author used the Spirit-Paraclete concept to link the contemporary life of the church with the historical roots of the faith.

The Church

In spite of the charges that it has no ecclesiology, scholars have shown that John contains a fascinating understanding of the community of faith (Bultmann, *Theology* 2:91; contrast, for example, Dahl; O'Grady, "Individualism"; de La Potterie, "Wort Jesu," and "Parole et Esprit"). The relationship of the church to the world is found expressed, think a number of critics, in chapter 17. P. Le Fort points out that Johannine ecclesiology is fundamentally dualistic: The church constitutes one pole over against the world (102, 180). Käsemann, of course, agrees. The presence of the word divides humanity into two camps; and the believer has no interest in the world except to pull the elect from its grasp. The church is comprised of those who belong to God and to Christ, as opposed to the world (*Testament* 63–69; cf. Schnackenburg, "Strukturanalyse"; Le Fort, 101; Rigaux, 202–4; Jaubert, "L'image"; and Heise). Käsemann finds no evidence for the moral distinction between the Christian and the world, which M. Vellanickal argues is so characteristic of the children of God in the gospel (Vellanickal, e.g., ch. 8).

The unity of believers in the church arises out of the unity of the Father and the Son. That christological unity is what Le Fort calls "the root of ecclesial unity," (Le Fort, 108; cf. Randall; and Pancaro, "People"), and M. Appold has found the oneness morphology running like a unifying thread throughout the theology of the Fourth Gospel. For Kuhl and Käsemann the Father-Son relationship provides the evangelist with a prototype of the relationship among believers. Beyond this christological origin of the Johannine view of the church, Käsemann argues love characterizes the community and expresses the unity of believers. The unity is itself a heavenly reality realized among humans (*Testament* 69; and Kuhl 198). Le Fort holds much the same view but expresses it differently—the unity of love is the actualization of divine life. Both agree that this unity is an eschatological phenomenon, and Käsemann connects it with the expectation of heavenly perfection that he finds in chapter 17 (Le Fort, 106–13; Käsemann, *Testament* 57–73; cf. F.-M. Braun, "Quatre"). M. Lattke finds a similar reciprocality in the love between the Father and the Son and among believers. Love is then the otherworldly unity of the Father and Son and becomes the commandment of the new community. This love is not a moral or ethical matter; nor is it a mystical relationship. It is, Lattke argues, unity in the word. The Father, Son, and believers are a chain of beings in the unity of the living word (see esp. 132–245).

On the mission of the church in the Fourth Gospel, there is also a great deal of agreement. Kuhl demonstrates the correlation of the sending of three agents—the Son, the Spirit, and the disciples (141–74). J. McPolin sees a fourth, namely the Baptist. Radermakers, Käsemann, and Kuhl all understand the missions of the Son and of the disciples to comprise one total mission, the latter fashioned on the model of the former. The object of the mission, says Kuhl, is the world, even though the distinction between the world and the believers is never compromised (Radermakers; Käsemann, *Testament* 65; Kuhl, 141–74; cf. Baumbach). Le Fort, however, sees another dimension of the mission of the church in John. He contends that in the Johannine view the church has a clearly polemic character. The evangelist designed chapters 10 and 15 to defend the believers from gnostic distortions. The church maintains the purity of the kerygma against the onslaughts of Gnosticism (77–78, 83–88, 90–94, 97–100, 180–81).

There is less agreement regarding the matter of church order. Le Fort finds no references to the order of ministry in John but is confident that it does present Peter as the prototype of ministry. The Fourth Evangelist did not mean thereby to deny the importance of the orders of ministry but only to focus upon the responsibilities of the whole community of the church (81–83, 161–62, 182). Käsemann's findings are far more radical. The evangelist assayed to de-emphasize the role of Peter and his authority. The Johannine church was a pneumatic congregation. Consequently, its leadership was Spirit-led and democratized. This description does not fit the picture we have of the emerging institution of the church in the late first century; therefore, Käsemann concludes, the Johannine community was a conventicle beyond the main stream of the Christian church (*Testament* 27–32, 45–46).

There is little need to issue critical appraisals of much of what we have just surveyed, for it is relatively harmonious. The ecclesial view of the Fourth Gospel is of a community united in love around its christocentric faith and set in opposition to the world beyond, while still feeling some sense of mission to that world. The most remarkable thing about the view of the community is, I think, the manner in which the author links it with the Father-Son relationship and the way in which that linkage gives heavenly status to the community (Kysar, *John* 266, and " 'As You Sent Me' "). Le Fort exaggerates the evidence in his insistence that there is an antignostic polemic in the Johannine view of the church; it is more likely that chapters 10 and 15 reflect the strong sense of the community that stands exposed and endangered by the world around it. As radical as Käsemann's analysis of church order may appear, it seems clear to me that he has mustered persuasive evidence that his view reflects the real intent of the gospel. Whether or not an anti-Petrine polemic was part of the early Johannine church is uncertain. Probably the truth is that there is only a concern to elevate the tradition of the Johannine community and not necessarily denigrate the Petrine tradition.

The Sacraments

One of the points at which there is the most debate and the least agreement among theological critics of John is the matter of the sacraments. To
be sure, the gospel presents us with peculiar problems in this area. We will
try to simplify the range of scholarship on the question of the sacraments
and speak of four major positions: 1) The Fourth Evangelist was indeed a
sacramentalist; 2) this figure was concerned to revise an understanding of
the sacraments held in Johannine community; 3) not the evangelist but
a later redactor is responsible for the sacramental passages in the gospel;
and 4) there is no sacramental teaching in the gospel at all. Our discussion will be concerned with the interpretation of specific passages as well
as some general positions.

Among those who find *a clear, explicit sacramental teaching in the Fourth
Gospel* is M. Rissi, who understands 2:1-11 to be an intentional effort to
evoke eucharistic associations. The wine of the wonder story recalls the
messianic joy and declares the reality of the new covenant ("Hochzeit"
80-81, 91; cf. Feuillet, *Johannine* ch. 1). R. Brown finds the eucharistic
meaning of this passage "incidental" but real. In much the same way,
he thinks there is baptismal meaning in 3:5 but as a secondary or incidental reference, not a primary one (*Commentary–Gospel* 2:109-10, 143).
K. Klos thinks 3:5 is clearly baptismal, for it declares that baptism is the
concrete act by which one gives expression to the faith in Christ required
for rebirth (69-73; cf. Schnackenburg, *Gospel* 1:369-71; Lindars, *Gospel of
John* 152; and Pesch). I. De La Potterie, too has argued that this passage is
the evangelist's statement on baptism. He does a tradition analysis of the
passage and decides that the tradition contained only the word "Spirit"
and the evangelist added "water and" (*hydatos kai*), thus making it speak
of the sacrament of baptism (*Naître*).

The most arguments for sacramental meaning in the gospel center
around 6:1-13 and 6:51c-59. Indeed, we would have to say that a majority
of scholars find eucharistic references here (e.g., Blank, "Brotrede"; Bligh;
Brooks; Feuillet, *Johannine* 118-27; Schlier, "Johannes 6"; Worden; Preiss;
Borgen, *Bread from Heaven* 188-92; Brown, *Commentary–Gospel* 1:287-
91). Among them is G. H. C. MacGregor, who thinks the terminology of
the sacramental ritual resounds throughout chapter 6 ("Eucharist in the
Fourth Gospel" 114-16, and *Gospel* 153-58). Klos is more careful, limit-
ing his claims to verses 51c-59. These passages transfer the christological
and soteriological discussion of verses 48-51b to a eucharistic level. Once
again, Klos finds that the sacramental meaning is a concretization of the
faith (66-69, 73). U. Wilckens argues that verses 51c-59 are an interpretation of the last meal tradition with a strong christological interest. Sound-

ing similar to Klos, Wilckens claims the eucharistic message here is that the sacrament is a concrete execution of remaining in Christ. F. Moloney insists that the eucharistic language of chapter 6 is intended to remind the readers that it is in the sacrament that one encounters the revealer and the revelation, and hence it fits neatly the subject of the previous verses ("John 6"). M.-F. Berrouard is still another who finds the Eucharist spoken of here. He is particularly concerned to explain the use of the word "flesh" (*sarx*) in verses 51 and 53 instead of the traditional eucharistic term "body" (*sōma*). He finds a number of reasons for this change of terminology. For instance, he suggests that the original Aramaic of Jesus' original words might have been rendered into Greek in two different forms (70).

Lindars cautiously argued that 13:1-17 is baptismal. Brown finds secondary baptismal meaning in 19:34—that is, the evangelist intended to communicate another meaning but was aware that his language was suggestive of baptism and affirmed that implication (Lindars, *Gospel of John* 451; Brown, *Commentary–Gospel* 2:566-68).[6]

We find fewer who argue for the theory that the *Fourth Evangelist was attempting to do some kind of revision of current sacramental views*. G. Richter is persuaded that 3:3a and 5 are bits of *Grundschrift* which the Fourth Evangelist incorporated and revised. That conclusion arises from what he regards as the wider context of 3:1-13. The passage reflects more concern with the revision of the Christology implicit in the text than with the baptismal teaching ("Sogenannten Taufetext"). In another connection, we have already mentioned J. D. G. Dunn's proposal that 6:51c-59 is the author's effort to refute a literalistic interpretation of the Eucharist.

R. Bultmann argued that *a redactor and not the evangelist was responsible for the sacramental passages of the Fourth Gospel*. He claims that the words "water and" were added to 3:5 by the redactor to introduce baptism to the gospel. Likewise, the redactor added 19:34b and 6:51b-58 in an effort to include the Eucharist. All this was done by the later "ecclesiastical redactor" in order to make the gospel read like a more "orthodox" statement of the faith (*Theology* 2:58–59, and *Gospel* 138–39, 234–37, 677–79). F.-M. Braun seems to follow the Bultmannian view with regard to 3:5 ("Don"), and G. Bornkamm agrees with Bultmann's assessment of 6:51c-59 ("Vorjohanneische," and "Eucharistische"; Richter, "Formgeschichte"; Lohse; contrast Boren, "Unity"; and Schurman). M.-E. Boismard contends that the original form of 13:1-17 was a simple moral teaching, but that this form dissatisfied some who then added words and phrases to give the passage a baptismal sense as well ("Lavement").

Those who argue *there is no sacramental meaning* in certain passages may find such meaning elsewhere, but are concerned that we not read into the gospel sacramental allusions not intended. For example, Schnackenburg strongly disagrees with the proposal that the wine of the Cana wonder (2:1-11) is eucharistic. The evangelist intended the wine to symbolize wisdom now present in Christ and not the Eucharist (*Gospel* 1:338-39; cf. Lindars, *Gospel of John* 125). D. W. B. Robinson has an elaborate argument against the baptismal reference of 3:5. He contends instead that water symbolizes the rebirth from the old religion and the spirit rebirth into the Christian religion. A number of scholars object to the sacramental reading of 19:34. Klos, who finds sacramental references elsewhere, insists that 19:34 refers solely to the redemptive significance of the death of Jesus (85-93). J. Wilkinson thinks that the meaning of this passage is simply that the body of Christ was a real, human body and that the mention of blood and water is an anti-docetic theme ("Incident"; cf. Venetz). Richter, too, thinks it is an anti-docetic and not a sacramental statement, but believes that it is an insertion into the text by his proposed anti-docetic redactor ("Blut").

Finally, let us mention briefly *some general views of the sacraments in John*. Brown has taken the position that the Fourth Evangelist has a strong commitment to the sacraments, which the later redaction emphasized. For Brown the institution of the Last Supper has been excluded and the eucharistic explicated in 6:51c-59 in order to elevate the sacrament to a theme on the lips of Jesus throughout his ministry (*Commentary–Gospel* 1:cxiii–cxiv; cf. Schlier, "Johannes 6" 123). MacGregor understands that the creator of the gospel was greatly concerned to give the sacraments a spiritual interpretation in order to stress their importance ("Eucharist" 118). Klos contends that this author wanted to stress the sacraments as the believer's concrete expression of faith (97–99). C. L. J. Proudman reasons that person was trying to cut the tie between the sacraments and primitive Christian eschatology, and hence deals with them differently than do the Synoptics or Paul. Lindars likewise thinks that the evangelist's teaching on baptism (especially 3:22) was part of an effort to shift the belief in the eschatological blessings out of the future into the present. The evangelist in no sense wants to belittle the sacraments but to link them with the proclamation of the word ("Word").

It is difficult to decide among the arguments made for each of the positions outlined above. There are those who seem to find sacramental references almost everywhere in the gospel and who are inclined to assign sacramental meaning to any passage which contains a word related to sacramental practice (e.g., the use of "to wash" in 13:1-17). On the other hand, there is a note of dogmatism in the arguments of some who refuse to see sacramental allusions anywhere. The truth doubtless lies somewhere in between. I suggest that at some points a later redactor may have highlighted the sacramental features of the gospel (especially at 3:5 and perhaps 6:51c-59). The evangelist may not have been so antisacramental as asacramental (cf. Kysar, *Fourth Evangelist*, and "Sacraments and Johannine Ambiguity," in the part 4 of this volume). As Brown argues, however, it is possible that the Fourth Evangelist made indirect and secondary allusions to baptism and Eucharist. If this is true, we might conclude that the author of the gospel did not believe the sacraments were important enough to the community to give them a prominent place in this document.

Conclusions

A few observations will have to suffice as a way of concluding the discussion of the framework of Johannine theology. First, as a way of generally characterizing the religious thought of this document, note how the gospel's themes are tightly interwoven with one another, but it is obvious too that the connecting threads are almost exclusively christological ones. The unifying theme of the gospel is surely its consistent christocentricity. Further, the thought of the Fourth Gospel seems to represent a form of early Christianity that was quite distinct and probably independent of other expressions of the young faith. Connected with that observation, we may safely conclude that the peculiar occasion for the writing of the gospel, and more generally the unique history of the community represented there, account for its original brand of Christian thought. The most crucial areas for future theological investigation of the Gospel of John, I believe, are four in number.

First, if the uniqueness of Johannine thought reflects in large part the history of the Johannine community itself, then it is certain that scholars need to do theological analysis of the document hand in hand with a study of the history of the community. "Community theology" is the method demanded by the thought of this gospel, if our investigations are to yield lasting and fruitful results.

Second, this means that the area of the relationship of history and faith is a vital one for all theological criticism of the gospel. Until we understand the hermeneutic employed by the evangelist, until we comprehend how this author viewed the community in relation to the historical tradition stretching back to Jesus of Nazareth, we shall not crack the enigmatic nut of Johannine thought.

Third, Johannine Christology continues to represent an equally significant means of approach. If the gospel is as christocentric as our survey has shown, then it behooves the investigators of the thought of the document to understand first of all the view of Christ expressed there and to make that understanding the cornerstone of their constructions of any aspect of Johannine thought.

Finally, (and to repeat the point) we must pursue adequate categories through which to grasp the thought of the evangelist and the Johannine community. As long as we are trying to make the Fourth Evangelist think in our categories, our theological analyses will be hopelessly doomed to failure. The document itself must yield up to us the modes of thought by which we can best investigate it.

PART III

Literary Criticism

In the second half of the twentieth century, a new emphasis on the literary qualities of the Bible arose. It followed what is called the "new literary criticism" in the broader field of literature and, in biblical studies, was led by scholars who informed themselves of the features of the wider literary movement. Of course, the cross-disciplinary influence was slow in coming into biblical studies and even slower in being widely accepted. Moreover, as usual Johannine studies were among the last to experience the fresh approach. Even though there were some predecessors (cf. the discussion by Olsson in "Literally Problems," ch. 5 of this volume), R. Alan Culpepper holds the distinction of having introduced the literary criticism of John. His 1983 book, *Anatomy of the Fourth Gospel: A Study in Literary Design* initiated what many of us experienced as a revolution in Johannine studies. What Culpepper called "literary design" was the early Johannine equivalent of the emerging "narrative criticism" known in other fields of New Testament studies (Powell).

As more and more scholars adopted some form of this critical method for their work, the nature of the discipline became more complicated and diverse. Narrative, reader-response, structural, rhetorical, as well as other critical methods, which expressed the new literary interest, arose. The whole of the movement known as "poststructuralism" is really a broad label for all interpretative enterprises that deny the theory that meaning is implanted in the text and instead emphasize the role of the reader in the discernment or creation of meaning (Kysar and Webb, *Postmoderns*).

Behind the welcome, however, this new criticism received in Johannine studies was a haunting, if sometimes unspoken, uneasiness with the results of historical criticism in the study of John. To some it seemed that scholars had exhausted the possibilities of historical studies to deal with the enigma of the Fourth Gospel. Some biblical scholars were beginning to feel what Walter Wink had the courage in 1973 to label "the bankruptcy of historical biblical criticism" (1). Certain scholars were uneasy with the historical criticism because it tended more and more to stress the dismantling of biblical texts rather than treating them in their entirety. Others were becoming suspicious of the historical method employed in critical biblical studies. However, the movement toward other critical biblical methods, at first, did not necessarily entail the denunciation of historical studies, and in many cases literary criticism was used hand in hand with the older critical methods (indeed, as is still sometimes the case). It became clear, however, historical criticism now had an equal partner, if not a competitor.

One way to express the difference between historical and literary criticism is to consider "where" or how we find "meaning" from a passage. *Historical studies* take for granted that the author of the passage intended to implant meaning in the passage. Hence, to discover the meaning of a text, one had to go *"behind"* it to expose the author's intention and explore its history—when and why the text was written and how (if at all) that meaning was changed in the transmission of the text through its own history. The text, therefore, functions as a kind of window through which the reader looks to discover the text's origin and its meaning. This view stresses the author's "intention" in writing the passage.

Literary critics, on the other hand, assume that the meaning of a text resides *in the text* as it stands before us and may be discerned without going behind it to investigate its origin. In some cases, literary critics think that the text bears its meaning and that this meaning may be determined in the study of the present text (without recourse to the history behind it). In other cases, literary critics maintain that readers, and not texts, create meaning in the reading process. The emphasis in this case may be on the text's influence on the reader, or it may be entirely the reader's creative act without the influence of the text itself. Some have put the distinction between historical and literary studies in terms of the relationship each has with time. Historical criticism is "diachronic," because it attempts to move through time and back to the origin of the text. Hence, it focuses on changes over the course of time and operates in two times—the present and the past. Literary criticism, on the other hand, works exclusively in the present—one time—and is "synchronic."

A nearly unconscious dissatisfaction with historical studies spurred my own interest in literary studies. Moreover, a number of colleagues in Johannine studies (including Culpepper) motivated my interest. For me the movement away from historical to literary studies was gradual and cautious. It began, I now realize, with the invitation from Fortress Press to write *John's Story of Jesus* (1984), which would join the series of "story of" volumes (including those of Werner H. Kelber, Richard Edwards, and eventually Richard I. Pervo). In effect, Fortress wanted a volume that would be a kind of narrative analysis at a rudimentary level. Notwithstanding the quality of that publication (which went out of print only in 2001), it ignited a new interest in me which gradually became a full blaze.

Beyond that book, my entry into literary criticism came by way of my fascination with metaphor. For some years, I had been interested in the use of metaphor in religious language, and it finally dawned on me that the fourth evangelist was a master of metaphor. The second, and third articles reprinted in this section concentrate on metaphors in specific passages from John: "The Meaning and Function of Johannine Metaphor (John 10:1-18)" (1991) and "The Making of Metaphor (John 3:1-15)" (1996). In both of these, I experiment with my own versions of reader response criticism, which intentionally tried to avoid some of the new jargon in the field (e.g., implied author, implied reader). What interested me then and now is the reader's experience of the text. What does the text do to the careful reader? This interest was further expressed in "The Dismantling of Decisional Faith (John 6:25-71)" (1997) and in a paper written for a subgroup on biblical interpretation for preaching of the Academy of Homiletics entitled "Matthew 20:1-16: A Narrative Reading" (1997). A comparison of the article on John 6 in this section with chaper 4 provides an interesting and sharp contrast. The earlier one ("Pursuing the Paradoxes of Johannine Thought") was a conscious use of redaction criticism based on historical reconstructions of both the gospel itself and the Johannine community which was responsible for it. The article included in this section begs all the historical questions to concentrate on the way one reader experiences the text. The difference between these two mirrors the drastic change taking place in biblical studies at that time.

By the mid-1990s my own personal commitments had moved to literary criticism, so that when I wrote on John for the collection *Anti-Semitism and Early Christianity* (Evans and Hagner, eds.) in 1993, I felt compelled to begin the article by trying to analyze how the "Jews" are presented on the *surface of the text*. Only after having done so do I turn to theories of the historical situation out of which the gospel may have come and for whom it was written. Thus, in this article, I made a conscious effort to use both forms of criticisms in tandem, and it represents a sort of transition from one to the other. I might say the same about the revised edition of my book *John, the Maverick Gospel*. When I wrote the book (1976), I was thoroughly immersed in historical-critical studies. By the time I chose to revise it (1993), however, my interest in literary studies required that I add sections that view the gospel from a strictly literary perspective.

As I gradually became more and more disillusioned with historical studies (see the introduction to part 4: "Postmodern Criticism"), my commitments to literary and other more contemporary forms of interpretation sprouted into full-grown devotion. When I moved into literary studies, I did not feel as dissatisfied with historical studies as I came to later on. Still, it was clear to me that our historical investigations were becoming more speculative and (even worse) were taking our attention off the text as it stands before us. I now believe that literary studies are the wave of the future and that historical-critical studies will become fewer and fewer in this new century. (Later I will try to explain how I combined my use of literary techniques with postmodern views.)

Chapter Nine

Anti-Semitism and the Gospel of John

Over twelve years ago Samuel Sandmel correctly observed, "John is widely regarded as either the most anti-Semitic or at least the most overtly anti-Semitic of the gospels."[1] Little has been done to ameliorate that harsh judgment since it was first written.[2] While efforts have been made to soften the impact of the tone of John when it comes to Jews and Judaism, the fact remains that a reading of the gospel tends to confirm Sandmel's judgment. Still, recent theories for understanding the historical setting of the writing of the Fourth Gospel do offer some ways of interpreting the harshness with which the gospel treats Jews and Judaism. Such theories do not change the tone of the gospel but offer a way of explaining that tone. Whether explaining the tone of a literary piece in fact alters the effects of the writing itself is a fundamental question that we must confront.[3]

The task of examining John in relationship to anti-Semitism requires several projects.[4] The first is to investigate the surface of the text and its implications for the question before us. The second is to explore the relevance of a theory for the historical origin of the gospel that affects our consideration. The final, and most difficult, endeavor is then to ask in conclusion if historical theories have any significance for assessing the relationship between this product of early Christianity and anti-Semitism then and now. My major thesis is that the text of the gospel itself nurtures an anti-Semitism that is properly understood (but not necessarily endorsed) only in the light of the historical origin of the document.

The Surface of the Text of the Fourth Gospel

When we raise the question of how the implied author[5] of John treats Jews and Judaism, a clear impression is possible, although one with some ambiguity. The effort here will be to observe the ways in which anti-Semitism surfaces in a reading of the text and how it is cast into shades of ambiguity by the strategies of the narrative. In this context, however, we can do no more than undertake a summary of the experience of the reader in following the text of the gospel as it stands before us without recourse to the history behind the text. This chapter will only isolate and articulate a series of impressions one gains from the reading of the text. I believe that this sort of analysis of the text of the gospel is especially important for the issue under consideration, since it affords a way of understanding how the Johannine story of Jesus is received by careful readers (and hearers). Thus, it is a way of comprehending how it is that the lay reader, untrained in biblical criticism or perhaps unsophisticated in theology, will respond to the story. Such a reader-response criticism is an avenue, I suggest, into a more popular and natural understanding of the gospel story.

The first impression the reader gains is the way in which the narrator is detached from and consequently distances the implied reader from Judaism.[6] This is accomplished through such expressions as "the Passover of the Jews" (2:13; 11:55) and "a [the] festival of the Jews" (5:1; 6:4; 7:2). We find other examples of this detachment in 2:6 and 3:25. The effect is to align the reader with the perspective of the narrator, who is separated from Judaism. Those who "own" the festivals are "Jews," and the narrator is neither a Jew nor leads the reader to Jewishness.[7]

Readers gain a second and more complex impression by the portrayal of the "Jews" (*Ioudaioi*) as characters in the narrative. The clearest impression is that these characters are antagonists of the hero of the story. The Jews consistently fail to understand Jesus (e.g., 3:1-4; 6:52; 7:35: 8:57). Such misunderstanding is not unusual in this gospel, but most often the Jews are cast in the role of Jesus' overt opponents (e.g., 2:18, 20; 6:41; 8:48). Very early in the narrative they are described as those who persecute and seek to kill Jesus (5:16-18; 7:1), and such motives continue to be attributed to them as the narrative proceeds (10:31; 11:8). Their hostility results in fear of the Jews among those who are interested in Jesus or believe in him (7:13; 9:22; 19:38; 20:19).

Furthermore, the gospel presents the Jews as untrue to their own faith and tradition. They do not keep the Torah (7:19) and are not truly children of Abraham but of the devil (8:39-44). They do not understand their own Scriptures (5:39-40; 10:31-39), and their leaders abrogate their loyalty to their God for fidelity to Caesar (19:15).

The impression the reader gains of the Jews, however, is blurred with ambiguity by several other features of their portrayal. They are sometimes present in the narrative as neutral inquirers or even admirers of Jesus (7:15; 10:24; 11:36; 12:9). One of their leaders, Nicodemus, seeks Jesus out but cannot understand him (3:1-15), defends Jesus against the Pharisees (7:50-52), and eventually assists in the burial of Jesus' body (19:39). The narrative sometimes represents the Jews as believing in Jesus (8:31; 11:45; 12:11). In the first case (8:31), however, they eventually become Jesus' opponents, and in the second case (11:45), while some believe, others take action that begins the death plot against Jesus. Most confusing to the reader is the fact that at one point in the narrative Jesus identifies himself as a Jew (4:9; see also 4:22).

The reader is further kept off balance by the manner in which these characters labeled Jews are distinguished from other groups in the narratives. The narrator leads the reader to think that the Jews are not to be identified with people of Jerusalem (7:25), the crowds (7:13; 12:17), the Pharisees (7:32-35; 9:13, 18), Ephraimites (11:54), Galileans (4:43-45), or other individual characters in the narrative such as the parents of the blind man (9:18), Martha (11:19, 31), Caiaphas (18:14), and Joseph of Arimathea (19:38). Readers discover no clue which might lead them to recognize these groups or individuals as Jews.

Out of this ambiguity, the story leads readers to conceive of Jews as those persons in the narrative who are most often predisposed to unbelief, rejection, and even hostility toward Jesus. The vague name "the Jews" becomes in the reader's mind representative of opposition to Jesus and his mission.[8]

Another of the reader's impressions is that the leaders of Judaism are also, in general, opponents of the Christ figure. The Pharisees are blind (9:40-41) and false leaders who guide the people away from the truth, even as do the Jews (9:40; and the discourse in 10:1-18). The Pharisees along with the council and the chief priests plot the death of Jesus (11:46-53) and seek to have him arrested (11:57), eventually succeeding in doing so (18:3). While not unified in their response to Jesus (9:13-16), the Pharisees are most often presented as opponents of the Christ figure (4:1; 7:32; 8:13; 12:42). Strangely, however, the reader is told not to confuse the Pharisees with the "authorities" (*archontōs*), many of whom believe in Jesus (12:42).[9]

The chief priests fare no better in the narrative. As with the Pharisees, the narrator leads the reader to believe they are opponents of Jesus. The chief priests are depicted as plotting to have Lazarus killed as a way of diminishing the movement toward Jesus (12:10), cry out for Jesus to be crucified (19:6), and declare that Jesus is not their king (19:15) and that they do not want him labeled as such (19:21). Consequently, the reader is left with the impression that these characters are hostile adversaries of Jesus.

One cannot read the passion story of the Fourth Gospel and escape the impression that the Jewish leaders alone are responsible for the arrest, conviction, and death of Jesus (18:3, 12, 19ff.; cf. Granskou, "Anti-Judaism and the Passion Accounts" 1:201–16). In his deliberations Pilate is shown caving in to the desires of the Jewish leaders (18:31, 38-40; 19:45, 12-16), even though he declares no less than four times his own judgment that Jesus is innocent (18:38; 19:4, 6, 12). Even the execution itself seems to be carried out by Jewish leaders and/or their representatives (see 19:16, where the antecedent for "they" appears to be found in the chief priests of 19:15)—an incredible implication.

Finally, the impression gained by the reader is that Judaism in general is degenerate and untrue. A number of the features of the narrative contribute either explicitly or implicitly to this impression. Those who believe in Jesus will be put out of the synagogue (9:22; 12:42; 16:2). While the Jews and leaders of Judaism are most often opponents to Jesus, the Samaritans readily receive and confess him (4:39-42).

In contrast to the falsity of Judaism, the gospel everywhere presents the message of Jesus as superior to the religion of the Jews (2:1-10; 4:21; 5:39, 45; 6:58; 8:31, 58). Jesus' relation with the temple suggests the superiority of his message (2:19-22; 7:14ff., 28). The preface to John's story of Jesus functions to give the reader those essential insights that will lead her or him properly to understand the entire story (Culpepper, *Anatomy* 168). The importance of 1:17, therefore, cannot be overemphasized. The "grace and truth" revealed in Christ is superior to the Law of Moses. Consequently, the use of the words "true" and "truth" throughout the narrative (e.g., 1:9; 6:32; 14:6; 18:37) may lead readers to infer that Judaism is "untrue," i.e., false. While Jesus stresses the continuity between himself and his message and Hebrew Scriptures (5:39; 6:45; 8:56; 10:34), Judaism is depicted as a faulty understanding of those Scriptures. The true "Israelite in whom there is no deceit" is one who goes on to become Jesus' disciple (1:47).

This summary of impressions drawn from a reading of John is not without shades of ambiguity. Overall, however, the conclusion is inescapable that the surface of the text (the narrative of the gospel taken by itself) persuades a reader to cast Jews and Judaism in an unfavorable light.

- The reader is encouraged to stand detached from Judaism;
- to take the terms "Jews," "Pharisees," and "chief priests" to refer to Jesus' opponents;

- to infer that the leaders of Judaism (and perhaps even the Jewish people themselves) alone were responsible for the execution of Jesus;
- and to believe that Judaism is untrue and that Christ is superior in every way to that religion.

The conclusion is inescapable that the text of the narrative nurtures a negative mentality toward Jews and Judaism.

The Historical Origin of the Fourth Gospel

To this point, we have focused exclusively on what appears on the surface of the text of John. Now it is necessary to try to move "behind" the text to examine two related questions. The first is the historical identity of the expression "the Jews" in the Gospel of John, and the second is the historical occasion for the production of the document.

The Identity of the "Jews"

Efforts to identify the historical referent for the term *the Jews* as used in the Fourth Gospel have occupied a good deal of Johannine scholarship. *Ioudaioi* ("Jews") occurs some seventy-one times in the gospel, as compared with only sixteen occurrences in all the Synoptic Gospels but more than eighty in the Acts of the Apostles. The synoptic occurrences of the expression appear most often on the lips of Gentile characters, as opposed to John where it is most frequently in the comments of the narrator. In the contemporary reading of John, the expression is naturally taken as a reference to the religious-ethnic group we know as modern Jews. But to whom was the evangelist referring when speaking of "the Jews"?[10]

In the framework of the evangelist's dualism, it is clear that the Jews belong most often (but not with absolute consistency) to the "world" (*kosmos*). That means that "the Jews" are part of the realm of unbelief, the reality that opposes Jesus and the revelation of God. They are the main constituent of the negative pole of the dualistic scheme of the gospel, the opposite of which is the Christian believer. As D. M. Smith has observed, Johannine dualism and the theological use of the expression *the Jews* "mythologizes the distinction between two modes of existence, the believing and authentic over against unbelieving and unauthentic, by identifying them with two historically and empirically distinct communities, the Christian and the Jewish" ("Judaism" 77).

Yet when we ask to what existent, historical group the expression refers, the answer is less clear. Few, if any, responsible scholars today would argue that the reference is to the entire Jewish people, for such a view would make no sense given the fact that nearly all of the characters—certainly

Jesus and the other main characters—of the gospel are themselves Jews. In 9:22, for instance, surely the parents of the blind man are themselves Jews. Moreover, 20:19 leads us to assume unquestionably that the disciples are also Jews. Judaeans, as opposed to Galilean Jews and the religious leaders of the Judaism contemporaneous to the Fourth Evangelist are the most frequent nominees for the position as referent of the expression (Fortna, *Fourth Gospel*, and "Theological Use" 58–95). The argument that the term refers to Judaeans alone does not prove persuasive, as von Wahlde has shown (cf. "Johannine 'Jews'" 33–60, and *Earliest Version* 31–36). His own argument is the more convincing. It is likely that "the Jews" in the Fourth Gospel refers to those leaders who hold some influence over their Jewish constituency in the region known to the author. To summarize again in the words of D. M. Smith: "'The Jews' is, then, a term used of a group of Jewish leaders who exercise great authority among their compatriots and are especially hostile to Jesus and his disciples. . . . It refers to certain authorities rather than to the people as a whole" ("Judaism" 82; cf. Granskou, 202–9).

The Historical Setting for the Composition of the Fourth Gospel

Our conclusions regarding the use of the expression "the Jews" lead only to a second question: what situation would result in such a slanderous and stereotypical reference to Jewish leaders—equating them with the force of evil? In what occasion would Jewish leaders have evoked such an attitude as that of the Fourth Evangelist's? In other words, what was the historical situation in which the evangelist wrote?

Unfortunately, the endeavor to identify that situation is fraught with numerous problems. The most important of these is the obvious fact that we must deal with imaginative historical reconstructions armed only with the explicit text, its implications, and our relatively scant knowledge of the history of the period. Hence, it is with *theory* that we must now deal—theory that may commend itself at best with some degree of probability but never with absolute conclusiveness. Nonetheless, a theory of the historical origin of the gospel seems essential to an effort to assess the relationship between the Fourth Gospel and anti-Semitism. I shall summarize a theory for the historical setting of the writing of John that holds persuasive credibility for many Johannine scholars today[11] and then attempt to view the anti-Semitic quality of the text in the light of that theory.

Over two decades ago J. L. Martyn and R. E. Brown each proposed that the occasion for the writing of the Fourth Gospel was an experience of expulsion of a Christian community from their synagogue home.[12] While they differed in the details of their proposals, each took the references in the gospel to expulsion from the synagogue (*aposynagōgos*, 9:22;

12:42; 16:2) as indications that the Christian community of which the author was a part and for which the gospel was written had been part of a Jewish synagogue but was then expelled from its religious community there. The precise reasons for the expulsion are speculative, and Brown and Martyn offered differing theories.[13] Yet both understood John (in at least one of its editions) as a response to the experience of the expulsion.

Both Brown and Martyn, however, further understood that the present gospel reflects the ongoing dialogue between Jews and Christians after their separation. Martyn, for instance, asserts that the gospel "seems to reflect experiences in the dramatic interaction between the synagogue and the Johannine church" (*History and Theology* 37). The central focus of that interaction appears to have been the identity of Jesus and in particular the high christological claims made by the Johannine Christians.[14]

In the years since Brown and Martyn offered their proposal, there have been numerous studies that embraced and attempted further to confirm and expand the theory. These have come from disparate types of works on various Johannine themes.[15] Their effect has been to offer impressive demonstration of the plausibility of what Brown and Martyn had hypothesized.

An increasingly clear picture emerges from all these studies grounded in the hypothesis that the gospel was written in response to the exclusion of the Johannine church from the synagogue and the subsequent dialogue between these two religious parties. The subject of the picture is a defensive and threatened Christian community, attempting to reshape its identity isolated from the synagogue and its Jewish roots. The picture is trimmed in vigorous debate over issues central to both Jews and Christians. It is shaded with hostility toward the Jewish parents of this Christian offspring, hostility highlighted with sometimes violent language.[16] The center of the picture, however, seems to be the subject of Christian identity. Who are the Johannine Christians now that they can no longer claim the synagogue as their home? In the background of the picture, I propose, we may dimly perceive a synagogue in which there is a similar identity crisis. It may be that the Jewish brothers and sisters who found it necessary to separate themselves from the Christians in their midst were struggling to understand themselves amid the trauma of the destruction of their Jerusalem temple (ca. 70 C.E.) and what that might mean for the future nature of their faith. In other words, the expulsion of the Christians from the synagogue may have been an effort to declare what Judaism was when stripped of its cultic center. The picture, then, is of two sibling religious communities, each with its own identity issues.

Armed with this imaginative reconstruction of the setting for the writing of the gospel, one returns to the text enabled to see many of its features in a new light. Foremost it is the polemical tone of the gospel that is suddenly made understandable, and to which we shall return for discussion that is more extensive. (Cf. the essay, "The 'Other' in Johannine Literature" in part 4 of this volume.) The light of the proposed setting for the document also illumines the gospel's concentration on the identity of Christ. Presumably that was the primary issue under consideration in the dialogue with the synagogue, and it is clear why the document would seek to clarify and stubbornly insist on its community's affirmations concerning Christ. The theory also illumines the danger-fraught dualistic thought of John. If basic Christian identity is at stake in order to clarify that identity, the evangelist resorts to a drastic either/or schema to define the distinction between the Christian and the Jew.

Most important for our purposes is how this hypothesis for the historical origin of the gospel informs the anti-Jewish tone of the text. First, it makes clear that the language regarding Jews and Judaism is polemical in nature and typical of classical polemic. If its expulsion from the synagogue threatens the very existence of the Christian community, it is natural that the stance toward Judaism be polemical. Some have proposed that the gospel also implies the existence of "crypto-Christians" who had renounced their Christian allegiance and remained in the synagogue. Apostasy may also have threatened the Johannine church. Consequently, the tone of the writing is hostile and argumentative.

The Jewish-Christian relationship standing within the shadows of history behind the Fourth Gospel was perhaps as much a social phenomenon as a religious one.[17] The issue at stake was the social repositioning of the Christian community. By being expelled from the synagogue, they had experienced the trauma of social dislocation. Their task was now to make a new place for themselves in a society that appeared to them to be hostile and unaccommodating of their views. The tendency was to conceive of themselves as the in-group, defending itself against the out-group (in effect, the rest of their society). Hence, so much of the tone and language of the gospel suggest this insider-versus-outsider perspective (e.g., the negative use of the word "world" [*kosmos*] at such places as chapter 17).

In summary, the posture of the church was that of defensiveness amid the self-doubt of uncertain identity. The polemical quality of John tells the interpreter more about the evangelist and the Johannine community than it witnesses to the ontological status of the Jews or Judaism. The gospel's view as the result of Jewish-Christian dialogue following the expulsion of the Christians from the synagogue explains why Judaism is painted in such unfortunate colors and why Christian faith is presented as superior to Judaism. If this hypothesis for the origin of the gospel is sound, the Johannine Christians occupied a precarious position. They had been Christian Jews who understood themselves as part of the ancient people of God. Their messianic affirmations concerning Jesus of Nazareth were made in the context of the faith of Israel. Now, however, with their expulsion from the synagogue, they were trying to affirm and express that they did not need Judaism. Their Christian faith could stand on its own without the support of Judaism, even while it appealed to the Jewish Scriptures as evidence of its truthfulness. It was a formidable (and perhaps impossible) task.[18] The approach taken to the task was to argue that Judaism was in error, degenerate, and unfaithful to its God. Christ offered the true revelation of that God, and hence Christianity apart from Judaism was the truth. The leaders of Judaism had beguiled the people into falsehood; they were the "hirelings" and "robbers" of the sheepfold (10:1-15). When confronted with the true revelation of their God—a revelation anticipated in their own Scriptures—they executed the revealer. The vitriolic attack on Judaism is nothing more or less than the desperate attempt of the Johannine Christians to find a rationale for their existence in isolation from Judaism.

The proposal for the historical origin of the Fourth Gospel advocated here makes at least two additional facts somewhat more comprehensible. These two each have to do with the fact that those characteristics usually associated with Judaism before the advent of Christianity are notably absent from or diminished in importance in the form of Christian thought advocated by the Fourth Evangelist. First among these is the absence of any central role assigned to Torah. While Torah is invoked in the argument that Jesus' message is truth and he himself is the Son of God (e.g., 5:39), the authority of Torah plays no role in the life of the believer.[19] Its moral teachings are in no way employed as a basis for the believer's behavior. The absence of a covenantal theology is another feature of Johannine thought that might be considered "un-Jewish." The word "covenant" (*diathēkē*) is entirely absent from the gospel.[20]

In spite of the best efforts of the evangelist, the basic Jewishness of the perspective of the Johannine community is visible between and behind the lines of the text (Kysar, *Fourth Evangelist* 144-46). Hence, an older tradition in which Jesus clearly identifies himself as a Jew and affirms Judaism as the source of salvation (4:22) slips past the watchful eye of the evangelist-redactor to confuse the reader.[21] Hence, the fundamental christological statement of the gospel (1:1-18) is modeled on the Jewish understanding of wisdom (Brown, *Commentary–Gospel* 1:25–36). Even in their desperate need to understand themselves over against Judaism, the Johannine Christians were not able to speak of their faith without recourse to its Jewish roots.

Finally, this hypothesis for John's origin helps us understand the role it assigns to the Jews and the leaders of Judaism. In the midst of this discussion of the historical origin of the gospel, we need a literary observation. An effective narrative needs an antagonist as much as it needs a hero figure. The author could tell the story of Jesus most powerfully only with a negative figure set over against the Christ figure in the dynamics of the narrative. The situation of the Johannine community provided such an antagonist ready at hand in the figure of the Jews. Since the opponents of the evangelist's own community were members of the synagogue, it was easy to make Jews, and in particular the leaders of the synagogue, the opponents of Jesus in the narrative.[22] Martyn's insight that John presents a two-level drama is helpful at this point. He contends that, while the evangelist told the story of Jesus, the opponents of Jesus in the narrative were only thinly disguised opponents of the writer's own contemporary Christian community. Hence, the character of the Pharisees in 9:13-17 could so easily become the Jews in 9:18 (*History and Theology* 24–36). The first readers of the gospel were thereby able to identify their own struggles with the struggles of their Master. The gospel supplied them sanction to understand their own conflict with members of the synagogue as conflict with the forces that had been responsible for the death of their Lord. It was a powerful literary tool in that historical setting, however unfortunate the consequences have become for succeeding generations of Christians and Jews.

The puzzling and perplexing portrayal of the Jews as the opponents of Jesus in the Fourth Gospel, therefore, owes its existence to a literary necessity and a historical accident. The evangelist, I suggest, did not intend to issue a universal indictment against Jews and Judaism. (Note the use of the words *Israel* and *Israelite*, e.g., in 1:31, 49; and 12:13.) The author was attempting to be as effective as possible in aiding the community for which the writing was intended. To ensure the continued existence of the Johannine church there may have seemed no alternative to indicting the Jews. To give expression to the loss and hurt of the Christian community, there may have seemed no alternative than to strike out at their former religious brothers and sisters of the synagogue. Oddly enough, the community that was founded on the sacrifice of an innocent person for their salvation now sacrificed their former Jewish brothers and sisters for the sake of their self-identity.

Conclusions

The persuasiveness of the argument that the Fourth Gospel was written in the wake of the expulsion from the synagogue and in the backwash of a lively dialogue between the Christian and Jewish communities is impressive. Yet it remains a theory—at best a hypothesis that commends itself to us in a number of ways. Weighed against the evidence of the experience of reading the text itself, however, the theory of the historical origin of that text seems weak. The evidence we have are the facts of the text, on the one hand, and the plausibility of a historical theory, on the other. The latter looks rather puny when compared with the former. Furthermore, a fundamental question lurks in the background.

Does historical contingency count for anything when dealing with the issue of the posture of a Christian document in relationship to Judaism? The answer must surely be yes in one sense but no in another. The historical origin of John makes its anti-Semitic tone understandable—and some would even say excusable. However, as one reads and hears the gospel read, the historical origin of the document does not alter its basic tone. In other words, contingency may count for something in the classroom but for little in the place of worship and even less in the privacy of the individual layperson's reading of the gospel.[23]

The reality is that an occasional writing has become canonical literature. The document we know as the Gospel of John was written within, out of, and for a very concrete and specific situation involving a particular Christian community in a given time and place. It may have served an admirable purpose in its origin. We might even conclude that this document made possible the continued existence of Christianity in a certain locale. Out of that community have come invaluable resources, woven together with others to produce the rich tapestry we know today as the Christian church and its faith. Without the preservation of the Johannine community and without its heritage to later generations of Christians, there is little doubt that the church today and, perhaps even the world, would be the lesser. We can, therefore, be grateful to that individual (or group) who produced the gospel.

Still, an occasional piece designed for a particular situation and to meet certain needs has become part of the canon of the Christian church. That means that it is read and interpreted outside of its original situation and beyond its original purpose. With the passing of centuries, the historical origin becomes more and more remote, less and less known and knowable. The result is that John stands on its own in isolation from the situation that occasioned its writing. Its canonization as Holy scripture means that the divine truth speaks through its words regardless of the historical setting or time in which it is read. However valuable it may be as a vehicle of divine truth, canonization means that the shortsightedness as well as the insight of its author and its message may now be taken as divinely sanctioned. It is now most often read and understood without reference to its first purpose. With those results comes a dreadful danger!

That danger is inherent in the risk of the canonization of historically contingent literature. It is a danger that is not exclusive to John but endemic to the principle of canon. Much of what we have said about this gospel might be said of certain other documents of the Christian canon, say the "tables of household duties" found in Colossians 3:18–4:1, Ephesians 5:21–6:9, and 1 Peter 2:13–3:7. Those passages written within one cultural setting were perhaps helpful and even liberating for their first readers but now are an embarrassment and oppressive in a culture that tries to correct the sins of a tradition of slavery and subjugation of women.

In its canonical status the Fourth Gospel has nurtured (or even conceived) repugnant attitudes and evoked abhorrent actions on the part of Christians toward their Jewish colleagues. Shall we blame those readers who used the document to sanction their own prejudices and ignorant hatreds? Shall we blame the interpreters who know better but still allow the gospel to speak its devilish words to others who are willing to hear them as truth? Shall we blame the principle of canon that may expect more and attribute more authority to individual pieces than is reasonable or possible? Or, shall we blame the document itself and its producers for having been so parochial in their views as not to have imagined the use to which their work might be put?

Fortunately, ours is not the awesome task of placing blame. It cannot go unstated, however, that the Christian church and Western culture have been amiss in not understanding the dangers inherent in the process of positing universal authority in documents that were never intended to carry such weighty importance. Responsibility for a misunderstanding of the nature of canon must rest at the doorstep of those in the past and the present commissioned with the duty to nurture a proper sense of canon and the interpretation of Scripture. Rather than placing blame, perhaps, the task is to issue a challenge to those of us who would read, interpret, and place authority in the Gospel of John. That challenge is simply that we question the gospel's authority in certain areas. The task is to define carefully and control meticulously its authoritative value. The commission is to conceive and foster a new and more precise understanding of canonical authority. Yet it is also to advocate that canonical authority resides only within an interpretive context.[24]

J. Christiaan Beker has stated the issue and the challenge with precision. He argues that we must formulate what constitutes the "coherence" of the New Testament and confess *that—and that alone—*to be the normative content of its message. Likewise, we must clearly and explicitly distinguish the "contingent situational factors" interwoven with that normative message so that we are able to differentiate between the normative and the situational.

> For Christians today, the crucial question is whether, in their present theological reflections on Judaism, they shall accord normative canonical status to those contingent factors . . . thus elevating [them] to a normative canonical status. . . . In other words, a sensible Jewish-Christian dialogue depends on a crucial theological decision: Where do we locate the authority of scripture? . . . thus the task of the Christian theologian with respect to "the Jewish question" is a foundational task. ("View of Judaism" 63–64).

Beker's challenge is, to be sure, fraught with risks and difficulties. Not least among those risks is the delicate question of distinguishing between the normative and the contingent. It also risks all that is involved in the classical issue of "a canon within the canon."[25] Most certainly too the challenge can be addressed not alone in the rarefied atmosphere of scholarly discussion. It must reach the congregations and the classrooms where the Fourth Gospel is read and valued. Still, the risks and the difficulties are worthwhile. In precisely the program that Beker proffers we can find our way to a new understanding of the issue of anti-Semitism in the Fourth Gospel and in the New Testament as a whole, while in the process bringing new clarity to the ever-troublesome question of the authority of Scripture for Christianity. In other words, it is in addressing the issue of anti-Semitism in the New Testament that we are forced to deal with a question on which Christian self-identity hinges. Ironically, but appropriately, wrestling with the Johannine effort to define Christian identity compels us to address the issue most fundamental to our own Christian identity.[26]

Only in a creative and diligent response to this challenge to define more sharply and interpret more effectively the doctrine of Christian canon is there the possibility of overcoming the tragic burden of the anti-Semitic tone experienced in the reading of the Gospel of John.

Chapter Ten

The Meaning and Function of Johannine Metaphor (John 10:1-18)

Introduction

In the past several decades, a great deal has been written on the nature and function of the parables of Jesus in the Synoptic Gospels.[1] Thanks to the abundant attention they have received, we have gained a new appreciation for their literary character. It is curious that the literary qualities of the Johannine metaphors on the lips of Jesus have received far less attention. One might speculate as to the reasons for this apparent lack of interest in figurative speech in John. Perhaps it is rooted in the now dated presupposition that this gospel affords no avenue to the historical Jesus, while the synoptic parables are often claimed to represent his original genius.[2] Or, maybe it arises from the presupposition that John's symbolism is purely and simply a theological vehicle, contrived for that purpose alone.[3] Possibly, too, it is merely the case that John is seldom the beneficiary of the newer scholarly interests until those fresh methodologies have been tested on the synoptic proving grounds.[4] Whatever the reason for this neglect, it is time to open a long overdue discussion of the literary qualities of the Johannine metaphors.

This article purports to do little more than initiate a discussion and arouse a new interest in the literary character of the Johannine metaphors. My thesis is that from the perspective of the reader the Johannine metaphors function in a manner not dissimilar to those functions assigned to the parables of Jesus in the Synoptic Gospels except that they are marked with peculiar Johannine characteristics and purpose. It is not the intent of this paper to make any claims regarding the authentic voice of Jesus in the Johannine metaphors. Such a question is far too complex and distinct from the literary analysis I have in mind.[5] I do, however, purport to make a case for the originality of the metaphors (whatever their origin), their character as poetic symbols, and their use in the implied author's literary scheme.

To make this preliminary probe it is necessary to select a sample case of metaphor in the Fourth Gospel. John 10:1-18 comes to mind for several reasons. The first is that it is a passage in which some clear parabolic features are present, e.g., the use of vehicles from daily life to illuminate a significant reality for Christian belief. Another reason for choosing this passage is, of course, its problematic features. Some discussion of those features will follow, but suffice it for now to say simply that it appears to be an instance in which metaphors are mixed in a confusing way.

Specifically, the objective of this paper is to investigate the interrelated concerns of the structure, integrity, and genre of the images found in John 10:1-8. My methodology is admittedly elementary and eclectic. I would like to bring little more than the tools of observation and query to this sampling of Johannine metaphor. I want to ask what happens to one as she or he reads this passage with care and sensitivity. My effort is, then, an attempt to inquire after the response of the reader to the passage as it stands without recourse to the classical critical questions that have informed its interpretation in the past. This investigation, therefore, is conceived as an elemental form of reader-response criticism. It is synchronic (i.e., in "one time") in that it brackets the historical questions of setting, sources, redaction, and the intent of the "real author." It is intratextual in its initial interests at least and concerned primarily with the strategies and the rhetoric of the text. There is also implicit attention to the temporal quality of the text as the implied reader experiences it.[6] I will attempt to produce a reading of the passage that might arise from an intimate participation in the text in which the reader allows him or herself to become vulnerable to its influence. In such an enterprise, the text is experienced more as an event than as an object (Moore, *Literary Criticism* 20). This, it seems to me, might be the place to start a new conversation regarding Johannine metaphors.

Two additional methodological observations are appropriate. The first is to venture into the foggy terrain of the locus of meaning. Without any attempt to peer through that fog, I am still committed to a modified essentialistic or realistic appraisal of the role of the text. The text is not entirely a creation of the reader but has an integrity of its own—a givenness. Readers, however, do not mine meaning out of the text, as one would dig for worms on a damp summer morning, as much as it is constructed through imaginative intercourse with the text. Meaning is the result of reading, but that reading is in response to the demands of the text. I assume the text occasions a unique experience for the reader. A concern for how the text does what it does is the professed method with which I begin. This does not necessitate believing that meaning is set in the objectivity of the text but only that it is the consequence of an engagement with the text. We transcend the subject-object dichotomy between reader and text insofar as meaning is possible only as the text and the reader become one reality. The reader enters the world of the text to become one with it, bringing his or her own subjectivity into it, or pulling the text out of its objectivity into the reader's own consciousness. Still, the text is more than the creation of the reader's imagination. In the momentary union of subject and object, the text is enabled to do its work within the world of the reader's subjectivity. Mine is a modified essentialist position—modified by the absolute dependence on the reader for meaning.[7]

The second methodological observation is to alert the reader to shifts in the methods among the constituent parts of this essay. After a brief summary of the historical-critical views of the passage, there follows an analysis of the surface structure of the verses. Methodologically the second of these sections attempts to summarize what the reader experiences in terms of the way the passage flows but also to epitomize what it evokes from the vulnerable reader in the course of participating in this structure. The third part of the paper discusses the reader's encounter with the passage and how the text evokes a sense of unity in the reader's mind. The fourth section deals with how the reader experiences the images of the passage and what that means for the genre of those images. Here it is necessary momentarily to abandon a purely intrinsic, intratextual approach when we ask how the genre of the images compares with those encountered in the parables of Jesus found in the Synoptic Gospels. Still, even here I have attempted to keep a reader focus in the discussion.

The Structure, Integrity, and Genre of John 10:1-18 in Contemporary Johannine Scholarship

The formal structure of John 10:1-18 gives us clues to the way in which the images of the passage are used and their meaning.[8] However, the precise understanding of the structure varies considerably among contemporary commentators. Most common is the assumption that there are two main parts, verses 1-5 and 7b-18 with verses 6-7a serving as a transition between the two. The relationship between these two parts is conceived in a number of different ways. Most commentators, however, see the latter part as some sort of exposition of the former. Raymond E. Brown's analysis suffices as an example of such a view. According to Brown, verses 1-5 contain first the parable of the gate (vs. 1-3a) and then the parable of the shepherd (vs. 3b-5), the two comprising what he calls "twin parables." Verses 7-18 are "allegorical explanations" of those two parables. Verses 7-10 explain the parable of the gate and verses 11-16 the parable of the shepherd.[9]

The tendency, then, is to see a shift in the nature of the language between these two halves, with only the first having the character of parable in any proper sense of the word. Whatever the character of the metaphorical language of the second half of the passage, it is implicitly demeaned by speaking of it as allegory, interpretation, expansion, or some such term.[10] Commentators generally tend to see the passage in two major halves, each employing a different genre, the second of which departs significantly from the first.[11]

Not surprisingly, then, the integrity of the passage is often questioned in contemporary research. Bultmann understood the passage as a composite of at least four independent units (*Gospel* 363–75). Brown contends that "a simple parabolic expression has been applied by the evangelist to a later church situation" (*Commentary–Gospel* 1:396).[12] Lindars agrees with the analysis of J. A. T. Robinson that in verses 1-5 two originally distinct parables have been meshed (Lindars, *Gospel of John* 354–55; Robinson, "Parable" 69). Barrett suggests that the passage contains numerous pieces, which the evangelist has reworked (*Gospel According to St. John* 368). Dodd immortalized his analysis of the passage when he described it as "the wreckage of two parables fused into one, the fusion having partly destroyed the original form of both" (*Historical Tradition* 383).[13]

Commentators are divided over the question of the relationship of verses 17-18 to earlier parts of the passage. A good number of them, however, understand these verses to stand separate from and independent of the images of verses 1-16. Bultmann insists that 17-18 leaves "aside for the most part the metaphors in the parable" (*Gospel* 368). Brown speaks of them as "a short commentary on the phrase in v. 15, 'I lay down my life,' rather than on any element of the pastoral symbolism" (*Commentary–Gospel* 1:399; cf. Haenchen, *John* 2:49). "The allegory is now almost abandoned, as Jesus expands the point made in verse 15," writes Lindars (*Gospel of John* 363; cf. Haenchen, *John* 2:49). Others, however, are inclined to view verses 17-18 as integral to the whole passage and stress the relationship of this christological statement to the symbolism of the discourse.[14] As a whole, however, they are not able to agree on the integrity of the entirety of 10:1-18.

In general scholars have tended to see within the complexity of the passage evidence of tradition and redaction and theorize that the fusion of the two have produced the disunity of the whole. Consequently, Bultmann's impression that there is "confusion of the various images" (*Gospel*

359) is widely shared,[15] even when such a severe judgment is withheld.[16] Scholars have tended not to find integrity in the passage, however gentle their expression of such a discovery may be.

When the issue of the genre of the component parts of the passage is pressed, the disagreement among commentators intensifies. It is widely agreed that the use of *paroimia* (translated "figure of speech" in the NRSV) in verse 6 has roots in the Hebrew *mashal* ("riddle," or "figure") and that the latter word is represented in both the New Testament words, *paroimia* and *parabolē* ("parable") (e.g., Brown, *Commentary–Gospel* 1:390; Beasley-Murray 164). Some insist that verses 1-5 are truly parabolic (e.g., Brown, *Commentary–Gospel* 1:390; Bultmann, *Gospel* 370, n. 4; Dodd, *Historical Tradition* 383), while others deny that is the case,[17] and others seem uncertain.[18] Generally, one must conclude, the labeling of the genre is done without recourse to clear distinctions among various kinds of metaphorical language and arises almost exclusively from an effort to understand *paroimia* in terms of its Hebraic roots. Little or no attempt is made to ask how the images of the passage function for the reader.[19]

The foregoing discussion is sufficient to illustrate some of the difficulties of the passage for contemporary interpreters. We may draw three general conclusions from a survey of the contemporary interpretations of John 10:1-18. (1) The structure of the passage is comprised of two main parts with a shift in the kind of comparative language employed between the two. (2) The passage lacks a basic unity and probably reflects the presence of both tradition and redaction. (3) Interpreters identify the genre of the parts in varied and evasive ways. The lack of agreement among commentators and the occasional vagueness of their remarks about it warrant a new look at the passage in terms of its literary features. The inadequacies of what has become the traditional historical-critical methodology are evident enough in the study of John 10:1-18. Whether or not a strictly literary approach entirely overcomes those deficiencies remains to be seen.

A Literary Reading of the Structure of John 10:1-18

My own view is that the passage is composed of four interlocking "human images" with an expansion of the last of those images, followed by an explicitly "theological image." I have chosen to use the word, "image," here in a neutral way, so as not to prejudge the genre of the pictures used in the passage. I mean to suggest that we understand genre only after the structure and unity or disunity of the passage is considered. Genre arises from function. I use the word "human" only as a way of distinguishing the images having to do with Jesus' relationship with humans as opposed to the "theological image" in verses 17-18, which directs attention to the relationship between Jesus and God. All five of the images are contrastive in form, in each case posing a positive image (A) over against a negative one (B). The structure of the passage appears thus (in the New Revised Standard Version):

THE IMAGE OF ENTERING THE SHEEPFOLD (vs. 1-3a)

1   "*Very truly I tell you,*
    B   anyone who does not enter the sheepfold by the gate
            but climbs in by another way
            is a thief and a bandit.
2   A   The one who enters by the gate is the shepherd of the sheep.
3   The gatekeeper opens the gate for him";

THE IMAGE OF WHAT THE SHEPHERD DOES AND WHAT THE SHEEP DO (vs. 3b-5)

    A   "and the sheep hear his voice,
          He calls his own sheep by name
          and leads them out.
4   When he has brought out all his own,
5   he goes ahead of them,
            and the sheep follow him,
               because they know his voice.
5   B   They will not follow a stranger,
          but they will run from him
            because they do not know the voice of strangers."

THE NARRATOR'S COMMENT AND TRANSITION (vs. 6-7a)

6   Jesus used this figure of speech with them,
        but they did not understand what he was saying to them.
7   So Jesus again said to them,

THE IMAGE OF THE DOOR TO THE SHEEP (vs. 7b-10)

    "*Very truly, I tell you*
    A   **I am the gate for the sheep**.
8   B   All who came before me are thieves and bandits;
            but the sheep did not listen to them.
9   A   **I am the gate.**
          Whoever enters by me will be saved
            and will come in and go out
               and find pasture.
10   B   The thief comes
          only to steal and kill and destroy;

A   I came
          that they may have life,
                  and have it abundantly."

THE IMAGE OF THE GOOD SHEPHERD (vs. 11-15)

11 A   **"I am the good shepherd.**
                  The good shepherd lays down his life for the sheep.
12 B   The hired hand,
                  who is not the shepherd
                          and does not own the sheep,
                          sees the wolf coming
                          and leaves the sheep
                          and runs away—
                  and the wolf snatches them
                          and scatters them.
13   The hired hand runs away
                  because a hired hand does not care for the sheep.
14 A   **I am the good shepherd.**
                  I know my own
                          and my own know me,
15   just as the Father knows me
16   and I know the Father.
17   And I lay down my life for the sheep."

AN EXPANSION OF THE IMAGE OF THE GOOD SHEPHERD (v. 16)

16   "I have other sheep
                  that do not belong to this fold.
          I must bring them also,
                  and they will listen to my voice.
          So there shall be one flock, one shepherd."

A THEOLOGICAL IMAGE (vs. 17-18)

17 A   "For this reason the Father loves me,
                  because I lay down my life
                          in order to take it up again.
18 B   No one takes (or has taken) it from me,
    A   but I lay it down of my own accord.
                  I have power to lay it down,
                          and I have power to take it up again.
                  I have received this command from my Father."[20]

Three characteristics emerge from this analysis. The first regards *the way in which the contrasts appear and are varied*. In the first image the pattern is B/A; in the second A/B; in the third A/B/A/B/A; in the fourth A/B/A; and in the theological image A/B/A. In each case, except the second, the image concludes with a positive statement (A). The series begins with a negative image, continuing the polemic quality of the context of the passage found in chapter 9 and specifically 9:40-41. The first two images are symmetrically formed with a B/A/A/B pattern. After the negative conclusion of the second image, the narrator's comment in verses 6-7a addresses the reader. The entire series of images begins with the negative and concludes with the positive. The variation of the pattern keeps the reader off guard and surprised. But the concluding positive statement of each (but the second) of the images and the entire series continuously emphasizes the affirmative in the reader's mind. This alternation between the positive and the negative tends to continue the same variation begun in chapter 9. The general impact, however, of the affirmative tone of the whole of 10:1-18 moves the reader away from the polemical conclusion of the previous narrative in chapter 9.

The text keeps the reader off guard by the variation of the affirmative and negative comparisons. However, the second characteristic of the passage is *the rapid transitions among the images* that also challenges the reader. The transition between the first image (entering the sheepfold) and the following complex image (what the sheep and shepherd do) is abrupt and without forewarning or notice. First, Jesus is the one who enters the gate (v. 1) then the gate itself (v. 7). While the narrator imposes an explanatory transition at verses 6-7a, the image of Jesus as the gate of the sheep (v. 7b) gives way unexpectedly to that of the good shepherd (v. 11) without any metaphoric preparation or guidance from the narrator. The images leads the reader on from a discussion of

- how unauthorized as opposed to authorized persons enter the sheepfold,
- to the behavior of the sheep and shepherd,
- then on to the consideration of the gate to the sheepfold,
- next to the good shepherd,
- and finally to the relationship of the Father and Son.

All of this in the course of eighteen verses (Kysar, *John* 164–65).

The expansion of the image of the good shepherd found in verse 16 moves the reader swiftly to consider another dimension of the previous image (vs. 11-15). The metaphorical language of the previous images is sustained ("sheep," "fold," "voice," "flock," and "shepherd"), but the image is expanded. However, verse 16 does more than expand the image of the good shepherd. Readers are subtly made aware of the fact that here they come to some conclusion of the human images in which they have been moving. The language of the image (which in terms of content is an expansion of the fourth image, as commentators have observed) serves to draw the first four images together. (See the discussion of the integrity of the passage below.)

Likewise, the theological image in verses 17-18 continues the readers in the world of sheep and shepherds ("because I lay down my life," v. 17), but now leads them into a new imaginary realm. This conclusion does not summarize the "meaning" of the previous images. Those images stand on their own without theological abstraction. Rather the theological language offers a new image, which one might label "divine relationship." The metaphorical language continues in the theological statements regarding the relationship between the divine Parent and child. The "logic" of the implied author at verses 17-18 is no longer confusing when one realizes that the verses are not an attempt to summarize the preceding images but are a continuation of imagery, which drags the reader into still another picture world.

A final characteristic of the passage emerges: John 10:1-18 is not without *aids to reading*, the first of which are all betrayed by a consideration of the surface structure of the passage. Each image begins with a key word that facilitates the reader's shift of imagination (however abrupt the shift may be). The participle, *ho eiserchomenos* ("the one who enters"), announces the central focus of the first image. "The sheep" in verse 3b redirects the reader's attention to the subject of the second image. The "I am" sayings of verses 7 and 11 aid the reader's attention. "The Father" in verse 17 hints that the object of the imagery has now changed from the human realm to the divine. The implied author effectively leads readers through the seeming maze of imagery of the passage.

In conclusion, from the perspective of the reader and her or his response, the structure of the passage moves consistently and artistically, if unanticipated, through four consecutive images and even through the theological image. The narrator's comment at verses 6-7a is less a division between two main parts as it is an aid to reading the images. The division created by the comment invites the reader on to further word pictures. The commentary at verses 6-7a should be seen in terms of its function to aid the reader's center of attention as well as an indication that some sort of change of genre is about to occur.

A Literary Reading of the Integrity of John 10:1-18

When viewed intratextually, there is a remarkable unity in the passage, in spite of commentators' reservations concerning the issue. Both the total passage and its component parts evidences unity.

Each of the subunits has integrity of its own, while at the same time each is bonded to others. The words "gate" (*thyra*) and "entering" (*eiserchomai*) internally unites the first image. Complete antithetical parallelism further forms the image, so that the reader is led from the negative to the positive. The images of the behavior of the sheep and the shepherd are coupled by the theme of "voice" (*phōnē*) in verses 3b, 4, and 5, as well as by "hear his voice" in verse 3b and "do not know the voice of strangers" in verse 5. The word *voice* thus forms closures around the pair of contrasting images of the familiar voice of the shepherd and the alien voice of the stranger.

Yet the first two images are interlocked in several ways. Most obvious is the fact that both invite the visualization of sheep and sheepfold, as well as legitimate and illegitimate personnel caring for the sheep. However, the persona of the "thief/bandit" in the first and the "stranger" in the second further tie them together, and the two identifications create bookends around the pair of images.

The unity of the image of the gate to the sheep is attained by repetition of the "I am" (*egō eimi*) sayings at verses 7 and 9, as well as the theme of "coming" (*ēlthon* in v. 8 and 10b and *erchetai* in v. 10a). Add to those occurrences the use of "entering" (*eiselthē* in v. 9), and "going in and out" (*eiseleusetai* and *exeleusetai* in v. 9) and the reading is saturated with representations of motion. Therefore, the reader is caught up in a world of movement. Moreover, three "I statements" unite the passage (vs. 7, 9, 10), adding a tone of personal immediacy to the two images.

The image of the good shepherd repeats the "I am" saying in verses 11 and 14, again forming the opening and closing of the subunit between which is sandwiched the representation of the "hired hand." The allusion to giving up life for the sake of the sheep occurs twice (vs. 11 and 15). The pair of expressions *idia* ("his own," v. 12) and *ta ema* ("mine," twice in v. 14) unifies the passage while at the same time further fostering a tone of intimacy.

The image of the good shepherd is linked to its predecessor thematically through the figures of the thief/bandit in the first and the hired hand in the second. Linguistically the two images are linked through the recurrence of the "I" sayings. The third and fourth images are each formed around "I am" expressions. The "I am" is repeated in each (vs. 7b, 9 and 11, 12). Consequently, the reader subtly gains a sense of the unity of the two images through their formal similarity. The "I" sayings also bind the images of the gate and the shepherd with one another through their emotional tone of personal immediacy. The movement characterized by the image of the gate to the sheep is continued in that of the good shepherd ("lays down," v. 11; "coming," "leaves," and "scatters," v. 12; and "flees," vs. 12 and 13). The reader continues to inhabit a world filled with motion in time and space.

The expansion of the image of the good shepherd in verse 16 is hardly read as anything more than a further dimension of the fourth image. This is due in part to the use of the words "sheep," "shepherd," and "fold." Formally, the verse pulls images from the previous units together to create a new whole. The word "other" (*alla*) in verse 16 directs the reader to another perspective of the good shepherd. Yet the word "sheep" welds all four of the images together. "Voice" joins this image with the second and "listen to" (or "heed," *akouō*) links this verse with both the second and third images. "Shepherd" not only ties this verse closely with the fourth but also recalls the first of the images (v. 2). Finally, "fold" (*aulē*, v. 16) provides closure to the beginning of the human images in verse 1. Consequently, verse 16 serves a double function. First, it expands the imagery of the good shepherd, but, second, it also brings to a closure the imagery drawn from the human realm of sheep, flocks, shepherds, and strangers in the midst of the sheep.

That verses 17-18 constitute a new subunit is evident both from the shift of language and by their own integrity as a pericope. A new and single image arises in these verses. The word *Father* introduces the new image at verse 17a and concludes it at 18b. One might think the theological language of verses 17-18 is intrusive in the passage or even that it belongs outside the unity of verses 1-16. This is so only if the reader is bound to the human realm, exclusive of the divine. The invitation of the four human images, however, has been precisely to tantalize the reader with the possibility that the human dimension betrays the presence of the divine. Hence, the four human images tease the reader into the consideration of the divine represented by the human. Now in the conclusion of the passage the imagery shifts to the divine, and explicitly addresses the relationship of Jesus and God in a new imagery. The previous verses anticipate that shift in several ways. First, they highlight the function of the figures to break open the human realm to reveal the divine presence in the human, and, second, by the seemingly misplaced verse 15. ("[J]ust as the Father knows me and I know the Father. And I lay down my life for the sheep.") The appearance of that verse in the midst of the fourth image anticipates and prepares the reader for the theological image of verses 17-18.

While I have chosen to speak of verses 17-18 as a "theological image," that label has limited usefulness. While the content of the verses has to do with a theological dimension (the relationship of Jesus to God), the language—like the preceding images—is imaginative. The language asks the reader to *picture* that relationship as one between a parent and a child. It evokes images of the parent's command (*entolē*) for the child and the parent's love of the child who obeys even the most demanding of parental requests. Even more fundamental to the imagery of verses 17-18 is the human experience of relationship. Relationship is something the reader knows from interchange with others. The verses solicit the reader's reflection on Christology in terms of the experience of relationship. In light of these considerations, the concluding image is theological but theology done with an anthropological metaphor.[21]

The concluding theological image then continues the imaginative character of the entire passage while passing beyond the pictures used in the four human images. It leads the reader into a new frame of reference. While doing so, it brings to a conclusion the use of the first-person pronouns of the passage and distinctly articulates the christological subject of the previous images.

As disparate as the images may seem ("mixing metaphors"), the five images are packaged as a whole. Obviously, their unity involves the metaphorical vehicle of sheep, shepherds, and dangerous persons. Nevertheless, beyond the obvious, the contrastive form also joins the five. The "very truly" (*amēn amēn*) formula holds the first pair of images together with the second. The images change swiftly and imaginatively, but they are so linked together that the reader is firmly guided by the author. The move is from the human images to the theological image of verses 17-18, but not without consistency and preparation.

The narrator's comment in verses 6-7a seems at first disruptive in the structure of the passage, but on further consideration we can see how it adds significantly to the movement of the discourse. The narrator declares that the "figures" (*paroimia*) were not understood and verse 7 continues, "So (*oun*) Jesus again said to them. . . . " In the figures which precede these verses the metaphors are implicit and in those which follow they are explicit. Distinct from the figures in verses 1-5, those in 7-15 include *eimi* ("I am"). Thus the figures in the first section are implicitly metaphorical but in the second explicitly metaphorical.[22] Commentators are correct in their identification of verses 6-7a as transitional. A reader-response interpretation, however, confirms that the transition is not as radical or as intrusive as sometimes claimed. Far from a distracting intrusion in the passage, the narrator's comment prepares the reader to be led more deeply into the universe of the escalating images.

Verses 6-7a prepares the reader for the increasingly intimate character (the personal immediacy) of the succeeding images that function to draw her or him closer to Jesus in the discourse. The reader experiences a crescendo of the first-person pronouns as she or he is led through verses 7b-18. Verse 7b begins with the first of four "I am" statements, and the first use of "me" is encountered immediately in verse 8 (*pro emou*, "before me"). Thereafter the first-person pronoun occurs with increasing frequency, its acceleration enhanced by the liberal use of the "me" and "my" from verse 14 on. (In English translation the reader counts sixteen uses of "I" and ten occurrences of "me" or "my" in vs. 7b-18.) The third-person pronoun recurs in verse 11, recalling its dominance in verses 1-5, but then is used only of the antagonist figure of the hired hand (v. 12). In the experience of this gradual enlargement of the role of the first person the reader's sense of the power of the immediate presence of the speaker is intensified, climbing incrementally to the theological image of verses 17-18 which invites the reader to imagine the identity of that speaker.

The omniscient narrator (who knows the hearers do not understand) provides another clue to the strategy of the passage. Verses 6-7a supply the middle member of three interlocking statements of the absence of understanding among the hearers. Thereby the verses anchor the whole of 10:1-18 in its context. In 9:40-41 immediately preceding our passage the "Pharisees" struggle to understand the meaning of Jesus' words regarding seeing and blindness. In 10:19-20 the narrator reports that the words of Jesus provoke "a division among the Jews."

Commentators are correct then in their insistence that verses 6-7a mark a transition. The insistence, however, that the verses signal a transition from parable to allegory (or some other transition beyond the simple difference between implicit and explicit metaphor) is less than satisfactory, as we shall see. That the verses indicate the shift from tradition to a redactional explanation is even less satisfying, since such a view does not take seriously enough the integrity of the entire passage. A reader's response to verses 6-7a most likely concludes that the comment functions as an authorial guide into the next set of images. There is indeed a transition at this point in the passage, but two things argue against verses 6-7a as demarcating a major division in the passage. The first is the unity of the whole series of images which makes unnecessary any explanation for a major shift at verses 6-7a. The fundamental similarity in the functional nature of the images before and after verses 6-7a constitute the second argument against viewing the narrator's comment as a break in the passage. Granted there is a transition from implicit to explicit metaphor at this juncture, but I shall argue below that the images before and after verses 6-7a all have a common character. The genre of the images must now be considered.

A Literary Reading of the Genre of John 10:1-18

An appreciative reading of the genre of the passage involves some grasp of the function played by each of the images. However, before attempting to determine the precise genre of the images, it is necessary to investigate the strategy of their use. If genre arises from function, the reader needs to become conscious of how the implied author leads the reader through the complex of images. I am concerned at this point to explore further how the implied author has employed the set of images to lead the implied reader toward some desired destination. The passage asks the reader to construct meaning in and among the images as they invade her or his consciousness. Still, an even more complex strategy is at work.

The Strategy of the Use of the Images

Jeffrey L. Staley has argued that the narrative of the Gospel of John in general tends to draw the implied reader "into the bosom of the implied author" (*Print's First Kiss* 91). Our passage accomplishes this strategy but only with considerable tension. The tension exists between the implied reader's astonishment at the series of metaphors, on the one hand, and, on the other hand, her or his pleasure in not entirely sharing the lack of understanding characteristic of the hearers alluded to in verse 6 and identified as "Pharisees" in 9:40 and some of the "Jews" in 10:19.

On the one hand, as a consequence of this passage, the implied reader experiences a distancing from Jesus and the narrator. The abrupt series of images works to confuse the implied reader. First, the reader thinks she or he understands the metaphor, but then the metaphor changes, and the reader is left behind, struggling to keep up with the temporal flow of the discourse. Verse 6 warns the reader that the danger of not understanding the images is real and threatening. The reader stands on the brink of becoming identified with those who lack the insights to grasp the meaning of the images—on the precipice of identification with unbelief. In a sense, the reader becomes a victim of the implied author at this point. "The victimization of the implied reader" is a frequent strategy in the Fourth Gospel. It is designed to force the reader, if only momentarily, out of his or her status as an insider into that of an outsider (Staley, *Print's First Kiss* 97–98, 116).[23] In this case the entrapment of the reader is accomplished by allowing him or her to believe that she or he understands the image, only to be confronted with the next image which challenges the first understanding. Readers come to the passage with some confidence, equipped with the previous narrative (most especially the prologue, 1:1-18). Therefore, the reading pilgrims of the narrative have been led to feel that they have the crucial key to comprehend the enigmatic words of Jesus and consequently are dissociated with the misunderstanding and unbelief of the characters in the narrative. Except the successive images of our passage call that confidence in comprehension and dissociation into question.

Hence, the implied author creates a situation of suspense. Will we succumb to misunderstanding? The enigmatic images evoke a sense of conflict, and they drive us on in search of the resolution of the conflict. The images put us off guard while urging us on toward clarification. Unlike elsewhere in the narrative, the implied author or narrator does not immediately unlock the meaning of Jesus' words (e.g., 2:21-25). On the other hand, the setting of the passage clearly suggests that it is the outsiders—the Pharisees and the unbelieving Jews—who fail to grasp the sense of the images. The reader gains pleasure from knowing (to some degree at least) the clue to the images that the characters in the narrative do not have. The images may victimize readers, but do not alienate them. Readers possess enough understanding to continue on in the journey with confidence that the narrator will be faithful in bringing them to harmonious understanding with the teller of the story, even as that allusive figure has done previously.

Therefore, the images create a tension between readers' failure to understand and their complete identification with the opponents of Jesus. While not debilitating the reader, the implied author keeps the reader off balance by challenging any smugness and annihilating any complacency. This strategy keeps the reader close to the narrator—clinging to the coattails of the storyteller—if not in the narrator's bosom. It functions to lead the reader further into the narrative in search for resolution without utterly destroying the relationship which the narrator has established with the implied reader.

The reader's apprehension of the images is, therefore, an *affective experience* as well as a *cognitive* one. The series of images in our passage does elicit cognitive confusion (which is surely part of its strategy), but the images evoke an emotional instability as well. The sense of being thrown off balance, of being cast into the realm of uncertainty, of being dangerously close to the antagonists of the narrative summons forth an affective response in the reader (Moore, *Literary Criticism* 96).

The implied author employs an effective strategy in the use of this series of images—one that propels the reader on in the narrative. The passage is far more potent than we sometimes realize.

The Genre of the Images

Still, the genre itself of the images is important to the strategy of the text. Therefore, we need to ask further what the precise nature of those figures is. How shall they be categorized? The discussion underway is a test of the hypothesis that genre arises more out of the function an image performs for the reader than its nature abstracted from the text in which it is found. That is to say, we cannot ascertain the precise nature of the images in John 10:1-18 in isolation from their performance in the strategy of the passage. Hence, we must ask if the effort to label the images of verses 1-5 parable and those of 7-15 allegory (or the lot of them as allegories) makes any sense in terms of the function they play in the reading of the passage. What genre best describes the images when their function for the reader is considered? In effect one might say this experiment intends to ask whether images can ever be helpfully defined "essentialistically" at all or whether "functional" (that is, by a reader's response to them) definitions are not both more descriptive and helpful.

The implied author has treated the reader to a series of rapidly changing images, asking the reader to shift visions abruptly and unexpectedly, drawing four distinct comparisons from one metaphorical field, a fifth from another realm, and in the process bombarding readers with provocative pictures. The first observation pertinent to the genre of the images is the simple fact that readers are asked implicitly or explicitly to make a comparison in each of the figures of the passage. The text asks readers to compare Jesus with the entry to the sheepfold, with the shepherd who tends and cares for the sheep, and with the obedient child of a loving parent. We are enticed into comparing life under the care of Jesus with life in the sheepfold under the care of a responsible and devoted shepherd. In contrast, the threats besetting readers are compared to illegitimate persons who enter the sheepfold (i.e., a thief, a bandit, and a hired hand) who do not care whether the sheep are scattered and killed.

So, what is the character of these comparisons? Our response is hampered by disagreement about the correct use of words such as "image," "simile," and "metaphor."[24] The question I want to ask is whether or not we have in these Johannine figures something like what contemporary scholars have claimed is the metaphorical character of at least some of the parables of Jesus. Do the images function for the reader in a way comparable to the synoptic parables?[25]

It is the identification of parable and metaphor, B. B. Scott suggests, that has set off new appreciation for the synoptic parables ("Essaying" 61; cf. Wheelwright, 78-79). That new appreciation roots in understanding the metaphor as more than an illustration or simple teaching device.[26] In the classification of P. Wheelwright, the parabolic metaphors are tensive language used "diaphorically." This is to say that the metaphor is indispensable to the truth it conveys. Truth is "in and through" the image itself. The image is not a "throwaway" tool to communicate a truth knowable independent of the metaphor itself (i.e., an "epiphor"). In Scott's words, "parable as metaphor demands the parable never be done away with. . . . We cannot state what a parable means, for it has no meaning separate from itself" ("Essaying" 15).[27] J. D. Crossan has advanced this understanding of poetic metaphor by further distinguishing between the two kinds of metaphors. The poetic metaphor is not chosen as a means of expression, Crossan writes, but rather the truth received is the metaphor itself, so that no discursive summary of that truth can be extracted from the metaphor.

> The thesis is that metaphor can also articulate a referent so new or so alien to consciousness that this referent can only be grasped within the metaphor itself. The metaphor here contains a new possibility of world and of language so that any information one might obtain from it can only be received after one has participated through the metaphor in its new and alien referential world . . . this primacy of participation over and before information is most profoundly relevant. (*In Parables* 13; cf. McFague, *Speaking in Parables* 49)

Consequently, one must speak of two types of metaphor: those in which information is first received which allows one to participate in the metaphor and those "in which participation precedes information so that the function of metaphor is to create participation in the metaphor's referent." A "true metaphor," Crossan insists, is of the second kind. Jesus used such metaphors to break open the world of his listeners with a new world (*In Parables* 14; cf. Funk, *Parables and Presence* 34). R. W. Funk has claimed that a metaphor, "because of the juxtaposition of two discrete and not entirely comparable entities, produces an impact upon the imagination and induces a vision of that which cannot be conveyed by prosaic or discursive speech" (*Language* 136).

On the basis of a reader-response experience of them, are we able to say that the images of John 10:1-18 are such poetic metaphors? Are they "true metaphors" or more prosaic comparisons? The latter has often been thought to be the case. Johannine scholarship has sometimes referred to such figures as these as *mashal* (Brown, *Commentary–Gospel* 1:390; cf. Scott, *Hear Then* 7–62) or as "allegories."[28] There has been a concern to distinguish the figures used in John from those of the synoptic parables, rightly attempting to protect the distinctiveness of both the Johannine and the synoptic portrayals of the message of Jesus.

Still, it is clear that, in the images in John 10:1-18, there is a remarkable and even startling series of comparisons. When the commentator tries to summarize the meaning of the figures, the results are puny and sometimes almost comical. The figures defy our attempts to translate them into discursive language.[29] They carry their own truth which resists generalization. They evoke from the reader a participation which in turns nourishes a "knowing" far different from illustrative comparisons, which are dispensed with once they have served their purpose. The metaphors in our passage invite readers into the flock of Jesus, there to share an intimacy with the shepherd and to benefit from protection from the threatening forces around them. This *participatory* feature is characteristic of each of the images individually but of the entire series as well. That is, the mosaic of images draws the reader in, constantly provoking with each abrupt move to a new figure (Kysar, "Promises and Perils" 215-16). The series of images forms a single experience in which readers are lured into the picture world as members of the sheepfold and confronted with the decision as to whether their world can survive the onslaught of this new world dominated by the image of the sheepfold and the shepherd/son. That participatory experience resists any effort to reduce them to discursive language.

The series of images also shares the *shock* of true metaphorical language.[30] The poetic metaphor startles the imagination by the comparison it offers and thereby opens a new and unanticipated possibility of truth. "In the metaphor," writes A. Wilder, "we have an image with a certain shock to the imagination which directly conveys visions of what is signified" (*Language* 80). The series of metaphors in John 10:1-18 produces that shock, that splitting of the ordinary reality which allows the possibility of the new.[31] This is part of what R. A. Culpepper has called the "deformation of language" in the Fourth Gospel—the use of the familiar in unfamiliar ways (*Anatomy* 198).[32]

Beyond this, there is something more in the Johannine metaphors of this passage that shares a functional resemblance to the metaphorical parables. The parables attributed to Jesus in the first three gospels are often characterized by shock or surprise in the use of certain vehicles, and we find the same in our passage.[33] A part of the experience of that shock is the *irresolvably paradoxical characteristic* of the synoptic parables (Crossan, *Cliffs of Fall* 58). If that is indeed the response to the parables, it is clearly also one shared by the reader of John 10:1-18. The images of the passage spark a paradoxical response to the portrayal of the divine in the mundane images of shepherd, sheepfold, and child. Paradoxical, too, is reaction to the feature so often labeled as the "mixture of metaphors." The passage drives the reader to imagine Jesus as the gate to the sheepfold as well as shepherd of the sheep himself. If the reader is faithful, however, the shepherd-gate must also be visualized as the son of a Parent. Maybe more significantly, the paradox of the images is the ambivalent posture into which metaphors innocently lead the reader—the posture of insider and outsider, protagonist and antagonist, companion and alien to the narrator.[34]

The participatory, shocking, and paradoxical qualities of the images of John 10:1-8 suggest that they are experienced not merely as similes or teaching vehicles. They are rather *"true metaphors" with poetic power* to initiate a new kind of experience. The implied author creates a new reality with these metaphors, a reality impossible without them.[35] Indeed, the entire Gospel of John might be considered an extended metaphor in which the author tries less to communicate some universal truths through individual narratives and speeches than to create a reader's experience of a world at the center of which stands the Christ figure. The individual metaphors of 10:1-18 become part of a whole metaphorical reality. The language of the gospel reveals a new world of meaning. Typical of this gospel, however, that new universe of meaning is Christ himself.

The metaphors of John 10:1-18, however, serve a *contrastive* role as well, posing opposites, utilizing bipolar images. This oppositional nature of the metaphors in John 10:1-18 (e.g., the good shepherd opposed to the hired hand) reminds one of certain synoptic parables in which such a feature is betrayed (cf. e.g., Luke 18:9-14; Matt 7:24-27; Luke 6:47-49; cf. Dodd, *Historical Tradition* 383). The setting of the images of John 10:1-18 in the entirety of the narrative of John however gives them a role for the reader that is distinct from the synoptic parables. Not unlike the so-called dualism or bipolarity of John, the metaphors of 10:1-18 function in the reader's imagination to distinguish two realities. They pose the alternatives in polar opposites, much as does the light/darkness theme of the gospel. The implied author imposes a duality upon the reader, insisting by the imagery that there are two and only two realities, one true and one false, one life-giving and one life-threatening. Consequently, the reader is forced to respond to the two options without any alternatives. Participating in the images of the sheepfold with its good shepherd and menacing strangers, the implied reader must evaluate experience in terms of shepherd or thief/bandit/hired hand. Do I want to live in the world of the sheepfold of Jesus or another? The metaphors smash the complacency of or the resignation to the reader's world with another world possibility. This suggests that the metaphors of the Gospel of John share a role in the broader compass of the document, contributing to the either/or strategy of the implied author.

This polar contrastive feature suggests the *decisional* character of the metaphors in our passage which in turn echoes the eschatological urgency of the synoptic parables.[36] In the first three of the gospels that urgency is related to the new age that is dawning in the ministry of Jesus and his disciples; it is part of the kerygmatic content of the message attributed to Jesus concerning the rule of God. The metaphors before us in John 10:1-18 betray a similar kind of urgency, even if they are cast in a very different context. These metaphors force upon the reader the necessity of response to the claims of Jesus. The issue at stake is nothing less than the "life" of the reader. Shall the reader embrace the claim of Jesus or allow existence to be threatened by the thieves/bandits/strangers? The decision thrust upon the reader is simply this: shall I choose life or death, light or darkness? The Johannine metaphors do evoke a sense of urgency, even if the eschatological setting is different in John.[37]

In summary, the comparisons asked of the reader in John 10:1-18 function as poetic metaphors (diaphors) by virtue of their demand for participation before knowing, their shocking impact, and their thrust of the reader into irresolvable paradox. Moreover, like the true metaphorical parables of the Synoptics, they elicit contrastive images and provoke decision.

Certain other similarities between the metaphors of our passage and the synoptic parables merit mention. We momentarily abandon our reader-response orientation to note these resemblances. First, it is frequently observed that the pairing of parables in the synoptic tradition is a common feature (e.g., Luke 14:28-32; 15:3-10) (Brown, *Commentary–Gospel* 1:393). The passage under investigation pairs images (vs. 1-5 and 7-15), but carries that assemblage further to produce a complex of metaphors.[38] (Should we compare this complex with the collections of parables such as the one in Matthew 13?)

Second, the metaphorical field of farming, sowing, and harvesting is prominent in the synoptic parables, as is that of a master's leaving servants in charge during his absence (e.g., Mark 4:3-8 and parallels; Matt 24:45-51; Luke 12:42-46). In John 10:1-18 we witness two other metaphorical fields, in this case the field of sheep, shepherds, and dangerous persons, as well as that of the parent-child relationship.

Third, it is well known and often emphasized that the authentic parables of Jesus have a realism about them. They speak of the mundane, daily reality of their hearers, lifting up the most common activity or occurrence. As Wilder claims, "One can even speak of their secularity" (*Language* 81, and *Jesus' Parables* 90). If that is true, it is surely correct to speak of the secularity of sheep and shepherds and the threat posed to the flock by intruders. Or further, the secularity of the relationship of parent and child is evident. The figures of John 10:1-18 draw on common realities of the first-century world and use ordinary common-sense knowledge as the occasion for new meaning.[39]

The effort to analyze the genre of the images of the passage has led to the conclusion that they function as poetic or true metaphors (diaphors), rather than simple vehicles of truth (epiphors). I have contended on the basis of a reader response to the passage that these images share the characteristics claimed for at least certain of the synoptic parables, including their participatory character, their shocking effect, their paradox-inducing consequence, their contrastive feature, and their decisional quality. In terms of their function for the reader the images are poetic metaphors and as such they share much with the parables attributed to Jesus in the Synoptic Gospels quite aside from the question of how and to what degree they invite allegorization on the part of the reader. Less important for our investigation is the fact that, like the synoptic parables, the metaphors in our passage exhibit the practice of pairing, the employment of metaphorical fields, and the application of the secular to open the sacred.

Conclusion

Notwithstanding the tendencies of the commentaries, John 10:1-18 appears to the reader as five interrelated images, flowing one after the other with abruptness and unexpectedness but with skillful guidance in the text. The passage functions as a single whole in both content and form, in spite of attempts to fragment it and find divisions based on either content or form. The functional genre of the images (i.e., the readers' experience of them), I suggest, is that of poetic or true metaphor quite apart from the question of where they provoke simple comparison and where they stimulate allegorizing.[40] The passage shares much with the literary quality of some of the parables attributed to Jesus in the Synoptic Gospels, so that the sharp distinction between the Johannine metaphors and the synoptic parables is to be seriously qualified. This is not to deny a difference between the metaphorical function of a story parable and the images of John 10:1-18. It is to argue, however, that in terms of a reader response both may and do perform as true or poetic metaphor.

This experiment has purported to be no more than a "literary case study" in Johannine metaphor. Whether or not the conclusions regarding John 10:1-18 are typical of Johannine metaphor in general requires further investigation.[41] The findings of our study, however, are significant enough to merit a new and different kind of probe of the vast reservoir of imagery in John—one that takes as its focus the literary function of those metaphors within the scope of a reader-response criticism.

This initial study has been set within the context of a dialogue with the contemporary historical-critical investigations of the Fourth Gospel, particularly as we find that method employed in the standard commentaries on the document. Such a dialogical setting has proven to be a way by which reader-centered attention to the text might be defined in distinction from the historical focus of traditional critical scholarship. Indeed, every attempt at a new methodology needs to work in conversation with the prevailing methods. I do not conceive the relationship between the methodology attempted above and the historical-critical methods as mutually exclusive. What I have attempted begs the questions of sources, redaction, and most especially the intent of the "real author." My interpretation of the passage addresses only the shape of the text as it stands and this reader's response to it. The historical-critical questions may still be appropriate, but on another level or in a different mode. It is hoped that a new literary criticism of the Fourth Gospel can serve as a corrective to the traditional historical-critical approach and take its place alongside those methodologies as a equal partner, allowing us still more tools with which to investigate this rich and intriguing gospel.[42]

Chapter Eleven

The Making of Metaphor (John 3:1-15)

Commentaries on John 3:1-15 have become nearly tiresome. The passage has been interpreted and reinterpreted until one would almost wish for a moratorium on the wearisome rehash of the Jesus-Nicodemus discussion with the standard repertoire of insights and observations. So, why still another reading of the passage? For one thing, the passage merits further discussion from the perspective of the author's strategies, that is, from a reader-response perspective. A number of recent publications have moved contemporary reading of the passage in that direction, especially those of F. Moloney (*Belief*, and *Gospel*) and M. W. G. Stibbe (*John as Storyteller*, and *John*). More importantly, little attention has been paid to the way in which the metaphors in the passage are developed in the process of the dialogue-discourse. While it is commonplace to point out the use of puns and double entendre in the passage, less effort has been made to analyze how the surplus meanings of those words function metaphorically and what result they have in the reader's experience of the passage. How are they metaphorical and in what way does the author create their metaphorical quality?

Methodology: First-Time Reader

This reading of John 3:1-15 attempts a first try at such an examination. The method of my reading, however, is not formal reader-response. I am not primarily interested in using these formal methods, although I am indebted to them in ways that will be obvious. What I shall do employs a far less formal method. I want to imagine myself—as best I can—an innocent, virginal contemporary reader, encountering the passage for the first time and to explore it from that perspective. I shall ask what this hypothetical reader might experience in a journey through the passage and how that reader might perceive the work of the author.

Naturally this effort is at best risky![1] Who of us can successfully put aside all we think we know about this passage and take on the role of a first-time reader? Risky as it may be, I should like to attempt it with the belief that some fresh understanding might be gained. So, for the most part I shall dispense with the standard categories of "implied" reader and "implied" author (Moore, *Literary Criticism* 78–81).

For methodological clarity, however, two descriptions are necessary at the beginning. The first is in regard to the interpreter of the text and the second to the imaginary reader the interpreter employs. A first-reader methodology requires description of the one who attempts such an imaginative encounter with the text. As with any interpretative process, the social location of the interpreter is crucial. No reading is possible without a specific reader, and no reader's endeavor is without a peculiar perspective, shaped by her or his ethnic, social, and economic situation (Segovia and Tolbert, *Social Location*, vol. 1). The location of the reader is, therefore, an indispensable methodological presupposition and all the more significant if some imaginative first reading of the text is undertaken.

This particular interpreter is an affluent, empowered, white male who works as a full, tenured professor within an academic setting in the service of the church. My history provides little in the way of social or cultural oppression. I was born and raised in the United States primarily in the middle class. I know social marginalization and disenfranchisement only indirectly, and hence am nearly blind to the possible meanings a passage might render for those who know firsthand oppression by virtue of gender, race, class, or economic condition. Furthermore, I assume that the passage functions within the context of the Christian community (specifically within the Lutheran tradition) as a source of authority and that academic inquiry is a servant of the faith community. Moreover, I have in the past served the scholarly and confessing communities primarily through the traditional historical-critical methods of biblical study. My use of a synchronic, literary methodology reflects a new commitment and hermeneutical enterprise.

My imagined first reader will reflect my own social and ethnic experiences, as well as my religious convictions. Hence, the first reader I imagine will be predisposed to questions of faith. Motivated by concerns of a religious nature, I will read the text with a personal intensity, searching for resolutions to the issues surrounding the story's central characters. The fictitious reader, however, is also astute and remembers what he has read earlier in the story, and he tries to use his earlier reading as a framework of comprehension for the present passage. I imagine a careful and sensitive reader, responsive to the nuances of the text. Moreover, my method requires a first-time reader who becomes vulnerable to the text. Immersed in the movement of the passage, this reader allows himself to be drawn into the text and to be subjected to its influence. Such an imaginative first reading experience is a productive enterprise only in terms of this sort of understanding of the invented participant in the procedure.

To accomplish the sort of reading I have in mind, I will first move through the passage, suggesting the possible experiences of the first-time reader. Then, the second part of the essay will reflect on what this reading experience offers in terms of our understanding of the (implied) author's enterprise in chapter 3. Finally, I will consider the way in which the author has fashioned the metaphors of the passage, what sort of metaphors they are, and what role they play. For the purposes of this paper, I have arbitrarily defined the perimeters of the text as vs. 1-15. No clear closures (however partial) are detectable before 3:21. Indeed, 3:1-21 functions, I think, as a literary whole.[2] I confess then that the division after v. 15 is irregular, made simply because vs. 1-15 offers a workable unit for the sake of this essay and includes the four major metaphors I wish to examine. I will conclude, however, that the reader experiences a climatic insight in v. 15, even though the literary unit continues through v. 21.

A First-Reader Examination of John 3:1-15

Our imaginary first reader approaches the passage with a naive optimism. The prologue of the narrative rings in memory's ear, and the reader comprehends, however vaguely, the identity of the story's hero. Nothing in the succeeding passages has diminished the bright image of the Word now made flesh. I have heard the baptizer's witness, watched Jesus call disciples, marveled at his insight, wondered at the transformation of water into wine, and heard with awe his majestic (if puzzling) pronouncements. True, the promise of the early verses that the hero would suffer rejection still haunts me (1:10-11). However, that troubling promise remains abstract with the one exception of a mention of the hero's death (2:22). Nearly everything has worked toward encouraging a simple optimism and excitement in our reader.

Everything, that is, except the immediately preceding verses (2:23-25). On the one hand, the excited anticipation is enhanced by the declaration that "many believed in his name." On the other hand, the narrator's insistence that Jesus would not trust himself to these believers begins to temper our reader's enthusiasm. I can only wonder what dreadful evil lurks in the human heart that would necessitate Jesus' reserve. Nonetheless, the first two verses of our passage rekindle my optimism. Anticipation is piqued by the possibilities of a conversation between Jesus and a religious leader. Nicodemus takes the initiative to come to Jesus and acknowledges that Jesus must be a teacher from God because of the quality of his wondrous works. He immediately attracts me, for I share his view of Jesus. Now a prominent Pharisee will come to understand Jesus and believe in him, and the story will continue to unfold the pattern of Jesus' glorious success.[3]

In that hopeful expectation, v. 3 shocks me! After the solemn, "Very truly, I tell you," Jesus speaks opaquely (again). This is his chance to win over a powerful leader. Why confuse the process with such a stern pronouncement? I am utterly puzzled by "born *anōthen* [again, from above, or from the beginning]." What possible meaning could it have? The juxtaposition of *ginomai* ("born") and *anōthen* creates an ambiguity. It crosses two experiences with a shocking result: To be born and from above or again. I am to consider how one might be born but born either from above or born again. I suddenly feel distanced from Jesus—alienated from this one with whose cause I have become identified. I cannot understand his words and feel threatened by that sense of confusion.

Moreover, Jesus now redefines the issue of the conversation around entering "the kingdom of God." I hear that such an entrance depends on an *anōthen* birth. However, the dominion of God itself has its own ambiguities. It conjures up a whole series of different references—among them God's power, the ideal human society, a political transformation. So, I am faced with one vague image (born *anōthen*) used along with another (the kingdom of God).[4] One metaphor refers the reader to another. I am forced to ask how it is that an *anōthen* birth empowers one to experience God's dominion. Does one illumine the other? If so, how?

Nicodemus' question in v. 4 triggers several different responses in me. First, his query somewhat calms my anxiety and puts me at ease. He, too, is puzzled by Jesus' words. Like Nicodemus, I wonder, "How is it possible?" I am, therefore, drawn to him, identify with him in his confusion, and become hopeful that with his help the obscurity of the saying will be clarified. In one sense, I now feel a comradeship with this character as a co-inquirer with me. Still, second, Nicodemus' question ridiculously narrows the meaning of born *anōthen*. How is a second physical birth possible? At Nicodemus' expense, I recognize that born *anōthen* cannot refer to a second physical birth. The reference of the image is narrowed, and its literal meaning eliminated. Finally, now I feel superior to Nicodemus. Like him I am puzzled by Jesus' words, but I would not suppose that they refer me to a second physical birth. My sense of alienation from Jesus is eased just a bit by the failure of Jesus' dialogue partner. Hence, while I feel distanced from Jesus, I do not yet feel abandoned by the discussion.

The intent of Jesus' words in the next verses (vs. 5-8) at first seems to confirm my renewed sense of companionship with Jesus. That new affirmation is short-lived, however. Once again I read, "Very truly, I tell you," and ready myself for difficulty. Born *anōthen* is paralleled with birth out of water and Spirit. The metaphor is enriched, but the reader is confused and again pushed away from the speaker. Little more is accomplished than to replace the puzzle of *anōthen* with that of *hydatos kai pneumatos* ("water and Spirit"). To be sure, I remember John the Baptist's distinction between his baptism with water and Jesus' baptism with the Spirit (1:33). But still, as I was first forced to ask what kind of *anōthen*, I am now compelled to ask what kind of water and what kind of *pneuma* ("spirit")?

Verse 6 still further narrows the possible reference of the enigmatic *anōthen* birth. Confirming Nicodemus' erroneous impression that the birth is physical, Jesus distinguishes between being born of flesh and born of spirit. I feel still further encouraged. But *sarx* ("flesh") clouds the light and introduces yet another of the accumulating ambiguous terms. Is it pejorative in this context? Or is it neutral? Is the contrast of birth by flesh and birth by Spirit meant only to distinguish the first, physical birth from a second birth; or is it intended to demean the physical? If we know what being born of the flesh is, what then can born of Spirit mean? Jesus has led me to think of born *anōthen* as a spiritual birth. That conclusion is consistent with the distinction of the prologue between born of God and born of flesh (1:12-13). The questions, however, of what more precisely a spiritual or divine birth is and how such a birth is possible compel me on in my reading.

I have managed to squeeze some satisfaction out of Nicodemus' question and Jesus' distinction between spiritual and physical birth. Still, Jesus' words in v. 7 mock both Nicodemus and me in our lack of understanding. How can we not be astonished? Now I sense that I once again stand with the Pharisee in my struggle to understand. My alienation from Jesus is reestablished.

Yet Jesus goes on now, seeming to promise clarification. His words concerning the *pneuma* ("Spirit," in v. 8) encourage me to expect an elucidation of entering God's dominion through an *anōthen* birth by the spirit. Spirit is the key to unlock the meaning imprisoned in Jesus' image. How disappointing and puzzling, then, is the fact that the key itself comes locked away in its own prison. The tiny metaphor of v. 8 stretches my mind between *pneuma* as Spirit and *pneuma* as wind. Jesus speaks of the freedom of the *pneuma*, the perception of the sound of the wind, but the mystery of its origin and destination. An implied comparison of wind and spirit is supposed to illumine the *anōthen* birth by water and the Spirit. But precisely how still evades me.

By v. 9 I feel that Nicodemus is inside my mind and speaks for me. My identification with him in his puzzlement and our mutual alienation from Jesus is complete. I, too, repeat Nicodemus' query, "How can this be?" ("this" referring to the entire discussion thus far). Consequently, Jesus' stern reprimand of Nicodemus is his reprimand of me as well: "Are you a teacher of Israel" (or, have you read this far), "and yet you do not understand this?"

The distance between Jesus and me increases with v. 11. It begins again with that signal that what follows is important and (in my experience) demanding: "Very truly, I tell you." I have heard the speeches and the witnesses, but now, by virtue of my failure to understand, Jesus says, I have rejected the witness. As a first-time reader, the first person plural of v. 11 is not troublesome, for I acknowledge the plurality of the speakers—witnesses thus far in the narrative (e.g., the narrator, John the Baptizer, and others). However, beginning with this verse, I experience the conversation opening into a community. Jesus speaks, but now from within a group that has "seen" and here "bear witness" to their experience.

The hole gets deeper. Jesus has spoken of "earthly things," and I did not believe? What are these earthly things, and what might the heavenly things be? My mind is driven back to the flesh-spirit distinction. However, I am led to think that both of those are earthly, not heavenly things. Still clinging desperately to the hero's verbal coattails, I suppose that Jesus speaks of heavenly things in v. 13. Yet I am ill-equipped to receive his words. Added to the quandaries already piled on me by the discussion thus far comes another distinction: ascending and descending. Plus with the distinction a title, "Son of Man." Yet I recall the promise to Nathanael: "You will see heaven opened, and the angels of God ascending and descending upon the Son of Man" (1:51). Again, here is an ascending and descending. Now, however, it is the Son of Man who descends and ascends. The connection between the two, plus the encouragement of the prologue, nurtures my identification of Jesus with the Son of Man. The descent, I suppose, speaks in a veiled way of the Word's becoming flesh. But what might the ascent be? Am I to assume that Jesus will ascend? What has all of this to do with *anōthen* birth?

I feel as if I am listening to a foreign speaker in a language of which I have only a few scraps of vocabulary. The sojourn thus far has left me with a sense of having been shoved rudely away from the story's hero. Still I have been thrown enough scraps of meaning that I continue to trail along, still hoping to reach the banquet table.

Immediately on the heels of the hint that Jesus has descended and therefore must once again ascend comes the enigmatic v. 11. The promise now is that the Son of Man will be "lifted up" in a way comparable to Moses' lifting up of the serpent in the wilderness. Sparks fly as this text rubs against another (Culler 1387) and I struggle to grasp those tiny hints of light. I am now confident that Jesus speaks of himself with the title Son of Man. "Ascending" and "lifting up" correspond with one another in their verbal image of spatial movement. I know I am working with spatial imagery for something else, but I have no other clue as to the meaning of the *hypsoō* ("to lift up").

Again, the reader is asked to wrestle with a puzzling, ambiguous expression. Along with *anōthen*, and *pneuma*, *hypsoō* is another hurdle. From it I might conclude that Jesus anticipates enthronement, and my mind races back to God's dominion. Or, I might venture the dreadful possibility of crucifixion, only to be forced to recall the dire prediction of rejection in the prologue and the mention of death in 2:22. I, however, cannot choose between enthronement and crucifixion. I have no clues to help me.[5] Along with the other ambiguous terms of the passage, I am left to suspend judgment concerning the sense of *hypsoō* until further reading. But the puzzling word occasions another recollection from my reading experience: "Destroy this temple, and in three days I will raise it up" (2:19, although the Greek expression is *egerō auton* and not *hypsoō*). Raise up. Ascend. Lifted up. Could these enigmatic sayings illumine the earlier one? Or, the earlier one, these?[6]

Verse 15 jolts me with the seriousness of the matter at hand. The one who believes in the lifted up Son of Man may have eternal life. I feel more threat than promise in those words, for, in my confusion, I have no basis for belief. I cannot believe, if I do not understand. My understanding, therefore, takes on ultimate significance.

At this point, let us suppose that our imaginary reader puts the text down, exhausted by the strenuous demands of these fifteen verses. As that reader, my head is spinning with ambiguity, stretched by obscure references, exhausted by the pace of the discussion, and confused by its movement. Still feeling distance between myself and Jesus, I nonetheless have been intrigued by the puzzles in the passage. Moreover I have taken seriously the claim that something vital is at stake. I shall in the future take up the text again to resume my pursuit.

Reflections on a First Reading Experience of John 3:1-15

On the basis of our journey through the passage as an imaginary first reader, we are ready to make some observations regarding the text and the implicit strategies of the author encountered there.

Presuppositions Imposed on the Reader

The first of these observations concerns what is presupposed of the reader in the passage (Culler). Those presuppositions are of at least two basic kinds. *First,* the text presupposes a prior reading of other texts. This pre-supposed intertextuality involves at least the earlier parts of the narrative. Further, the passage seems to assume that the reader will complete the remainder of the story, that is, that the reader is reading the whole gospel and the fullest meaning of the present passage is known only in the con-text of the whole document. The passage leads the reader to hope that the remainder of the narrative will produce satisfaction with the present portion. Beyond the text of the gospel, v. 14 presupposes the reader's knowledge of another passage in the canon, namely, Numbers 21:4-9.

The *second* kind of presupposition burdening the reader of this text has to do with values. It assumes from the very first the implicit worth of the kingdom of God and eternal life. "Seeing" or "entering" the kingdom and having "eternal life" are implicitly desirable. Without adherence to God's dominion and the quest for a higher quality of life as important values, the engine of the passage is rendered impotent. The passage also takes for granted a certain willingness on the part of the reader to recog-nize and deal with polyvalence. The reading experience is moved along by the ambiguity of key words. Without the reader's desire to pursue the sense of this language for the sake of understanding what is required to enter or see the reign of God and have eternal life, the passage would have no motivating power.

The imagined reading experience I have sketched demonstrates that the passage makes enormous demands on the reader. There are discour-agements, disappointments, confusion, and alienation from the story's hero. The text implicitly trusts its own intertextuality and the reader's val-ues to sustain the reading. The reader survives the text only if and because, as a result of the previous two chapters, her or his imagination has been captured by the fascinating hero of the story.[7] The reader endures the abuse of the passage only if and because he or she senses that the king-dom of God/eternal life are of utmost importance. With the obscurity of the passage, its implied author risks the loss of the reader—endangers his or her patience. So stressful and bewildering is the passage that only its intertextuality and subject matter render it passable.[8]

On the positive side, what I have addressed as the author's risk might also be understood in terms of the enticement of the reader into partici-pation. The arduous demands on the reader force her or his involvement, if the passage is to be other than pure nonsense. The "gaps" of mean-ing are bridged only if the reader ventures some preliminary sense that enables progress (Botha 190).[9] The striking thing about the first-reader examination is how tenuous the reader's constructions of meaning are and what thorough and imaginative participation is required for a successful reading.

The Role of Nicodemus

The second reflection focuses on the steadily decreasing role of Nicodemus in the discussion. On the one hand, he stands at the head of the section, taking initiative in the meeting and stirring the anticipation of the reader. On the other hand, he rapidly slips from prominence. He is assigned three speeches in the passage. In the Greek, the first of these in v. 2 is comprised of twenty-four words, the second in v. 4 of eighteen words, and the third at v. 9 of only four words. In the end, the reader's anticipation that Nicodemus would lead the way to understanding and faith is disappointed.

Without trying to engage the whole question of how the author employs characters, at the level of experience the reader is subtly encouraged to identify with Nicodemus as well as to draw excited anticipation from his entrance. Once the reader has identified with Nicodemus, she or he begins to be distanced from him, beginning with his first response to Jesus' words. Finally, however, in his last speech Nicodemus articulates the reader's experience.[10] However, then the figure disappears. Nicodemus is a bridge character, that is, a means by which the reader begins to hear Jesus' words and to try to understand them. He is a scout who leads the reader into the midst of the skirmish. Once the reader has become involved in the process of the discussion—once the reader begins to struggle with the images of Jesus' words—Nicodemus' function has been accomplished, and he becomes an obsolete accessory to the reading process.[11]

The reader's relationship with Nicodemus amounts to what J. Staley calls "reader victimization" and what J. E. Botha terms more simply "manipulation" (*Print's First Kiss* 95–118; Botha 191–92). In particular, my reading experience led me to view the advent of Nicodemus as promising and as the beginning of a significant acknowledgment of Jesus' identity—a view that the passage utterly annihilates.[12] Consequently I felt as though I had become a victim of the text.[13] Furthermore, my relationship with Nicodemus moved from identification to superiority and back to identification. As a result there is a sense in which the text manipulated my attitude toward this character in what Botha calls "involuntary association and disassociation."[14] The reader's posture toward Nicodemus may, however, be only one of several ways in which the text subtly misdirects the reader.

The Language of the Passage

The peculiar language of the discussion shapes the reader's experience in several different ways. Verbs of knowing (*oida* and *ginoskō*) are prominent in the whole of the discussion. Nicodemus knows (v. 2), and then does not know (vs. 8 and 10). In v. 11 Jesus and others know. Verbs of knowing dominate the discussion through v. 11 and then give way to belief (*pisteuō*), with which the passage climaxes (vs. 12 and 15). This shift skillfully leads the reader from a concern for knowing to one for believing and to the ultimate importance of knowing for belief (an important theme in the Fourth Gospel as a whole). The reader's experience of struggling to understand (that is, to know) is vital in order that she or he might believe. On the basis of the reading experience of this passage, knowing and believing appear intertwined, if not synonymous.

Another feature of the language of the passage consists of the words referring to the use of the senses. The verb see (*horaō*) occurs twice (vs. 3 and 11). On the other hand, words of sounds and hearing govern the passage: In v. 8 the verb "to hear" (*akouō*); "said" and "say," seven times (vs. 2, 3, 4, 5, 7, 9, and 11); "answered," three times (vs. 3, 5, and 10). "Sound" (v. 8), "speak" (v. 11), "witness" (v. 11), and "told" (v. 12, twice) complete the repertoire of auditory expressions in the passage.

Of course, a dialogue-discussion passage is going to use many of these terms, so their prominence does not surprise us. Still, I propose that the reader has an important auditory experience as a result of the passage. Not surprisingly, Jesus is made to refer to the sound (*phōnē*) of the pneuma, so important is the experience of hearing. Combined with the use of the verbs of seeing, the reader's experience is essentially a sensory one. This suggestion is important, since the passage pivots around four metaphors, each of which has a sensory basis. "To be born," "to be born of water," "to hear and feel the wind," "to see the Son of Man lifted up"—all of these appeal to an experience of the senses. By means of sensory experience (among other things) the text opens the reader to the transformation effected by the metaphors. (Of course, the author of this gospel consistently appeals to the senses, beginning the document with seeing the incarnation of the Word [1:14] and concluding it with a discussion of Thomas' seeing [20:24-29]. Kysar, *Maverick Gospel* [1993], 86–90).

The language of the passage also subliminally bathes the reader in contrasts: knowing and not knowing (vs. 2, 8, 10, and 11); spirit and flesh (vs. 5, 6, 8); earthly and heavenly things (v. 12); ascend and descend (v. 13); born *anōthen* by spirit (vs, 3, 6, and 7) and natural birth (vs. 4 and 6); and the implicit contrast between lifted up for enthronement and for crucifixion. Still, another contrast is fundamental to the reading of the passage, namely that of the possible and the impossible. The use of the word *dynatai* in the Greek text creates this contrast. It begins with Nicodemus' confession in v. 2, "no one can do (*dynatai*) these signs that you do, unless God is with him." Jesus claims that participation in God's dominion is possible (*dynatai*) only if one is born *anōthen* (v. 3) of the water and the Spirit (v. 5). Three times Nicodemus asks how such a birth is possible (*dynatai*, twice in v. 4 and again in v. 9). Jesus' interrogator begins with an affirmation of what is possible but disappears behind his last puzzling question in v. 9, "How is it possible (*pōs dynatai tauta genesthai*)?" The contrast is between what is impossible from the human perspective and what is possible and necessary from the divine perspective.[15]

Meeting contrast after contrast, the reader gradually becomes aware of a fundamental opposition to which the passage propels her or him, namely, a contrast of belief and unbelief which becomes explicit only in v. 12: "If I have told you about earthly things and you do not believe, how can you believe if I tell you about heavenly things?" In general, *the author frames the whole narrative with polarities*, which find their literary expression in the kind of contrasts we see in this passage. Verse 15 gives the passage a deadly seriousness in part by the polarities with which the reader must deal. The sense of seriousness is experienced because, in the environment of the contrasts of the passage, there is no alternative to the polarity of belief and unbelief.[16]

The unity of the passage is attained on one level by its language. The author takes the reader by the hand to lead her or him on from one to another thought by means of something like catchwords. We have already observed this feature in the use of several words in the text:

see, leading from v. 3 to v. 11;
know, leading successively from v. 2 to v. 8 to v. 10 and finally to v. 11;
believe, directing the reader from v. 12 to v. 15.

Two other bridge words are worth noting:

God in v. 2 recurs in Jesus' words in v. 3;
born is first used in v. 3 but then sequentially in vs. 4, 5, 6, 7, and 8.

Establishing such a repertoire of words focuses the reader's attention and formulates a theme. Using them to lead the reader on provides transitional bridges, holding tightly to the reader's mind as the passage races on.

One more linguistic observation is necessary. In the passage as I have delimited it, Jesus is introduced with a saying about birth (v. 3). Jesus concludes the passage with a saying about life (v. 15). It is not accidental, I think, that my reading experience directed me from consideration of the origin of life to a claim about the authentic quality of life. The character of human existence is a journey from physical birth to a search for the meaning and quality of genuine life. Therefore, the *anōthen* birth is implicitly about the authentic existence, i.e., eternal life.

Reading Structure

The reader is carried through a threefold dialogue (Stibbe, *John* 53–54). Each of the three parts is comprised of a statement or question by Nicodemus followed by Jesus' words. As Nicodemus' participation in the discussion is steadily shortened, Jesus' words become more lengthy. In each of the first two of the three components, Jesus begins his speech with the solemn *amēn, amēn* ("truly, truly" or "very truly"). In the third component, v. 10 intrudes before "Very truly, I tell you." In the reading experience itself, the double *amēn* signals the reader that the forthcoming words are of vital importance but also that they will be puzzling.

In reading the passage, one begins only as an interested observer of a dialogue between Jesus and Nicodemus. The dialogue, however, soon evolves into a triangular discussion, including the reader's participation. Finally, it shifts abruptly to a dialogue between the reader and Jesus, who now stands within and speaks for a witnessing community. Hence, the tripartite structure entails three reading modes: observer; participant with Nicodemus and Jesus; and dialogue partner with Jesus and his community.

The Making of a Metaphor—The Metaphors of John 3:1-15

I have traced the experience of our imaginary first reader through the passage and drawn from that experience a number of observations about the text and the strategies of its author implicit therein. Only now are we ready to turn to the central topic of the reading: the making of the metaphors found there. The passage, I suggest, epitomizes the way in which this author creates a metaphor, fashions a metaphorical experience for the reader, and places the reader in the midst of a metaphorical ecosystem. In this case, the construction of the metaphor is through what I would like to call mini-images, that is, short uses of language (sometimes single words) to refer to something beyond the commonplace referent of the words. The process of that construction has a number of features, a few of which describe the way the text constructs metaphor.

Earthly Phenomena and Transcendent Realities

Obviously the making of a metaphor in this case, as always, begins by daring the reader to consider two phenomena placed side by side. In this passage the phenomena are four pairs: birth and *anōthen*; birth and *pneuma*; wind and spirit; lifted up for enthronement and lifted up for crucifixion. Additionally, the rule of God is compared with an earthly kingdom and authentic human existence is named "eternal" (*aiōnion*). In each case, the metaphorical experience resides in the strangeness of the comparison, the shock of being asked to consider one by reference to the other, and the provocative and open-ended character of the comparison. In this passage, metaphor is created by aligning phenomena from this earthy existence with those of a transcendent realm. In particular, physical birth and birth from above (or by *pneuma*), physical wind and the divine spirit, and crucifixion and enthronement. In this way, the metaphors have an earthly quality about them, which in turn transforms the earthly into something more.

This leads us to a related feature of the passage, "defamiliarization" (Scott, *Parable* 427).[17] Obviously, the text requires the reader to deal with the familiar phenomenon of birth and wind in unfamiliar ways. In the process the power of the familiar is altered and a new potency infused. Birth becomes new creation in a novel sense. Wind is broken open to reveal the work of the Spirit. Two ordinary meanings of "lifted up" are challenged by the possibility that the two may become one. The text imposes on the reader the necessity to see the old and daily in new ways. Their entrance into the reader's consciousness is through their very familiarity. Once having gained entrance into the fortress of the reader's mind, they wreak havoc in his or her worldview.

The category of defamiliarization, however, is not quite appropriate to what we have witnessed in the experience of the reader. The familiar is not finally destroyed to make room for the new. Better, it is transformed by virtue of the metaphors, something more akin to *transfamiliarization*. The result is that the phenomena of birth and wind remain familiar and daily. Yet now the familiar threatens to carry within itself a transfamiliar reality—the reality of *anōthen* birth and the spirit. The familiar meaning of the image is not cast aside, once it is defamiliarized. Rather, the familiar retains an essential role in the process of transfamiliarization and ever carries the peril of becoming unfamiliar.

Metaphor out of Ambiguity

Even more characteristic of the metaphors before us in the passage is the fact that they are constructed from the raw material of ambiguity (as all poetic metaphors are). By ambiguity I mean the "verbal nuance . . . which gives room for alternative reactions to the same piece of language."[18] The nuances of Jesus' language breed tension and constantly compel the reader on in the text. What is clarified leaves something else vague. One hand offers the reader some advancement in understanding, while the other hand rudely takes it away by providing still another ambiguity.

In this passage it is precisely in ambiguity or surplus of meaning that the metaphorical quality of the words of the Johannine Jesus is found. That is, the comparison of the new origin from above with physical birth arises from the imprecision (or the overflow of meaning) of the word *anōthen*. Does it refer to another physical birth or another beginning occasioned by transcendent forces? Therein, as the reader, I am forced to ask how a spiritual rebirth is like a physical birth. The ambiguity of *pneuma* allows for an image of the Spirit as wind. The double meaning of *hypsoō* ("lifted up") invites the reader to anticipate the meaning of the crucifixion by comparing it with a royal enthronement.

The surplus of meaning in the speeches of Jesus, in this case at least, gives the language its metaphorical quality. Metaphor is crafted out of ambiguity. That should not surprise us, since metaphor feeds on excess of meaning, often excess that is never conscious until the poet is brave enough to hint at it. Hence, the surplus meaning residing in a simple story of a shepherd who leaves ninety-nine sheep to search for a single stray lamb evades pedestrian thought and explodes our consciousness when it is offered. On the other hand, the metaphorical use of ambiguity in this passage is linguistic rather than narrative. That is, it feeds on the ambiguity of single words and phrases, rather than an ambiguous plot line. There is no narrative of one who is born and then experiences a new beginning, or of a child wondering about the sound and comings and goings of the wind. The metaphors of the passage are linguistic as opposed to narrative.

Still, that distinction may not be quite adequate, since each of the words or phrases miniaturizes a single basic story. The narrative quality of the metaphors in this passage then may be implicit. (How easy it would be, for instance, to create a story out of each of the ambiguous expressions of the passage.) However, such a thesis demands further and separate attention which we cannot afford on this occasion. Whether or not that thesis can be defended, it is still the case that metaphor in our passage is fabricated with the stuff of ambiguity.

Stacked and Progressive Metaphors

Another feature of the making of metaphor in John 3 is the way in which the images are "stacked." The reader is systematically led to quest the resolution of the earlier metaphor in the next. Hence,

> BORN *anōthen* TO ENTER THE KINGDOM OF GOD
>   leads to

BORN OUT OF WATER AND SPIRIT
   leads to
SPIRIT IS LIKE WIND
   leads to
THE SON OF MAN BEING LIFTED UP.

The strategy of the author is to pile image upon image, letting each illumine and each conceal the others. Image is superimposed on image, creating a literary ecosystem of metaphor. Such a strategy is not limited to our passage, for one can witness just such a stacking of images in 10:1-18[19] as well as elsewhere in the Fourth Gospel.

Yet there is an implicit progression discernible in the sequence of the images of our passage. The Spirit appears to be the key to the image of the *anōthen* birth. Spirit is, however, only understandable in the context of the event of the crucifixion-enthronement of the Son of Man. There is no resolution of the metaphors, no explanation of the parable, no delimitation of the reference. Yet there is direction for the reader's contemplation of these mysteries. Ultimately, the passage suggests that all the previous images must be considered in the light of the crucifixion-enthronement and witnessing the communion of heaven and earth in that event. From a theological perspective, the author has placed the cross at the apex of the images of the passage and of the discussion of entering the kingdom of God. From a literary perspective, the author has tantalized the reader at this point with the grand climax of the entire narrative (the crucifixion-resurrection). The reader's anticipation of Jesus' glorious triumph has been drastically qualified by the promise of a conclusion at the foot of the cross.

Johannine Metaphor and Synoptic Parable

A final, concluding observation about the making of metaphor in John 3:1-15 entails consideration of Johannine metaphorical language and the narrative parables attributed to Jesus in the Synoptic Gospels. My suggestion is simply that the two share a fundamental functional similarity. What we have come to think of as distinctive about the synoptic narrative parables is subtly evident in the metaphors of this passage. Like the best of Jesus' synoptic parables, the metaphors of this passage are diaphorical as opposed to throwaway epiphors. They are both participatory in the sense that they clearly invite the reader to share in the discovery of meaning and surprising in that they both make startling comparisons. The narrative parables and the metaphors of 3:1-15 both explore another metaphor (the dominion of God) in relationship with very different earthly phenomena. Moreover, the Johannine metaphors share a paradoxical quality with the narrative parables, if only in the sense that meaning resides in the tension among the four images of our passage. The poetic quality of the Johannine mini-images and the parables is evident insofar as the metaphors of this text have power to initiate new experience, as do the narratives told by Jesus. The realism so well attested in Jesus' parables is retained in John 3:1-15 in the use of the familiar to invite consideration of the transcendent. The pairing of parables common in the Synoptics (e.g., Mark 4:26-32) is witnessed here in the "stacking" of metaphors. The implicit narrative character of the Johannine images, hinted at above, might add still another possible common feature between them and the synoptic narrative parables.

I do not wish to venture a historical conclusion to a literary study. However, I propose only the possibility that the parabolic tradition associated with Jesus may be preserved in a very different way in the metaphors attributed to him in the Gospel of John.

Chapter Twelve

The Dismantling of Decisional Faith (John 6:25-71)

The discourse segment of John 6 has been the subject of frequent investigations. (For a recent bibliography on John 6, see Beasley-Murray 81–82.) Often it has been read in terms of its relationship with Hebraic and Jewish themes (cf. e.g., Borgen, *Bread from Heaven*) and often in search of its sacramental meaning.[1] The symbolism of the language attributed to Jesus in these verses has intrigued scholars for centuries, and its pivotal role in the whole narrative of chapters 1 through 12 is clear to some interpreters.[2]

This interpretation of 6:25-71 does not intend to minimize the importance of other investigations but only to supplement them. My interest here is in the exploration of the general function of the language of the passage on and in readers. The method used in this essay asks how the discourse/dialogue of verses 25-71 functions in its narrative context; how the language performs in a particular reading experience. Hence, I am concerned only with what the text does to a particular reader. The conviction underlying this method is that the whole of the passage may impact readers in some unusual ways.[3]

In particular I seek a greater self-consciousness in the reading of this text. Consequently, this witness to the reading is intentionally and intensely personal. In this passage I was struck by the way in which Jesus persistently and gradually dismantles the inquiry and the pretense of faith exhibited by his dialogue partners and demolishes the beginnings of some kinds of faith. I experienced this passage as a challenge to one's understanding of faith or of the beginnings of faith.[4] To anticipate my conclusion, the text may have the effect of questioning the notion that belief or faith is rooted in personal decision in response to Jesus, a theme that is sometimes attributed to the Fourth Gospel (cf. e.g., Forestell, 103–13).

Of course, a description of the way in which this reader experiences the text is but one among many possibilities, and I make no claim for its being a "true" reading of the text (if there is such a thing). This paper is a witness, if you will, to what the text did to this particular reader at one particular time.[5] One purpose of the paper is to discover what value, if any, there might be in this sort of experiment.

The essay will move through three stages. The first is a summary of a reading experience of the passage. The second stage will reflect on the performance of the text in the reading experience. Finally, the study will offer some theological and hermeneutical conclusions.[6]

A Reading of John 6:25-71

The general context for the passage includes a number of encounters with previous portions of the gospel.[7] Most important for our interests is the fact that the reader has seen certain characters engaged in significant discussion with Jesus on at least two occasions—one as remarkably unsuccessful as the other was fruitful. In chapter 3 Nicodemus comes to Jesus with what appears to be an interest in learning from him (i.e., he calls Jesus "teacher," 3:2). The reader, however, watches as Nicodemus fails to understand Jesus—fails even to be able to ask significant questions—with the result that he is gradually brought to silence and disappears entirely from the discussion. In chapter 4 the reading experience is very different. Here a Samaritan woman engages Jesus in vital issues of tradition and theology. By the conclusion of this dialogue, the woman is brought to some degree of faith and shares her new faith with members of her village with the result that they confess Jesus to be "Savior of the world" (4:42). (S. M. Schneiders describes the Samaritan woman as "a genuine theological dialogue partner," 191.) The impression is that discussion with Jesus is possible but not always realized.

The immediate context of the passage under consideration is the experience of reading two wondrous stories. First, Jesus has successfully fed the crowd in 6:1-15, then walked across the chaotic waters to come to his distressed disciples and brought them safely to shore (6:16-21). The reader is filled with a sense of awe as a result of these two episodes and anticipates the popular reception of Jesus, even as 6:15 suggests. So, I enter the discussion that ensues after verse 24 with anticipation of the hero's glorious acclamation by the people. The anticipation is qualified, however, by the fact that 6:15 implies that the crowd's enthusiasm had been wrongly motivated. Still, by this time in the reading of the gospel, the reader is prepared to be surprised by developments in the plot.

In the light of the two previous attempts to hold discussion with Jesus, the reader wonders what success the "crowd" will have in engaging Jesus in dialogue. (The antecedent of "they" in verse 25 appears to be the *ochlos*, "crowd," of verse 24.) Will it be a profitable discussion, like the one with the Samaritan woman, or a futile one as witnessed in 3:1ff.? Like the discussion with Nicodemus, the crowd, not Jesus, initiates this conversation; and, like Nicodemus (3:2), they call Jesus "Rabbi" (v. 25). The Pharisee's failure to engage Jesus in discussion looms large in the reader's mind. The crowd's initial question is enigmatic,[8] but Jesus' response is challenging. Rather than answering their inquiry, he seems to chastise them for their motives in seeking him (v. 26)—Beasley-Murray calls Jesus' response "brusque" (90)—and then commands them to labor for "food that endures to eternal life" (v. 27). The reader is not sure what that food might be but remembers the "living water" that wells "up to eternal life" (4:10-14). The inference is to compare the feeding story earlier in the chapter with some other form of nourishment still to be discovered.

The crowd responds to Jesus' exhortation to "labor" (*ergazesthe*) for food that "endures for eternal life" with a very rational question: "What must we do to perform the works (*erga*) of God?" It is an honest inquiry that has also occurred to the perceptive reader. To their question, however, Jesus answers that the work of God is to believe in the one sent by God (v. 29). What does "the work of God" mean? Is this an invitation to believe?

His remark evokes the crowd's second question in verse 30: "What sign (*sēmeion*) are you going to give us then, so that we may see it, and believe you?" They want to believe. I remember that experiencing a "sign" occasions faith (2:11) and like this reader, the crowd wants some grounds for believing in Jesus (although one may wonder why the marvelous feeding is not sign enough). They support the legitimacy of their question with appeal to their tradition. God had fed their ancestors in the wilderness. Jesus' reply shocks this reader with its polemic tone and his attack on the crowd's sacred tradition.[9] It was not Moses who fed them but the Father, who gives the true bread for "life." God's bread comes down from heaven (vs. 32-33). Therefore, the food that "endures (a form of *menō*) for eternal life" (v. 27) is not to be identified with God's feeding of Israel.

Even though Jesus has assaulted their religious heritage, the crowd responds with a request for such bread, and the conversation begins to sound as if it will be a productive encounter (compare the Samaritan woman's request in 4:15). Jesus' dialogue partners in this case express an authentic quest and an openness to receive that of which Jesus speaks.[10] The crowd has won this reader's sympathy and even admiration.

Jesus then proceeds to say that he is the bread of life and that those who come to him and believe will never hunger or thirst again (v. 35). Apparently, the people have not believed, even though they have followed him some distance to this locale. Those who are given (*didōsin*) to him by the Father come to him, Jesus says (v. 37). Verses 38-40 go on to make claims for the special relationship Jesus has with the Father. This is followed by God's will that nothing should be lost, that those who believe should have "eternal life," and that believers will be "raised up at the last day." Belief becomes vitally important, since it entails eternal life. The conversation has now moved to the crucial matter of faith, life, and the "last day."

While the reader acknowledges that Jesus is offering himself as the bread of life, his words appear harsh and obscure (not unlike the words spoken to Nicodemus), especially given the fact that the people have demonstrated what seems to this reader to be a genuine receptivity. On the other hand, the reader hears echoes of Jesus' conversation with the Samaritan woman. There Jesus claims that he is the source of "living water" (4:10); here he claims to be "bread of life" (v. 35). As he told the Samaritan woman that whoever drinks of the water he gives "will never thirst" (4:14a), he now says to the crowd that those coming to him "shall not hunger" and "shall never thirst" (v. 35). The dialogue has promising possibilities.

Still, the reader is puzzled when the "crowd" of verses 25-40 suddenly disappears, and at verse 41 another group—"the Jews"—enters the conversation. More important is that the reader has felt some sympathy for the crowd to this point and experienced their questions and requests as genuine inquiry. Whatever promise their exchange with Jesus might have had is unfulfilled. This new group "began to complain (*egoggyzon*) about him" (v. 41). Inquiry has shifted to skepticism: "Is not this Jesus, the son of Joseph?" (v. 42). This reader finds himself an observer, distanced from the new dialogue partners, when earlier he had some sense of participation with the crowd. These "Jews" discern a conflict between what they know about Jesus and what he is now claiming for himself. The reader cannot entirely share that conflict, since he has read 1:1-18 and—at least believes—he knows Jesus' true identity.

Jesus' response to the complaint of "the Jews" is the assertion that they cannot believe unless they are drawn by the Father (*oudeis dynatai elthein pros me ean mē ho patēr ho pempsas me helkysē auton*—"No one can come to me unless drawn by the Father who sent me"). He accompanies his response with the repetition of the promise that the believer will be raised up (v. 44). Those who are taught by God come to him, Jesus says (vs. 45-

46). He contrasts his offer of bread with the tradition of the manna given from heaven, for this bread provides a life freed from death (vs. 47-51a).

The dialogue has brought me to a dilemma. Faith is clearly of utmost importance. Yet faith seems contingent on matters beyond human will. The Father "gives" believers to Jesus and "draws" them. What role then does the reader have in responding to Jesus? The disturbing words, "the bread that I will give for the life of the world is my flesh" (v. 51b), intensify my dilemma. This seems an even more drastic claim than those made to the crowd. Strangely, this reader begins to feel some identification with the complaint of the Jews, for I too ask, "How can this man give us his flesh to eat?" (v. 52). Jesus' answer to what the Jews ask confuses this reader all the more. His speech heightens the bewildering identification of his flesh with the life-giving bread. One must "eat" (*phagein*) his flesh (v. 53), even "feed on" (*trōgō*) it (v. 54), and drink his blood. (The word in 6:53 is *phagēte*, which is the second aorist subjunctive of *esthio*.) Those who do not do so "have no life," and those who do have "*eternal* life" and resurrection (vs. 53-54), for his flesh and blood are "true" (*alēthēs*) food and drink (v. 55). They are promised that they will "abide in" Jesus, and he in them (v. 56). Then, the speech ends reiterating again the benefit of such a feeding—eternal life (vs. 57-58).

This reader wonders. How am I to eat this flesh and drink this blood? Faith is the vital link and is invited. On the other hand, it seems to transcend the reader's own volition. Believers are "given" and "drawn" by God, so what am I left to do in order to believe and hence eat and drink as Jesus commands? I am left feeling powerless to act in the face of the radical words I have read.

Struggling with those radical words and the feeling of helplessness given what has been said about God's role in believing, I am surprised—yet in another sense reassured—when the identity of the discussion partners shifts again in verse 60. The unbelief among the disciples surprises me, since I had been led to think that they were the ones who believed in Jesus (e.g., 2:11). Yet I am reassured, because now it is even the disciples who "complain" about their master's words. With me, they ask who can accept (*akouō*—literally, "hear") such words (v. 60)? In Jesus' response in verses 61-62 he says in effect: "You haven't seen anything yet! If this offends you, how will you respond to the Son of Man's ascension to where he originated?" But his next words are the cause of more reflection than offense. He claims that the "spirit gives life; the flesh is useless" and that his words are spirit (v. 63). What can this mean in the light of what he has just said about the importance of eating his flesh? The shift to spirit suggests that the previous speech should not be taken literally; but that leaves unresolved what sense it makes if one looks for the "spirit" in it.

The last segment of the speech begins with what should be obvious but is striking: "among you there are some who do not believe" (v. 64a). The storyteller explains that Jesus knew "from the first" (*ex archēs*) who believed and who would betray him (v. 64b). Jesus seems to elaborate the narrator's words by reiterating that those who come to him do so only because it is "granted (*ē dedomenon*) by the Father" (v. 65). Again, this reader must ask what it means to believe, given the fact that some disciples do not believe, that Jesus knew it all along, and that one is able to come to him only because of the Father's "granting" (i.e., "giving") it. The discussion moves toward a tragic conclusion with many of the disciples leaving Jesus (v. 66). Their abandonment of Jesus threatens the reader, since the whole narrative to this point had nurtured his identification with this group. The discussion has failed, it seems, as did the one with Nicodemus. The fact that not all disciples believe weakens my sense of any power to contribute to my believing, as does Jesus' claim that he has foreknowledge of who the believers are, and (again) that faith must be given. I recall 1:11 and wonder if my own uncertainty about my faith takes me with the departing disciples. There is no security in counting oneself among the disciples. I see myself, along with Nicodemus and the disciples, walking back out into the darkness (1:5).

Yet there is one more installment in the passage. This time Jesus takes the initiative and addresses the Twelve. This is the first time in the discussion Jesus has initiated a conversation with a group. Without extratextual information, this reader would have no idea who the Twelve are, since this is the gospel's first use of that designation. Jesus asks if they will also leave (v. 67), suggesting that the twelve are not identical with the disciples who have just joined the Jews in being offended by Jesus' words. Peter makes his bold statement of faith on behalf of the others (vs. 68-69). Faith is possible! One can will (exercise volition) to believe in the face of the difficulties of the words of this puzzling Jesus!

Or, so I may think, until I read Jesus' response to Peter's words. Jesus has "chosen" (*exelexamēn*) the twelve, not they him. Yet one of them is a devil (v. 70)! The narrator eases this reader's discomfort a bit by explaining that the "devil" is Judas who will betray Jesus (v. 71). Verse 64 is the first the reader hears of betrayal, and now the betrayer is named. He is among the intimate faithful circle of disciples, but with some knowledge of the story of Jesus told elsewhere I am inclined to put this Judas in a special category among the group. Still, the believers are the chosen, and even then there may be "devils" among those who are chosen.

With some such uncertainty and discomfort, the reader comes to the conclusion of the conversation. I am left still pondering the words about

Jesus' identity as the bread of life and about eating his flesh and drinking his blood. Equally disturbing is how one comes to this banquet at all. Coming to Jesus and believing in him is required for such "eating." Yet the only believers in this discussion are those selected by Jesus and, even then, there is the possibility of devils among the selected ones!

However, what is faith? How am I to understand the origin of this all-important believing? Can one ever know with any confidence that they believe?

Reflections on the Performance of the Text

This sketch of my witness to the experience of reading 6:25-71 provides a basis on which to reflect on what the text does—at least to one reader. Even if my own reading experience is alien to others, perhaps these reflections help to understand the performance of the text. Several different kinds of reflections are important for elucidating the way the language of the text works.

First in importance is *the movement of the passage* as it is experienced in the reading. It is comprised of eight discrete movements, with four distinct groups engaging Jesus in dialogue.

A == vs. 25-27

B == vs. 28-29 $\longleftrightarrow$ JESUS AND THE CROWD

C == vs. 30-33

D == vs. 34-40

E == vs. 41-51 $\longleftrightarrow$ JESUS AND THE "JEWS"

F == vs. 52-58

(v. 59 ===Narrator's Comment)

G == vs. 60-66 $\longleftrightarrow$ JESUS AND THE DISCIPLES

H == vs. 67-71 $\longleftrightarrow$ JESUS AND THE TWELVE

With the exception of the last unit, each segment begins with a statement or question by a dialogue partner to which Jesus then responds. In H Jesus takes the initiative to begin a conversation with the twelve.

The groups designated as dialogue partners shift in the process of the development of the passage. Those who begin the conversation appear sincere, receptive inquirers. They have sought Jesus out (6:24), an act associated with the beginnings of discipleship. (The verb, *zēteō*, is used of discipleship in 1:38 and 20:15 but elsewhere of those who desire to persecute Jesus, e.g., 5:18. Therefore, the word is ambiguous of itself and apart from its context.) To be sure, their motives for pursuing Jesus are mixed (v. 26). They ask how Jesus got to this side of the lake (A), ask what they are to do to do God's works (B), and request a sign as a basis for the faith (C). In D they are portrayed as making a pious appeal for the bread Jesus has mentioned.[11]

In E and F, however, the discussion partners are clearly hostile. Jesus' words in D (not least of all the *egō eimi* ["I am"] in v. 35) evoke the complaint of "the Jews." They appear in the discussion as those who cannot accept Jesus' claims for himself and as clearly distinguished from the crowd (*ochlos*) of the previous units. In both E and F they are represented as skeptical of Jesus' words, and Jesus' response to them in E only intensifies their grumbling. In F it is their understanding of Jesus' identity that evokes his radical words about eating his flesh and drinking his blood.[12]

The dialogue partners change to the disciples in G, and their complaints implicitly identifies them with "the Jews" (v. 61). The reading effect of having the hostile opponents suddenly become disciples (v. 60) powerfully suggests that unbelief is not limited to Jesus' opponents. The introduction of the phenomenon of unbelieving disciples blurs the distinction between "the Jews" and "the disciples."

Finally, Jesus opens a conversation with the Twelve in H. This group is portrayed as a faithful collection among the larger circle of the disciples, in spite of the scandalous quality of their master's words. The pattern of movement betrays an increasingly hostile role attributed to the discussion partners in segments E through G, but is suddenly reversed in H.

The narrator plays an increasingly important role as the passage moves toward a conclusion. That voice first sets the stage for the dialogue and moves the text from narrative to discourse in verse 25a. After that, the narrator introduces the speakers in each of the sections. The storyteller's role becomes more frequent and more important in sections A through H. The guiding voice identifies the reaction of the Jews in verse 41 and describes their response in verse 52. When the discussion shifts to the disciples, that voice gives the reader insight into Jesus' unspoken knowledge: Jesus knows the disciples are murmuring (v. 61) and which of them does not genuinely believe (v. 64b). Finally, in section G the narrator tells the reader that "many of the disciples" disowned Jesus. In the final segment of the discussion, the narrator explains Jesus' comment in verse 70 and names Judas as the betrayer (v. 71).

The information about locale in verse 59 is the most puzzling of the narrator's words.[13] In terms of the reader experience, this intrusion serves as a buffer between the grumbling of the Jews and that of the disciples! Functionally the verse separates disciples (even unbelieving ones) from the religious institution, the synagogue. Does it then suggest boundaries between disciples, on the one hand, and the crowd and the Jews on the other? Yet verse 59 hardly breaks the flow of the whole passage, since the passage continues with grumbling and rejection. Location does not, it seems to me, figure prominently in the performance of the text.

The sections move steadily toward more and more extreme claims for Jesus' identity, reaching their climax in F. The movement of the discussion is essentially tragic in structure. It begins with genuine inquirers (if not believers), but Jesus becomes more and more offensive in each of the dialogue units until his words result in the loss of many of his disciples at the conclusion of G (v. 66). The discussion is, then, similar to the one with Nicodemus in which Jesus' dialogue partner fades away, in that case more because of incomprehension than unbelief.[14] The totally tragic quality of the structure of the discussion is qualified with Peter's confession in H. The final unit, however, has a still more tragic tone, insofar as it ends with the mention of Judas as one among the "faithful group."[15]

The *style* of the whole tragic passage is repetitious dialogue. The passage is genuine dialogue, as has been shown in the reflections on the movement of the passage. It is important to note, too, that the discussion partners frequently introduce the theme of a section. The crowd first raises the theme of the bread from heaven (v. 31), and Jesus' words about his identity in section F are occasioned by the Jews assertion that they know who Jesus is (v. 52).

More significant is the fact that the passage is filled with repetition while still progressing in thought.[16] Indeed, those who argue that the Johannine discourse style is spiral find evidence for their view here.[17] The major motif of the discussion is hunger and food as they are related to life. That theme moves toward a transformation in verse 63. Food is immediately introduced in verses 26-27 as is the theme of nourishment that yields "eternal life." Certain words and phrases are repeated almost tiresomely through the sections of the dialogue. "Eternal life" (*zōē aiōnios*) appears in verses 27, 40, 47, 51, 54, 58, and 68 and "life" (*zōē*) in verses 33, 53, 57, and 63. "Bread from heaven" (*artos ek tou oupanou*) or "bread of life" (*artos tēs zōēs*) is introduced in verse 31 and reoccurs in verses 35, 41, 48, 50,

51, and 58. Since belief is connected with the relationship between bread and eternal life, the verb, "to believe" (*pisteuō*) debuts early (v. 29) and is then used at least seven more times—verses 35, 36, 40, 47, 64 (twice), and 69. The bread that has eternal consequences is from heaven, hence it "descends" (*katabainō*, e.g., v. 33), even as Jesus claims he has descended (e.g., v. 38).[18] The combination of the descending bread and descending Jesus is found in verse 51. (The verb, *katabainō*, is also used in vs. 38, 42, 50, and 58.)

One may discern subtle connections between Jesus' identification with the nourishment that provides eternal life. The emphasis on the descent of Jesus and the bread climaxes with Jesus' reference to his own ascension (*anabainō*, v. 62). The crowd is urged to seek the food that "remains" (*menō*) in verse 27, and in verse 56 Jesus promises that those who feed on his flesh and drink his blood "abide (*menō*) in me, and I in them." In the climax of the discussion belief and eternal life are found together (vs. 68-69).

Other expressions are emphasized through repetition. Jesus speaks of himself as sent from God five times (vs. 29, 38, 39, 44, 57). The promise of the eschatological resurrection (*anastēsō auto en tē eschatē hēmera*—"I will raise him on the last day" and its variations) appears four times (vs. 39, 40, 44, and 54). The solemn *amēn, amēn legō humin* ("truly, truly I say to you") is used four times (vs. 26, 32, 47, and 53), and the *egō eimi* ("I am") expression three times (vs. 35, 48, and 51).

All of this documents what the reader experiences as a continuous use of key expressions in the conversation—hammering away at the passage's themes. However these repetitions also suggest the way in which terms are nuanced in slight ways to further the progression of the themes of the passage. For example, the verb "eat" (*esthiō*) is used consistently through the discussion (e.g., vs. 26, 31, 50, 53), but then is replaced by "feed on" (*trōgō*) in verses 54-58. Eating is supplemented by references to thirst (e.g., v. 35) and drinking (vs. 53 and 56). The discussion spirals up from the food the Son of Man gives (v. 27) to the Father's giving the bread from heaven (e.g., v. 32) to Jesus' identity as the bread of life from heaven (v. 51). There is clear progression, therefore, even amid the repetitious style of the passage.

The role of reader identification is complex, for the reader's identification with the various groups changes even within their respective sections. This reader gradually became identified with the crowd in their quest and was sympathetic toward their queries. At first distanced from the Jews, I was brought closer to them by the time of verse 52. This was in part due to the reader's own uneasiness with Jesus' statements and to my discovery of myself in some of the reactions of the Jews. There was mixed attraction and repulsion toward the disciples. At first, I was surprised, since the reading had never revealed unbelief in the characterization of this group. Still, this reader felt reassured by the fact that they too were offended by Jesus' words. The disciples, however, also posed a certain threat to this reader, because of the possibility of my being one of these unbelieving disciples. The Twelve elicited immediate identification. This reader wants to think of himself as the faithful believer modeled in Peter's confession in verses 68-69. Then, however, the Twelve become threatening when Jesus says that he had chosen them and that there is a devil among them.

This tracing of the reader's shifting identification is a witness to the text's power, as well as to the reader's vulnerability to the text. At times, I experienced the text almost toying with me. It first enticed, teased, pulled me close and finally pushed me away. The strategy of the text is to keep the reader's response off guard and in a state of flux. While it is dangerously subjective to speak of emotional responses to a text, it seems to me obvious that the work of the text entails such response, especially in a religious document. If the text intends to evoke the response of the whole person, as I believe 20:31 implies, then it will influence the reader at an emotional as well as cognitive and volitional level. At least in the Fourth Gospel, that influence is most often found in the text's characterizations. In my own case, this text invites the reader to struggle with the characters in the plot to discover at a deeper level what was read in the prologue concerning Jesus' identity. That struggle goes on through the process of identification with and distancing from the persons portrayed in the narrative. In the case of the passage under consideration, the process entails the pulsation between, on the one hand, finding oneself in each of the four groups with whom Jesus converses and, on the other hand, disavowing association with those groups. John 6:25-71 is a prime example of Johannine characterization and its impact on the careful reader.[19]

As a result of the reading, *the function of metaphor in the passage* is also obvious. The bread that results in eternal life is the central metaphor, and the passage's performance is largely due to the comparative language around that theme. The passage steadily expands the metaphor and strengthens its intensity as the dialogue progresses. Finally, the exaggeration of the metaphor renders the language of the passage offensive to the discussion partners, as well as puzzling to this reader.

The metaphoric language begins in verse 27 with a simple comparison of perishable food that satisfies hunger and "the food that endures to eternal life" (*tēn brōsin tēn menousan eis zōēn aiōnion*)—a comparison not entirely impossible to imagine. Then Jesus speaks of that potent food as God's "bread from heaven" (v. 32) and identifies it with that which gives life to the world (v. 33). With the mention of life, the comparison begins

to threaten the reader's world view. Next in verse 35, for the first time
Jesus equated the bread with himself and contrasts it with manna from
heaven in verses 49-50. The identification of the bread from heaven with
Jesus' own flesh (v. 51b) further embellishes the metaphor. Verse 53 first
extends it with the insistence that one must eat (*esthiō*) then feed on (*trōgō*)
the flesh of Jesus (vs. 54-58). Second, the metaphor is extended to its final
extreme with the inclusion of "drinking my blood" in verses 53-56 and
the conclusion that "my flesh is food indeed (*alēthēs estin brōsis*) and my
blood is drink indeed (*alēthēs estin posis*)" in verse 55.

"Feeding on" the food that is Jesus' own flesh and "drinking" his
blood is the climactic offense of the passage for the dialogue partners
(even the disciples). The passage pursues a simple metaphor beyond its
ordinary limits. A simple comparison has become a shocking juxtaposing
of realities. In doing so, the passage violates a common sense view of metaphor, namely, that any comparative language has intrinsic limitations.
The comparison of one commonly known reality to illumine a lesser-
known (or unknown) reality works, but only within certain boundaries
of similarities. (For example, to say that he ran like a frightened rabbit is
illuminating, but we do not then normally speak of the way the person
hopped with his hind legs!)[20]

Clearly "feeding/drinking" is no simple metaphor (i.e., simile), even
though one could say that it begins as such. The language births new
meaning through its radicality. (McFague describes the category as "radical metaphor"; *Speaking in Parables* 50–56.) The very absurdity of its even-
tual form in the passage entices human imagination into new possibilities
for construing reality. In P. Ricoeur's terms, the metaphor of the passage
exploits the sense in which such language uses *dissimilarity* rather than
similarity ("Biblical Interpretation" 77).[21] In this passage the literal sense of
Jesus' words compels the reader to imagine a possible meaning in which
Jesus' body is bread, struggling with the obviously ridiculous sense of the
equation. The result of the dissimilarity in the metaphor questions the literal meaning while inviting the construction of another meaning. Consequently, the metaphor challenges the reader's construction of reality and
implies a new construction, without ever describing that new understanding of reality. In sum, the metaphor functions to endanger the reader's
security in the truth and ignite the pursuit of some new world, yet only
insinuated. Its functional nature, then, might be called, "root metaphor,"
in the sense that the tension between the two terms of the language (bread
and flesh) is never resolved and is inexhaustible. The tension is felt most
immediately in the fact that we can never reduce the metaphor to a simple
propositional statement. That very tension energizes the quest for a new
construction of meaning (Ricoeur, *Interpretation Theory* 64).

Therefore, the heart of the scandal of Jesus' words is a metaphorical language that violates its own limitations. The offense results from the metaphor's questioning of the boundaries of human knowledge. Radical metaphor entices and teases the human imagination to conceive beyond the limits of ordinary language, i.e., language that is supposed to name reality. This sort of absurd metaphor is language pushed beyond the outer limits of that which can be spoken and signifies the unknown and mysterious, promising the possibility of new knowing. As it is found here, metaphor may be part of what others have called Johannine "overlexicalizing," which I take to be the density of reference structured into language (Malina, "Sociolinguistic Perspective").[22] In just such a way, the language of our text tests the reader's capacity for imagination and—more fundamentally—calls into question the adequacy of language's signification. Thereby it challenges the adequacy of the reader's conception of reality, since that conception is constructed and expressed in language. (See Kysar, "Johannine Metaphor," reprinted in part 3 of this volume.)

This raises the final and crucial reflection on this reader's experience of the text. The central metaphor challenges the readers' construction of reality and invites new structures of meaning. Adjunct to this challenge is another: *the demolition of human confidence in decisional faith.* A reader gains the total impact of the passage through its movement, the use of repetitious dialogue, identification with its characters, and the performance of the central metaphor. For this reader, at least, the text works to call into question the human capacity for faith and undermines any confidence that of their own volitional powers one can will belief. I acknowledge that this is not the sole function of the passage, or the one that commentators most often identify as the "meaning" of the text. Certainly, the heart of the passage is christological, and no careful reading of the text can avoid that conclusion. Nonetheless, for at least some readers one possible result of a close reading of this christological text is a serious questioning of the assumption that faith is solely a human responsibility.

To understand how the text performs this demolition of decisional faith it is necessary, first, to observe how believing is treated throughout the passage. Belief is among the first themes introduced in the passage. In section B Jesus declares, "This is the work of God, that you believe in him whom he has sent" (v. 29). Following that announcement, the value and importance of believing is scattered throughout the passage. In verse 35, faith is equated with coming to Jesus and never hungering or thirsting. Faith is crucial, for it entails eternal life (e.g., v. 40). Believers even "have eternal life" (*ho pisteuōn echei zōēn aiōnion*, v. 47). Hence, to feed on Jesus' flesh and drink his blood is the nature of faith that gives life (v. 53).

But, second, we must ask what the passage suggests with regard to the origin of faith. This all-important belief appears at times in the course of the discussion to be the result of the human will—the individual's response to Jesus. In verses 28-29 the crowd asks what they must do, and Jesus responds that belief is the work of God. When taken as a statement of what God demands, this is an invitation to obey through believing. "Coming" and "believing" seem to be human acts (e.g., v. 35). God wills "that all (*pas*) who see the Son and believe in him have eternal life" (v. 40). Furthermore, the climax of the passage has Jesus asking the Twelve if they too will leave, implying that it is their decision. What it means to believe seems clearly to entail understanding who Jesus is and accepting his claims.

Yet the language of the text also works to challenge the assumption that human will alone is the origin of faith in response to Jesus, or, at the very least, to question any human confidence in the will to believe. The challenge begins in verse 29 with the ambiguous phrase, *to ergon tou theou* ("the work of God"),[23] and that ambiguity immediately teases the reader's assumptions about the origin of faith.[24] Do I do God's work when I believe, or is God's work the creation of faith in me?[25]

The questioning of willful belief continues, then, in a number of the passage's recurring themes. The first is in that enigmatic expression regarding the Father's "giving" the Son those who believe. We find this first in verse 37: "Everything that the Father gives me (*pan ho didōsin moi*) will come to me." Verse 39 repeats the theme in connection with the God's will: "that I should lose nothing of all that he has given me (*pan ho didōken moi*), but raise it up on the last day." However, this divine giving remains ambiguous throughout the passage.

Verse 44 is equally ambiguous. It speaks of faith being dependent on a divine "drawing" (*helkysē*). In response to the unbelief of the Jews, Jesus seems here to acknowledge that belief is possible only as a result of God's magnetic attraction of humans. That mysterious "drawing" is perhaps explicated in the next verse. In what appears to be a free citation of Isaiah 54:13 (Brown, *Commentary–Gospel* 1:271), Jesus speaks of those who are "taught by God." Then he declares, "Everyone who has heard and learned from the Father comes to me." Those who are drawn by God are those who have been taught by God. How is one, however, taught by God?

The final segments of the discussion only enhance the ambiguity of these expressions of the origin of faith. First, because of the narrative, the reader has come to think of those who follow Jesus as examples of the faith response to his words and deeds (e.g., 2:11). Yet verses 60-66 declare that there are disciples who do not believe. That declaration implicitly undermines this reader's confidence in his own supposedly believing response to Jesus. Verses 60-66 also announce that only those to whom it is "granted" (e.g., v. 65, *dedomenon*—again, "given") are able (*dynatai*) to come to Jesus (v. 45). That Jesus knows who will not believe (v. 64b) suggests his foreknowledge. Still, the haunting phrase "from the first" (*ex archēs*) may suggest something more. In 1:1 *en archē* ("in the beginning") implies that "the first" is the mysterious beginnings of reality. The possibilities of some divine determination rooted in eternity menace the reader.[26]

Even with its ambiguity, this language has, at best, shaken this reader's confidence in any faith decision. Still, the concluding segment seems to promise the reconstruction of confidence that decisional faith is possible. The Twelve are free to choose, and Peter models the faith response (v. 69). On the other hand, Jesus has chosen the Twelve, not they him, and there is a "devil" among the chosen faithful (v. 70).

When the whole of the passage is in view, one sees that in the discussions with each of the four groups Jesus utters ambiguous statements that may be construed as qualifications of the volitional quality of faith. To *the crowd* he speaks of the "work of God" (v. 29) and insists that believers are "given" to him by the Father (vs. 37 and 39). He tells *the Jews* that no one can believe unless they are first "drawn" by God (v. 44). The *disciples* are unbelieving, and Jesus knew *ex archēs* (from the first) who were believers and who were not (v. 64). Jesus also repeats to the disciples the claim that believers are given to him by the Father (v. 65). He reminds *the Twelve* that he had chosen them. The theme of God's role in originating the faith response runs through the whole discussion and is represented in the dialogue with each group of participants.

The text works to nurture the importance of believing. The issue at stake is nothing less than life, eternal life, and resurrection. Then, however, it works subtly to chip away at the foundation of confidence that faith is possible, at least through human will alone. Is it within human ability alone to respond to Jesus in faith? Does this divine work, giving, drawing, and teaching refer alone to God's initial act in Christ, or to some other activity in the human spirit? Is it enough that one wills faith? Faith may be as ill motivated as that of the crowd that seeks Jesus out, not because they saw signs but because they had eaten their fill earlier as a result of his wondrous feeding. Faith may be as fragile as that of the disciples who followed Jesus until they hear him expand this metaphor of bread to his own flesh and blood, and then they find their faith demolished by his words. Faith may even be genuine and steady, but there are "devils" among the believers. *The passage performs the demolition of any confidence in faith conceived as human decision.*[27]

Conclusions

The effort has been only to witness to a single reading of John 6:25-71 without any claim to the universal value of my experience of the text's work. Yet this witness has uncovered a haunting and muffled subtext within the passage that may perform the dismantling of human confidence and the construction of uncertainty. A few theological and hermeneutical observations are appropriate in conclusion.

First, an essentially christological passage has impact on the issue of faith. Christology cannot stand in isolation from the human response to claims made for Christ's identity. Not accidentally, our passage weaves the thread of faith into the fabric of Jesus' identity, for explication of that identity is whole cloth only with the inclusion of belief in that which transcends human experience. This is to say both that Christology evokes human response (belief or unbelief) and that Christology is in itself faith language—the assertion of faith.

Second, to speak of faith is always to speak of a response to divine presence. The Fourth Gospel is clear about that. The prologue speaks of response, both the rejection of the Word and his acceptance and belief in his name (1:11-12). Faith is always the result of what God does. The issue at stake in this essay is how much God does in evoking faith. The design of 1:14 ("the Word became flesh and lived among us") is to evoke faith. Still the faith response remains mysterious, insofar as something more in terms of God's activity seems at stake. A mysterious "drawing" by some power beyond human will plays a role in the faith response. That something more, for this reader at least, intrudes itself into the text of 6:25-71. Whether the text performs this function of itself or only because of a reader's location and condition or as some strange combination of both is beyond the scope of this inquiry. In its historical context the gospel may have sought among other things to account for why it is some believe while others do not. This much is certain: the work of the text for this reader has undermined any confidence and certainty in the human will alone to believe. In the place where that confidence and certainty in human will had grown, there is confidence and certainty only in the Word that still lives among us.[28]

Third, this reading of the passage solicits a hermeneutical observation. The readers' presuppositions about faith shape the way they experience the performance of the text. Readers predisposed to conceive of faith as individual decision in response to God's presence, in all likelihood, will not interpret the text as I did. Perhaps only those of us who have had the certainty of our faith challenged and who have experienced something of what might be called the "mystery of believing" will read the text in ways similar to this discussion of the passage. One is forced, I believe, to acknowledge that any such effort to elucidate the performance of the text's language has to take into account the reader's precondition. The reader's "social location" needs also to include matters such as religious tradition and faith experience, as well as gender, ethnicity, and class.[29]

Finally, then, the reader of 6:25-71 has still to experience those provocative words of 12:32: "I, when I am lifted up from the earth, will draw all people to myself." As disabling as 6:15-71 may seem to the human desire to believe, 12:32 suggests the hope that the cross in some enigmatic way is the Father's "drawing" (helkō) referred to in 6:44.[30] If our passage functions to dismantle all human pretense to the capacity for faith, the reader may gain hope that, in the Gospel of John, the cross makes faith possible. John 6:25-71 points beyond itself to the conclusion of the narrative of which it is only one part.

PART IV

Postmodern Criticism

A good many cultural critics and others believe that our North American culture stands on the brink of radical change. Few would deny this, although they cannot always agree on the nature of the change currently underway. A considerable number, however, believe we are entering a "postmodern" era. By postmodern, they mean the period following the demise of the assumptions that arose and held sway with the advent of modernism in the period of the so-called Enlightenment (the seventeenth and eighteenth centuries). Others contend, to the contrary, the changes we are experiencing are actually a new and more vigorous modernism that will reinforce the assumptions of the Enlightenment.

This is not the place to argue for my contention that we are, indeed, entering a postmodern period in our history. Rather, I should like only to sketch my view with special attention to what the changes may mean for biblical interpretation. Actually, my view of those changes arises from attempts to understand and practice a workable method of reading a text. I now realize that my affinity for the features of biblical interpretation that today we call postmodern have their origin in the convictions that date back to my graduate years. The first article in this collection argues that Bultmann's interpretation of the prologue of John underscores the contention that there is no such thing as an entirely objective, unprejudiced reading of Scripture. My dissertation was an attempt to demonstrate the influence of the exegete's perspective (shaped by his or her theological views) on his or her interpretation of John 1:1-18. On the other hand, Bultmann convinced me of the merger of the objective and subjective in exegesis. Moreover, my interest in philosophy eventually made historical research seem ineffectual.

Gradually, through the forty years of my career as teacher and scholar I came to three conclusions. *The first has to do with the way in which texts arise from the author's own assumptions and perspectives, shaped by her or his position of power, and the way that texts tend to sustain social structures.* This is why I am now interested in what is called ideological criticism—the analysis of the structures an author seeks to propagate (cf. Yee). I now believe that interpreters of biblical texts have the obligation to ask how our interpretations (1) reflect and sustain our positions of power and (2) will work to strengthen the status quo (cf. Schüssler Fiorenza).

The second conclusion is that most historical reconstructions done for the sake of interpreting the Fourth Gospel are excessively speculative and beyond provability. First I grew less and less enamored with the Q hypothesis. This was largely so because of the detailed pursuit of the historical setting, various editions, and origin of the presumed collections of sayings. These efforts seemed to construct a vast edifice on nothing but the tip of a needle. Then, the same sort of disillusionment overtook my interest in isolating the sources used in the composition of John. Where once I was an ardent advocate of the possibilities of identifying those sources (cf. Kysar, "Source Analysis"), I am now convinced that any such effort is futile and reflects more of the scholars' commitments than of actual history. Again, this conclusion was a reaction to the excessive detail proposed on the basis of the thinnest of evidence.[1] This suspicion of historical reconstructions resulted in my abandonment of the theory of the expulsion of the Johannine Christians from the synagogue (cf. the article "Tale of a Theory" in this collection) and the effort to reconstruct the Christian community related to the Fourth Gospel (cf. Kysar, "Whence and Whither").

The third conclusion to which I have been driven is "the instability of language" to such a degree that every text is hopelessly multidimensional. In describing Paul de Man's view of language, Stephen D. Moore wrote, the "self-deconstructing drive in text is to be explained with reference to language. Because language is a bottomless quicksand of rhetorical figures (such as metaphor), it is fatally unstable" (*Mark and Method* 87; cf. ch. 5 of Kysar and Webb, *Postmoderns*). Such a view of language means that a reader can never "pin the meaning of a text down," that the meaning of language is an ever-changing kaleidoscope of suggestion and implication, and that the "true meaning" of a text (if there is even such a thing) can never be discovered.

This radical (and self-deconstructive) nature of language flowed out of my increasing interest in ambiguity and metaphor in the Johannine texts. Several of the articles in the previous section chronicle my gradual movement toward what might be called "a postmodernist view of language."

This autobiographical sketch of the change in my views in the last ten years suggests why I have gathered some of my recent articles and grouped them under the title "Postmodern Criticism." I am not concerned to argue that my tendencies in recent years are accurate predictions of the future in biblical interpretation, nor would I offer these essays as models of postmodern criticism. My only interest is to whet your appetite for what the future decades in biblical studies might bring. If the tenants of postmodernism become the norm, it will radically revise the process of interpreting a text. It remains to be seen, even, if interpretation will be possible at all or whether we should surrender it as an unrealistic goal. In which case, of course, we would have to label the act of reading a text something other than interpretation. What is clear now is simply that new trends in interpretation are indications of what may be fully realized only in the future.

The four essays in this section represent some of the themes in Johannine studies that are likely to be significant, in one form or another, in the next several decades. The first of the articles ("The Gospel of John in the Twenty-first Century") is no more than a brief glimpse at some of the ways in which John may be important for the future church in the United States. It is no more than a description of some possibilities for the interpretation of John and their consequences and reflects my very earliest venture into the question of what the future might hold. "The 'Other' in Johannine Literature" is a kind of ideological interpretation that includes both the Gospel of John and the epistles of John. It gives expression to the "ethics of interpretation" in our day, as well as raising the issue of "the other" in postmodernist thought. Third, "The Expulsion from the Synagogue: A Tale of a Theory" exemplifies the issues entailed in one historical reconstruction of the situation in which the Fourth Gospel was written and the concrete issues it supposedly addresses. It challenges a theory that I once held but which has become increasing difficult for me as the whole matter of doing history has been called into question by postmodernists. Finally, "The Sacraments and Johannine Ambiguity" emphasizes the role of the dense ambiguity of John as it affects the interpretation of passages that some have argued refer to the sacraments of the Lord's Supper and/ or baptism. It exemplifies the instability of language as it is used in the Gospel of John.

Time alone will determine whether these four articles foreshadow the kind of Johannine research we will do and read in this new century. While I do not pretend to know the degree to which postmodernism will be realized, I do contend that in the future decades of biblical interpretation critics will have to grapple with the matters exemplified in the following essays.

Chapter Thirteen

The Gospel of John in the Twenty-first Century

In the course of the twentieth century, interpreters of John have experienced one earthquake after another—shaking the hermeneutical earth under our feet. The future promises to be no less tumultuous. The "big one" may be yet to come for readers of John (cf. Kysar, "Living at the Epicenter"). Of course, predictions are risky and cheap, but my reflections on the Gospel of John at the close of the twentieth century serve as an invitation to consider the future. I propose that in the twenty-first century, at least in North America, the interpretation of the Gospel of John will be reshaped still more. At least two essential questions are likely to play key roles in this basic change. Opposing and sometimes contradictory features of John, I suggest, arouse those questions. The two questions involve these matters: first, the sectarian, exclusivistic over against the trans-sectarian and inclusivistic themes; second, the ambiguous contrasted with absolute truth-claims.

Sectarian and Trans-sectarian Themes

The first question has to do with the Fourth Gospel in the context of the changing religious scene in North American and evolves around sectarianism. How will the sectarian nature of Johannine Christianity function for a church that finds itself in a sectarian relationship with its culture? This question, of course, assumes that in the twenty-first century the whole Christian church in North America will be forced to take its place as just one more religious option in a fully pluralized and globalized culture (cf.

Hughes and Kysar). The final remnants of the Constantinian era of the church will fade away, and the church will find itself to be something of a sect group in relation to its culture. By sectarian I mean that Christians will constitute a social minority in the culture—a marginal group—and will tend to understand themselves over against the world (cf. Mead). In such a setting as this, John is likely to sound newly relevant. Its sectarian language and ideas (for which it is infamous) will appeal to a church under siege and offer sanction and even empowerment for that kind of mentality. The outsider-insider distinctions implied in so much of the gospel may encourage a new otherworldliness.

The essential question is whether we can and will interpret the Gospel of John in ways that appropriate the *best* of that sectarian strain without succumbing to what I take to be the *worst* of such a perspective. Can we find empowerment for a mission to the world—a mission that subverts the powers of injustice and oppression, on the one hand, and refuses, on the other hand, to be seduced by a hostility and hatred toward others? Can we think of ourselves as sent into the world that God so loves, and can we say no to the texts that invite us to regard opponents as demonic?

Clearly, the dangers of a contemporary sectarian view have surfaced since the tragedies of 9/11. The demonizing of the Islamic terrorists has sometimes encouraged an "us and them" mentality toward Islam in general. Or, at best we have had to resist the temptation to adopt such a mentality. The inclination is often to isolate ourselves from all Muslims and perpetuate the idea that Christianity contains truth and Islam falsehood. The inclination has been accelerated by the rhetoric of our nation's leaders which denounces the Islamic radicals as evil and touts North American democracy as the only worthy form of government. (Cf. the article "The 'Other' in Johannine Literature" in this section.)

In this kind of atmosphere, will the church be able to read and appropriate the gospel's trans-sectarian motifs? Will the Johannine witness to the Creator's love of the *kosmos* ("world"—see 3:16) sufficiently qualify the gospel's sectarian strains? Will the often-muted strains of mission in the gospel drown out the implicit hostility toward the church's opponents?

Inherent in this first question is a second matter that focuses on the exclusive versus inclusive tension of the narrative of the Gospel of John. In a remarkable way, this gospel often sounds so very exclusive and sectarian (e.g., love only one another—15:12). Yet it also witnesses to a radical inclusion of at least some of the socially marginalized (for instance, the gospel's attention to women and Samaritans). Still, with this ironic contradiction the Fourth Gospel may provide sanction and empowerment for *either* the church's inclusive stance or exclusive posture toward others. Which will it be?

My first question about this pair of contradictory emphases does little more than suggest the importance of how John will be read and understood in a new cultural context. By what process will the church determine which side of these opposing motifs should guide its life, or in what kind of balance will they function as authoritative? That process will need to produce some clearer and bolder distinctions between the "normative" and the "contingent" in the text (if I may use that way of speaking of the different value of biblical ideas and teachings; see "Anti-Semitism and the Gospel of John" earlier in this collection).

A canonical reading of John may also be helpful in using the whole of the canon as a corrective to the contingent character of the Johannine themes. We will need a new courage to stand at times against the text and to practice a hermeneutic of suspicion that challenges the text's contingencies. At the same time, the hermeneutical process will need to allow the text to shape Christian life and witness in ways consistent with the word made flesh.

Ambiguous/Absolute Truth Claims

This second question relates to another polarity in the Fourth Gospel, namely, the ambiguous nature of much of its language, on the one hand, and the absolute character of some its declarations of what is truth, on the other. We might pose the issue in this way: Can the language of John continue to function in a revelatory way?

In this new century, the media are likely to become the most decisive factor in shaping human consciousness and reshaping language. The question is, then, how will that reformed consciousness read the language and imagery of John? Can that language and those images still convey the presence of a transcendent reality? In a curious way, I believe, the very ambiguities and polyvalence of John may become even more relevant than they have been in the past. My belief is rooted, admittedly, in a guess! It is a guess that in a culture dominated by the visual media and drowning in information, truth will become generally uncertain and far more ambiguous. Has it not already become so?

In such a culture, where truth is experienced as ambiguous and uncertain, the paradoxes, ironies, and enigmatic declarations of the Fourth Gospel may all take on a fresh quality. This gospel will speak more clearly through its ambiguities than we have allowed it to do in the twentieth-century culture.[1] The paradoxical quality of much of the gospel will begin to have an increasing ring of truth about it, I believe. Therefore, the language and the imagery of John, which has so often stopped us in our tracks, may provide us frames of reference for life in a new culture. What of those truths, however, for which the gospel makes absolute claims with

near-dogmatic certainty? How shall we read and hear that Johannine feature in twenty-first century North America? (Cf. "The Sacraments and
Johannine Ambiguity" below, and "'He Gave up the Spirit.'")

If Johannine ambiguities of language and imagery take on a new
power, the absolute claims for truth in the same gospel may gradually
appear more and more problematic, if not anachronistic. (Or, it is equally
possible that these absolute claims will be seen as ambiguous in themselves.) At least, I think, this much is true: the way in which the Gospel
of John has served as a wellspring from which the church drew one after
the other of the great dogmas cannot survive. With no little personal fear
and trembling, I suggest that the christological and Trinitarian dogmas so
decisively formed in the ancient church under the influence of the Fourth
Gospel may become threatened. We Christians will no longer be able to
document our view of Christ based on the Johannine text—at least not
in the way we have done in the past. Our new sensitivity to the variety of
religious views in our world will force us to reevaluate our previous self-
assurance. We will no longer be comfortable in reducing the Johannnine
discourse material to creedal statements. That ease with which we once
ladled rationale for our faith statements from the flowing water of the
gospel narrative will end. What we may once have read as creed will be
seen for what it is, namely, polemic poetry.

How, then, will this gospel function as a resource for Christian theology in the twenty-first century? Johannine language may help us revise
our understanding of theological language and method as a whole and
may provoke a more profound appreciation for the symbolic nature of all
articulations of faith. We may increasingly recognize Johannine language
as parabolic poetry, fashioned in the midst of controversy. That recognition may then lead us to another recognition. It may help us acknowledge
that *all* expressions of religious truth are metaphorical, pointing but not
describing (cf. Kysar, *Stumbling*). As a consequence of these insights we
may gradually begin to locate the authority of Scripture for theology, not
in propositions, but in images (or pictures) that hint and tease at ultimate
reality and that consequently are vulnerable to varieties of responses. We
will search, not for grand propositions, but for controlling and fundamental images, or (if one prefers) formative stories.

Still, there will be no such thing as a single authoritative interpretation of John—no such thing as a true reading of the text. Instead, the
church will be forced to recognize the validity of a wide variety of interpretations, and truth found in a range of readings arising from a multicul-
tural body of readers. We will have to redefine biblical authority in ways
that more honestly recognize the tenuous and culturally formed character

of all authority. In some such way, we may be able to claim an authority that liberates and empowers rather than oppresses and controls some for the benefit of others.

Conclusions

Whether or not the church and its scholars will succeed in such an ambitious enterprise remains to be seen. The church as we know it today may splinter even more with the splintering of the various readings of biblical texts, including John. The challenge of interpretation of John in the future century is formidable. I suggest, however, that the Fourth Gospel should play a featured role in the drama of the church in the twenty-first century in North America. My suggestion is based on three features of John: its representation of the issues inherent in an early Christian sectarianism, its portrayal of the nature, function, and authority of religious language; and its presentation of the ambiguity of truth in a postmodern age.

Chapter Fourteen

The "Other" in Johannine Literature

The increasing diversity of persons in our society and the shrinking world have both contributed to a new interest in what has been called "the other" (cf. Spongheim). For purposes of this paper, I define "the other" simply as *the awareness of a person or group of people who appear in some way to be different from me and my group, and thereby may pose some sort of threat to me and the group to which I belong.* For both social and theological reasons, it is important that we rethink much of what has become an almost unconscious attitude toward "the other."

My interest in this paper, however, is a much narrower single issue raised by the prominence of "the other." What obligations do interpreters have for dealing with biblical presentations of "the other," and, in this case, the Johannine portrayal of "the other"? I assume that such a question is a matter of the ethics of interpretation. Borrowing in part from feminist interpretation (cf. Plaskow), I take for granted that an ethics of interpretation involves the interpreter's responsibility in four important steps or topics.

First, the ethics of interpretation demands *honesty* with the text. More specifically, it demands that we are candid with others and ourselves about what the text seems to mean within our social and theological settings.

Second, an ethics of interpretation requires that we *name* certain biblical teachings and themes for what they are and what they mean for us. If we believe the issue at stake in the text has implications for the church and society, we are obliged to raise that issue in clear and forceful terms.

Third, the ethics of interpretation, in some cases (like feminist interpretation), *problematizes* a text or some part of it. This entails analyzing the impact of the biblical theme in our society and suggesting what difficulty it poses for its appropriation today. In this sense, the ethics of interpretation entails, at least for me, a specific faith community and its understanding of the broader society.

To problematize a text or biblical theme at the same time involves the *fourth* part of the ethics of interpretation, namely, to *raise the consciousness* of our public (whoever that may be) regarding the implications of that theme (cf. Colonnese). In this case, I propose to be honest about the limitations of certain dimensions of the Johannine literature regarding "the other," to name what I find there, to treat it as a problem, and therefore to raise consciousness concerning that subject.

One final note about method: any use of the ethics of interpretation raises the question, "Whose ethics?" The ethics of interpretation varies among interpreters and does not necessarily reflect the cultural morals of a time and place. Therefore, I cannot pretend to be speaking for others in my analysis, nor even to claim that any group shares my ethics in its entirety.

Since I propose that in these documents there is a similar attitude toward certain "others," our attention will focus on 1 and 2 John as well as the Fourth Gospel. This paper will isolate and describe the attitude the texts nurture toward some "others," first in the gospel and then in 1 and 2 John. The conclusion will suggest some ramifications these texts have for our posture toward "others" today.

The Fourth Gospel

The Gospel of John speaks in radically different ways of different groups (cf. the previous article). On the one hand, the gospel gives the impression that women play an equally important role as do men (cf. Kysar, *Maverick, Gospel* [1996], 147–54), and the narrative presents both Samaritans and Gentiles in a relatively favorable light (e.g., ch. 4). On the other hand, its presentation of the Jews is remarkably mixed. It is curious that a gospel story treats the "otherness" of women, Samaritans, and Gentiles so favorable, while its portrayal of the Jews is so often negative. To be sure, that portrayal is ambiguous, but, on the surface of the text, it is far more negative than positive.[1]

There is a common consensus, I think, that the gospel often (but not always) uses the term *the Jews* in such a way as to align this group with those opposed to Jesus. There is, however, no consensus as to who these Jews are. Does the expression refer to a certain segment of the population, to those who live in a certain region, to a religious group, to religious leaders, or what? What is the historical referent? D. M. Smith represents a common view in saying that in the conflict between Jesus and the Jews "[w]e see . . . the reflection of the mortal tension between the Johannine community and the Jews who had rejected their claims" (*John* 187).[2] I will not try, however, to answer the question of the identity of the Jews nor argue for a historical referent for the expression "the Jews," but I will ask what kind of attitude toward these "others" the language of the text advocates.

It is neither necessary nor possible in this setting to rehearse all the gospel has to say about Jews and Judaism. As a summary of that question, for the most part, the text of the Gospel of John encourages readers:

1. to stand detached from Judaism,
2. to take the references to "Jews," Pharisees, and chief priests as Jesus' opponents,
3. to infer that the leaders of Judaism alone are responsible for Jesus' arrest and execution, and
4. to believe that Judaism is untrue and that Christ is superior in every way to that religion. (Cf. "Anti-Semitism and the Gospel of John" in part 3 of this collection.)

We are particularly interested in two features of the presentation of the Jews. First, the text gives us the impression that "the Jews" were responsible for the death of Jesus. In 19:16 the antecedent of "them" (*autois*) seems to be "the chief priests" mentioned in the previous verse. "Then [Pilate] handed [Jesus] over to *them* to be crucified. So, they took Jesus. . . ." This might be no more than the result of simple carelessness on the part of the author, since it is obvious that the Roman soldiers are responsible for carrying out Pilate's sentence, as verse 23 makes clear. Still, such carelessness with regard to the religious leaders is inexcusable.

The second important feature is even more serious. In 8:39-47, the crowd, which was earlier labeled "the Jews who had believed in him" (8:31), declares that their father is Abraham. Jesus replies, "you are from your father the devil,"[3] who "was a murderer from the beginning and does not stand in the truth" (v. 44). This is one of only three places in John where the word "devil" (*diabolos*) appears. In 6:70 it is used to refer to Judas, one of the Twelve, and in 13:2 we are told that "the devil" inspires Judas to betray Jesus. (In 13:27 the narrator tells us Satan [*ho satanas*] entered Judas.) The Fourth Gospel does not make as much of the leader of the forces of evil as do the Synoptics, but it does fashion the polarity of God and the devil into another expression of the dualism for which the gospel is so famous.

Jesus uses three other terms in 8:44 to name the devil, all of which are traditionally related to the figure of Satan: "murderer" (*anthrōpoktonos*, i.e., slayer of humans), "liar," and "father of lies" (*pseustēs estin kai ho patēr autou*). The three labels—devil, liar, and murderer—arose from the interpretation of the Genesis account of the fall as is evident by the use of the phrase "from the beginning" (*ap' archēs*) in connection with "murderer" (cf. Wisdom 2:24). All these designations describe one who is opposed to God, who alone gives life and is truth.[4]

For whatever reason, with these words the Johannine Jesus "demonizes" the Jews. The gospel claims he equated the Jewish crowd with the forces of evil in the world. One commentary on John says this about 8:43-47: "In a culture that considers the devil to stand at the opposite pole from God, to call someone the offspring of the devil in an honor and shame society is a truly harsh and demeaning insult" (Malina and Rohrbaugh, 162).

Suggestions have been made about the historical setting of the Gospel of John that try to mollify the harshness of the presentation of the Jews somewhat, and sociological readings take the hostility in terms of social rejection and the effort to reestablish identity (Peterson, 80-82). However, the fact remains that there was a group toward which the evangelist and possibly the Johannine churches felt this kind of intense disdain. What would compel such a depiction?

We cannot answer this question with any certainty. What needs to said, however, is that, pushed to the wall, the Fourth Evangelist chose to blame this group for Jesus' death and equate them with offspring of the devil, thus claiming *there was nothing of worth—no truth—in them or their views.* An ethics of interpretation requires us to name such a posture toward "another," who was different from the Christians and posed a significant threat to them. In a word, it is *deplorable and inexcusable!*

First and Second John

With all of the similarities and differences between the Gospel of John and 1 and 2 John, perhaps among the most striking is that these epistles characterize their opponents in the manner similar to how the Fourth Evangelist characterizes the Jews, namely, by equating them with evil. If the Gospel of John was written amid a crisis with the synagogue, as many (but not all) have thought (cf. Reinhartz, "Johannine Community"), the first two epistles (and especially 1 John) seem to have been occasioned by another crisis. First John gives us some indication of the nature of the crisis, although even then we still have only the vaguest notion of what actually transpired and assuredly only one side to the story. For one reason or another, it seems a group has withdrawn from the Johannine congregations. In 2:19, the author says, "They went out from us, but they were not of us." We cannot know with certainty what precipitated this separation, nor can we know the exact nature of the separatist group (cf. Kysar, "John, Epistles of," 3:900–912).

It appears the author of 1 John attempts to accomplish a number of things. First, the document reflects a pastoral concern to quiet the anxiety stirred up in the congregations by the splintering of their group. Second, it exhibits a clear intent to distinguish the life and faith of those still in the congregations (the writing addresses) from those of the separatists. The distinction lies in both doctrine and practice.

Second John reflects a situation that may have resulted from the same separation implied in the first epistle. At least, the "elder" of 2 John seeks to diminish the influence of "another" group on the congregations addressed in this short document. That influence clearly pertains to morality and Christology, as it does in 1 John (cf. Brown, *Commentary–Epistles*).

Consequently, both 1 and 2 John have a polemical as well as a pastoral tone. They are concerned to discredit the faith and lifestyle (later to be what the church labeled as "heresy") of "another" group of believers, while at the same time nurturing what the authors regard as true faith and practice. Both equate with the forces of evil anyone who teaches that the Christ was not a flesh and blood human being. The author of 1 John labels the separatists "antichrists" (*antichristoi*, e.g., 2:18) and "liars" (*ho pseutēs*) because they did not believe that the Christ came in the flesh (2:18-19).[5] The elder in 2 John echoes the same view, calling those who do not "acknowledge the coming of Jesus Christ in the flesh" "the deceiver and the antichrist" (*ho planos kai ho antichristos*, v. 7). The belief that Christ was a flesh and blood human is so important that a failure to believe it betrays a demonic nature and constitutes the eschatological lie associated with the final days.

First John also names "liar" any who do not believe or practice faith as the author understands it (1:10; 2:4, 22; 4:20; 5:10). Most interesting to us is its use in connection with the "antichrists." (These two epistles are apparently the first to use this title, *antichristoi* and offer the only occurrences of the term in the New Testament).[6] Just as the Fourth Gospel equates the devil with liar, so now 1 John equates antichrist and liar. Likewise, this author uses "murderer" (*anthrōpoktonos*) to describe those who hate rather than love others (3:15).

The similarity between the Gospel of John and 1 and 2 John on this matter is striking. In 1 John we find the same three labels used in John 8:44: Liar, children of the devil, and murderer. One difference stands out. While the language of the Fourth Gospel may imply eschatological significance by titles used for the Jews, 1 and 2 John are explicit in equating the separatists with the resurgence of evil in the last days. First and 2 John speak five times of the "antichrist" of the last days. Moreover, note that 1 John speaks of the "other" group with the language of affiliation, just as the evangelist says of the Jews "you are *of* your father the devil" (literally, "you are out of your father," *humeis ek tou patros*, 8:44). In the first epistle, it is the lack of affiliation with the Christian community—"not *of* us" (*ouk ēsan ex hēmōn*, 2:19). Elsewhere the author also says that those who sin are "of the devil" (*ek tou diabolou*, 3:8) and those who do not practice righteousness are "children of the devil" (*ta tekna tou diabolou*, 3:10). In the gospel and first two epistles, the language of affiliation expresses the source of people's identity. In this case, the preposition *ek* (translated simply "of") denotes origin or cause.[7]

If we assume that the separatists are also in view when the authors of 1 and 2 John attack others for their views of morality, there are still further connections between the Fourth Evangelist's condemnations of Jews and Judaism and the condemnation of the separatists in 1 and 2 John. For example, the author of 1 John condemns those who do not love others and declares that they "do not know God" (*ouk egnō ton theon*, 4:8), are "in the darkness" (*en tē skotia*, 2:9), as well as "liars" (*pseustēs estin*, 4:20). In a similar way, the gospel says that the disciples' opponents "have not known the Father" (*ouk egnōsan ton patera*, 16:3) and that believers "should not remain in darkness" (*en tē skotia mē meinē*, 12:46). One could even imagine a direct literary dependence when 1 John claims that "the devil has been sinning from the beginning" (*ap' archēs ho diabolos hamartanei*, 3:8), while John 8:44 claims that the devil has been a "murderer from the beginning" (*ap' archēs*). The similarities do not surprise us, yet it is interesting how some of the views of evil in the Fourth Gospel are transferred in 1 John to those who may have been among the separatists.

1 and 2 John suggest that unless you agree with the views of the authors, you are aligned with eschatological forces trying to lead humanity away from the truth. Both of these documents attempt to determine the outer boundaries of Christian faith. They each claim to distinguish what is authentic Christianity from what is an erroneous expression of the faith—that is, in their opinion. The issue these writings advance is what the church eventually called orthodoxy as opposed to heresy. *The dynamics of the Johannine reaction to the splintering of their community created a precedent for how for centuries the church would regard those of differing beliefs and moralities.*

Implications for Today

Three of the four New Testament documents attributed to John (not including Revelation) label "other" groups instruments of evil. The first group named in the gospel seems to be outside the community, and the threat it poses is external. The second group was comprised of Christians who had been a part of the congregations addressed in 1 and 2 John, and hence they posed an internal threat. It is, however, remarkable that in both cases the Johannine writings demonize the "others."

All three of these documents may reflect a situation of crisis and thereby suggest that labeling an opponent evil may often arise from the pressures of crisis. Ironically, the opponents in the gospel may have been former colleagues of the Johannine Christians in the synagogue, and the separatists were members of the Christian communities to which 1 and 2 John were written. In the epistles, the separatist group is damned. The gospel demeans another religious group—the very religious tradition from which Christianity came. First and 2 John, however, condemn another group that (presumably) still calls itself Christian.

One of the worrisome things about the gospel and 1 and 2 John is that they each declare another *group* evil. What about "another" group would ever justifiably lead us to take such an extreme view of them? We may sometimes call an individual or a circle of individuals within a larger group evil. However, are we ever justified in demonizing *whole groups*? The fact that the Johannine literature does so may be related to the fact that such condemnation of whole groups has become a common practice in Western culture. (Remember the President who identified three whole nations "an axis of evil.") However, when is such an action necessary to protect others and when is it simply an expression of bigotry? These questions arise when we problematize the Johannine condemnation of opponents.

The Johannine predilection to demonize "others" who disagree with the leaders of the churches actually roots deeply in a fundamental view of "others" and of themselves. The tendency to condemn those who are different is part of the sectarian mentality of the churches represented in the Johannine literature. That mentality is especially evident in the Gospel of John. Believers are set over against the "world." They have the truth and stand opposed to those who live in error and falsehood. (See, e.g., John 17.) This "us-against-them" mentality hints at the radical dualism of the gospel's thought. There are but two forms of existence possible—live in the light or walk in the darkness—and there is no middle ground!

Another feature of Johannine thought which nurtures a readiness to declare "others" are erroneous and evil is the absolute exclusivity it claims for the Christian view. John 14:5 expresses this view with infamous words: "I am the way, and the truth, and the life. No one comes to the Father except through me." This perspective cultivates the exclusion of those who are wrong and discourages encounter with other belief systems. Furthermore, it mandates that any encounter with another belief system should and must be aimed at converting the "other"—making the "other" like us.

These views set within the context of the dualistic schema of Johannine thought makes it impossible to deal openly and respectfully with others who hold different views from our own. If there is only one truth, then all else must be false. The task before us today, it seems to me, is to rethink the nature of truth in order to recognize the diversity of thought and belief in our world. To do so means to jettison the Johannine exclusivity and absolute certainty in favor of openness to others.

Having become conscious of the seriousness of the gospel's portrayal of "the Jews" and 1 and 2 John's words about the separatists, interpreters are required to call into question the attitude toward the "other" promoted by these writing. In a day when the church and our culture are dealing more and more with groups of different religious traditions, the Johannine examples are unfortunate and dangerous. Those who hold an ethic that values respect and dialogue with those who are different need publicly to question the value of the Johannine perspective, at least on this matter.

For years I have tried to defuse the Fourth Gospel of its power to nurture anti-Semitism and have done so in terms of a hypothetical setting for its composition. I have grown, however, less and less comfortable with such efforts and now believe that I must in honesty more explicitly challenge and even denounce the postures of both the gospel and 1 and 2 John toward "others" who are different from us. I know the language of these documents is an example of classic polemic in the conventions of the time (cf. e.g., L. T. Johnson, "Anti-Jewish Slander"). However, if that is the case, perhaps we need to raise serious questions about such polemic and not use it as a way of justifying the language of the Johannine literature. The challenge of the "other" in our contemporary society is made all the worse by these documents in our religious heritage.

To challenge these features of the Johannine writings means that we are willing and required to assess critically the value of particular portions of Scripture for our contemporary lives. That is to say, we need to practice a kind of *resistance* in our reading of the Bible that allows us to reject as irrelevant ideas and teachings that are out of harmony with what we understand to be the substance of God's act in Christ.[8] Unless we are equipped to do so, portions of our Bible are likely to lead us away from a faithful public witness. If we cannot deal with Scripture in this way, it seems to me we need to reassess our understanding of the authority of the Bible.

The most serious issue facing the church and our culture is how we perceive and relate to those "others" who are in one way or another different from us—i.e., what we take to be the majority. We cannot simply mimic the view of much of our Scripture. We can, however, I believe, seize upon the image of the Christ and, guided by that image, shape our public witness in ways that reflect the gospel.

Chapter Fifteen

The Expulsion from the Synagogue: The Tale of a Theory

I have recently realized how my Johannine scholarly career parallels and has been entangled with the proposal that the Fourth Gospel was written soon after the Johannine community was expelled from the synagogue. With that realization in mind, I want to sketch—from my perspective—the narrative of the theory of the expulsion from the synagogue from its rise to prominence until the present.

With the initial introduction of the proposal by Raymond E. Brown and J. Louis Martyn, it rapidly became the most commonly held view of the occasion for the gospel's writing—at least in North American scholarship. In recent years, however, the tale of this theory has taken another, and somewhat surprising turn. I would like to trace what seems to me the gradual decline in the credibility of the hypothesis. Let us suppose that the tale of the rise and decline of which I speak has a number of distinct chapters.

Chapter One: The Rise of the Theory

Of course, the theory has roots earlier in the middle of the twentieth century (cf. Carroll) and to some degree drew on the work of W. D. Davies. However, it was the 1960s when the proposal captured the attention of the scholarly world—just about the time I was completing my doctorate. Raymond Brown cautiously offered the excommunication of Christians from the synagogue as an influence on the fourth stage of the development of the finished gospel and suggested the Fourth Gospel implied the existence of "crypto-Christians," who remained in the synagogue because they were too cowardly to confess their faith in Christ. Furthermore, Brown proposed that the hypothetical edict of excommunication issued at the Council of Jamnia (80–90 C.E.) provided the last possible date for the completion of the gospel.[1]

In 1968 between the publication of the two volumes of Brown's commentary (1966 and 1970), Martyn published his proposal (*History and Theology*). He argued that the expulsion of the Johannine Christians from their synagogue was the most likely reason for the two layers of much of the gospel's message—Jesus' time and the later time of the church (*History and Theology* 104–5). Martyn tried more clearly and precisely to tie the event with a formal ban against Christians in the synagogue, originating at the Council of Jamnia (*Gospel* 104–5). He proposed that the expulsion made Jewish Christians out of the Christian Jews of the Johannine church. However, Brown and Martyn postulated different reasons for the expulsion. Brown held that "a group of Jewish Christians of anti-Temple views and their Samaritan converts" entered the community and provided the "catalyst" for christological developments in the Johannine church. Furthermore, the presence of this group resulted in the breakdown of relations between that community and the synagogue (*Community* 23, n. 13, and "Johannine Ecclesiology") Martyn, on the other hand, was content simply to suppose that the rapid growth of the Jewish Christians provoked the ban against them.[2]

In the next years, the rise of the popularity of this proposal was remarkable. For a time, the theory appeared confirmed by different sorts of studies, including history of religions (Meeks, e.g., "Man from Heaven"), form-critical (Leroy), redaction-critical, and others (Kysar, *Fourth Evangelist* 149–56). Moreover, each of these publications increasingly gave the impression that the theory addressed a good number of the most different and troubling issues regarding the Fourth Gospel.

Nearly twenty-nine years ago, I pronounced the theory of the expulsion from the synagogue the most promising proposal for the concrete setting for the Gospel of John. I wrote, "A proposal (for the situation and purpose of John) which seems steadily to be gaining an increasing degree of consent among critics . . . is that the evangelist was related to a community of Christian believers engaged in a serious and perhaps even violent dialogue with the synagogue" (*Fourth Evangelist* 149). I dared even to call the new understanding of the setting for John resulting from the theory "the lasting contribution of the last quarter of the twentieth century to Johannine scholarship."[3]

The proposal swept through Johannine studies and took deep and healthy roots that grew until it was regarded almost as a given fact. By the 1990s in many circles, it was often a foregone assumption that this was the setting for the writing of the Gospel of John. Like other hypotheses, this one was so widely embraced that at times many of us may have forgotten that it was *only a hypothesis*. Indeed, along with the speculative Q document, the theory has now become one of the best examples of how scholarship tends to transform hypotheses into truth. The tale of this theory demonstrates the necessity to keep reminding ourselves of the difference between truth and hypothesis, as well as the fact that we never *really prove much of anything*.

Chapter Two: The First Sign of Flaws

Martyn argued that the expulsion of the Johannine Christians from the synagogue witnessed in the text of John was the result of a formal revision of the twelfth benediction of a liturgical Jewish prayer (the *birkat ha-minim*, "the blessing of the heretics"). Along with others, he claimed that the rabbis gathered at Jamnia toward the end of the first century produced the revision and that the Fourth Gospel evidences the use of a more formal ban against Christians in the synagogue than those mentioned in Acts. In contrast to the formal edict put in force by members of the "Jamnia Academy," Martyn thought that references in Acts were "*ad hoc* measures taken in one city after another." The benediction against the heretics "is intended, therefore, to weld the whole of Judaism into a monolithic structure by *culling out* those elements which do not conform to the Pharisaic image of orthodoxy" (*History and Theology* [2003] 51, 55, 59). For both Martyn and Brown, this supposed revision was instrumental in creating a new and unfriendly environment for the Christian Jews who continued to worship in the synagogue.

In the early 1980s, however, historians decisively challenged this key part of the theory of the expulsion and (in my opinion) showed it to be imaginary. Reuven Kimelman demonstrated that there was no such "benediction" or any other formal act that would have resulted in the expulsion of Christian Jews from their synagogues. Furthermore, there is uncertainty as to what the original text of the "blessing" might have been and a great deal more doubt about when—if ever—it was actually put into use. However, *there is no uncertainty that the blessing did not seek the exclusion of the Christians as much as it sought the unification of the Jewish community*. The heretics about whom it spoke were not coerced to leave their synagogues, and, if they chose to leave, it was by their own volition. Speaking of the division between Christians and Jews, Kimelman wrote,

> Apparently there never was a single edict which caused the so-called irreparable separation between Judaism and Christianity. The separation

was rather the result of a long process dependent upon local situations and ultimately upon the political power of the church.[4]

Not surprisingly, those of us who had committed ourselves to the importance of the theory of the expulsion from the synagogue were able quickly to make the necessary adjustments. For instance, I simply contended that the exclusion of Christians Jews was not the result of any formal decree from a council of rabbis but the decision of the leadership of a local synagogue or number of synagogues.[5] In other words, we argued that the Johannine Jewish Christians suffered from one of those ad hoc actions taken by synagogue leaders in the Acts of the Apostles. Then, of course, we had to claim that John was written for a limited number of Christian congregations within a defined region.[6] Still, the retreat was orderly and did not entail surrendering the whole fort.[7]

Chapter Three: Further Deterioration of Confidence

I think the next chapter in this tale of a theory came with a hermeneutics of suspicion that forced some of us to ask about the exact meaning of the key passages on which proponents of the expulsion theory based their suppositions. The proposal hangs precariously on three threads, that is, the uses of *aposynagōgos* ("put out of the synagogue") in John 9:22; 12:42; and 16:2. Read these three passages and then those that are so vitriolic toward the Jews (e.g., 8:39-47). One need not be an unrepentant skeptic to wonder if "expulsion" *identifies a historical action or an emotion.* The Jewish Christians *may have felt* the leaders of their synagogue had kicked them out of the community. That is really as much as those passages may tell us (Kysar, *Preaching John* 24). The feelings expressed by the Johannine Christians might have been much like some discontent Christians or Jews today who claim that a particular congregation "drove them out."

What we can know from these three passages is little more than that some Christians and Jews separated themselves from one another in some way and for some reason. I suggest the obvious, namely, that the text of the gospel presents readers with only one side of a story to which there most assuredly is another side. Therefore, it seems to me, this chapter of the theory's story necessitates that we significantly revise our imaginary picture of the situation. There was no formal and widespread ban against Christians participating in synagogue worship, *and* the division between the church and synagogue more likely occurred little by little on a local basis. Moreover, we are in no position to discern who took the initiative in bringing about the division or what caused the separation.[8]

Chapter Four: Evidence of Fatal Flaws

This chapter is comprised of critics of the theory and their contribution to the weakening of confidence in it. In my experience, Adele Reinhartz has been the most effective of those critics and little by little has chipped away at our overconfidence in it. She has persistently claimed that the expulsion theory does not fit the rhetoric of the *whole gospel*. She cites the external evidence against a formal banning of Christians from the synagogue, but goes further to examine the internal evidence against the theory.

Reinhartz's arguments appear in a number of different publications, but (if I may summarize) in each case she usually makes several interrelated points. First, she invites us to consider other passages where John presents a different picture of the relationship between Jews and Christians. In those cases, the evidence does not support the expulsion theory. One of these passages is 11:1-44, where "many of the Jews" comforted Mary and Martha on the occasion of their brother's death (11:19). Clearly, the two sisters are among Jesus' disciples, but that fact does not alienate them from other Jews. If the expulsion theory shaped the portrayal of Christians and Jews in the gospel, there would be no comforting Jewish presence.

Reinhartz also cites 12:10-11 as testimony against the theory. "So the chief priests planned to put Lazarus to death as well, since it was on account of him that many of the Jews were deserting and were believing in Jesus." If we are to read this passage at the two levels, as Martyn and others propose, the desertion and belief of the Jews seems incongruous. Apparently, these Jews were not expelled from their synagogue, but rather made the decision to believe in Jesus. Reinhartz recognizes that these verses are not necessarily incompatible with those which speak of Christians being expelled from the synagogue, but the fact that Jews are said to be "deserting" (or "leaving," *hypēgon*) suggests that their departure from the synagogue was their own doing, not that of a Jewish congregation. When these two passages are set alongside 9:22, 12:42, and 16:2, the picture of Jewish-Christian relationships painted by the gospel becomes more complicated and ambiguous. In this and other ways, the expulsion theory is not exegetically sound (Reinhartz, "Johannine Community," "'Jews,'" and *Befriending* 40-48).

It seems to me that this challenge to the dual level nature of the text raises a fundamental question for the historical-critical method in general. Martyn's theory is a prize example of what we have come to call using the text as a "window."[9] We have assumed that we can look through the text to reconstruct its original context and this will enable us to understand what the text was *intended* to mean! While Reinhartz does not take her argument this far, she hints at the question of whether the text is indeed a window on the past (cf. Conway, "Production").

On this very matter of reconstructing the history of the community behind the text by looking through the text, Reinhartz's efforts have received support from what might seem an unlikely source. Another part of this chapter on "evidence of fatal flaws" in the theory entails the nature of historical research itself. T. L. Johnson scrutinizes those of the "Jesus Seminar" and challenges the concept of history operative in what he called "the Misguided Quest for the Historical Jesus." In the course of deconstructing the historical method of Dominic Crossan and others of the Jesus Seminar, he also denounces the efforts of Johannine redactional critics to identify sources used by the Fourth Evangelist and to reconstruct the history of the community responsible for the gospel. Johnson charges R. E. Brown with using the same flawed method discernible in the new quest for the historical Jesus. Brown's reconstruction of sources and stages in the composition of John are, Johnson asserts, the result of unrestrained imagination in the guise of historical research. "*There are no controls,*" he writes, "there is only imagination hitched to an obsessive need, somehow, anyhow, to do 'history.'"[10] To be sure, L. T. Johnson never directly addresses the supposition that the Johannine Christians were expelled from their Jewish worshiping community,[11] but the implications of his general critique of Brown's reconstruction are clear. Because of its entanglement in the historical method responsible for the theory, it is seriously and perhaps fatally challenged.

Chapter Five: The Theory in a New Age

Johnson's critique of the speculative nature of most of our historical endeavors, including the historical reconstructions of the Johannine community, may indicate a new direction for biblical criticism. We are, perhaps, entering an era in which "history" itself may necessarily play a different role in biblical interpretation, and the reign of history as the key to interpretation may be brought to an end.

C. M. Conway's 2002 article in *Journal of Biblical Literature* gives us a glimpse of the future direction of Johannine studies from the perspective of one who embraces the "new history." She suggests that we think of interpretations as *productions* of the drama of the Gospel of John and examines Martyn's reading of John as one such production. He sought both to preserve the gospel's authority and at the same time demonstrate how it relates to current cultural values. In the last century, many of us felt a desperate need to explain the Johannine portrayal of the Jews, since, in the wake of the Holocaust, anti-Jewish attitudes were correctly judged abhorrent. What interests Conway is the fact that Martyn's theory and its use by others was "intended to function ideologically in the contemporary context. The point is to make clear what is not relevant in order to preserve the part of the gospel that is." She goes on to describe what seems to her would be a more viable method of interpretation.

> Rather than making the meaning of the text dependent on the specific circumstances in which it was written, one would investigate the ways in which various productions of the gospel participate and contribute to particular historical/cultural circumstances. Indeed, instead of seeking *the* meaning of the text, one would examine how particular readings of the gospel are generated by and participate in the complex "textualize universe" at any given moment, thereby contributing to the management of reality. ("Production" 494).

Conway forces us to ask if (perhaps unconsciously) our historical methods have in large part been devised to separate the contingent and relevant in a biblical text. The new history challenges our motives and our participation in the ideologies of our culture and time.[12]

Postmodernism deals with the past in a much different way than did the modernism that arose from the Enlightenment. The postmodernist perspective is inclined to believe (1) that a "factual history" is impossible, (2) that the origin of a document is not necessarily definitive in terms of its meaning, and (3) that the past is forever unstable and uncertain. An investigation of the past usually tells us more about the investigator than about the past. Of course, no one doubts that there are events in the past. What postmodernist thinkers question is our ability to reconstruct them in anything approaching what actually happened. If it is true that modern historiography is not dependable, it has significant implications for the historical critical method of biblical interpretation. Biblical criticism as a whole, and Johannine scholarship in specific, cannot evade the troublesome questions that seem to be emerging in our culture and discipline: Whose history does historical criticism assume? Who determines what counts as history and what does not count? How is that history told? Who is empowered to do the telling? What ideologies do biblical interpreters bring to their task?

Of course, at stake in all of this is the nature of meaning itself (cf. Kysar and Webb, *Postmoderns*, ch. 6). The sort of criticism responsible for the formulation and application of the theory of the expulsion from the synagogue assumes both (1) that every text has a single determinate objective meaning and (2) that we can learn that meaning by looking through the text itself to its historical origin. The crisis before us, it seems to me, is whether there is ever such a thing as a single and objective meaning of a text and whether using the text as "a transparent window to an extra-textual referent" is the golden path to its meaning. Is it the case that meaning is in the past and in what the text implies about the past? Or, is meaning always the product of reading?[13]

A. K. M. Adam has shown the role modernity has given to the past and its discovery, as well as demonstrating the fallacies of efforts to reconstruct the past. He urges those of us in New Testament theology to take seriously what many secular historians seem to have admitted sometime ago, namely, that there is no pure history, only individual views of the past. Specifically Adam suggests that biblical scholarship needs to abandon "[t]he illusion that there is something behind or within the biblical texts that we might get at by way of sufficient research or the right method." The efforts to "locate the world *behind* the text" and discover an "original" meaning, he says, are not only impossible but unnecessary (*What Is Postmodern*, 32–33; cf. *Making Sense*).

The likely future status of historical research in biblical studies will gravely undermine the theory of the expulsion from the synagogue, and for many of us that theory now remains interesting but problematic. I think that the time may come in the near future when the modern method of biblical study will necessarily be revised in significant ways in favor of attending to the text as it is before us and how we respond to it. Therefore, the prognosis for such theories as the expulsion from the synagogue is not good. Soon they may no longer interest interpreters who believe it is not necessary to take a trip behind every text they wish to read.

Conclusion

I admit there is a transparently autobiographical quality to my telling of this tale of a theory. As my interests gradually turned more and more toward the literary methods, my confidence in the expulsion theory faded. In that process, the degree of speculation entailed in the historical reconstructions of the Johannine community and the written sources behind the gospel increasingly struck me (cf. Kysar, "Whence and Whither"). As grateful as I am for the work of scholars like Brown and Martyn, I now find abstract speculative constructions irrelevant and needless.

So, how will this tale conclude? In spite of my pretense to knowledge, I have no crystal ball that informs me of the final destiny of this hypothesis. Indeed, I certainly have no stake in pronouncing its death. If and when the theory is entirely discarded, most of my publications on John will also end up in the scarp pile. Still, what might have been our overconfidence in it has now been radically compromised, and properly so. Given the story I have just told, I think I will always have to remind everyone, including myself, that this theory and all the others are nothing but that—theories. Are they then necessary to our reading of the Gospel of John?

Chapter Sixteen

The Sacraments and Johannine Ambiguity

The purpose of this paper[1] is to suggest briefly how one recent trend in Johannine interpretation impacts Raymond E. Brown's view of the question of John and the sacraments.[2] The aged distinction between sacramental and nonsacramental interpretations, along with speculations about the difference between the evangelist and some redactor, are now tiresome, exhausted, and largely irrelevant. There is, I believe, a more significant trend in biblical studies that calls for an entirely different consideration of the sacraments. I have in mind the movement toward literary criticism with all of its interest in metaphor, polyvalence, and ambiguity. Father Francis Moloney has carefully edited Brown's manuscript to suggest the new importance of what he calls "narrative criticism," but he is also careful not to abandon the historical-critical methods.[3] I refer to a more radical kind of reader-oriented criticism that for the most part denies the effectiveness of the older classical methods. My goal is to do no more than suggest how this new method in some ways revolutionizes the treatment of the question of the sacraments in John.

First, these new approaches radically revise the criteria for discerning John's references to the sacraments. Brown criticizes his colleagues for not being sufficiently "scientific" in their decisions about the gospel's references to the sacraments (cf. Brown, *Commentary–Gospel* 1:cxiii). The issue, he says, is whether a passage is "intended" to be sacramental (*Introduction* 232). Not surprisingly, Brown believed that an interpreter could be objective and scientific in reading the gospel and that the goal was always to determine the intention of the author.

Recent movements in biblical interpretation have concluded, however, that there can be no purely objective and scientific interpretation of Scripture. The Bible and Culture Collective say of ideological criticism that it "is a critical mediation between the text and reader which contends *that there can never be a pure, ideology-free, uninvested meeting between text and reader*" (*Postmodern* 302, italics mine). This is most surely true of meetings of sacramental-sounding Johannine texts and their readers. In the history of scholarship, one can easily recognize that interpreters writing out of a sacramental orientation (such as Roman Catholic, Anglican, or Lutheran) tend to identify both the Eucharist and baptism in Johannine passages, while those who are affiliated with nonsacramental traditions are inclined to deny or minimize such identifications. Ideological commitments obviously influence the interpretative process.

Moreover, among many literary critics there is seldom any pretense of discerning the author's original intention. While there are a number of different views of the relationship between a text and authorial intention, the recognition of the "intentional fallacy" has radicalized interpretation for many of us (cf. Adam, "Author" 8–13). What an author actually "intended" by a text is concealed from readers. If the goal of interpretation is to read a text with the author's original intention in mind, we must first create an imaginative construct of the "real author" before taking the next step of proposing her or his intention. To appeal to the author's intent as a means of interpreting a passage's potentially sacramental meaning is simply to appeal to the *interpreter's intention for the passage*.

Therefore, by the most recent standards of criticism, Brown's effort to construct a means of adjudicating among different interpretations of texts that may speak of the sacraments is seriously flawed. Reader response criticism and postmodernist interpretation, however, make a number of additional points clear when it comes to the determination of sacramental references in the Fourth Gospel. The following theses might form the basis of a new approach to the sacraments in John.

The first thesis: The riddle of sacramental references in John is simply part of the general Johannine ambiguity. In this case, I mean by ambiguity a multitude of possible meanings.[4] We have all recognized the use of double-entendre and misunderstanding in John, and they have become nearly indisputable elements of this gospel. We have, however, sometimes been tempted to believe that there is an implicit "intended meaning" to such passages, so that theoretically all we have to do is work through the false meanings to arrive at the "true meaning." This may require identifying what appears to us as the "obvious" or "first meaning" of a word or phrase and on the basis of that we construct the "second meaning." The basic distinction between physical and spiritual meanings is an example of such solutions, for instance, of "water and blood" (*haima kai hydōr*) in 19:34.[5]

There is, however, no resolution to most instances of ambiguity in this perplexing document and to insist on some resolution does violence to the text. The invitation of Johannine ambiguity (or multiple meaning) is to live with it and allow it to continue to stimulate our imaginations. The delicate uncertainty implied in most (if not all) of John must be maintained and become the focus of our pondering. Therefore, for instance, we continue to live with the multiple meanings of the words like (*anōthen*) in chapter 3, the vagueness of Jesus' promise, "I will come again" (*palin erchomai*) in 14:3, or the meaning of "spirit" (*pneuma*) in 19:30 (cf. Kysar, "'He Gave Up'").

The second thesis: Johannine symbolism is part of the ambiguity of the gospel. Brown points out that nearly all of the passages that have been interpreted sacramentally entail symbolism. He proposes that this is the case,

> because only through symbolism could the evangelist teach his sacramental theology and still remain faithful to the literary form of the gospel in which he was writing. He could not interpolate sacramental theology in the gospel story by anachronistic and extraneous additions, but he could show the sacramental undertones of the words and works of Jesus that were already part of the gospel tradition. (*Introduction* 234)

Such symbolism is often—if not always—ambiguous. That is, to propose a singular meaning of any symbol, such as water, is fruitless and actually minimizes the effectiveness of the language. Symbolism is not simply a code which is suddenly clear once we have found the key to the code. Of course, one could ask further how else but through symbolism could the sacraments be discussed? Do not the sacraments, as understood in the Christian tradition, defy any "literal" description or representation? Some literary critics have gone so far as to maintain that all language is by nature metaphorical, so that we can no longer distinguish between what is symbolic (or metaphorical) and what is "literal," for nothing is "literal."[6]

If these theses are true, what do they mean for the interpretation of the Gospel of John? If the passages that are so often argued either to be or not be sacramental participate in the ambiguity we have been discussing, then every suggestion that a passage is sacramental may be correct, provided we recognize that there is *another sense in which it is nonsacramental.* Yes, 6:51-56 does call to mind the eucharistic, and, yes, the verses *need not* be read as referring to the Eucharist. They are hopelessly ambiguous and no amount of research or study will (or even should) finally resolve that ambiguity.

If this is the case, then we must agree to acknowledge that the interpretation of Johannine passages both sacramentally and nonsacramentally have a degree of truth. Both are true and both must be respected by interpreters. This means too that there may be reading communities (just as Fish suggested; and Moore, *Literary Criticism* 116) which emphasize the sacramental meaning and others who do not. If we acknowledge the basic ambiguity of the key passages, we may legitimately read the texts sacramentally in communities that are so inclined to do so or we may legitimately read them as nonsacramentally in other communities. Of course, we cannot declare absolutely that we are right and the other reading communities wrong without thereby denying the ambiguity of the passages.

Conclusion

I have little doubt that Brown would not be happy with the view I have here advocated. He graciously acknowledged that new approaches have influenced the interpretation of John but was none too patient with what he calls "extravagant claims" that these approaches "supplied messianic deliverance from a barren past totally concerned with sources and reconstructions." Nonetheless, he acknowledges that these approaches provide "complementary enrichment" of historical criticism (*Introduction* 29). In this sense, Moloney's incorporation of narrative along with the historical criticism was indeed in Brown's spirit.

Notwithstanding the likelihood of Brown's rejection of my view of Johannine ambiguity and its implications for the sacraments, I maintain that literary criticism opens revolutionary and provocative ways of addressing the issue and does so in a more productive way than has been the case with the traditional historical-critical methods of reading.

Conclusion

Looking Over One's Shoulder

In all likelihood, everyone at one time or another looks over her or his shoulder and considers their personal past. This part of the collection attempts to do something of the same thing—looking back over the years during which I wrote and published (most) of the previous sixteen articles. Standing on the "other side" of these "voyages with John" gives one a different sort of view. What follows are a few reflections on the past during which I wrote these pieces.

The main reflection entails the setting in which the writing was done and in particular *what a rich and exciting time the past fifty years have been for Johannine scholarship*. Some voyages are dull—just trying to get from point A to point B. Others feel more as if the journey itself is the whole purpose of the voyage. As I have already said, the first years of my career during my doctoral work were the beginnings of what proved to be an amazing journey in biblical studies. The historical-critical method of exegesis had been around for many years, but in the 1960s through the 1980s the method was vastly expanded and developed, as a number of the articles reprinted as part of this book demonstrate.

The most striking example of that expansion and development of historical criticism, it seems to me, was in the area of form and redaction-critical studies. "Form criticism" entails the identification and analysis of the various types of language formations in the Bible. Easy examples are the healing stories in the Synoptic Gospels and how they tend to betray a certain pattern. The analysis of form dates back to the beginning of the twentieth century and the work of Hermann Gunkel in the Old Testament. It was refined, however, and advanced only later. Bultmann stole the show in this matter as in others. His monumental *History of the Synoptic Tradition* did not please a good many scholars but it nonetheless demonstrated the importance and possibilities of form critical studies. (Cf. Bultmann and Kundsin, *Form Criticism*; McKnight, *Form Criticism*.)

The Europeans were already vigorously at work in redactional studies (that is, identifying what was added in the editing process by the evangelists), particularly of the Synoptics. Actually W. Marxsen was first to use the expression *Redaktionsgeschichte*, but the practice arose earlier. The first of a number of remarkable studies of this kind came from the then young K. Stendahl. His work on the Qumran documents aroused his interest in the use of the Old Testament in the gospels. In 1954, Stendahl published *The School of St. Matthew and Its Use of the Old Testament* and sounded chords that were to resonate through the whole of the century. Stendahl proposed that a group of interpreters (a "school") stood behind the Gospel of Matthew and that they and the First Evangelist worked on the sources that came to them. Matthew was also the theme of the 1960 study by E. P. Blair (my major advisor for the dissertation) about which he wrote, "My objective is . . . to identify and characterize the distinctive element in the author's [i.e., Matthew's] Christology" (8).

Although the English translation of the collection of redactional studies by Bornkamm, et al., *Tradition and Interpretation in Matthew*, was published in 1963 (while I was still trying to get my dissertation done), many of us gobbled it up like starving wanderers in the desert (cf. Stanton). These authors attempted to separate the tradition received by Matthew and the evangelist's interpretation. Two redaction-critical studies that have influenced research on the Synoptics long after the aforementioned volumes were published are Marxsen, *Mark, the Evangelist* and Conzelmann, *The Theology of Luke*. Redaction criticism flourished from these early years to the present time.

The most recent critical methods are often slow in coming to Johannine studies. In the Synoptics, the scholar can compare one with the other two, and armed with a theory of the sources employed in the composition of the first three gospels, make a case for what is redactional. In the case of John, however, comparison with the Synoptics does not aid much in determining what was in the Johannine tradition before the composition of the gospel. So, except for a few passages (e.g., the passion story), all we have is the gospel itself. The exception, of course, was C. H. Dodd's remarkable *Historical Tradition* which ventured into a form-redaction study of the Fourth Gospel in relationship with the Synoptics.

This leads us to the efforts of source criticism in the Gospel of John, an enterprise that blossomed in the second half of the twentieth century, but about which we have already said enough. However, like so many trends in Johannine criticism in this period, we may lay source-redaction criticism at the feet of the giant, Rudolf Bultmann. However, Robert Fortna and others followed along in only a few years. Fortna's source proposal has proven to be the most influential and lasting of the source analyses done on the Gospel of John. Thanks to Bultmann and Fortna, Johannine redaction studies were launched and developed throughout the remainder of the century and continue today.

The period from the 1960s through today was rich with redaction-critical studies of John, and as a result the historical-critical method in general prospered. The voyages seemed to take us deeper and deeper into our destination—understanding John. For example, the reconstruction of the history of the community (out of which and for which the evangelist wrote) became a dominant theme in Johannine studies. This was due in large part to the work of Brown and Martyn (cf. "The Expulsion from the Synagogue" in part 4 of this book). That vast reconstruction has been the principal hypothesis and only in the last few years has been seriously challenged (cf. Kysar, "Whence and Whither").

Two new kids on the block, however, began to change things. *Literary studies* gradually drew more and more attention. As was the case with redaction criticism, the Fourth Gospel was nearly the last portion of Scripture to become the subject of literary studies. In the 1930s a "New Criticism" (aroused in the study of literature in general) protested how critics understood literature exclusively in terms of the historical context of its author. The New Criticism sought to read and interpret literature as pieces of art. Years later the same kind of revolt occurred in the study of Scripture. One scholar summarizes the new literary movement in biblical studies this way: "the approach of literary criticism is to accept the form of the work, *and the reader's participation in the form,* as an intrinsic part of entry into the imaginative world of the work" (Beardslee, 13, italics mine). In biblical studies, this new literary study took a multitude of new forms, each of which has brought new excitement (cf. Kysar and Webb, *Postmoderns*). From the evidence of the last twenty years, we may safely conclude that the literary movement will continue to spawn new methods.

As if literary criticism were not enough, another "new kid" moved in down the street and brought the advent of still another type of criticism in the last half of the twentieth century. One could argue that the social science methods of interpretation are rooted in earlier decades, but in its newer form it has brought an enormous number of studies. These two new types of criticism—literary and social science—each has its own unique relationship with the older historical-critical method. Literary criticism constitutes an intentional turn away from the long-held assumptions of the older methods. Insofar as it entails investigation of the biblical societies, the social science methods seemed at first a way to deepen and enrich historical criticism. In time, however, it is clear that the social approach is radically different from its predecessor.

The richness of the developments of these new methods thickened with what we call postmodern criticism. As I have already made clear, I think no one is quite sure what sort of critical methods (if any) we can properly label "postmodern." However, a number of movements in contemporary biblical studies have arisen around characteristics of postmodern thought (cf. Adam, *Handbook*). The group of ten scholars who called themselves "The Bible and Culture Collective" worked together (in a manner they believe is postmodern) to write *The Postmodern Bible*. The book draws together a large number of movements related to the new era and critiques each of them. It may prove to be the most important scholarly work of the turn of the centuries. In Johannine studies, the work of S. D. Moore and J. L. Staley signal what postmodern criticism might look like.

I have two other reflections about the half century we have been discussing. When I was in seminary and then graduate school (1956–1964), the European and English superscholars dominated New Testament studies. We could never discuss John without knowing Bultmann, Cullmann, Dodd, Bernard, Schnackenburg, and Hengel, to name just a few of the giants in scholarship at the time. Just remember that the doctoral programs in biblical studies at mid-century required students to at least read both German and French. The assumption was that the classics of both the past and the future were likely to be written in one of those two languages. In that era, every biblical scholar of any promise had to study in Europe for at least one year.

In the final five decades of the twentieth century, however, *North American Johannine scholarship came into its own.* Most certainly, Brown exemplifies how we could and did produce scholars of top caliber. This is not to say that there were no North American Johannine scholars until midcentury! The focus, however, has clearly shifted to the United States since the early years of my career. North American scholars have now become the leaders in Johannine studies!

Far more important than the rise of North American scholarship is *the diversification of scholars who are among those leading the way in Johannine studies.* First, and after centuries of exclusion, women broke through the door to biblical scholarship. Thankfully, their voices are now common and highly respected. However, the diversity is not just in gender. African Americans are now colleagues with the rest of us.

Another expansion of biblical scholarship is no less important. Roman Catholic scholars have made significant contributions to the revolution of our disciple. The bibliography of this volume is filled with Roman Catholics, and clearly some of the greatest names in English biblical scholarship are among them. This transition is one of the most remarkable of my career, and we have now come to take for granted the common commitments of scholars of all parts of the Christian church.

By virtue of the new world in which we live, scholars of *all* races, nationalities, and backgrounds have come to the table with white Europeans and North Americans. Johannine scholarship has become globalized, as have other specializations in research. The multitude of interpretative perspectives has transformed our search for biblical insight and understanding far from anything most of us could imagine. (Cf. Segovia and Tolbert, *Reading from this Place*, 2 vols.) What an exciting day to engage in the scholarly enterprise!

Within the course of fifty years, biblical scholarship (including Johannine) has changed dramatically. Hence, today the "voyages" are different. The sixteen articles in this collection are, I think, representative of some of the changes, but they represent only a tiny bit of the story. Yet, scholarship is never inert. You no sooner finish one "voyage," and you are off on another in a different direction. Looking over your shoulder to what has been motivates you to launch out into the future. In my few years of teaching graduate students in New Testament at Emory University, I have seen ample evidence that the future holds a good many more changes, and perhaps even radical ones. Looking over our shoulders to see where our earlier voyages took us may improve our vision of both the present and the future and launch a new voyage with John. Where will your voyages with John take you?

Notes

Introduction

1. The Northwestern University Philosophy department was largely responsible for the influential series, "Northwestern University Studies in Phenomenology and Existential Philosophy," edited by my major advisor in the department, John Wild, in the years following 1964.

Chapter One

Originally published in *Catholic Biblical Quarterly* 32 (1970): 77-78. Revised.

1. In contrast to Bultmann's view, C. H. Dodd argues that the evangelist intends to suggest the archetypal ideas of a speculative Platonism. Dodd fails to note any reference to creatio ex nihilo in the passage (*Interpretation* 203 et passim). C. K. Barrett's view is similar. He sees cosmology as the intent of verses 1-5 (*Gospel According to St. John* 125-27). R. E. Brown stands closer to Bultmann's position in his insistence, "The Prologue is a description of the history of salvation in hymnic form." Therefore, "the whole case of the hymn as salvific history removes it a distance from the more speculative Hellenistic world of thought" (*Commentary–Gospel* 1:23-24). Still, Brown makes no effort to find the doctrine of *creatio ex nihilo* in the prologue. Similarly, Schnackenburg stresses the hymnic, nonspeculative intent of the passage but is silent with regard to the classical doctrine of creation out of nothing (*Gospel* 1:232-33, 236-41).

2. It is interesting that Bultmann does not propose the distinction between "natural" and "eternal" life as do some commentators (e.g., Brown, *Commentary–Gospel* 1:7, 507). Moreover, he maintains that it is possible to

257

distinguish between the meaning of *zōē* ("life") and *zōē aiōnios* ("eternal life") (Bultmann, *Gospel* 152, n. 2). In contrast, Dodd claims that the first is but an abbreviation for the second "without any apparent difference of meaning" (*Interpretation* 144).

3. On the other hand, Dodd clearly understands *phōs* ("light") to be a metaphysical term which refers to the eternal as opposed to the phenomenal order (*Interpretation* 201–2). Unlike the "subjective" reference Bultmann gives the word, Hoskyns and Davey stress the "objective" allusion of *phōs* ("light"). For them it is, "that by which [humans] are enabled to recognize the operation of God in the world" (143).

4. "Creation is at the same time revelation, inasmuch as it was possible for the creature to know of his [or her] Creator, and thus to understand [her or] himself" (Bultmann, *Gospel* 44). (*Die Schöpfung ist zugleich Offenbarung, sofern das Geschaffene die Möglichkeit hatte, um seinen Schöpfer zu wissen und so sich selbst zu verstehen* [Bultmann, *Johannes* 25]).

5. Bultmann's existential reading of the passage is distinctive when compared with the "history of salvation" interpretation (e.g., Brown, *Commentary–Gospel*). For Bultmann's discussion of the history of salvation position, cf. *Existence* 226–40.

6. Cf. Bultmann, *Faith and Understanding* 1:55, where Bultmann writes, "If one wishes to speak of God, one must clearly speak of [her or] himself."

7. See also Bultmann's interpretation of redemption of which the essay "Grace and Freedom" (*Essays* 168–81) is one example. His understanding of faith as obedience would appear to be a logical extension of the concept of utter dependence. For example, his discussion of faith and related terms (along with A. Weiser) in *Theological Dictionary* 6:174–228, as well as his other contributions to this work.

8. It would be interesting to build a case for the significance of an implicit concept of creation in the philosophical system of M. Heidegger. To Christian readers of Heidegger the concepts of authenticity and inauthenticity necessitate some original intention for existence. Of course, Heidegger himself would not care to go this far in the direction of a Christian interpretation of existence. Yet if there is an evaluative distinction between modes of existence, it would seem fair to infer that there is a kind of "essential" origin of proper existence, i.e., creation. J. Macquarrie writes that the Christian life understood as authentic existence entails "the restoration of the original possibilities" God gave humans in creation (137). Such an evaluation of modes of existence sets the Heideggerian apart from the Sartrian system with its radical concept of "nothingness."

Chapter Two

Previously appeared in *Perspective* 13 (1972): 23–33. Revised.

1. The problem of Johannine eschatology was concisely stated by C. K. Barrett some years ago when he suggested the problem could be summarized in

four essential points: (1) "'Futuristic' eschatology is exceptionally rare in the fourth Gospel." (2) "Apocalyptic is entirely absent from John . . . [except for occasional images such as the one occurring at 16:2]." (3) "The language of eschatology, and sometimes of apocalyptic, is taken over for the purpose of mysticism." He defines mysticism in this case as "the whole range of immediate, personal, religious experience, in which a [person] is conscious of contact with God (or Christ)." (4) "[T]he introduction of a new idiom [e.g., "rebirth"]." ("Unsolved" 302–3).

2. Among those who hold to such a "tensional" (already and not yet) solution to the problem of Johannine eschatology, there are at least four different kinds of premises used to understand the evangelist's theology: (1) A tensional eschatology is suggested by M.-E. Boismard on the basis of a hypothesis regarding the literary history of the gospel ("Lévolution"). (2) In another group of interpreters this sort of now-not yet eschatology is read from the perspective of salvation history. Examples include Cullmann, *Salvation*, and "L'Évangile"; Holwerda, *Holy Spirit*; Ricca; and Corell. (3) Still others understand that the evangelist intended to apply the appropriate eschatology to the appropriate situation. See Stauffer; and van Hartingsveld. (4) Finally, another large group of scholars proposes that the tensional eschatology is a result of the evangelist's utilization of new language and/or categories of thought. One example is Moule, "Individualism." Bland (*Krisis*) is among continental interpreters who defend this position. E. Käsemann has suggested that the futuristic passages represent a kind of naive contradiction in the theology of the gospel. He writes, "the evangelist . . . failed to outgrow completely the relics of the past" (*Testament* 13–14).

3. Early in his commentary Bultmann suggests that evidence sufficient for concluding that the gospel has undergone redaction is to be found in two obvious facts. The first is that the text is clearly disarranged in its present form and the second that chapter 21 is the addition of a redactor(s) (*Gospel* 17, n. 2).

4. Cf. *Epistles*, e.g., 19–20. A thorough statement and valuable criticism of Bultmann's method has been done by D. M. Smith (*Composition*).

5. E. M. Good offers this definition of demythologizing. "[D]emythologization is the interpretation of the New Testament in terms that contemporary [people] can comprehend. In the more specific way that Bultmann means the term, it is a method of interpreting the mythological understanding of [humans] held by the New Testament so that it becomes understandable to its contemporary hearer and compels him [or her] to make a decision for him [or her] self with regard to it" (Kegley, 22).

6. See also *Faith and Understanding* 1:165–83. Representative of the many criticisms of Bultmann's interpretation of Johannine eschatology is P. Minear's article in which he claims that Bultmann presupposes a basic dichotomy between the cosmic and the historical reality. Minear would opt for a "Christological eschatology" which overcomes this dichotomy (Kegley, 80–81).

7.   The validity of Bultmann's method has, of course, been frequently challenged. D. M. Smith has quite correctly raised the question as to whether or not Bultmann's critical methods do not demand of the evangelist undue consistency in style and in content (Smith, *Composition* 241).

8.   Most notable are J. A. Bailey and Williams. Although very cautious, Williams suggests "that before looking for special sources or independent traditions behind the Fourth Gospel, investigators ought to scrutinize their material very carefully for possible connections with the synoptic tradition" (319). Cf. Noack; and Shulz, *Komposition.* E. Haenchen also concedes that the sources used by the Fourth Gospel may have been oral ("History" 207, n. 24, and "Johanneischen"). Van Iersel grants that the evangelist used both oral and written sources (265–66). For a general example, see Kysar (*Maverick Gospel* [1976], 12–14). Another example of the theory that oral tradition explains both the similarities and the differences between John and the Synoptics is found in the work of P. N. Anderson ("Interfluential," and "John and Mark").

9.   In 1963 D. M. Smith expressed the general state of scholarship on the issue of John's use of the Synoptic Gospels when he says, "the evidence that [the Fourth Evangelist] did not use [the Synoptics] as a principal source, if he knew them at all, has been mounting in recent years. It has now reached such a point that the burden of proof may be said to lie upon the scholar who wishes to maintain that John knew and used them" (*Johannine Christianity* 105). Smith furthers this view in *John.* More recently, however, he has made a case for John's use of the Gospel of Mark and the value of the Fourth Gospel as a source for knowledge regarding the historical Jesus (*John* 195–242).

10. See now the third edition of Martyn's book, *History and Theology.* As early as 1916, J. M. Thompson found what he called a mystical use of *zōē* ("life") imposed upon a more primitive apocalyptic use of the term and argued from this discovery that the evangelist had utilized a source in composing at least the first twelve chapters of the gospel ("Composition"). See the essay "Expulsion from the Synagogue: A Tale of a Theory" in the final section of this book. There I describe the case for questioning Martyn's influential proposal.

11. My argument is similar to B. Childs's contention that the Old Testament writers often employed myth of non-Israelite origin but reinterpreted it in light of the "reality" which Israel knew. The result was an unresolved tension between the mythical elements of a passage and those elements arising out of Israelite interpretation. Childs calls the result "broken myth" (cf. Tillich, *Dynamics* 50–51). Furthermore, Childs contends that the authors of the material were in full control of their material and that their use of the mythical material was conscious (*Myth and Reality*, passim). Cf. the article, "Pursuing the Paradoxes of Johannine Thought," ch. 4 below.

Chapter Three

Originally published as "Christology and Controversy: The Contributions of the Prologue of John to New Testament Christology and Their Historical Setting." *Currents in Theology and Mission* 5 (1978): 348–64. Revised.

1. Two useful summaries of the questions involved in the prologue and scholarly research on them are Schnackenburg, *Gospel* 1:221–81, and Brown, *Commentary–Gospel* 1:29, 18–23. For more recent literature on the subject see Kysar, "Community" 364, and "Gospel of John" 314–23.

2. For a summary of efforts of scholars to isolate the intellectual background of the term *logos*, see Kysar, *Fourth Evangelist* 107–11 and J. T. Sanders, *Christological Hymns* 29–57.

3. For a different view, but one which I think is less likely, see Berger.

4. M. R. Vincent writes, "The phrase, *en morphē theou hyparchōn* [in the form of God existing] is then to be understood of Christ's preincarnate state. To say that he was *en morphē theou* [in the form of God] is to say that he existed before his incarnation as essentially one with God, and that, objectively, and not merely in God's self-consciousness as the not yet incarnate Son . . ." (843).

5. R. E. Brown is correct in saying that "the beginning . . . is a designation, more qualitative than temporal, of the sphere of God" and that the beginning of creation does not come until verse 3" (*Commentary–Gospel* 1:4). However, elsewhere he claims, "only John makes it clear that the preexistence was before creation." ("'Other Sheep'" 16, n. 37.) We have seen, of course, that the theme of Christ's role in creation is not unique to the prologue. Hence, we must say that preexistence prior to creation is clearly implied especially in Colossians 1:16 and Hebrews 1:2, but the prologue affirms a preexistence that supersedes even creation.

6. For examples of proposals that the present hymn is comprised of two separate poems (see Rissi, "Logoslieder," and "John 1:1-18") as well as Deeks. On the debate over where in the prologue the reference to the historical appearance of the logos begins, contrast, e.g., Dodd, *Interpretation* 270, with Bultmann, *Gospel* 54–55.

7. Dion points out the way in which the Fourth Evangelist has altered the sequential form of humiliation and exaltation and transforms the crucifixion into a glorification (56–57).

8. E.g., Bernard 1:cxliv–cxlvi. On the other hand, see the view of Barrett, *Gospel According to St. John* 126.

9. This interpretation stands in contradition to that of Lightfoot (85) who reads 1:14 in the light of the kenotic Christology of Philippians 2:7.

10. That the glorification of the Son of Man is already present in his earthly life is one of the distinctive marks of the Johannine view. Ruckstuhl, "Menschensohnforschung" 281. For a similar view see Tremel, 65–92.

11. An article that stresses that the Fourth Evangelist presents Jesus in a multidimensional manner—the Jewish man of Galilee and the spiritual Christ present in the church—is found in D. M. Smith, *Johannine Christianity* 175–89.

12. On the theme of the resistance to Jesus see the argument of Harvey, who sug-
    gests that the whole of the gospel contains a prolonged trial of Jesus. While
    he makes a good point, he tends to exaggerate the evidence.

13. Talbert presents a tenable case for the Fourth Gospel having its roots in a
    Hellenistic Jewish mythology of the descending and ascending divine agent,
    which stands in contrast to the mythic patterns used in the Synoptic Gospels
    (ch. 3). His argument helps us understand the evangelist's distinctive use of
    the gospel genre, for he points out that, unlike the mythic patterns employed
    in the Synoptic Gospels, the descending-ascending motif has no parallel in
    Greco-Roman biographies (*What Is* 77). This may mean that the biography
    genre was not the literary form employed by the Fourth Evangelist, in dis-
    tinction from the synoptic evangelists.

14. Pancaro points out the Johannine Christians transferred to Christ a number
    of the symbols associated with the Law in first-century Judaism, including
    that of "light." Other examples include "bread," "water," and "life" (*Law*
    452–53).

15. This understanding of the disclaimers concerning the Baptist need not
    exclude the possibility that there is also an implicit polemic against a Baptist
    messianic movement in these verses. However, Bultmann probably exagger-
    ated the significance of the anti-Baptist polemic in *Gospel* 51–52.

16. This proposal gains some support from the trend in recent scholarship
    toward the view that first century Judaism offers the most illuminating con-
    text in which to understand the thought of the prologue. See Kysar, "Com-
    munity" 364.

17. Müller writes, "John 1:14, 16 is stamped with a one-sided Christology of
    glory which ignores the possible offense of the death of Jesus (*Geschichte*
    69)." His discussion of the combination of a community hymn (1:14 and 16)
    with the gospel narrative that stresses a theology of glory is closely akin to the
    interpretation of the prologue I am proposing.

18. Mastin sees 1:1 and 18 as two of three verses in John (the third being 20:28)
    in which Jesus is called God. They are "best understood as a result of the
    controversy between Jews and Christians over claims made about Jesus . . . it
    does not describe his function, but indicates who he is" (32–51, quote 51).
    While I share Mastin's understanding of the setting for the Christology of
    the prologue, I think that he has de-emphasized the functional dimensions
    of what the prologue means by calling Christ God.

19. The theory that the early Christians associated with the Fourth Gospel were
    engaged in a heated controversy with Jews is a potentially dangerous idea. It
    can easily be interpreted in ways that foster a contemporary anti-Semitism. If
    this historical reconstruction has any truth in it, we should remember, first,
    that the Johannine Christians were themselves Jews with roots in the syna-
    gogue. Second, if there was such a conflict between them and their broth-
    ers and sisters in the synagogue, it was more like a family argument than a
    fierce battle. See the essay in part 3 of this book entitled, "Anti-Semitism
    and the Gospel of John," for an analysis of the evidence for the Christian-

Jewish dialogue influencing John and for an exploration of its contemporary relevance.

20. J. A. T. Robinson is correct in challenging the view that the Christology of the prologue reflects a "high Christology" which could only have emerged late in the first century; but he is not correct in concluding therefore that John can be dated before 70 C.E. (*Redating* 282-25). That the Christology of the prologue makes no advances beyond the passages in Philippians and Colossians, as Robinson claims, seems to me to miss the important differences I have pointed out above. I would deny that the Christology of the prologue is so close to that of Paul's that we need not date it in a different decade, but I would also demur before the necessity of postponing the emergence of such a Christology to the 90s simply on the grounds of an evolutionary scheme.

21. Moule argues that the Christology of the New Testament is better understood as a "development" than as an "evolution" (*Origin* 2-3).

Chapter Four

Originally published in *The Living Text: Essays in Honor of Ernest W. Saunders*. Edited by D. E. Groh and R. Jewett. Lanham, Md.: University Press of America, 1985. 189-206. Revised.

1. P. N. Anderson has used the thesis of the "dialectical theology" of the Fourth Evangelist seriously and thoroughly in his study of John 6 (*Christology*). Among other things, Anderson relates such dialectical thought to J. Fowler's understanding of faith development and the ability to think dialectically (e.g., Fowler, *Stages of Faith*).

2. This is to view the theology of gospel as "community theology (*Gemeinde-theologie*)," to borrow the expression of U. Müller (*Geschichte*, esp. 69-72). Examples of this approach are found in J. Becker's study of Johannine dualism ("Beobachtungen") and J. Coppens's thesis regarding the Son of Man motif in John's gospel ("Fils").

3. For a brief survey of this and other methods of distinguishing tradition and redaction employed in contemporary scholarship, see Kysar, *Fourth Evangelist* 15-24. One can best see the use of the "content criterion" or "ideological tension" in Lindars, *Behind*, and *Gospel of John*; Schnackenburg, *Gospel*; and Haenchen, *John*.

4. In the literature discussing Fortna's enterprise three contributions are especially worthy of note: Freed and Hunt; Carson, "Current"; and D. M. Smith, *Johannine Christianity*, 80-93.

5. For other support of Martyn's general thesis, see the surveys in Kysar, *Fourth Evangelist* 149-56; "Community" 273-74; "John in Current" 316-18. Some critics are appropriately raising serious questions and challenges to Martyn's insistence that the expulsion of the Johannine community from the synagogue was a result of the formal propagation of the *Birkat ha-Minim* ("Blessing the Heretics"). See esp. Kimelman; and Katz. It is much more likely that the experience of expulsion for John's church occurred as a result of a localized and informal decision on the part of a single synagogue and that it took

place much earlier than Martyn has proposed (perhaps as early as 70–80 C.E.). That expulsion, as I image it, was part of an "intra-family" argument reflective of conditions in John's city and not necessarily of the general Jewish-Christian relationship in the second half of the first century. An earlier dating of the expulsion also allows one to see it as a result, in part, of the reaction of Judaism to the destruction of the temple. Still, Martyn's thesis has proven helpful in elucidating the setting of the gospel. However, see the essay, "The Expulsion from the Synagogue," in part 4 of this collection for a statement of my own reevaluation of Martyn's thesis.

6. We leave to one side for now those cases in which we find not simply one pair of contradictory concepts in a passage but a myriad of countervailing ideas, such as I think are present in the christologies of the gospel. I am content for now to show how this proposed method might handle a simple pair of opposing ideas.

7. The major work on this theological theme has been done by Carson (*Divine Sovereignty*) and Bergmeier. The article on chapter 6 in the literary criticism section of this collection is more representative of my current view of the issue.

8. Fortna says of this narrative, "The source may have continued here (after v. 25) with material which is now buried in the rest of chap. 6, notably in the episode with Peter in 6:67ff." (*Gospel of Signs* 238).

9. Commentators tend, for the most part, to minimize the conflict among these passages and to harmonize them with hasty generalizations. Typical of such are the following: Brown, *Commentary–Gospel* 1:277; Schnackenburg, *Gospel* 2:50; Lindars, *Gospel of John* 263; and Barrett, *Gospel According to St. John* 295. Notable, however, are these comments by two very different scholars. Bultmann writes of verse 44, "faith has no support outside itself." (*Gospel* 232). F. F. Bruce comments on the same verse, "The divine initiative in the salvation of believers is emphasized. The responsibility of men and women in the matter of coming to Christ is not overlooked (cf. John 5:40); but none at all would come unless divinely persuaded and enabled to do so" (56). See also Kysar, *Maverick Gospel* (1976) 70–74.

10. It is interesting to note that we do not find this tension in verses 51-59. These verses are by almost common agreement a second form of the bread of life discourse and, according to some interpreters, one in which we encounter the eucharistic interpretation of the discourse. The fact that it is devoid of the ideological tension with regard to the issue of faith may be a further suggestion of its separation from the discourse form in verses 25-50 and the narrative in verses 60-71. However, verses 51-59 do contain the tension between future and present eschatology (see the chart below). If the section is a somewhat later eucharistic interpretation of the words of Jesus, then it becomes clear that the redactor has dropped any interest in the question of the responsibility for the faith-act in favor of the sacramental motif. The continued presence of the eschatological tension may be because the Eucharist was an experiential expression of the "now and not-yet" quality of God's

11. Although his understanding of the signs source is considerably different from Fortna's, Nicol shares the view that the source was designed primarily as a missionary document. (*Sēmeia* 44).

12. Fortna's proposed source was, of course, a collection of narratives, and we are discussing discourse materials (for the most part). I am supposing that the point of view found in the signs source pervaded the whole of the Johannine tradition, discourse as well as narrative. As we have seen, the discourse materials of the chapter, as well as in the narrative piece in verses 60–71, exhibit the presumption of human responsibility for faith.

13. It is equally feasible that someone introduced the proposed second layer of material before the evangelist incorporated it into the gospel, in which case the evangelist inherited the tension between the two views and preserved it as he or she found it in the tradition. Clearly, however, the second layer arose in the community after the experience of expulsion from the synagogue. It is more likely, then, that this second stratum comes from the evangelist and/or the community and reflects the critique of the tradition at the time of the composition of the Gospel of John.

14. Martyn offers a proposal that supports the argument developed here. Behind 1:35-49, he suggests, lies an early sermon adapted by the evangelist from the community's tradition. That sermon stressed Jesus' "passivity" expressed in the invitations "to come" and "to find." Such an emphasis on human initiative is in contrast "with key passages in the Fourth Gospel in which the initiative of Jesus (or of God) is polemically affirmed," Martyn says, and cites 6:44 and 6:65, and 15:16 and 15:19 in particular. Most likely the latter reflects the redactional work of the evangelist (*Gospel* 93 and 95).

15. Many commentators today correctly reject the view that this refrain betrays the hand of a later redactor (e.g., Bultmann, *Gospel* 219–20). E.g., Barrett, *Gospel According to St. John* 294; Schnackenburg, *Gospel* 2:48; Bruce, 154; Lindars, *Gospel of John* 261; and Brown, *Commentary–Gospel* 1:276. More recently, some have argued on the basis of Greek grammar that the expression does not imply a present eschatology. E.g., Caragounis, 125–34.

16. See "The Eschatology of the Fourth Gospel: A Correction of Bultmann's Redaction and Hypothesis," reprinted in part 1 in this collection. *Maverick Gospel* [1993] 97–127.

17. Paul's thought illustrates the likelihood that such a tension between the present and future was represented in Christian tradition very early (Rom 10:9-10). The Christian is already justified (Rom 3:24) and yet looks forward in hope for salvation (Rom 8:24). Such a tension may have its roots in Jesus' own proclamation that the kingdom of God is both present and yet to come to power. More recently G. B. Caird has maintained that the New Testament presents "three tenses of salvation"—past, present, and future (*New Testament Theology* 118–35).

18. If the thesis of this article were correct, a strict "trajectory" view of the Johannine community (like the theory proposed, for instance, by J. A. T. Robinson and Koester in *Trajectories*) would suggest that we would probably find only a present eschatology emphasized in the later Johannine epistles. Instead, we find a futuristic eschatology strongly attested in 1 John (e.g., 2:18-20), although remnants of the present eschatology of the gospel are also clear (e.g., 1 John 3:14 and 5:11). A number of factors account for the preservation and even revitalization of the older eschatology in later stages of the history of the community. First, closer associations with other Christian churches after the writing of the gospel may have brought the community to a renewed affirmation of the future promises of God. Second, this affirmation was natural after the intense dialogue with the synagogue had subsided and the necessity of Christian self-definition over against Judaism had passed. Third, the occasion of the internal division within the community, which precipitated the writing of the epistles, stirred apocalyptic expectations (e.g., the "antichrist"). In search of a defense against those who had separated themselves from the community, the author of 1 John sought an eschatological context for understanding the experience. Cf. Brown, *Commentary–Epistles*.

19. D. Aune demonstrates the importance of social experience for early Christian thought, especially eschatology (*Cultic Setting*). See also the seminal work by Meeks, "Man from Heaven." Schnackenburg discusses other possible causes for the emergence of John's realized eschatology in *Gospel* 2:435–37.

20. This view has much in common with that of Wengst. My own reflections on the Johannine propensity for paradox in contemporary preaching is found in *Preaching John* 52–56.

21. Recently a fundamental challenge to much of the investigation into the history context of the Gospel of John and the other New Testament documents has come from Bauckham and others. They maintain that the gospels were not written for particular communities but for circulation within the whole of the Hellenistic world.

22. For a very effective challenge to the idea that contradiction and other anomalies indicate editing and use of sources, see Kellum. Woll proposed a rather different setting for chapters 13 and 14. While intriguing, his thesis is not entirely convincing, although we should take it seriously as an indication that the proposed setting for the gospel employed in this essay is not the whole picture, nor necessarily a true one. Cf. "The Expulsion from the Synagogue" in part 4 of this volume, which gathers some of the major criticisms of Martyn's proposal.

23. Even Martyn demurs before a radical statement of the social roots of Johannine Christology. Of conclusions drawn by Aune cited above (110) he writes, "One can easily imagine the Fourth Evangelist shuddering at such statements" (Martyn, *Gospel* 105, n. 168).

Chapter Five

Originally published in "The Fourth Gospel, A Report on Recent Research." *Aufstieg und Niedergang der Römischen Welt*, Teil II: *Principate*, 3. Teilband. Edited by Wolfgang Haase. Berlin/New York: Walter de Gruyter, 1985. 2391–2411. Revised.

1. This overlooks the efforts to analyze the Gospel of John in terms of *Gattungen*. For a research report on the attempts to deal with the literary forms of John, see the article in ANRW by Beutler (2506–2568).

2. M. Làconi's work is known to me only through the survey of displacement theories in Teeple, *Literary* 106–11.

3. Olsson's approach has received confirmation and appreciative use in some of the recent work of de Jonge, "Signs" 122–24.

4. H. Lona, 446–49, 451–56. Cf. *FV* 73 in which one issue is devoted to structuralism, esp., Jaubert, "Comparution"; Escande; and Geoltrain. For an explanation of semiotics, see Cook.

5. L. Dupont, C. Lash, and G. Levesque reflect another kind of structural analysis. Cf. Festuriere; Vouga; and Vanhoye, "Interrogation."

6. For a summary and critique of Bultmann's source theory, see D. M. Smith, *Composition*.

7. Cf. D. M. Smith, *Composition* 38–44. Bultmann's signs source depends heavily upon Faure, 107ff.

8. A number of scholars believe the presentation of Jesus in the Fourth Gospel betrays a parallel with the Hellenistic concept of the "divine man," e.g., Fuller *Interpreting*; Koster; Schottroff, *Glaubende* 257ff.

9. Cf. D. M. Smith, *Composition* 23–34, and 48–51. A more thorough defense of the *Offenbarungsreden* source is attempted by H. Becker.

10. We find confirmations and criticisms of Fortna in the following: Martyn, *Jesus*; Freed and Hunt; O'Rourke "Historic"; D. M. Smith, *Johannine Christianity*; Schnackenburg, *Johannesevangelium* 3:463ff.; Lindars, *Behind* 32–33; and Kysar, *Fourth Evangelist* 33–37.

11. E.g., van Belle. Among those who reject source criticism are De Jonge, "Variety,"and Schneider, 24–25. An excellent survey of source criticism of the Gospel of John is Teeple, *Literary* 1–116. Nicol's proposal receives critical appraisal by Richter in "Sogenannten Semeia-Quelle."

12. Brown defends and utilizes his hypothesis throughout the two volumes of his commentary. Cf. Làconi. In the revisions of his commentary Brown made just before his death, however, he condensed the proposed stages to three: (1) the origin in the public ministry or activity of Jesus; (2) the proclamation of Jesus in the post-resurrectional context of the community history; and (3) the writing of the gospel and its redaction. (*Introduction* 64–85.)

13. Cf. D. M. Smith, *John*. Smith revised this book and retracted his conclusion that the Fourth Evangelist did not depend on the Synoptics for the writing of John. Instead, Smith makes a case that the Fourth Evangelist was

independent of the Synoptics but nonetheless may have known at least the Gospel of Mark.

14. A persuasive and careful case for this is made by Fortna "Jesus."

15. D. M. Smith's summation written in 1975 still seems both concise and helpful: "The distinctive character of the Johannine narrative material within the gospel strongly suggests a principal source (or sources) and one independent of the Synoptics" ("Johannine Christianity" 229; cf. Lindars, "Traditions").

Chapter Six

Originally published in "The Fourth Gospel, A Report on Recent Research." *Aufstieg und Niedergang der Römischen Welt*, Teil II: *Principate*, 3. Teilband. Edited by Wolfgang Haase. Berlin/New York: Walter de Gruyter, 1985. 2411–2439. Revised.

1. Cf. Schulz, *Stunde* 323, 331, and *Untersuchungen*. Contrast Fascher. On the personification of the logos, contrast Langkamer.

2. E.g., E. Freed argues that the Fourth Evangelist cites the Old Testament from memory (*Old Testament*, and "Some Old Testament"). Schnackenburg maintains that the Fourth Evangelist made free use of the Old Testament (*Gospel* 1:123). F.-M. Braun contends that the evangelist used a Palestinian canon and the later redactor of the gospel a Greek translation of the Old Testament (*Jean le théologien. II* 17). Reim argues that the Old Testament citations in John are exclusively from the tradition used by the evangelist (*Studien* 93–96, 188–89, 231–32). Richter proposes that the citations at 6:31b and 45 are not OT at all but from a contemporary Jewish haggadah ("Alttestamentlichen"). Cf. Aaletti; O'Rourke, "Fulfillment Texts."

3. Scholars frequently argue the proposal that John 10:34 reflects a rabbinic background of the citation of Psalm 82: Hanson "Citation of Psalm LXXXII," and "Citation of Psalm LXXXII Reconsidered"; Ackerman; Boismard "Jésus"; Emerton. Cf. Schirmer, esp. 207; Laurentin; McNeil; Wilcox.

4. Space will not permit us to discuss the general criticism of the prologue of the gospel. I refer you to the following works which are representative of the research being done on 1:1-18: Bultmann, *Gospel* 13–83; Brown, *Commentary–Gospel* 1:3–37; Schnackenburg, *Gospel* 1:221–81; Rissi "Logoslieder"; Deeks; Trudinger "Prologue"; Hooker; Aatal, esp. 79f. and 52–54; King; Zimmermann; Richter "Strukturbildendes"; and Ramaroson. For a survey of scholarship on this passage cf. Thyen, "Literatur" 222–52.

5. Cf. Borgen "Observations—John 6"; Schnackenburg, "Rede"; Blank "Brotrede," and "Ich bin." Contrast Richter "Formgeschichte," and Bornkamm "Vorjohanneische."

6. Jaubert, *Date*; Ruckstuhl, *Chronology*; and Strand. Other studies relevant to the Passover motif of John include R. H. Smith; Brown, *Commentary–Gospel* 1:ix, 529; and Riga.

7. Cf. the imaginative but unconvincing article by Bowman, *Fourth Gospel and the Jews*. Other studies related to Old Testament-rabbinic background of the

gospel are Mealand; Ruddick; Boismard, *Baptême*; and Hanson, "John I.14-18."

8. For a survey of views of the dualism of the Fourth Gospel and Qumran, cf. H. Braun, *Qumran* 2:119–32; and Bergmeier.

9. Martyn was not the first to propose that exclusion from the synagogue was connected with the writing of John. Cf., e.g., Carroll; Schnackenburg "Origin;" and Beutler, 345.

10. Cf. the introductory studies of the theology of the Fourth Gospel that employ this setting, e.g., Painter; and Kysar, *John*. For a different and more contemporary view of Martyn's proposal see "The Expulsion from the Synagogue" in part 4 of this collection.

11. Cf. Bratcher; Shepherd; and the article "Anti-Semitism in the Gospel of John" in part 3 of this collection.

12. Others who propose that an anti-Jewish polemic is one of the purposes of John include the following: Riesenfeld "Johanneischen"; Neugebauer 14; Richter "Gefangennahme." However, Richter later declared that he believes the Christian-Jewish conflict visible in the Fourth Gospel is actually a conflict between Jewish Christians and Johannine Christians ("Gemeindebildenden"). J. P. Miranda sees the conflict as one between Christians and rabbinic Judaism (*Sendung* 71–80). T. C. Smith has reaffirmed his view that the purpose of the gospel is missional rather than polemic in regard to the Jews ("Christology").

13. Richter also finds evidence of an anti-baptist polemic ("Bist" 13–15, and "Frage" 309–10). Cf. Schnackenburg, *Gospel* 1:67–169; Brown, *Commentary-Gospel* 1:lxviii–lxx. Schnackenburg earlier assigned a more significant role to the anti-baptist theme (*Evangelium*). G. F. Snyder offers an anti-petrine thesis.

14. For further studies of the Samaritan religion, see MacDonald; Bowman, *Samaritanische*; Ben-Hayyim; Kippenberg; Purvis, *Samaritan*; Collins; and Spiro.

15. More recently, J. A. T. Robinson has argued in detail for an earlier date. See his *The Priority of John*. Moloney attacks Robinson's proposal in "Fourth." Cf. the highly speculative and tenuous argument of Gericke.

16. Cf. Bruns "Confusion," and "John Mark"; L. Johnson, "Who Was the Beloved Disciple?", and "Reply"; Porter; and Rogers.

Part II

1. A historical survey of the development of the views in the Bible is more accurately termed history of religions than theological, even though both use the same data. A comparison of Ringgren's *Israelite Religion* and von Rad's *Old Testament Theology* makes the distinction clear.

Chapter Seven

Originally published in "The Fourth Gospel, A Report on Recent Research," *Aufstieg und Niedergang der Römischen Welt*, Teil II: *Principate*, 3. Teilband.

Edited by Wolfgang Haase. Berlin/New York: Walter de Gruyter, 1985. 2391–2480. Revised.

1. Other works which might be considered in this category include the theological insights of those scholars who deal with the history of the Johannine community, see esp. Richter "Präsentische."

Chapter Eight

Originally published in "The Fourth Gospel, A Report on Recent Research." *Aufstieg und Niedergang der Römischen Welt*, Teil II: *Principate*, 3. Teilband. Edited by Wolfgang Haase. Berlin/New York: Walter de Gruyter, 1985. 2443–2464. Revised.

1. Cf. Jaubert, "L'Image" 93–99, and *Approches*. Contrast Brown, "Kerygma" 395–96, and Bultmann, *Theology* 2:8. Cf. on the general subject, Carnegie; and Morris, *Studies* 65–138.
2. Cf. for example, these studies: de La Potterie "L'exaltation"; Caird "Glory of God"; de Kruijf; van Boxel; and Feuillet, *Le prologue*. More specifically relevant to Käsemann's view, cf. Schweizer, "Jesus" 186; Bornkamm, "Interpretation"; Brown, "Kerygma" 396–400; and most recently, M. M. Thompson.
3. For other studies of the Son of Man, cf. Ruckstuhl "Menschensohnforschung"; Dion; Freed, "Son of Man"; Lindars "Son of Man"; De Jonge "Jesus"; Beauvery; and De Oliveira.
4. Other works relevant to the humanity of Christ in the Fourth Gospel include: Kinniburgh; Howton; Smalley, "Johannine"; Schnackenburg, *Johannesevangelium* 2:166–67; Gryglewicz; Hill; Weise; Negoitsa and Daniel; and Richter, "Fleischwerdung."
5. For other attempts to stress this inseparable equality of flesh and glory, cf. Harner, 53–65; Schnackenburg, *Johannesevangelium* 2:69–70; Tremel; and Morris, *Gospel*.
6. Cf. Richter, *Fusswaschung*, and "Fusswaschung Joh 13." Other weaker arguments for sacramental references in the Fourth Gospel include Sandvik; Shaw, "Breakfast," and "Image."

Chapter Nine

Previously published in *Anti-Semitism and Early Christianity: Issues of Polemic and Faith*. Edited by Craig A. Evans and Donald A. Hagner. Minneapolis, Minn.: Fortress Press, 1993. 113–27. Revised.

1. Sandmel, *Anti-Semitism* 101. In his earlier introduction to the New Testament, Sandmel makes much the same observation: "In its utility for later Jew-haters, the Fourth Gospel is preeminent among the New Testament writings" (*Jewish Understanding* 269).
2. The tendency toward an anti-Judaistic presupposition operative in the tradition of New Testament interpretation is well documented in C. Klein. The persistence of the issue of Christian anti-Semitism was evidenced in 2004 with the opening of Mel Gibson's movie, "The Passion of Christ."

3. See the persuasive argument of E. V. McKnight, particularly for what he terms "the contemporary challenge of interpretation." McKnight points out, "Analysis of the various approaches to the Bible uncovers the same basic procedure: Readers make sense of the Bible in the light of their world, which includes not only linguistic and literary tools but also world views that influence the sorts of meanings and the methods that are satisfying" (*Post-Modern Use* 58).

4. For the purposes of this article I define anti-Semitism as any attitude, action, or social-economic structure which tends consciously or unconsciously to demean the Jewish people as a whole and to nurture negative attitudes toward them. Like any form of prejudice it constitutes a view of the Jewish people disregarding any and all facts about them.

5. For definitions of the terms *implied author*, *implied reader*, and *narrator*, as used in the following discussion, see Culpepper, *Anatomy* 71–73.

6. It is interesting that, while arguing against an anti-Jewish character of the gospel, Schnackenburg observes about 4:22, "The Gospel displays no hatred of the Jewish people, though it regards them with a certain aloofness." (*Gospel* 1:436)

7. Staley points out how the narrator's translation of Aramaic and Hebrew words (e.g., 1:38) makes "the implied reader feel like an outsider: They separate—as nothing else could—the narrator's and characters' world from that of the implied reader" (*Print's First Kiss* 82). This practice might also be viewed as part of the strategy of the implied author to distance the reader from Judaism.

8. Culpepper suggests that "the burden of unbelief which the Jews are made to carry is relieved in two ways. First, John affirms that belief must be given (6:37, 39). . . . Second, some of the Jews do believe . . . so John allows hope that for some at least (i.e., those who are 'given') belief is possible." But he concludes nonetheless that "the Jews carry the burden of the unbelief of 'the world' in John" (*Anatomy* 138).

9. Although the antecedent is vague, the reader gains the impression from 12:37–43 that the Pharisees are prevented by God from believing in Jesus. Cf. Mussner, *Tractate* 206–7.

10. See the recent and thorough collection, *Anti-Judaism and the Fourth Gospel*, edited by Bieringer, et al.. In these papers nearly every possible alternative for understanding the issue of the Jews in John is discussed along with theological reflection.

11. The limitations of space do not allow for a consideration of all of the many historical settings that have been proposed for the Gospel of John even in recent years. Therefore, I have chosen here to discuss only the hypothesis that seems to me to be the most widely endorsed and (in my view) the most convincing. Other proposals have been offered in recent years. See, Kysar *Fourth Evangelist* 147–65, "Community" 265–67, 273–74, "Gospel of John" 316–17, and the articles in this collection taken from *Aufstieg und Niedergang der römischen Welt*.

12. J. L. Martyn, *History and Theology* and *Christian History*; Brown, *Commentary–Gospel*, and *Community*. While Martyn and Brown brought this theory into prominence in recent Johannine studies, they were not the first to make such a proposal. See, e.g., Carroll, 19–32; and Parkes, 83.

13. Martyn's earlier contention that the expulsion should be related to the "Twelfth Benediction" (the *Birkat ha-Minim*) and the conference of rabbis at Jamnia was countered vigorously and effectively by historical investigations. Martyn himself has modified his earlier statements in this regard, and most Johannine interpreters deny any direct link between the expulsion of the Johannine Christians and the Twelfth Benediction. See Katz and Kimelman. Smith provides a helpful summary of the value of Martyn's first proposal ("Judaism" 84–67), although he assesses it more highly than I would be inclined to do. J. Koenig regrettably makes the Twelfth Benediction the basis of his approach to John (122–23), as also does Beck, 250–51.

14. For my earlier and own brief statement of the historical setting for the writing of the gospel, see *John* 13–15. For a more recent view, see the article "The Expulsion from the Synagogue: A Tale of a Theory" in part 4 of this volume.

15. Examples include the following: Meeks, *Prophet-King*; Beutler; Grässer; Pancaro, *Law*; Neyrey; Whitacre; Fortna, *Fourth Gospel*; and von Wahlde, *Earliest Version*.

16. P. S. Minear argues that the gospel was set within the context of a realistic fear of martyrdom at the hands of Jewish authorities (*John* 26–27). I doubt that such a conclusion is warranted on the basis of the evidence of the gospel, although the vigorous interaction of Jews and Christians may well have involved some degree of violence.

17. Increasingly more is being written regarding the sociological setting for the Gospel of John, much of it premised on the Martyn-Brown hypothesis for the origin of the gospel. Among the most important and influential of the published works to this date are the following: Meeks, "The Man from Heaven"; Malina, "Sociolinguistic Perspective"; and Neyrey.

18. L. Gaston correctly observes, "[The Fourth Gospel] is sectarian, even paranoiac, but it does not deny the central self-affirmation of Judaism" (174).

19. In this way the response of Johannine Christianity is markedly different from that represented in the Gospel of Matthew, which might also have been written out of an effort to define Christian faith in relationship to Judaism. See, e.g., Perrin, *New Testament* 169–75.

20. This is true in spite of Brown's efforts (e.g., *Commentary–Gospel* 2:614) to explicate the message of the gospel in covenantal categories.

21. My proposal that 4:22 represents part of an older tradition is not the most common understanding of this verse. Bultmann is an example of those who insist it was an "editorial gloss" (*Gospel* 189). Both Brown (*Commentary–Gospel* 1:172) and Schnackenburg (*Gospel* 1:436), among others, deny that view of the passage, the latter saying, "Jesus had to overcome the woman's

repugnance to the 'Jews.'" Neither Fortna (*Fourth Gospel* and *Gospel of Signs*) nor von Wahlde (*Earliest Version*) argues that 4:22 was an early tradition. While I cannot make a case here for the claim that it was, it does seem to me that for some of the reasons implied above it may very well represent a part of the narrative of chapter 4 that originated among the Johannine Christians while they were still part of the synagogue.

22. Kysar, *Maverick Gospel* (1976). In the discussion of the Jews in the Fourth Gospel I suggest they are "stylized types" used as a foil to demonstrate the revelation in Jesus (68).

23. Various remedies to the predicament occasioned by the anti-Semitic quality of John have been proposed. Beck argues for a new translation that reflects the theory of the historical origin of the gospel espoused in this essay (e.g., 267–68). In his chapter on the gospel, Smith responds to Beck's strategy by saying, "My conviction is that we cannot resolve these issues by removing offensive aspects of Scripture occasioned by the concrete circumstances of historical origins" ("Judaism" 96, n. 24). With Smith, I have grave reservations about such a proposal. To base a translation on a hypothesis for the origin of the Fourth Gospel is risky business, the result of which would necessitate a new translation every time a new theory gained prominence in scholarly circles. Furthermore, such a proposal amounts to an effort to deceive the lay hearers and readers and would result in more difficulty than it avoids. I find more helpful the suggestion of R. Fuller that the problem necessitates "careful teaching" of the laity ("'Jews'" 137). However, I think the solution is more complicated than making historical critics out of lay readers and hearers.

24. See the persuasive argument of Bauckham, however, that the gospels were not written strictly for single communities of Christians but for a larger Christian audience (*Gospel for All*). I have challenged the whole concept of the "Johannine community" in "Whence and Whither."

25. The challenge, I believe, is being addressed in such efforts as those of Jodock.

26. In a provocative article, C. M. Conway has challenged our usual way of reading and interpreting biblical documents. She argues for a keener sense and acknowledgment of how our interpretations both reflect and shape cultural attitudes and practices ("Production").

Chapter Ten

Originally published in *Semeia* 53 (1991): 81–112 as "The Fourth Gospel from a Literary Perspective." Edited by R. Alan Culpepper and Fernando F. Segovia. Atlanta, Ga.: Society of Biblical Literature, 1991. Revised.

1. For a summary of the developments see Perrin, *Jesus*, ch. 3. A more thorough bibliographical survey is found in Kissinger.

2. E.g., among others, Wilder, *Language* 90; Breech, 217. Scott has declared that the burden of proof is on those "who would claim a parable is not from Jesus" ("Essaying" 8).

3.   E.g., Leon-Dufour. In her excellent study of revelation and irony in the Fourth Gospel, G. O'Day proposes a more useful perspective. She writes, "The revelatory dynamic of the Fourth Gospel rests in the interplay between *en paroimiasis* ["in images"] and revelation *parresia* ["plain," "clear"], and in the transformation of categories and assumptions that takes place through the juxtaposition of these two modes" (*Revelation and Irony* 109). O'Day's work marks one of the important initial efforts to take the literary qualities of John seriously, especially as they relate to the theological message of the document.

4.   Gratefully, the gap between the applications of new methods in synoptic and Johannine studies has been narrowed due to the appearance of an increasing number of investigations of the Gospel of John from a literary perspective. This movement in its contemporary form perhaps began with Birger Olsson (*Structure and Meaning*). Its primary impetus in American scholarship arose from the publication of Culpepper's *Anatomy*. That seminal work has been followed by a stream of studies from a literary critical perspective, including O'Day, *Revelation and Irony*; Duke; Staley, *Print's First Kiss*; and less directly Moore, *Literary Criticism*. See also Mack. A number of structural studies have been done, examples of which include D. Patte, "Narrative and Discourse." See also Girard, "L'unite." Semiotic studies are represented in Colloud and Genuyt, *Discours*, and *L'Evangile*; and Boers. The 1991 *Semeia* volume in which this article was first published hoped to close the gap still further between the advances made in synoptic studies and those in Johannine research.

5.   Such claims for some of the metaphors attributed to Jesus in John have, of course, been made. Among the most notable and influential of such efforts are Dodd (*Historical Tradition* 366–87) and J. A. T. Robinson ("Parable" and *Priority of John* 67–75). Both Dodd and Robinson make excessive claims, it seems to me, for the historical reliability of the Fourth Evangelist's representation of Jesus' teachings. See also Sturch; and Lindars "Two Parables."

6.   For definitions of the terms *implied author*, *implied reader*, and *narrator* in the following discussion, see Culpepper, *Anatomy* 15–18, 205–11, and Staley, *Print's First Kiss* 27–47. See Moore, *Literary Criticism* 46. Moore later states, "To read any text is necessarily to engage, in and through its rhetoric (however overt or subtle), a projection of the reader that that text requires. This projection is proffered as a role, one which can be taken on or rejected but which can not be circumvented. . . . Indeed, if the hypothetical reader (or hearer) is thought of as one exposed to the text for the first time, then we have a working definition of reader-response criticism in the New Testament context" (72).

7.   I would no longer use the word "essentialist" to describe my concept of meaning and would put more emphasis on the creative role of the reader. See the last chapter of Kysar and Webb, *Postmoderns*.

8.   Recent and helpful bibliographies on the passage are found in Beasley-Murray, 162–63, and Haenchen, *John* 2:43–44.

9. Brown, *Commentary–Gospel* 1:390–96. See also Schneider, "Komposition." Bultmann calls 7-10 and 14-18 interpretations of the parables in verses 1-5 (*Gospel* 363–75). Lindars prefers to speak of verses 7-18 as expansions and developments of the parables in verses 1-5 (*Gospel of John* 354, 355). For Beasley-Murray verses 7-18 are "a meditation on the parable" (167). Schnackenburg refers to the component parts of verses 7-15 as "extensions of the imagery outlined in the *paroimia*" (*Gospel* 2:294). According to Dodd, the parables of verses 1-5 are "exploited" by the evangelist in verses 7-18 (*Historical Tradition* 385).

10. J. A. T. Robinson suggests that verses 7-18 are the result of the church's allegorization of the original parable in verses 1-5 and typical of the tendency in the early church to interpret the parables of Jesus allegorically ("Parable"). For a different interpretation see Meyer.

11. Some have proposed that the passage has suffered serious disarrangement. Examples include: Bultmann, *Gospel* 358–60; Bernard, 1:xxiv; Macgregor, 232ff. A careful analysis of Bultmann's proposal is found in D. M. Smith, *Composition* 163–66. Such disarrangement theories are widely rejected today, as a perusal of recent commentaries shows.

12. F. F. Bruce suggests that verses 7-9 comprise "a short parable" inserted into a longer one, verses 1-5 and 10-17, hence accounting for the sudden shift to the consideration of Jesus himself as the door (225).

13. A dissenting voice to the assumption that verses 1-5 are the composite of two separate parables is heard in Beasley-Murray (167), who cites in support J. Becker, *Evangelium* 1:325.

14. See, e.g. Schnackenburg, *Gospel* 2:299, who denies that verses 16-18 are redactional and claims that they "develop the idea of the good shepherd's offering of his life." Dodd seems to regard 7-18 as a single unit (*Historical Tradition* 384, n. 2), as does Beasley-Murray who understands verses 17-18 as the conclusion of the "meditation on the parable" found in verses 1-6 (171).

15. See also D. M. Smith, *Composition* 29 and von Wahlde suggests that 10:15b-16 betrays "a level of theology more appropriate to the later editions [of the Gospel]" (*Earliest Version* 125).

16. E.g., Barrett, *Gospel According to St. John* 367: "Meaning assigned to sheep seems to vary." The thought of the passage then "moves in spirals rather than straight lines." For an argument favoring the unity of verses 1-18, see Tragan.

17. For a discussion of the problem of the genre of 10:1-18, see Busse. In my commentary I labeled all the images of verses 1-18 allegories while admitting that the term is not the most descriptive of what appears in the passage. Kysar, *John* 159. Schnackenburg insists that the passage is neither parable nor allegory but "a figurative device of a mixed kind, a parable with symbolic features . . . a way of speaking that is *sui generis*" (*Gospel* 2:284–85). Haenchen argues that it is "a dark saying or figure of speech with a hidden meaning" (*John* 2:47). See also Barrett, *Gospel According to St. John* 367, and Bauer, et al., 613.

18. Lindars calls the whole passage an "allegory" (*Gospel of John* 352) but then says, "It is not so much an allegory as a discourse in monologue form" (354). Regarding verses 1-5 he concludes that they are "to some extent allegorized" because their features are "not simply drawn from life" (354). He then titles verses 7-18, "The Allegory" (357).

19. K. E. Dewey has correctly pointed out that the word *paroimia* in John covers a wide range of literary forms including parable, metaphor, allegory, and proverb (82). See also Simonis, 74–85.

20. For another and different analysis of the structure of the passage see Simonis, 20-22, and his concluding chart. While his analysis is helpful, it overlooks a number of important features of our project.

21. This effort to elucidate the theological language of verses 17-18 as image or metaphor is indebted in part to the work of S. McFague, especially, *Speaking in Parables*, *Metaphorical Theology*, and *Models*. See also ch. 2 of Kysar, *Stumbling*.

22. See N. Frye, 56. G. B. Caird speaks of the same distinction as the difference between simile and metaphor. "If a comparison is explicit we call it a simile. . . . If it is implicit we call it a metaphor" (*Language* 144).

23. J. L. Staley describes "reader victimization" or "entrapment" in this way: "It first presents the reader with the narrative 'facts' in such a way that the reader is induced to commit the character's or narrator's errors, then it forces the reader to recognize his or her misjudgments by supplying or implying the corrective perspective" (95-96). Moore argues "that the recipients of the Fourth Gospel are the ultimate victims of its irony" (*Literary Criticism* 168).

24. Compare for instance Caird, *Language* 144, and Frye, 56. See also Culpepper, *Anatomy* 182.

25. Scott, *Jesus* 13. More recently Scott has interpreted the parables in ways that might be called "metaphorical" (*Hear Then*). See also Kjärgaard.

26. Compare Ricoeur, *Essays*, and "Biblical Hermeneutics" 88, 93-101.

27. Wilder expresses a similar idea: "Now we know that a true metaphor or symbol is more than a sign, it is a bearer of the reality to which it refers." Hearers learn about reality by participating in it (*Language* 92). See also Tillich, *Systematic Theology* 1:239-41, and "Religious Symbols."

28. No better example exists than the comment of this author in comparing the synoptic and Johannine representations of Jesus: "The story parable is entirely missing. There are comparisons made, but they take on the form of elaborate allegories and lose the simplicity which their counterparts in the Synoptics have" (Kysar, *Maverick Gospel* [1976] 8). See also Kysar, *John* 158-59. Compare the second edition of *Maverick Gospel* (1993), 8.

29. Evidence of this is found in the way the image of the "good shepherd" functions in popular Christian mentality. While many Christian believers speak of Jesus as the good shepherd, few would be able to express in discursive language what they mean by that identification. The metaphor is its own truth, and it defies translation into propositional terms. The lay mentality may better grasp the nature of the metaphor than do scholarly enterprises!

30. The startling quality of the images suggests R. Alter's distinction among conventional, intensive, and innovative images. He uses as examples of innovative images the poetry of Job and makes several observations pertinent to our discussion. First, he observes how on occasion there is a "rapid flow of innovative figures" in Job. Such is surely the case as well in John 10:1-18. Second, he suggests that the force of the innovative image "colors our perception of its referent." Referring to the innovative metaphors of the Song of Songs, he writes, "imagery is given such full and free play . . . that the lines of semantic subordination blur, and it becomes a little uncertain what is illustration and what is referent" (189–90, 192–93). Those descriptions of innovative imagery could justifiably be made of John 10:1-18.

31. Brown speaks of what I have called shock as the "puzzlement" of the Johannine discourses. "Puzzlement is the way in which the readers/hearers are brought to recognize, however incompletely, who this Jesus is" ("Word for Preachers" 63). Scott writes, "Jesus' discourse changes or challenges the implied structural network of associations" (*Hear Then* 61). My suggestion is that the images in John 10:1-18 are shocking precisely because they violate the assumed system of associations.

32. Culpepper shares the expression with Beardslee (11). This literary insight is comparable to Malina's sociological suggestion that the language of the Fourth Gospel is "antilanguage," that is, the use of a culture's language by an antisocial group. Among the features of antilanguage is its relexicalization of vocabulary. See Malina, "Sociolinguistic Perspective" 11–17. See also Malina and Rohrbaugh, *Social-Science* 4–14.

33. E.g., the use of the shepherd. K. E. Bailey points out, "flesh and blood shepherds who in the first century wandered around after sheep were clearly 'am ha'aretz and unclean" (147).

34. Such is not an infrequent feature of the Johannine rhetoric. Moore argues briefly but convincingly that Johannine irony "collapse[s] in paradox" (*Literary Criticism* 163). See the importance of paradox in Kysar, *Preaching John* 52–56.

35. See E. V. McKnight's discussion of the values of deconstruction for biblical criticism (*Bible* 93–94).

36. In the words of J. Jeremias, "The hour of fulfillment is come, that is the urgent note that sounds through them all" (230). See also Via, 182ff.

37. In a sense then J. A. T. Robinson is correct in insisting that the parables of verses 1-5 have an eschatological urgency of their own, which he conceives of in terms of the "realized eschatology" of the Fourth Gospel ("Parable" 74). I prefer to think of the eschatological urgency of the passage and of the entire Johannine gospel as "existential" rather than temporal. Whether that emphasis constitutes a Johannine demythologizing of the early Christian eschatology as Bultmann argued is another question (Bultmann, *Theology* 2: pt. 3).

38. Caird speaks of "metaphor systems" in which groups of metaphors are "linked together by their common origin in a single area of human observation,

experience or activity, which has generated its own peculiar sublanguage or jargon" (*Language* 155).

39. E. Richard concludes his study of expressions of double meaning in John by saying, "Ultimately John's vision is ambiguous. . . . John's readers are constantly challenged to consider both the earthly and the heavenly" (107).

40. The distinction between simple comparison and allegory is at best a thin one, as Caird demonstrates (*Language* 165–67). The same argument is made in Klauck, *Allegorie*. When the metaphor functions poetically in the way we have described, the difference between singular comparison and allegory dissolves entirely, for both may perform as true metaphor. There surely is, however, a distinction between allegory and allegorizing.

41. Still, another avenue to be explored is the nature of some Johannine metaphors as "condensed stories" and the relationship between their abbreviated story character and that of the synoptic story parables. It may be that the distinction between Johannine metaphor and synoptic story parable is not as sharp as has sometimes been assumed.

42. Of course, my optimism about the continued use of the historical-critical method, especially in conjunction with reader-response, has faded considerably since writing this article. As the essays in the fourth part of this volume show, I now have far less appreciation for the historical-critical method.

Chapter Eleven

Originally appeared in *"What is John?" Readers and Readings of the Fourth Gospel*. Edited by Fernando F. Segovia. Society of Biblical Literature Symposium Series. Edited by Gail R. O'Day. Atlanta: Scholars Press, 1996.

1. See J. Fowler, 54–55. Since having written this paper, I have given up the effort to read the text as a first-time reader. Such a method now seems finally impossible. However, this sort of a method does share some things in common with autobiographical methods of interpretation. See Staley, *Reading*.

2. Moloney's division is more commonly proposed. He suggests that verses 1-10 and 11-21 constitute separate units (*Belief* 106). He is, of course, correct that in the latter Jesus speaks directly to the reader and Nicodemus is in the background.

3. Moloney suggests that, unlike my imaginary reader, the implied reader (on the basis of 1:5) recognizes Nicodemus' coming out of the darkness into the light (*Belief* 108). Hence, in his view the reader is even more optimistic about this meeting of the two figures.

4. See the seminal and still provocative discussion of the metaphorical character of "kingdom of God" in Perrin, 29–32. What the reader senses at this point is the "tensive" quality of the symbol.

5. Moloney argues (*Belief* 117) that the reader is expected to grasp the double meaning of *hypsoō* in verses 14-15, even though what the event is may be a puzzle. I am less sure of that expectation.

6. See the interesting work of Reinhartz, *Word*, esp. 19, 33, and 43. Reinhartz understands the language of vertical spatial movement in this and other dis-

courses in John as evidence of the "cosmological tale" of the gospel. Our reader is unknowingly immersed in a cosmic narrative.

7. Stibbe's enterprise (*John* 17) to demonstrate that the Johannine Jesus is "the elusive Christ" is clearly helpful and valid. See also "The Elusive Christ" 20–39. Our reading of 3:1-15 is an experience of that very elusiveness. But for the reader, the mystery of Christ's identity is also comprised of a certain fascination that compels her or him to pursue a resolution of Christ's words.

8. Moloney cites 3:1-15 as one example of where the author tries to accomplish too much (*Belief* 199). Stibbe points out that here Jesus is guilty of a "discontinuous dialogue by transcending the level of discourse used by his questioners" (*John* 55). These are others ways of saying that the text nearly demands too much of our imaginary first-time reader.

9. See also Talbert who suggests that the gaps are "invitations for readers or hearers to fill in the narrative" (*Reading John* 103). On such literary gaps, see J. Fowler, 61–65.

10. I cannot agree with Staley's suggestion that the implied reader joins the implied author in laughing together at Nicodemus and his obtuseness and thereby reestablishes a close relationship between them. The relationship between the reader and Nicodemus is, it seems to me, far more complicated and the reader's identification with either Jesus or the implied author made far more precarious than Staley seems to acknowledge (*Print's First Kiss* 92).

11. Moloney maintains that Nicodemus represents one who is not able to move beyond his own categories (*Belief* 116, 120). Unable to move him, Jesus shifts at verse 11 to a commentary on the whole discussion. Furthermore, for the reader he serves as an example of those described in 2:23-25. Stibbe calls Nicodemus "the embodiment of misunderstanding" (*John* 54). My view of Nicodemus differs only in that I see him far more as an authorial construct to lead the reader into a one-on-one dialogue with Jesus. However, he remains, I think, a thoroughly ambiguous character in the whole of the gospel. Conway makes a persuasive case that the minor characters in John are not flat and one-dimensional but ambiguious ("Speaking" 324–41). See also Bassler, 635–46, and M. Davies, *Rhetoric* 336–38.

12. Stibbe convinces me, however, that Jesus' identity emerges as the readers see characters such as Nicodemus respond to Jesus. As "foils . . . they speak and behave in such a way that our understanding of who Jesus really is is enhanced" (*John as Storyteller* 25). Therefore, even with the reader's disappointment in Nicodemus' failure, something of Jesus' identity may be clearer.

13. Staley concludes his fascinating study with the suggestion that the Johannine text betrays the fact that it is intended for "insiders." The reader is brought "inside" by virtue of the prologue, if nothing else. But "the reader victimization strategies" push the reader "outside" (*Print's First Kiss* 116). Verses 3:1-15 function primarily to evoke a sense of being an outsider and qualifying any sense the reader may have of being an insider.

14. Botha suggests that the reader victimization functions in two ways (192). On the one hand, it maximizes reader participation and involvement, because they never know what to expect next, and on the other, it enhances the communication in such a way that the message is actually formulated by the readers themselves because they are forced to evaluate and reevaluate their opinions, beliefs, and perceptions.

15. Stibbe points out that the author parodies Nicodemus' lack of knowledge (*John* 57).

16. Moloney expresses this point in terms of the necessity of decision and the impossibility of indifference (*Belief* 119). Such a view assumes the role of the reader's values, including those sketched above.

17. W. A. Beardslee speaks of the "deformation of language, a stretching of language to a new metaphorical meaning which shocked the hearer (the 'dialogue partner') into new insight" (11).

18. W. Empson, 1. This classic study of ambiguity explores seven different types. Jesus' metaphorical language in this passage appears to me to be a blending of Empson's fourth and sixth types. He characterizes the fourth type as "two or more meanings of a statement [that] do not agree among themselves, but combine to make clear a more complicated state of mind in the author" (133). The sixth type requires the reader "to invent statements of his [*sic*] own and they are liable to conflict with one another" (176). Our passage shows that the possible referents of Jesus' words disagree and are complicated. But it also invites the reader's own imaginative constructs. See the essay in the last section of this book, "The Sacraments and Johannine Ambiguity." See also Culpepper, *Anatomy* 26.

19. See Kysar, "The Meaning and Function of Johannine Metaphor," reprinted in part 3 of this volume.

Chapter 12

Previously published in *Critical Readings of John 6*. Biblical Interpretation Series, 22. Edited by R. Alan Culpepper and Rolf Redtorff. Leiden: Brill, 1997. 61–181. Revised

1. For instance, Barrett, "Flesh" 37–49. A more recent discussion is found in Koester, esp. 257–62. For the literature and interpretations of the issue of the eucharistic references of 6:25–71 see Kysar, *Fourth Evangelist* 252–55, 257–59.

2. For example, T. L. Brodie understands it to be the climax of Part 2 (2:23–6:71) of "Book One" (chs. 1–12) (13). W. Loader understands ch. 6 to begin the second half of the "christological structure" of chs. 1–12 (45–53). I have suggested that it is a pivotal point in the first twelve chapters at which the extent of Jesus' opposition emerges (*Maverick Gospel* [1993] 14–18). See also Kysar, *John's Story* 39–44.

3. In this way the goal of this paper is similar to that of G. A. Phillips, 23–56. There Phillips attends to the question of "The Text's Work" (51–53). Phillips's expressed method, however, is structuralist, while mine is more akin to

some forms of reader response. For a review of the most current methods in the study of the Fourth Gospel, see Gourgues, 230-306.

4. In this sense mine is a self-conscious "resistant reading"—one that resists the implications of the passage for faith. R. M. Fowler suggests the possibility of becoming "more self-conscious about our acts of assent and our acts of resistance" in reading (73–81, quote 81). Furthermore, by attending to my own response to the reading, I am following Anderson and Moore's injunction: "We are members of the critical guild, in other words, overtrained readers who need to unlearn as well as to learn" (*Mark and Method* 21). In my method, however, self-consciousness takes the form of autobiographical experience. The autobiographical turn in reader response criticism is the newest and fastest growing method and is found in its fullest and most honest form in Staley, *Reading*. Other important examples include: *Autobiographical Biblical Criticism: Learning to Read Between Text and Self*, edited by Ingrid Rosa Kitzberger. The considerable dangers in the autobiographical reading of a text are discussed in the Bible and Culture Collective, *Postmodern Bible* 20–69.

5. This reader is an affluent, empowered Caucasian Lutheran Christian male who works within an academic setting and interprets Scripture on behalf of the church and its ministry. Furthermore, I do not come as an innocent reader without presuppositions about the text but with an interest in the theme of the "origin of faith" already evident in several redactional critical analyses. Examples include *Maverick Gospel* [1993] 70-74, and "Pursuing the Paradoxes" (found in part 1 of this collection).

6. A summary of an earlier draft of portions of this paper was published in my article, "Is Faith Possible? A Reading of John 6:25–71 with Homiletical Considerations," in the collection of papers for the Work Groups of the 1995 annual meeting of the Academy of Homiletics.

7. I will refer to the reader here in the first person singular and the second person masculine singular, as well as simply "the reader," only because I wish to witness to my own reading experience. In this case, the reference to the reader as male does not imply gender exclusivity. This summary of my reading experience was first written without footnotes. The notes in the section were added later for the sake of the readers of this paper.

8. Most commentators find the crowd's question a combined effort to ask how long Jesus had been there and when he had come to this place. See, for example, Brown, *Commentary–Gospel* 1:261, and Barrett, *Gospel According to St. John* 286. Schnackenburg suggests that their question reminds the reader of Jesus' sea walk (*Gospel* 2:35).

9. In his provocative study of the Fourth Gospel, N. Peterson argues that this polemic quality is a part of the Johannine Jesus' "anti-language" (89–109).

10. J. Painter proposes that 6:1-40 is written in the genre of "quest story" (*Quest* 267–76).

11. My reading of the crowd is considerably different than that found in many commentaries. A. Plummer calls the crowd, "wrongheaded" (152). More

contemporary commentators tend to agree. Carson, for instance, uses adjectives such as "confused" and "uncertain" to describe the crowd and says of them, "they acknowledge [Jesus] as teacher though they are about to dispute his teaching, they clamor for him as king (v. 15) though they understand little of the nature of his reign" (*Gospel* 283). My own sense is that they are genuine seekers, even if they are confused by Jesus' words (as this reader was) and motivated by less than the ideal (as this reader most often is)!

12. My concerns are synchronic, so I leave aside the question of the text's history of composition. Whether or not verses 51b-58 were a later addition to the discourse by either a "friendly" or "unfriendly redactor," the passage exhibits unity as it stands. For my view of the redactional history of the passage at an earlier time see *John* 108–10, *Maverick Gospel* (1993) 122–26, and "Pursuing the Paradoxes" reprinted in part I of this this collection.

13. Some commentators take the narrator's statement of the locale as a division in the passage. Barrett, for instance, proposes that verse 59 ends the first discourse, "Bread from Heaven," and provides a transition to a second discourse comprised of verses 60-71 which he entitles, "Reaction and Confession" (*Gospel According to St. John* 300–301). A similar division is used by Lindars (*Gospel of John* 249–70). Stibbe has more recently proposed two different major movements in the passage. After what he understands to be an introduction to the theme of "the true bread from heaven" in verses 25-34a, he speaks of a first section having to do with "Coming to Jesus" (vs. 30-40 and 41-51) and then a second, "Staying with Jesus (vs. 52-59 and 60-71). The narrator's comment at verse 59 serves no more than to divide the two halves of the second section (*John* 87–88). Painter's analysis finds a "quest story" from first edition of the gospel in verses 1-40 and "rejection stories" added in later editions verses 41-71 with verses 36-40 redacted to make the transition. He says of verse 59 only that it moves the locale to an unspecified place. But it clearly delineates the conversation with "the Jews" from that with the disciples (*Quest* 267–84). On the basis of contemporary reading, I doubt that the whole dialogue should be fragmented. It is better, I think, to emphasize the dialogical pattern that continues through the final verses as unifying the whole passage. Painter and Stibbe agree with my contention that verse 59 need not be taken as a major division in the text.

14. Phillips is correct in saying that John 6 demonstrates "how one can engage or not engage Jesus in discourse, indeed the very possibility of having discourse with Jesus at all" (53).

15. Stibbe speaks of the "tragic irony" of the discourse but in terms of the elusiveness of Jesus (*John* 87–88).

16. Crossan describes the style of John 6 as "formulaic, hypnotic, and almost rhapsodic repetition" ("'It is Written'" 15).

17. Schnackenburg writes that Johannine "thought in 'circles', repeating and insisting, and at the same time moving forward, explaining and going on to a higher level" (*Gospel* 1:117). This may be a microstylistic feature of what

Staley argues is the "concentric structure" of the plot of the Gospel of John in its entirety (*Print's First Kiss* 58–71).

18. The substance of the dialogue is bracketed with descending and ascending. Verse 33 speaks of the bread's coming down (*katabainō*). After identifying himself as the "bread from heaven," Jesus speaks of the "Son of Man ascending (*anabainō*) where he was before" (v. 62). See the classic study by Nicholson.

19. See Staley, *Print's First Kiss*, esp. 93–118, and "Stumbling" 55–80. In a "Postscript" to the latter, Staley responds in interesting ways to some of the criticisms of reader response methods (69–70).

20. Crossan asserts that verses 53-56 make "it clear that something more beyond metaphor is happening. . . . The language of 6:49-58 is explicable only in terms of eucharistic formulae known from outside the chapter" ("It is Written" 15). To my mind his view illustrates one danger in the eucharistic interpretations of the metaphor in verses 51b-58, namely, that they sometimes tend to domesticate the gospel's language and thereby lose something of its subversive qualities. While I believe that the text subtly alludes to the Lord's Supper in some way and for some purpose, simply to close the metaphor by saying that its reference is the Eucharist does not take its ambiguity seriously enough. If the interpreter reads the metaphor in terms of the Eucharist, it is necessary then, I believe, to transfer to the sacrament itself something of the ambiguity and mystery intrinsic to the metaphor itself. See the article, "The Sacraments and Johannine Ambiguity," in part 4 of this collection.

21. S. M. Schneiders's words are helpful: "[Real metaphors] exist in and even as linguistic tension involving a simultaneous affirmation and negation of the likeness between the two terms of the metaphor. The metaphor contains an 'is' and an 'is not' held in irresolvable tension" (29).

22. Peterson points out that such a use of language is part of John's anti-language (141). See the more recent discussion of the "Features of the Language of John" in Malina and Rohrbaugh, 4–15.

23. The Gospel of John uses the word *ergon* and its plural in essentially four different ways: (1) In reference to the deeds done by humans (e.g., 3:19-21; 14:12). (2) In reference to Jesus' deeds (e.g., 7:3; 10:25; 15:24) and (3) the work(s) God has given Jesus to do (e.g., 5:36; 10:37; 17:4). (4) In reference to God's activity (e.g., 4:34; 5:20; 9:3). The ambiguity of *to ergon tou theou* in verse 29 is intrinsic to the evangelist's use of this language, especially since God's work is enacted in human form in Jesus' deeds. If we read the dialogues in 6:25-71 and 4:7-42 together, the reference to God's *ergon* in 4:34 may cast some light on the meaning of 6:29. (See also Brown, *Commentary–Gospel* 1:526-27.)

24. This contradicts my own easy statement that the expression constitutes an "invitation to believe" in *John* 98. Commentators generally use verse 29 as an occasion to discuss the relationship between faith and works and/or the difference between Pauline and Johannine thought. Some claim simply that

"the work of God" (what God demands) refers to the human faith response to Jesus. Examples include Beasley-Murray, 91, and Haenchen, *John* 1:290. Others recognize that human activity is the essential meaning of the expression but that what humans do is evoked by what God does in Christ. Examples include Brown, who acknowledges that the expression can mean either "the work that God requires of [humans]" or "the work that God accomplishes in [people]" (*Commentary–Gospel* 1:262). He writes, "this believing is not so much a work done by [humans] as it is submission to God's work in Jesus" (1:265). See also Barrett, *Gospel According to St. John* 227, and Schnackenburg, *Gospel* 2:39. Bultmann's qualification of the human *ergon* of faith is stronger. He claims humans find their "true being not in what [they themselves achieve], but in submission to what God works; [they find] it, that is to say, in what, by faith, [they allow] to happen to [them]" (*Gospel* 222).

25. A. Schlatter makes the strongest statement of sense of the text strictly in terms of what God does in human life to implant faith. "Gottes Werk ist auch hier das Werk, das Gott wirkt, nicht das, das er nur verlangt" (171).

26. Among the many discussions of Johannine determinism these are especially worthy of attention: Schnackenburg, *Gospel* 1:573–75; Carson, *Divine Sovereignty*; Bergmeier; and Dodd, *Essays*, esp. 54–55, 62–68.

27. A case could be made, I believe, for understanding these ambiguous expressions concerning faith as mini-metaphors. "The work of God," the Father's "giving" and "drawing," and even Jesus' knowing *ex archēs* and "choosing" are themselves radical metaphorical expressions. Their subversive effect on the reader is similar to the disorienting result of the passage's central metaphor—Jesus' flesh is bread and his blood drink. Therefore the challenge of the metaphorical nature of the expressions used of faith is of a piece with that of the central metaphor. Such an argument, however, requires an additional essay beyond the scope of the present one.

28. Carson summarizes the view of the gospel on this issue with these words: "John holds men and women responsible for believing; unbelief is morally culpable. . . . But in the last analysis, faith turns on sovereign election by the Son (15:16), on being part of the gift from the Father to the Son (6:37–44). And this, it must be insisted, drums at the heart of a book that is persistently evangelical. God's will is not finally breached, even in the hardness of human hearts (12:37ff.)" (*Gospel* 99–100). Bultmann's comments are even more interesting. "[F]aith becomes possible when one abandons hold on one's own security, and to abandon one's security is nothing else than to let oneself be drawn by the Father. . . . It occurs when [one] abandons his [or her] own judgment and 'hears' and 'learns' from the Father, when he [or she] allows God to speak to him [or her]." He goes on to characterize the faith of the disciples who are offended by Jesus' words and leave him as "only a provisional, unauthentic faith" (*Gospel* 231–32, 443).

29. See the two-volume collection of essays edited by Segovia and Tolbert. Segovia's article, "Social Location," is a useful summary of "reader constructs."

30. Carson warns against allowing 12:32 "to dilute the force" of 6:44 (*Gospel*

293). I agree that the sense of 6:44 should not be weakened but am convinced that the cross informs us how Johannine thought understands the divine "drawing."

Part IV

1. A good example is an article by S. C. Winter. Winter argues that one can identify glosses in the origin hypothetical Signs Gospel, as Fortna has isolated it. "Consideration of the Fourth Gospel as a whole shows that phrases and clauses in which the perfect tense occurs belong to a stage of composition between the Signs Gospel and the current text of John" (220). This is speculation based on other speculations.

Chapter Thirteen

Originally published as "The Coming Hermeneutical Earthquake in Johannine Interpretation" in *"What Is John?" Readers and Reading of the Fourth Gospel*. Edited by Fernando F. Segovia. Symposium Series 3. Edited by R. O'Day. Atlanta, Ga.: Scholars Press, 1996. 185–89. Revised.

1. See Conway, "Speaking." After examining the portrayal of minor chapters in the Johannine narrative, she concludes: "The stubborn resistance of the Johannine characters to be flattened into a particular type warns against the temptation to flatten our own lives into an over-simplified, unambiguous posture" (341).

Chapter Fourteen

Not previously published.

1. For discussions of the Jews in the Fourth Gospel, see the essay, "Anti-semitism and the Gospel of John" in part 3 of this collection. See also D. M. Smith, "Judaism." The most thorough and recent exploration of interpretations of Judaism and the Fourth Gospel are found in Bieringer, et al., *Anti-Judaism*.

2. D. M. Smith, *John* 187. We can no longer, however, be so certain that the tension Smith refers to was a result of the Johannine Christians' expulsion from the synagogue. See the article, "The Expulsion from the Synagogue" in this section.

3. There is a problem in the wording of this passage, and there are a number of different textual readings. Literally verse 44b reads, "You are descended from the father of the devil (*humeis ek tou patros tou diabolou este*)." However, the different possible translations are not relevant to our discussion. See Schnackenburg, *Gospel* 2:213.

4. These terms may also have been associated with the eschatological events, in particular, the birth pangs preceding the end. See Mark 13:21-22 and 1 Timothy 4:1-2. Also see O'Day's excellent discussion in "Gospel of John" 641–43.

5. "The deceiver" or "liar" (*pseustē*) seems to have been a metaphysical creature

who in the eschatological period ("the last hour"—see 2:18) would seduce believers into error. In the Johannine dualistic setting, the "liar" is the opposite of the truth (*alētheia*—see 1 John 1:8 and 4:6). If this figure is synonymous with the antichrist, the use of the plural in 2:18 suggests that they take the form of false teachers, who in this instance deny the flesh and blood reality of Christ. See H. Braun, *Planaō*; *Theological Dictionary* 6:228–53.

6. For the origins of the figure of the antichrist, see Schnackenburg, *Epistles* 134–39. Schnackenburg admits that we will probably never know the genesis of this title but offers an excursus on "The Expectation of the Antichrist: Its Earlier History" 135–39.

7. Bultmann describes Johannine anthropology by saying that a human's origin determines his or her life. "[T]he goal of [one's] life corresponds to [her or his] origin" (*Gospel* 137–38). The Johannine expression *ek* conveys that same idea. What one is "of" (or "out of") is their character. Another way of putting it is that what one is "of" describes their affiliation in life that, in turn, determines their character.

8. Cf. Reinhartz, *Befriending* 81–98.

Chapter Fifteen

Not previously published.

1. Brown, *Commentary–Gospel* 1:xxxvii, lxxxv. In a 1977 article, however, he wrote, "[t]he *Birkat ha-Minim* probably only formalized a break that had begun at an earlier stage" ("Johannine Ecclesiology" 391.) Later in his 1979 book, *The Community of the Beloved Disciple*, Brown clearly endorses Martyn's proposal, e.g., 22–23, 66. Still, in the unfinished manuscript of his revision of his Anchor Bible commentary on John, Brown repudiates any connection between the expulsion from the synagogue and any formal Jewish decree (see *Introduction* 213).

2. Martyn, *Gospel* 103. One of Brown's criticisms of Martyn's work is that "he does not explain why the Christian Jews from the early period developed a Christology that led to their expulsion from the synagogue and their becoming Jewish Christians" (*Community* 174).

3. Kysar, "Gospel of John" 318. Moreover, my introductions to John and my commentary consistently employed the theory of the expulsion from the synagogue. One study, I declared, "*convincingly exhibits the fact* that the Fourth Gospel was written in response to the expulsion of Jewish Christians from their synagogues and the condemnation of Christians as heretics" ("Community" 274, italics are original). Cf. "Historical Puzzles in John," in part 1 of this volume.

4. Kimmelman, 244. Cf. Katz, 43–76; and more recently van der Horst.

5. See the commentary by Keener who thinks the expulsion occurred earlier than *Jamnia*. Compare the two editions of *Maverick Gospel* to see the change in my position ([1976] 15, and [1993] 20).

6. As early as 1970, Brown admitted, "It is impossible from the adjective *apo-*

synaggos [expelled from synagogue] to be certain that John is not referring to one local synagogue" (*Commentary–Gospel* 1:690). Recently, however, the assumption that the gospels were each written for one local community is under attack. Cf. Bauckham, *The Gospel for All Christians* 9–48.

7. Of course, not all Christian scholars were so easily convinced and continued to adhere to Martyn's interpretation of the Benediction. Cf. e.g., Boring, Berger, and Colpe, 301–2.

8. In his recent dissertation, M. Labahn takes a position somewhat comparable to what I am suggesting here. In his study of the miracle stories in John, he postulates a multistaged development of the Johannine tradition into the completed gospel. However, he does not associate the passages referring to an expulsion from the synagogue (9:22; 12:42; and 16:2) with any Jewish action. Nonetheless, he maintains that debates with the synagogue eventually brought about a division between the two and formed an important stage in the history of the Johannine community. His proposal attempts to maintain the idea of conflict between the Johannine church and the synagogue without supposing that a formal expulsion occurred. (I am indebted to Moloney for my summary of Labahn's work; cf. "Where?" 223–51.)

9. The metaphors of window and mirror were apparently first suggested by Krieger.

10. L. T. Johnson, *Real Jesus* 100. Of Brown's reconstruction, he asks, "What guiding principles attend the discrimination between sources and stages? What reasons are there for arranging the pieces in the suggested sequence? . . . Once more, such exercises should be recognized as flights of fancy rather than sober historiography." His conclusion is that Brown's "entire reconstruction of Johannine 'history' rests upon no more solid basis than a series of subjective judgments and suspect methodological presuppositions" (100). To my knowledge Brown never published a response to Johnson's critique.

11. In the first edition of his introduction to the New Testament, L. T. Johnson uses John 9:22 as evidence that early Christians were expelled because of the *Birkat ha-Minnim* (cf. *Writings* 120). In the most recent edition (1999), however, he is more cautious, acknowledging only that 9:22, 12:12, and 16:2 suggest that the Johannine Christians may have been expelled from the synagogue for some reason by other Jews. Johnson regards this experience as only one of several experiences of the Johannine Christians in the background of the gospel (130–31).

12. Conway rightly criticizes my article, "Anti-Semitism and the Gospel of John" (reprinted in part 3 of this collection), for some of the same reasons she criticizes Martyn. Indeed, I do suggest that the gospel's portrayal of the Jews necessitates a more careful distinction between the contingent and the authoritative, along with a new understanding of biblical authority.

13. Bible and Culture Collection, *The Postmodern* 13, 41–42, quote 41, and is credited to Burnett, 53.

Chapter Sixteen

Not previously published.

1. This paper was first prepared as a response to Brown's treatment of the sacraments, in *Introduction* 229–34, to be delivered in the Section on Johannine Literature of the Annual Meeting of the Society of Biblical Literature, 2004. The intent of the papers was not to praise Brown for his work nor to demean it, but simply to ask how different views would affect his work.

2. In my opinion the section entitled "Crucial Questions in Johannine Theology" in Brown's introduction to his 1966 commentary is one of the weakest sections of the entire work (see *Commentary–Gospel* 1:cv–cxxviii). I was pleased then to find that, in his *Introduction*, Brown had rewritten and expanded most of what is in the commentary. When we look at the section on the sacraments, however, we find little substantial difference in his revision.

3. Moloney concludes his excursus on "Narrative Approaches to the Fourth Gospel" by declaring that the method is only a supplement: "the achievements of historical-critical scholarship are an essential part of sound narrative critical approaches to the Fourth Gospel" (Brown, *Introduction* 232).

4. Ricoeur is among those who distinguish ambiguity from multiple meanings. He limits ambiguity to literary situations in which "only . . . one meaning alone of two possible meanings is required, and the context does not provide us grounds for deciding between them." He goes on to distinguish those situations from others "where several things are meant at the same time, without the reader being required to choose between them" (*Figuring the Sacred* 53, 143). I prefer to use ambiguity to refer to both of these situations, i.e., both when one of two meanings is possible and when a number of meanings are possible but the reader has no way of determining which is the "intended meaning." Empson identified seven different types of ambiguity in the writings of poets and concluded that among the most complex of the types, "the reader is forced to invent interpretations" (176). This distinction in the meanings of ambiguity is important, because it involves the expectations of the reader when interpreting John.

5. E. Richard concludes his study of expressions of double meaning in the Fourth Gospel by saying, "Ultimately John's vision is ambiguous. . . . John's readers are constantly challenged to consider both the earthly and the heavenly" (107).

6. See Moore, *Literary Criticism* 139, who credits Crossan with this point. See Crossan, *Cliffs of Fall* 8–9.

Abbreviations Used in the Bibliography

AB	*Analecta Biblica*
AnB	Anchor Bible
ANRW	Aufstieg und Niedergang de römischen Welt
ATR	*Anglican Theological Review*
BANT	Schlier, H. *Besinnung auf das Neue Testament. Exegetische Aufsätze und Vorträge.* Freiburg: Herder, 1964. Vol. 2.
Bib	*Biblica*
BJRL	*Bulletin of the John Rylands Library*
BL	*Bibel und Leben*
BTB	*Biblical Theology Bulletin*
BZ	*Biblische Zeitschrift*
CBQ	*Catholic Biblical Quarterly*
CS	*Christ and Spirit in the New Testament.* Studies in Honour of C. F. D. Moule. Ed. B. Lindars, and S. Smalley. Cambridge: Cambridge University Press, 1973.
DR	*Downside Review*
EH	*Europäische Hochschulschriften*
EJ	*L'Evangile de Jean. Sources, redaction, theologie. Bibliotheca Ephemeridum Theologicarum Lovamensium* 44. Ed. M. De Jonge. Leuven: Duculot, 1977.
ET	*Expository Times*
ETL	*Ephemerides Theologicae Lovanienses*
FRLANT	*Forschungen zur Religion und Literatur des Alten und Neuen Testaments*
FTS	*Frankfurter Theologische Studien*
FV	*Foi et Vie*

GG   Bornkamm, G. *Geschichte und Glaube, 1. Teil. Gesammelte Aufsätze.* Vol. 3. *Beitrag zur evangelisch Theologie* 48. Munich: Kaiser, 1968, and *Geschichte und Glaube, 2. Teil. Gesammelte Aufsätze.* Vol. 4. *Beitrag zur evangelisch Theologie* 53, 1971.

GBS.NT   Guides to Biblical Scholarship. New Testament Series

Int   *Interpretation*

JBL   *Journal of Biblical Literature*

Jesus   De Jonge, M. *Jesus. Stranger from Heaven and Son of God.* Society of Biblical Literature Sources for Biblical Study 11. Missoula: Scholars, 1977.

JMH   *Jesus and Man's Hope.* Vol. 1. Pittsburgh: Perspective, 1970.

JTS   *Journal of Theological Studies*

JQ   *John and Qumran.* Ed. J. H. Charlesworth. London: Chapman, 1972.

LV   *Lumiere et Vie*

Neo   *Neotestamentica 6. Essays on the Jewish Background of the Fourth Gospel*

NRT   *Nouvelle Revue Theologique*

NT   *Novum Testamentum*

NTK   *Neues Testament und Kirche.* Festschrift for R. Schnackenburg. Ed. J. Gnilka. Freiburg: Herder, 1974.

NTS   *New Testament Studies*

Oik   *Oikonomia. Heilsgeschichte als Thema der Theologie.* Ed. F. Christ. Hamburg: Reich, 1967.

RA   *Religions in Antiquity. Essays in Memory of Erwin Ramsdell Goodenough.* Numen, suppl. 14. Ed. J. Neussner. Leiden: Brill, 1968.

RB   *Revue Biblique*

RSR   *Recherches de Science Religieuse*

SB   *Stuttgarter Bibelstudien*

SBLD   Society of Biblical Literature Dissertation Series

SBLMS   Society of Biblical Literature Monograph Series

SBLSem   Society of Biblical Literature Seminar Papers

SBLSS   Society of Biblical Literature Symposium Series

SBT   *Studies in Biblical Theology*

Sc   *Scripture*

SE   *Studia Evangelica*

SJe   *Studien zum Johannesevangelium.* Ed. J. Hainz. Biblische Untersuchungen 13. Regensburg: Pustet, 1977.

SJT   *Scottish Journal of Theology*

SNT   Supplements to *Novum Testamentum*

SNTSM   *Society for New Testament Studies* Monograph Series

Stujn	*Studies in John.* Presented to Professor Dr. J. N. Sevenster on the Occasion of His 70th Birthday. Supplement to *Novum Testamentum* 24. Leiden: Brill, 1970.
TW	*Theologie und Wirklichkeit*
TZ	*Theologische Zeitschrift*
VE	De La Potterie, I., and S. Lyonnet. *La vie selon l'Esprit, condition du chretien.* Collège Unam Sanctam 55. Paris: Cerf, 1965.
WUNT	*Wissenschaftliche Untersuchungen zum Neuen Testament*
ZNW	*Zeitschrift für die neutestamentliche Wissenschaft und die Kunde der älteren Kirche*

Bibliography

Aalen, S. "'Truth.' A Key Word in St. John's Gospel." *SE* 2.1 (1961): 3–24.

Aaletti, J.-N. "Le discours sur le pain de vie (Jean 6). Problèmes de composition et fonction des citations de l'Ancien Testament." *RSR* 62 (1974): 169–97.

Aatal, D. *Structure et signification des cinq premiers versets de l'hymne johannique au Logos.* Recherches africaines de theologie 3. Paris: Beatrice-Nauwelaerts, 1972.

Achtemeier, E. R. "Jesus Christ, the Light of the World. The Biblical Understanding of Light and Darkness." *Int* 17 (1963): 439–49.

Ackerman, J. S. "The Rabbinic Interpretation of Psalm 82 and the Gospel of John." *Harvard Theological Review* 59 (1966): 186–88.

Adam, A. K. M. "Author." In *Handbook of Postmodern Biblical Interpretation.* Ed. A. K. M. Adam. St. Louis: Chalice, 2000. 8–13.

——. *Making Sense of New Testament Theology: "Modern" Problems and Prospects.* Studies in American Hermeneutics 11. Ed. Charles Mabee. Macon: Mercer University Press, 1995.

——. *What Is Postmodern Biblical Criticism?* GBS.NT. Ed. Dan O. Via, Jr. Minneapolis: Fortress, 1995.

Agourides, S. "Peter and John in the Fourth Gospel." *SE* 4 (1965): 3–7.

Alter, R. *The Art of Biblical Poetry.* New York: Basic Books, 1985.

Anderson, J. C., and S. D. Moore, eds. *Mark and Method: New Approaches in Biblical Studies.* Minneapolis: Fortress, 1992.

Anderson, J. C., and J. L. Staley, eds. *Semeia* 72 (1993).

Anderson, P. N. *The Christology of the Fourth Gospel: Its Unity and Disunity in the Light of John 6.* Valley Forge: Trinity Press International, 1996.

293

Anderson, P. N. "Interfluential, Formative, and Dialectical—A Theory of John's Relations to the Synoptics." *Für und wider die Priorität des Johannesevangeliums*. Salzburg: Peter Hofrichter, 2002.

———. "John and Mark: The Bi-Optic Gospels." *Jesus in Johannine Tradition*. Ed. Robert T. Fortna and Tom Thatcher. Louisville: Westminster John Knox Press, 2001. 175–88.

Appold, M. *The Oneness Motif in the Fourth Gospel. Motif Analysis and Exegetical Probe into the Theology of John*. WUNT 2. Tübingen: Mohr-Siebeck, 1976.

Aune, D. E. *The Cultic Setting of Realized Eschatology*. Leiden: Brill, 1972.

Bailey, J. A. *The Traditions Common to the Gospels of Luke and John*. SNT 7. Leiden: Brill, 1963.

Bailey, K. E. *Poet and Peasant*. Grand Rapids: Wm. B. Eerdmans, 1976.

Bammel, E. "Jesus und der Paraklet in Johannes 16." CS 199–217.

Barrett. C. K. "'The Father is Greater Than I' (Jn 14:28). Subordinationist Christology in the New Testament." *NTK*. 148–59.

———. "'The Flesh of the Son of Man' John 6:53." *Essays on John*. Philadelphia: Westminster Press, 1982. 37–49.

———. *The Gospel According to St. John. An Introduction with Commentary and Notes on the Greek Text*. 2nd ed. London: SPCK, 1978.

———. *The Gospel of John and Judaism*. Philadelphia: Fortress, 1975.

———. "John and the Synoptic Gospels." *ET* 85 (1974): 228–33.

———. *New Testament Essays*. London: SPCK, 1974.

———. "Unsolved New Testament Problems: The Place of Eschatology in the Fourth Gospel." *ET* 59 (1948): 302–3.

Barrosee, T. "The Seven Days of the New Creation in St. John's Gospel." *CBQ* 21 (1959): 507–16.

Bassler, J. M. "Mixed Signals: Nicodemus in the Fourth Gospel." *JBL* 108 (1989): 635–46.

Bauckham, R., ed. *The Gospel for All Christians: Rethinking the Gospel Audiences*. Grand Rapids: Wm. B. Eerdmans, 1998.

Bauer, W., W. F. Arndt, F. Gingrich, and F. W. Danker. *A Greek-English Lexicon of the New Testament and Other Early Christian Literature*. 2nd ed. Chicago: University of Chicago Press, 1979.

Baumbach, G. "Gemeinde und Welt im Johannes-Evangelium Kairos." *Zeitschrift für Religionswissenschaft und Theologie* 14 (1972): 121–36.

Beardslee, W. A. *Literary Criticism of the New Testament*. GBS.NT. Ed. Dan O. Via, Jr. Philadelphia: Fortress, 1970.

Beare, F. W. *The Epistle to the Philippians*. New York: Harper, 1959.

Beasley-Murray, G. R. *John*. Word Biblical Commentary 36. Waco, Texas: Word, 1987.

Beauvery, R. "'Mon père et votre pere.'" *LV* 20 (1971): 75–87.

Beck, N. A. *Mature Christianity: The Recognition and Repudiation of the Anti-Jewish Polemic of the New Testament*. Selinsgrove, Penn.: Susquehanna University Press, 1985.

Becker, H. *Die Reden des Johannesevangeliums und der Stil der gnostischen Offenbarungs-rede*. Ed. R. Bultmann. Göttingen: Vandenhoeck & Ruprecht, 1956.

Becker, J. "Beobachtungen zum Dualismus im Johannesevangelium." *ZNW* 65 (1974): 71–87.

———. *Das Evangelium des Johannes*. 2 vols. Ökumenische Taschenbuch-Kommentar zum Neuen Testament 4:1, 2. Gütersloh: Mohn, 1979–1981.

———. "Wunder und Christologie." *NTS* 16 (1970): 130–48.

Beker, J. C. "The New Testament View of Judaism." *Jews and Christians*. Ed. J. Charlesworth. New York: Crossroad, 1990. 60–75.

Ben-Hayyim, A. *The Literary and Oral Tradition of Hebrew and Aramaic amongst the Samaritans*. Jerusalem: Academy of Hebrew Language, 1967.

Berger, K. "Zu 'Das Wort Ward Fleisch' Joh. 1,14a." *NT* 16 (1974): 161–66.

Bergmeier, R. *Glauben als Gabe nach Johannes. Beiträge zur Wissenschaft vom Alten und Neuen Testament*. Stuttgart: Kohlhammer, 1980.

Bernard, J. H. *A Critical and Exegetical Commentary on the Gospel According to St. John*. International Critical Commentary. 2 vols. Edinburgh: T&T Clark, 1928.

Berrouard, M.-F. "La multiplication des pains et le discours du pain de vie (Jean 6)." *LV* 18 (1969): 63–75.

Betz, O. *Der Paraklet. Fürsprecher im häretischen Spätjudentum, im Johannes-Evangelium und in neu gefundenen gnostischen Schriften*. Arbeiten zur Geschichte des Spätjudentums und Urchristentums 2. Leiden: Brill, 1963.

Beutler, J. *Martyria. Traditionsgeschichtliche Untersuchungen zum Zeugnisthema bei Johannes*. FTS 10. Frankfurt am Main: Josef Knecht, 1972.

———. "Literarische Gattungen im Johannesevangelium. Ein Forschungsbericht." *ANRW*. Ed. Hildegard Temporini and Wolfgang Haase. Part 2. Principat 25.3. Berlin and New York: Walter de Gruyter, 1984. 2506–2568.

The Bible and Culture Collective. *The Postmodern Bible*. New Haven: Yale University Press, 1995.

Bieringer, R., D. Pollefeyt, and F. Vandecasteele-Vanneuville, eds. *Anti-Judaism and the Fourth Gospel: Papers of the Leuven Colloquium, 2000*. Jewish and Christian Heritage Series. Vol. 1. Netherlands: Royal Van Gorcum, 2001.

Blair, Edward P. *Jesus in the Gospel of Matthew*. Nashville: Abingdon, 1960.

Blank, J. "'Ich bin das Lebensbrot.'" *BL* 7 (1966): 255–70.

———. "Die johanneische Brotrede." *BL* 7 (1966): 193–207.

———. "Der johanneische Wahrheits-Begriff." *BZ* 7 (1963): 164–73.

———. *Krisis, Untersuchungen zur johanneischen Christologie und Eschatologie*. Freiburg: Lambertus, 1964.

Bligh, J. "Jesus in Galilee." *Heythrop Journal* 5 (1969): 3–26.

Blinzler, J. "Johannes und die Synoptiker. Ein Forschungsbericht." *SB* 5. Stuttgart: Katholisches Bibelwerk, 1965.

Böcher, O. *Der johanneische Dualismus im Zusammenhang des nachbiblischen Judentums.* Gütersloh: Mohn, 1965.

Boers, H. *Neither on This Mountain Nor in Jerusalem: A Study of John 4.* SBLMS 35. Atlanta: Scholars, 1988.

Boice, J. M. *Witness and Revelation in the Gospel of John.* Grand Rapids: Zondervan, 1970.

Boismard, M.-E. "Aenon, pres de Salme (Jean 11, 23)." *RB* 80 (1973): 218–29.

———. "Du bapteme à Cana (Jean 1:19–2:11)." *Lectio Divina* 18. Paris: Cerf, 1956.

———. "L' évolution du thème eschatologique dans les traditions johanniques." *RB* 68 (1961): 507–24.

———. "Jésus, le prophète par excellence, d'après Jean 10, 24-39." *NTK*. 160–171.

———. "Le lavement des pieds." *RB* 71 (1969): 5–24.

———. "Saint Luc et la rédaction du quatrième évangile (Jn 4:46-54)." *RB* 69 (1962): 185–211.

———. "Un precédé rédactionnel dans le quatrième évangile: la Wiederaufnahme." *EJ*. 235–41.

Boismard, M.-E., and A. Lamouille. *Synopse des Quatre Évangiles en Français.* Vol. 3 of *L'Évangile de Jean.* Avec la collaborations de G. Rochais. Paris: Cerf, 1977.

Borgen, P. *Bread from Heaven: An Exegetical Study of the Concept of the Manna in the Gospel of John and the Writings of Philo.* Vol. 10 of SNT. Leiden: Brill, 1965.

———. "God's Agent in the Fourth Gospel." *RA*. 137–47.

———. "'Logos was the True Light.' Contributions to the Interpretation of the Prologue of John." *NT* 14 (1972): 115–30.

———. "Observations on the Midrashic Character of John 6." *ZNW* 54 (1963): 232–40.

———. "Observations on the Targumic Character of the Prologue of John." *NTS* 16 (1970): 288–95.

———. "Some Jewish Exegetical Traditions as Background for Son of Man Sayings in John's Gospel." *EJ*. 243–58.

———. "The Unity of the Discourse in John 6." *ZNW* 50 (1959): 277–78.

Borig, R. *Der wahre Weinstock. Untersuchungen zu Joh 15,1–10.* Studien zum Alten und Neuen Testament 16. Munich: Kosel, 1967.

Boring, M. E., K. Berger, and C. Colpe, eds. *Hellenistic Commentary to the New Testament.* Nashville: Abingdon, 1995.

Bornkamm, G. "Die eucharistische Rede im Johannes-Evangelium." *GG*. 1:60–67.

———. "Der Paraklet im Johannesevangelium." *Festschrift für R. Bultmann.* Stuttgart: Kohlhammer, 1949. 12–35. GG 1:68–69.

——. "Vorjohanneische Tradition oder nachjohanneische Bearbeitung in der eucharistischen Rede Johannes 6?" GG. 2:54–59.

——. "Zur Interpretation des Johannes-Evangeliums." GG. 1:104–21.

Bornkamm, G., G. Barth, and H. J. Held. *Tradition and Interpretation in Matthew.* Tran. Percy Scott. Philadelphia: Westminster, 1963.

Botha, J. E. *Jesus and the Samaritan Woman: A Speech Act Reading of John 4:1–42.* SNT 65. Leiden: Brill, 1991.

Bowman, J. *The Fourth Gospel and the Jews. A Study in R. Akiba, Esther and the Gospel of John.* Pittsburgh Theological Monograph Series 8. Pittsburgh: Pickwick, 1975.

——. "The Fourth Gospel and the Samaritans." *BJRL* 40 (1958): 298–308.

——. *Samaritanische Probleme. Studien zum Verhältnis von Samaritanertum, Judentum und Urchristentum.* Stuttgart: Kohlhammer, 1967.

Boyle, J. L. "The Last Discourse (Jn 13, 31–16, 33) and Prayer (Jn 17). Some Observations on Their Unity and Development." *Bib* 56 (1975): 210–22.

Bratcher, R. "'The Jews' in the Gospel of John." *Bible Translator* 26 (1975): 401–9.

Braun, F.-M. "Le Cercle johannique et l'origine du quatrième évangile d'après O. Cullmann." *Revue d'Histoire et de Philosophic Religieuses* 56 (1976): 203–14.

——. "Le don de Dieu et l'initiation chrétienne." *NRT* 86 (1964): 1025–48.

——. *Jean le théologien et son Évangile dans l'Église ancienne.* Collège Études Biblique. Paris: Gabalda, 1959.

——. *Jean le théologien. Les grandes traditions d'Israël. L'accord des écritures d'après le quatrieme Evangile.* Collège Études Biblique. Paris: Gabalda, 1964.

——. *Jean le théologien, III. Sa théologie, 2. Le Christ, notre Seigneur; hier, aujour'hui, toujours.* Collège Études Biblique. Paris: Gabalda, 1972.

——. *Jean le théologien, III. Sa théologie. Le mystère de Jésus-Christ.* Paris: Gabalda. 1966.

——. "Quatre signes johanniques de l'unite chretienne." *NTS* 9 (1963): 147–55.

Braun, H. *Planaō (and Related Terms).* Vol. 6 of *Theological Dictionary of the New Testament.* Ed. G. Kittel and G. Friedrich. Trans. and ed. G. W. Bromily. 10 vols. Grand Rapids: Wm. B. Eerdmans, 1968. 228–53.

——. *Qumran und das Neue Testament.* 2 vols. Tübingen: Mohr, 1966.

Breech, J. *The Silence of Jesus: The Authentic Voice of Jesus.* Philadelphia: Fortress, 1984.

Breuss, J. *Das Kanawunder. Hermeneutische und pastorale Überlegungen aufgrund einer phänomenologischen Analyse von Joh 2,1-12.* Biblische Beiträge 12. Fribourg: Schweizerisches Katholisches Bibelwerk, 1976.

Brodie, T. L. *The Gospel According to John: A Literary and Theological Commentary.* New York: Oxford University Press, 1993.

Brooks, O. "The Johannine Eucharist—Another Interpretation." *JBL* 82 (1963): 293–300.

Brown, R. E. *The Community of the Beloved Disciple*. New York: Paulist, 1979.

——. *The Epistles of John*. AnB 38. New York: Doubleday, 1982.

——. *The Gospel According to John*. 2 vols. AnB 29 and 29a. New York: Doubleday, 1966 and 1970.

——. *Introduction to the Gospel of John*. Ed. F. J. Moloney. AnB Reference Library. Garden City, NY: Doubleday, 2003.

——. "Johannine Ecclesiology—The Community's Origins." *Int* 31 (1977): 379–93.

——. "The Johannine Word for Preachers." *Int* 43 (1989): 58–65.

——. "The Kerygma of the Gospel According to John." *Int* 21 (1967): 387–400.

——. "'Other Sheep Not of This Fold': The Johannine Perspective on Christian Diversity in the Late First Century." *JBL* 97 (1978): 5–22.

——. "The Paraclete in the Fourth Gospel." *NTS* 13 (1967): 113–32.

——. "The 'Paraclete' in the Light of Modern Research." *SE* 4 (1965): 157–65.

Brownlee, W. H. "John the Baptist in the Light of Ancient Scrolls." In *The Scrolls and the New Testament*. Ed. K. Stendahl. New York: Harper & Row, 1957. 33–53.

Bruce, F. F. *The Gospel of John*. Grand Rapids: Wm. B. Eerdmans, 1983.

Bruns, J. E. "The Confusion Between John and John Mark in Antiquity." *Sc* 17 (1965): 23–26.

——. "John Mark. A Riddle Within the Johannine Enigma." *Sc* 15 (1963): 88–92.

Buchanan, G. "The Samaritan Origin of the Gospel of John." *RA*. 149–75.

Buhner, J.-A. *Der Gesandte und sein Weg im 4. Evangelium*. WUNT 2/2. Tübingen: Mohr, 1977.

Bultmann, R. "Analyse des ersten Johannesbriefes." *Festgabe für Adolf Jülicher zum 70. Geburtstag, 26. Janua 1927*. Tübingen: Mohr, 1927. 138–58.

——. *Essays: Philosophical and Theological*. Trans. J. C. G. Creig. London: SCM Press, 1955.

——. *Existence and Faith: Shorter Writings of Rudolf Bultmann*. Ed. S. Ogden. New York: Meridian, 1960.

——. *Faith and Understanding*. Ed. R. W. Funk. Trans. L. P. Smith. 4 vols. New York: Harper & Row, 1969.

——. *The Gospel of John. A Commentary*. Trans. G. R. Beasley-Murray. Ed. R. W. N. Hoare and J. K. Riches. Oxford: Blackwell, 1971.

——. *The History of the Synoptic Tradition*. Trans. John Marsh. Oxford: Basil Blackwell, 1963.

——. *Jesus Christ and Mythology*. New York: Scribner, 1958.

——. *The Johannine Epistles. Hermeneia—A Critical and Historical Commentary on the Bible*. Ed. R. W. Funk. Trans. R. P. O'Hara, L. C. McGaughy, and R. W. Funk. Philadelphia: Fortress, 1973.

——. *New Testament and Mythology*. Vol. 1 of *Kerygma and Myth*. Ed. H. B. Werner. 6 vols. New York: Harper & Row, 1971. 1–44.

——. *Primitive Christianity in Its Contemporary Setting*. Trans. R. H. Fuller. New York: Meridian, 1956.

——. *Theology of the New Testament*. Trans. K. Grobel. 2 vols. New York: Scribner, 1955.

——. *The Word and Beyond: Marburg Sermons*. Trans. H. Knight. New York: Scribner, 1960.

Bultmann, R., and K. Kundsin. *Form Criticism: Two Essays on New Testament Research*. Trans. F. C. Grant. New York: Harper & Brothers, 1962.

Bultmann, R., and A. Weiser. *Pisteuō, pistis, pistos, apistos, apisteuō, apistia, oligopistos, oligopistia*. Vol. 6 of *Theological Dictionary of the New Testament*. Ed. G. Kittel and G. Friedrich. Trans. G. W. Bromiley. 10 vols. Grand Rapids: Wm. B. Eerdmans, 1968. 174–228.

Burnett, F. "Postmodern Biblical Exegesis: The Eve of Historical Criticism." *Semeia* 51 (1990): 51–80.

Busse, U. "Offene Fragen zu Joh 10." *NTS* 33 (1987): 520–21.

Cadman, W. H. *The Open Heaven. The Revelation of God in the Johannine Sayings of Jesus*. Oxford: Blackwell, 1969.

Caird, G. B. "The Glory of God in the Fourth Gospel. An Exercise in Biblical Semantics." *NTS* 15 (1969): 265–77.

——. *The Language and Imagery of the Bible*. Philadelphia: Westminster, 1980.

——. *New Testament Theology*. Completed and ed. L. D. Hurst. Oxford: Clarendon, 1994.

Caragounis, C. C. "The Kingdom of God: Common and Distinct Elements between John and the Synoptics." In *Jesus in the Johannine Tradition*. Ed. R. T. Fortna and T. Thatcher. Louisville: Westminster John Knox, 2001. 125–34.

Carnegie, D. "The Kerygma in the Fourth Gospel." *Vox Evangelica* 7 (1971): 39–74.

Carroll, K. L. "The Fourth Gospel and the Exclusion of Christians from the Synagogue." *BJRL* 40 (1957): 19–32.

Carson, D. A. "Current Source Criticism of the Fourth Gospel." *JBL* 97 (1978): 411–29.

——. *Divine Sovereignty and Human Responsibility*. Atlanta: John Knox, 1981.

——. *The Gospel According to John*. Grand Rapids: Wm. B. Eerdmans, 1991.

Casey, M. *From Jewish Prophet to Gentile God: The Origins and Development of New Testament Christology*. Louisville: Westminster John Knox, 1991.

Cassem, N. H. "A Grammatical and Contextual Inventory of the Use of Kosmos in the Johannine Corpus with Some Implications for a Johannine Cosmic Theology." *NTS* 19 (1972): 81–91.

Charlesworth, J. "A Critical Comparison of the Dualism in 1 QS 3:13–4:26 and the 'Dualism' Contained in the Gospel of John." *JQ.* 76–106.

——. "Qumran, John and the Odes of Solomon." *JQ.* 107–136.

Charlesworth, J., and R. A. Culpepper. "The Odes of Solomon and the Gospel of John." *CBQ* 35 (1973): 298–322.

Childs, B. *Myth and Reality in the Old Testament.* SBT 27, old series. London: SCM Press, 1960.

Clergeon, C. H. "Le quatrième évangile indiqué le nom de son auteur?" *Bib* 56.4 (1975): 545–49.

Coetzee, J. C. "Life (Eternal Life) in St. John's Writings and the Qumran Scrolls." *Neo* 6 (1972): 48–66.

Collins, M. "The Hidden Vessels in Samaritan Traditions." *Journal for the Study of Judaism* 3 (1972): 97–116.

Colloud, J., and F. Genuyt. *Le discours d'adieu. Jean 13–17. Analyse sémiotique.* Lyon: Centre pour l'Analyse du Discours Religieux, 1987.

——. *L'Évangile de Jean (II). Lecture sémiotique des chaptres 7 à 12.* Dossiers du Centre Thomas More. L'Arbresle: Centre Thomas More, 1987.

Colonnese, L. M., ed. *Conscientization for Liberation.* New Dimensions in Hemispheric Realities. Washington, D.C.: Division for Latin America, United States Catholic Conference, 1971.

Colson, J. *L'énigme du disciple que Jesus aimait.* Bibl. de Théol. hist. 10. Paris: Beauchesne, 1969.

Conway, C. M. "The Production of the Johannine Community: A New Historicist Perspective." *JBL* 121 (2002): 479–95.

——. "Speaking Through Ambiguity: Minor Characters in the Fourth Gospel. *Biblical Interpretation* (2002): 1–19.

Conzelmann, H. *A Commentary on the First Epistle to the Corinthians.* Hermeneia—A Critical and Historical Commentary on the Bible. Ed. G. W. MacRae, S.J. Trans. J. W. Leitch. Philadelphia: Fortress, 1975.

——. *The Theology of St. Luke.* Trans. G. Buswell. New York: Harper & Row, 1960.

Cook, J. G. *Semiotics.* Vol. 2 of *Dictionary of Biblical Interpretations* Ed. J. H. Hayes. Nashville: Abingdon, 1999. 454–56.

Coppens, J. "Le fils de l'homme dans l'évangile johannique." *ETL* 52.2 (1976): 28–81.

——. "Les logia johanniques du fils de l'homme." *EJ.* 311–15.

Corell, A. *Consummatum Est.* Lund: Berlingska Boktrycheriet, 1950.

Cottam, T. *The Fourth Gospel Rearranged.* London: Epworth, 1952.

Countryman, L. W. *The Mystical Way in the Fourth Gospel: Crossing Over into God.* Philadelphia: Fortress, 1987.

Cribbs, F. L. "A Reassessment of the Date of the Origin and the Destination of the Gospel of John." *JBL* 89 (1970): 39–55.

———. *A Study of the Contacts that Exist Between St. Luke and St. John.* Vol. 2 of SBL-Sem. Cambridge: Society of Biblical Literature, 1973. 1–93.

Crossan, J. D. *Cliffs of Fall: Paradox and Polyvalence in the Parables of Jesus.* New York: Seabury, 1980.

———. *In Parables: The Challenge of the Historical Jesus.* New York: Harper & Row, 1973.

———. "'It is Written:' A Structuralist Analysis of John 6." *Semeia* 26 (1983): 3–22.

Culler, J. "Presupposition and Intertextuality." *Modern Language Notes* 91.6 (1976): 1380–96.

Cullmann, O. *The Christology of the New Testament.* Trans. S. C. Guthrie and C. A. M. Hall. Philadelphia: Westminster, 1959.

———. "L'Évangile Johannique et l'Histoire du Salut." *NTS* 11 (1964): 111–22.

———. *The Johannine Circle.* Trans. J. Bowden. Philadelphia: Westminster, 1976.

———. *Salvation in History.* Trans. S. G. Sowers and the editorial staff of SCM Press. New York: Harper & Row, 1965.

———. "Von Jesus zum Stephanuskreis und zum Johannesevangelium." *Jesus und Paulus. Festschrift für W. G. Kümmel zum 70. Geburtstag.* Ed. E. Ellis and E. Grässer. Göttingen: Vandenhoeck & Ruprecht, 1975. 44–56.

Culpepper, R. A. *Anatomy of the Fourth Gospel: A Study in Literary Design.* Foundations and Facets: New Testament. Ed. R. Funk. Philadelphia: Fortress, 1983.

———. *The Johannine School. An Evaluation of the Johannine-School Hypothesis Based on an Investigation of the Nature of Ancient Schools.* SBLD 26. Missoula: Scholars, 1975.

Dahl, N. "The Johannine Church and History." *Current Issues in New Testament Interpretation.* Ed. W. Klassen and G. F. Snyder. New York: Harper & Row, 1962. 124–42.

Dauer, A. *Die Passionsgeschichte im Johannesevangelium. Eine traditionsgeschichtliche und theologische Untersuchung zu Joh, 18,1–19,30.* Studies zum Alt und Neue Testament 30. München: Kösel, 1972.

Davies, M. *Rhetoric and Reference in the Fourth Gospel.* Journal for the Study of the New Testament Supplement 69. Sheffield: JSOT, 1992.

Davies, P. R., ed. *First Person: Essays in Biblical Autobiography.* London: Sheffield Academic, 2002.

Davies, W. D. *The Setting of the Sermon on the Mount.* Cambridge: Cambridge University Press, 1964.

De Boor, W. *Das Evangelium des Johannes.* 2 vols. Wuppertal: Brockhaus, 1971.

Deeks, D. "The Prologue of St. John's Gospel." *BTB* 6 (1976): 62–78.

De Jonge, M. "Jesus as Prophet and King in the Fourth Gospel." *ETL* 49 (1973): 161–77. Repr. in *Jesus.* 49–76.

——. "Jewish Expectations About the 'Messiah' According to the Fourth Gospel." *NTS* 19 (1973): 246–70. Repr. in *Jesus*. 77–116.

——. "Nicodemus and Jesus. Some Observations on Misunderstanding and Understanding." *BJRL* 53 (1971): 338–58. Repr. in *Jesus*. 29–48.

——. "Signs and Works in the Fourth Gospel." *Jesus*. 117–40.

——. "The Use of the Word *Christos* in the Johannine Epistles." *Stujn*. 66–74.

——. "Variety and Development in Johannine Christology." *Jesus*. 193–222.

——, ed. *L'Évangile de Jean, Sources, Rédaction, Théologie. Bibliotheca Ephemeridum Theologicarum Llovaniensium*. XLIV. Leuven: Louvain University Press, 1977.

De Kruijf, T. C. "The Glory of the Only Son (John 1,14)." *Stujn*. 97–110.

De La Potterie, I. "L'exaltation du Fils de l'homme." *Gregorianum* 49 (1968): 460–78.

——. "'Je suis la Voie, la Vérité et la Vie' (Jn 14,6)." *NRT* 88.9 (1966): 917–26.

——. "Naître de l'eau et naître de l'Esprit—Le texte baptismal de Jean 3:5." *VE*. 56–61.

——. "Le Paraclet." *VE*. 85–105.

——. "Parole et Esprit dans S. Jean." *EJ*. 177–201.

——. "La parole de Jésus 'Voici ta mère' et l'accueil du disciple (Jn 19, 27b)." *Marianum* 36 1974): 1–39.

——. "La verità in San Giovanni." *Rivista Biblica* 11 (1963): 3–24. Repr. in *San Giovanni*. Atti Delia 17 Settimana Biblica. Associazione Biblica Italians. Brescia, Italy: Paideia, 1964. 123–44.

——. "Das Wort Jesu, 'Siehe, deine Mutter' und die Annahme der Mutter durch den Jünger (Joh 19, 27b)." *NTK*. 191–219.

De Oliveira, C.-J. P. "Le verbe *didonai* comme expression des rapports du Père et du Fils dans le VIᵉ evangile." *Revue des sciences philosophiques et théologiques* 49 (1965): 81–104.

De Pinto, B. "Word and Wisdom in St. John." *Sc* 19 (1967): 19–27, 107–22.

De Solaces, B. "Jean, fils de Zébédée et l'énigme du 'disciple que Jesus airnait.'" *Bulletin de Literature Ecclesiastique* 73 (1972): 41–50.

Dennison, W. D. "Miracles as 'Signs.' Their Significance for Apologetics." *BTB* 6 (1976): 190–202.

Derrett, J. D. "The Good Shepherd: St. John's Use of Jewish Halakah and Haggadah." *Studia Theologica* 27 (1973): 25–50.

Dewey, Kim E. "*PAROIMIAI* in the Gospel of John." *Semeia* 17 (1980): 81–99.

Dibelius, M. "Joh 15:13. Eine Studie zum Traditionsproblem des Johannes-Evangelium." In *Festgabe für Adolf Deissmann*. Tübingen: Mohr, 1927. 169–89.

Dion, H.-M. "Quelques traits originaux de la conception johannique du Fils de l'homme." *Sciences Ecclesiastiques* 19 (1967): 49–65.

Dodd, C. H. *Historical Tradition in the Fourth Gospel*. Cambridge: Cambridge University, 1963.

——. *The Interpretation of the Fourth Gospel*. Cambridge: Cambridge University Press, 1953.

Dubois, J. "Chronique johannique." *Études Théologiques et Religieuses* 51 (1976): 373–81.

Duke, P. D. *Irony in the Fourth Gospel*. Atlanta: John Knox, 1985.

Dunn, J. "John VI–An Eucharistic Discourse?" *NTS* 17 (1971): 328–38.

Dupont, L., C. Lash, and G. Levesque. "Recherche sur la structure de Jean 20." *Bib* 54 (1973): 482–98.

Edwards, H. *The Disciple Who Wrote These Things. A New Inquiry into the Origins and Historical Value of the Gospel According to St. John*. London: Clarke, 1953.

Emerton, J. A. "Melchizedek and the Gods. Fresh Evidence for the Jewish Background of John X. 34–36." *JTS* 17 (1966): 399–401.

Empson, W. *Seven Types of Ambiguity*. New York: Directions, 1966.

Escande, J. "Jesus devant Pilate." *FV* 73 (1974): 66–81.

Eusebius of Caesarea. "Church History." *Fathers of the Church. A New Translation*. Ed. R. J. Deferrai. 86 vols. Washington D.C.: Catholic University of America Press, 1929.

Evans, C. A., and D. A. Hagner, eds. *Anti-Semitism and Early Christianity: Issues of Polemic and Faith*. Minneapolis: Fortress, 1993.

Facsimile Edition of the Nag Hammadi Codices. 10 vols. Leiden: Brill, 1972–1977.

Fascher, E. "Christologie und Gnosis im vierten Evangelium." *Theologische Literaturzeitung* 93 (1968): 725–30.

Faure, A. "Die alttestamentlichen Zitate im 4. Evangelium und die Quellenscheidungshypothese." *ZNW* 21 (1922): 99–121.

Fensham, F. C. "Love in the Writings of Qumran and John." *Neo* 6 (1972): 67–77.

Fenton, J. C. "Towards an Understanding of John." *SE* 4 (1965): 28–37.

Festugiere, A.-J. *Observations stylistiques sur l'évangile de S. Jean*. Étude et Commentaire 84. Paris: Klincksieck, 1974.

Feuillet, A. "Les christophanies pascales du quatrième evangile sont-elles des signes?" *NRT* 97 (1975): 577–92.

——. "Les *ego eimi* christologiques du quatrieme Evangile." *RSR* 54.1-2 (1966): 5–22, 213–40.

——. *Johannine Studies*. Staten Island: Alba, 1965.

——. *Le mystère de l'amour divin dans la théologie johannique*. Paris: Gabalda, 1972.

——. *Le prologue du quatrième évangile. Étude de théologie johannique*. Paris: Brouwer, 1968.

Fischer, G. *Die himmlischen Wohnungen. Untersuchungen zu Joh 14,2 f*. EH 23/38. Bern: Lang, 1975.

Fischer, K. M. "Der johanneische Christus und der gnostische Erlöser." *Gnosis und Neues Testament. Studien aus Religionswissenschaft und Theologie.* Ed. K. W. Trögee. Berlin: Evang. Verlagsanstalt, 1973. 245-67.

Fish, S. *Is There a Text in the Class? The Authority of Interpretative Communities.* Cambridge: Harvard University Press, 1980.

Fitzmyer, J. *Essays on the Semitic Background of the New Testament.* Sources for Biblical Study 5. Missoula, Mont.: Scholars, 1974.

Ford, J. M. "'Mingled Blood' From the Side of Christ." *NTS* 15 (1969): 337-38.

Forestell, J. T. *The Word of the Cross. Salvation as Revelation in the Fourth Gospel.* AB 57. Rome: Biblical Institute, 1974.

Fortna, R. "Christology in the Fourth Gospel. Redaction-Critical Perspectives." *NTS* 21 (1975): 490-94.

———. *Fourth Gospel and Its Predecessor.* Philadelphia: Fortress, 1988.

———. "From Christology to Soteriology. A Redaction-Critical Study of Salvation in the Fourth Gospel." *Int* 27 (1973): 32-45.

———. *The Gospel of Signs. A Reconstruction of the Narrative Source Underlying the Fourth Gospel.* SNTSM 11. Cambridge: Cambridge University Press, 1970.

———. "Jesus and Peter at the High Priest's House. A Test Case for the Question of the Relations between Mark's and John's Gospel." *NTS* 24 (1978): 371-83.

———. "Source and Redaction in the Fourth Gospel's Portrayal of Jesus' Signs." *JBL* 89 (1970): 150-66.

———. "Theological Use of Locale in the Fourth Gospel." *ATR*, suppl. 3 (1974): 58-94.

Fowler, J. *Stages of Faith: The Psychology of Human Development and the Quest for Meaning.* San Francisco: Harper & Row, 1981.

Fowler, R. M. "Reader-Response Criticism: Figuring Mark's Reader." In *Mark and Method: New Approaches in Biblical Studies.* Ed. J. C. Anderson and S. D. Moore. Minneapolis: Fortress, 1992. 73-81.

Freed, E. D. "Did John Write His Gospel Partly to Win Samaritan Converts?" *NT* 12 (1970): 241-56.

———. *Old Testament Quotations in the Gospel of John.* SNT 11. Leiden: Brill, 1965.

———. "Samaritan Influence in the Gospel of John." *CBQ* 30 (1968): 580-87.

———. "Some Old Testament Influences on the Prologue of John." In *A Light Unto My Path: Old Testament Studies in Honor of Jacob M. Myers.* Ed. H. Bream, R. Heim, and C. Moore. Philadelphia: Temple University, 1974. 145-61.

———. "The Son of Man in the Fourth Gospel." *JBL* 86 (1967): 402-9.

Freed, E. D., and R. Hunt. "Fortna's Signs-Source in John." *JBL* 99 (1975): 563-79.

Frye, N. *The Great Code: The Bible and Literature.* New York: Harcourt Brace Jovanovich, 1982.

Fuller, R. H. *The Foundations of New Testament Christology.* New York: Scribners, 1965.

——. *Interpreting the Miracles.* Philadelphia: Westminster, 1963.

——. "The 'Jews' in the Fourth Gospel." *Dialog* 16 (1977): 31–37.

Funk, R. W. *Language, Hermeneutic, and the Word of God.* New York: Harper, 1966.

——. *Parables and Presence: Form of the New Testament Tradition.* Philadelphia: Westminster, 1982.

Gaffney, J. "Believing and Knowing in the Fourth Gospel." *Theological Studies* 26 (1965): 215–41.

Gardner-Smith, P. *Saint John and the Synoptic Gospels.* Cambridge: Cambridge University Press, 1938.

——. "St. John's Knowledge of Matthew." *JTS,* n.s. 4 (1953): 31–35.

Gaston, L. "Retrospect." In *Separation and Polemic.* Vol. 2 of *Anti-Judaism in Early Christianity.* Ed. S. G. Wilson. Studies in Christianity and Judaism 2. Waterloo; Wilfrid Laurier University Press, 1986. 163–74.

Geoltrain, P. "Les Noces à Cana." *FV* 73 (1974): 83–90.

Gericke, W. "Zur Entstehung des Johannes-Evangeliums." *Theologische Literaturzeitung* 90 (1965): 807–20.

Giblet, J. "*Développements dans la théologie johannique.*" *EJ.* 45–92.

Girard, M. "La structure heptapartite du quatrième évangile." *Studies in Religion/ Sciences Religieuses* 5 (1975–1976): 350–59.

——. "L'unite de composition de Jean 6, au regard de l'analyse structurel." *Église et Theologie* 13 (1982): 79–110.

Glasson, T. F. *Moses in the Fourth Gospel.* SBT 40. Naperville: Allenson, 1963.

Gnilka, J. "Der historische Jesus als der gegenwärtige Christus im Johannesevangelium." *BL* 7 (1966): 270–78.

Gourgues, M. "Cinquante ans de recherche johannique: De Bultmann a la narratologie." In *De Bien des manières: La recherche biblique aux abords du xxie siecle. Lectio Divina* 163. Association Catholique des Ètudes Bibliques au Canada. Paris: Cerf, 1995. 230–306.

Granskou, D. *Anti-Judaism in the Passion Accounts of the Fourth Gospel.* Vol. 1 of *Anti-Judaism in Early Christianity.* Ed. P. Richardson and D. Granskou. Waterloo: Wilfrid Laurier University Press, 1986. 201–16.

Grässer, E. "Die antijudische Polemik im Johannesevangelium." *NTS* 11 (1964): 74–90.

Grelot, P. "Le problème de la foi dans le quatrieme évangile." *Bible et Vie Chrétienne* 52 (1963): 61–71.

Gryglewicz, F. "Das Lamm Gottes." *NTS* 13 (1967): 133–46.

Gundry, R. "'In My Father's House Are Many *Monai*' (John 14:2)." *ZNW* 58 (1967): 68–72.

Gunkel, Herman. *Einleitung in die Psalmen. Göttinger Handkommentar zum Altes Testament.* Göttingen: Vanderhoeck und Ruprecht, 1933.

Haacker, K. *Die Stiftung des Heils. Untersuchungen zur Struktur der johanneischen Theologie.* Stuttgart: Calwer, 1972.

Haenchen, E. "History and Interpretation in the Johannine Passion Narrative." *Int* 24 (1970): 198-219.

———. "Johanneischen Probleme." *Gott und Mensch.* Tübingen: Mohr, 1965. 78-113.

———. *John: A Commentary on the Gospel of John.* Ed. R. W. Funk with U. Busse. Trans. R. W. Funk. 2 vols. Hermeneia. Philadelphia: Fortress, 1984.

———. "'Der Vater, der mich gesandt hat.'" *NTS* 9 (1963): 210-16. Repr. in *Gott und Mensch. Gesammelte Aufsätze 1.* Tübingen: Mohr-Siebeck, 1965. 68-77.

Hahn, F. "Die Jiingerberufung Joh 1, 35-51." *NTK.* 172-90.

Hambly, W. F. "Creation and Gospel. A Brief Comparison of Genesis 1,1-2,12 and John 1,1-2,12." *SE* 5, pt. 2 (1968): 69-74.

Hanson, A. "*Hodayoth* xv and John 17: A Comparison of Content and Form." *Hermathena* 118 (1974): 48-58.

———. "John I. 14-18 and Exodus XXXIV." *NTS* 23 (1976): 90-101.

———. "John's Citation of Psalm LXXXII." *NTS* 11 (1965): 160-62.

———. "John's Citation of Psalm LXXXII Reconsidered." *NTS* 13 (1967): 363-7.

Harner, P. *The "I Am" of the Fourth Gospel.* Facet Books, Biblical Series 26. Philadelphia: Fortress, 1970.

Harvey, A. E. *Jesus on Trial. A Study in the Fourth Gospel.* Atlanta: John Knox, 1977.

Hawkin, D. "The Function of the Beloved Disciple Motif in the Johannine Redaction." *Laval theologique et philosophique* 33 (1977): 135-50.

Heer, J. "Glauben—aber wie?" *Geist und Leben* 46 (1973): 165-81.

Heidegger, M. *Being and Time.* Trans. J. Macquarrie and E. Robinson. New York: Harper & Row, 1962.

Heinz, D. "Kosmos-Men or Men for the Kosmos." *Concordia Theological Monthly* 41 (1970): 360-65.

Heise, J. *Bleiben. Menein in den Johanneischen Schriften.* Tübingen: Mohr, 1967.

Hickling, C. J. A. "Attitudes to Judaism in the Fourth Gospel." *EJ.* 346-54.

Higgins, A. J. B. "The Words of Jesus According to John." *BJRL* 49 (1967): 363-86.

Hill, D. "The Request of Zebedee's Sons and the Johannine *doxa* Theme." *NTS* 13 (1967): 281-85.

Hindley, J. C. "Witness in the Fourth Gospel." *SJT* 18 (1965): 319-37.

Hofbeck, S. *Semeion. Der Begriff des "Zeichens" im Johannesevangelium unter Berücksichtigung seiner Vorgeschichte.* Münster-Schwarzacher Studien 3. Münsterschwarzach: Vier Türme, 1966.

Holwerda, D. E. *The Holy Spirit and Eschatology in the Fourth Gospel.* Kampen: J. H. Kok, 1959.

Hooker, M. "The Johannine Prologue and the Messianic Secret." *NTS* 21 (1974): 40–58.

Hoskyns, E. C. *The Fourth Gospel.* Ed. F. N. Davey. London: Faber, 1940.

Howard, J. K. "Passover and Eucharist in the Fourth Gospel." *SJT* 20 (1967): 330–37.

Howard, W. F. *The Fourth Gospel in Recent Criticism and Interpretation.* Revised by C. K. Barrett. London: Epworth, 1955.

Howton, J. " 'The Son of God' in the Fourth Gospel." *NTS* 10 (1964): 227–37.

Hughes, R. G., and R. Kysar. *Preaching Doctrine for the Twenty-first Century.* Fortress Resources for Preaching. Minneapolis: Fortress, 1997.

Hunter, A. M. *According to John.* Philadelphia: Westminster, 1968.

———. *The Gospel According to John.* Cambridge: Cambridge University Press, 1965.

Ibuki, Y. *Die Wahrheit im Johannesevangelium.* Bonner bibl. Beitr. 39. Bonn: Hanstein, 1972.

Inch, W. "Apologetic Use of 'Sign' in the Fourth Gospel." *Evangelical Quarterly* 42 (1970): 35–43.

Irenaeus. *Against Heresies.* Vol. 1 of *The Anti-Nicene Fathers.* Ed. Alexander Roberts, James Donaldson, and Cleveland Coxe. Trans. Alexander Roberts. American ed. Grand Rapids: Wm. B. Eerdmans, 1956. 315–567.

Janssens, Y. "Une source gnostique du Prologue?" *EJ.* 355–68.

Jaubert, A. *Approches de l'Évangile de Jean.* Coll. Parole de Dieu 13. Paris: Seuil, 1976.

———. "The Calendar of Qumran and the Passion Narrative in John." *JQ.* 62–73.

———. "La comparution devant Pilate selon Jean." *FV* 73 (1974): 3–12.

———. *The Date of the Last Supper.* Staten Island: Alba, 1965.

———. "L'image de la vigne (Jean 15)." *Oik.* 93–99.

Jeremias, J. *The Parables of Jesus.* Rev. Ed. New York: Scribner's, 1963.

Jodock, D. *The Church's Bible: Its Contemporary Authority.* Minneapolis: Fortress, 1989.

Johnson, L. "The Beloved Disciple. A Reply." *ET* 77 (1966): 380.

———. "Who Was the Beloved Disciple?" *ET* 77 (1966): 157–58.

Johnson, L. T. "The New Testament's Anti-Jewish Slander and the Conventions of Ancient Polemic." *JBL* 108 (1989): 419–41.

———. *The Real Jesus. The Misguided Quest for the Historical Jesus and the Truth of the Traditional Gospels.* San Francisco: HarperSanFrancisco, 1996.

Johnson, L. T. *The Writings of the New Testament: An Interpretation.* Philadelphia: Fortress, 1986. 2nd. ed. 1993.

Johnson, N. E. "The Beloved Disciple and the Fourth Gospel." *Church Quarterly Review* 167 (1966): 278–91.

Johnston, G. "The Spirit-Paraclete in the Gospel of John." *Perspective* 9 (1968): 29–37.

———. *The Spirit-Paraclete in the Gospel of John.* SNTSM 12. Cambridge: Cambridge University Press, 1970.

Käsemann, E. "Aufbau und Anliegen des johanneischen Prologs." In *Exegetische Versuche und Besinnungen.* Vol. 2. Göttingen: Vandenhoeck & Ruprecht, 1964. 155–80.

———. *The Testament of Jesus According to John 17.* Trans. Gerhard Krodel. Philadelphia: Fortress, 1968.

Katz, S. T. "Issues in the Separation of Judaism and Christianity After 70 C.E.: A Reconsideration." *JBL* 103 (1984): 44–76.

Keener, C. S. *The Gospel of John.* 2 vols. Peabody: Henrickson, 2003.

Kegley, C. ed. *The Theology of Rudolf Bultmann.* New York: Harper & Row, 1966.

Kellum, S. *The Unity of the Farewell Discourse: The Literary Integrity of John 13.31–16.33.* Journal for the Study of the New Testament Supplement Series 256. Ed. M. Goodacre. London: T & T Clark, 2004.

Kilpatrick, G. D. "What John Tells Us about John." *Stujn.* 75–87.

Kimmelman, R. *Birkat Ha-Minim and the Lack of Evidence for an Anti-Christian Jewish Prayer in Late Antiquity.* Vol. 2 of *Jewish and Christian Self Definition.* Ed. E. P. Sanders. Philadelphia: Fortress, 1981. 226–44.

King, J. S. "The Prologue to the Fourth Gospel: Some Unsolved Problems." *ET* 86 (1975): 372–75.

Kinniburgh, E. "The Johannine 'Son of Man.' " *SE* 4 (1965): 64–71.

Kippenberg, H. G. *Garizim und Synagoge.* Berlin: Walter de Gruyter, 1971.

Kissinger, W. S. *The Parables of Jesus.* American Theological Library Association Bibliography, Series 4. Metuchen: Scarecrow, 1979.

Kitzberger, I. R., ed. *Autobiographical Biblical Criticism: Learning to Read between Text and Self.* Leiden: Deo, 2003.

———, ed. *The Personal Voice in Biblical Interpretation.* London: Routledge, 1999.

Kjärgaard, M. S. *Metaphor and Parable. A Systematic Analysis of the Specific Structure and Cognitive Function of the Synoptic Similes and Parable qua Metaphors.* Acta Theologic Danica; Leiden: Brill, 1986.

Klauck, H.-J. *Allegorie and Allegorese in synoptischen Gleichnistexten.* Neutestamentliche Abhandlungen, N.F. 13. Münster: Aschendorff, 1978.

Klein, C. *Anti-Judaism in Christian Theology.* Philadelphia: Fortress, 1978.

Klein, H. "Die lukanisch-johanneische Passionstradition." *ZNW* 67 (1976): 155–86.

Klos, H. *Die Sakramente im Johannesevangelium.* SB 46. Stuttgart: Katholisches Bibelwerk, 1970.

Koenig, J. *Jews and Christians in Dialogue: New Testament Foundations*. Philadelphia: Westminster, 1979.

Koester, C. R. *Symbolism in the Fourth Gospel: Meaning, Mystery, Community*. Rev. ed. Minneapolis: Fortress, 2002.

Koster, H. "One Jesus and Four Primitive Gospels." *Harvard Theological Review* 61 (1968): 203–47.

Kragerud, A. *Der Lieblingsjünger im Johannesevangelium. Ein exegetischer Versuch.* Oslo: Universitätsverlag, 1959.

Krieger, M. *A Window to Criticism: Shakespeare's Sonnets and Modern Poetics*. Princeton: Princeton University Press, 1964.

Kuhl, J. *Die Sendung Jesu und der Kirche nach dem Johannes-Evangelium*. St. Augustin: Steyler, 1967.

Kuyper, L. J. "Grace and Truth. An Old Testament Description of God and Its Use in the Johannine Gospel." *Int* 18 (1964): 3–19.

Kysar, R. "'As You Sent Me.' Identity and Mission in the Fourth Gospel." *Word and World* 21 (2001): 370–6.

———. "The Background of the Prologue of the Fourth Gospel. A Critique of Historical Methods." *Canadian Journal of Theology* 16 (1970): 250–55.

———. "Community and Gospel: Vectors in Fourth Gospel Criticism." *Int* 21 (1977): 355–66.

———. "The Eschatology of the Fourth Gospel. A Correction of Bultmann's Redactional Hypothesis." *Perspective* 13 (1972): 23–33.

———. *The Fourth Evangelist and His Gospel. An Examination of Contemporary Scholarship*. Minneapolis: Augsburg, 1975.

———. "The Gospel of John in Current Research." *Religious Studies Review* 9 (1984): 314–23.

———. "'He Gave up the Spirit.' A Reader's Reflection on John 19:30b." In *Transcending Bourdaries. Contemporary Readings of the New Testament. Essays in Honor of Francis J. Moloney*. Ed. R. M. Chennattu and M. L. Coloe. Rome: Liberia Ateneo Salesiano, 2005. 161–72.

———. *John*. Augsburg Commentary on the New Testament. Minneapolis: Augsburg, 1986.

———. *John, Epistles of*. Vol. 3 of *The Anchor Bible Dictionary*. Ed. David Noel Freedman. New York: Doubleday, 1992. 900–912.

———. *John, the Maverick Gospel*. Atlanta: John Knox, 1976, 1993.

———. *John's Story of Jesus*. Philadelphia: Fortress, 1984.

———. "Living at the Epicenter: Preaching and Contemporary Biblical Interpretation." *Taproot: Journal of Lutheran Theological Southern Seminary* 14 (1999/2000): 114–53.

———. *Opening the Bible*. Minneapolis: Augsburg, 1999.

Kysar, R. *Preaching John.* Fortress Resources for Preaching. Minneapolis: Fortress, 2002.

——. "The Promises and Perils of Preaching on the Gospel of John," *Dialog* 19 (1980): 215–16.

——. "The Source Analysis of the Fourth Gospel. A Growing Consensus?" *NT* 15 (1973): 134–52. Repr. in *The Composition of the Gospel of John. Selected Studies from Novum Testamentum.* Compiled by D. E. Orton. Brill's Readers in Biblical Studies 2. Leiden: Brill, 1999. 129–47.

——. *Stumbling in the Light: New Testament Images for a Changing Church.* St. Louis: Chalice, 1999.

——. "The Whence and Whither of the Johannine Community." On *Life in Abundance: Studies of John's Gospel in Tribute to Raymond E. Brown,* S.S. Ed. J. R. Donahue. Collegeville, Minn.: Liturgical, 2005. 65–81.

——. *I–II–III John.* Augsburg Commentary on the New Testament. Minneapolis: Augsburg, 1986.

Kysar, R., and J. Webb. *Preaching to Postmoderns: Persectives for Presenting the Message.* Peabody: Henrickson, 2006.

Labahn, M. *Jesus als Lebenspender. Untersuchungen zu einer Geschichte der johanneischen Tradition anhand ihrer Wundergeschichte.* Beihefte zur Zeitschrift für die neutestamentliche Wissenschaft 98. Berlin: Walter de Gruyter, 1999.

Lacomara, A. "Deuteronomy and the Farewell Discourses (Jn 13:31–16:33)." *CBQ* 36 (1974): 65–84.

Làconi, M. "La critica letteraria applicata al IV Vangelo." *Angelicum* (1963): 277–312.

Lamarche, P. "Le Prologue de Jean." *RSR* 52 (1964): 497–537.

Langkamer, P. H. "Zur Herkunft des Logostitels im Johannes-Prolog." *BZ* 9 (1965): 91–95.

Lattke, M. *Einheit im Wort. Die spezifische Bedeutung von agaapē, agapan, und philein im Johannesevanglium.* Studies zum Alt und Neun Testament 41. Munich: Kosel, 1975.

Laurentin, A. "*We-attah-kai nun,* formula charactéristique des texts juridiques et liturgiques Apropos de Jean 18:5." *Bib* 45 (1964): 168–97 and 413–32.

Lazure, N. *Les valeurs morales de la theologie johannique.Évangile et Épîtres.* Paris: Gabalda, 1965.

Le Fort, P. *Les structures de l'eglise militante selon Saint Jean.* Geneva: Labor et Fides, 1970.

Leaney, A. R. C. "The Historical Background and Theological Meaning of the Paraclete." *Duke Divinity School Review* 378 (1972): 146–59.

——. "The Johannine Paraclete and the Qumran Scrolls." *JQ.* 38–61

Leistner, R. *Antijudaismus im Johannesevangelium? TW* 3. Bern: Lang, 1974.

Leon-Dufour, X. "Towards a Symbolic Reading of the Fourth Gospel," *NTS* 27 (1981): 430–56.

Leroy, H. *Rätsel und Missverständnis. Ein Beitrag zur Formgeschichte des Johannesevangeliums.* Bonner Biblische Beiträge 30. Bonn: Hanstem, 1968.

Lightfoot, R. H. *St. John's Gospel: A Commentary.* Oxford: Clarendon, 1956.

Lindars, B. *Behind the Fourth Gospel.* Studies in Creative Criticism 3. London: SPCK, 1971.

——. *The Gospel of John.* New Century Bible. London: Oliphants, 1972.

——. "The Son of Man in the Johannine Christology." *CS.* 43-60.

——. "Traditions Behind the Fourth Gospel." *EJ.* 107-24.

——. "Two Parables in John." *NTS* 16 (1970): 318-29.

——. "Word and Sacrament in the Fourth Gospel." *SJT* 29 (1976): 49-63.

Linnemann, E. "Die Hochzeit zu Kana und Dionysos." *NTS* 20 (1974): 408-18.

Loader, W. *The Christology of the Fourth Gospel.* Beiträge zur biblischen Exegese und Theologie 23. Frankfurt am Main: Lang, 1989.

Locher, G. "Der Geist als Paraklet." *Evangelische Theologie* 26.11 (1966): 565-79.

Lohse, E. *A Commentary on the Epistles to the Colossians and to Philemon.* Hermeneia—A Critical and Historical Commentary on the Bible. Philadelphia: Fortress, 1971.

——. "Wort und Sakrament in Johannesevangelium." *NTS* 7 (1961): 110-25.

Loisy, A. *The Origins of the New Testament.* New York: Macmillan, 1950.

Lona, H. *Abraham in Johannes 8 in Beitrag zur Methodenfrage.* EH 23/65. Frankfurt am Main: Lang, 1976.

Longenecker, R. *The Christology of Early Jewish Christianity.* SBT, Series 2, 17. London: SCM Press, 1970.

Lorenzen, T. *Der Lieblings| jünger im Johannesevangelium. Eine redaktionsgeschichtliche Studie.* SB 55. Stuttgart: Katholisches Bibelwerk, 1971.

MacDonald, J. *The Theology of the Samaritans.* London: SCM Press, 1964.

MacGregor, C. H. C. "The Eucharist in the Fourth Gospel." *NTS* 9 (1963): 111-19.

——. *The Gospel of John.* Moffatt New Testament Commentary. New York: Harper, n.d.

Mack, B. L. *Rhetoric and the New Testament.* GBS.NT. Ed. Dan O. Via, Jr. Minneapolis: Fortress, 1990.

Macquarrie. J. *An Existential Theology: A Comparison of Heidegger and Bultmann.* London: SCM Press, 1955.

MacRae, G. "The Ego-Proclamation in Gnostic Sources." In *The Trial of Jesus. Cambridge Studies in Honour of C. F. D. Moule.* Ed. by E. Bammel, SBT, Series 2, 13. London: SCM Press, 1970. 123-39.

——. "The Fourth Gospel and Religionsgeschichte." *CBQ* 32 (1970): 17-24.

——. "The Jewish Background of the Gnostic Sophia Myth." *NT* 12 (1970): 86-101.

Mahoney, R. *Two Disciples at the Tomb. The Background and Message of John 20: 1-10.* TW 6. Frankfurt am Main: Lang, 1974.

Malina, B. "The Gospel of John in Sociolinguistic Perspective." In *Center for Hermeneutic Studies in Hellenistic and Modern Culture.* Colloquy 48. Ed. H. C. Waetjen. Berkeley: Graduate Theological Union and University of California, Berkeley. 11–17.

Malina, B., and R. L. Rohrbaugh. *Social-Science Commentary on the Gospel of John.* Minneapolis: Fortress, 1998.

Manns, F. *La Vérité vous fera libres. Étude exégétique de Jean 8/31-59.* Studium Biblicum Franciscanum, Analecta 11. Jerusalem: Franciscan, 1976.

Marsh, J. *Saint John.* Pelican Gospel Commentaries. Baltimore: Penguin, 1968.

Martin, J. P. "History and Eschatology in the Lazarus Narrative. John 11:1-44." *SJT* 17 (1964): 332–43.

Martyn, J. L. "Glimpses into the History of the Johannine Community." *EJ.* 150–75.

——. *The Gospel of John in Christian History: Essays for Interpreter.* New York: Paulist, 1978.

——. *History and Theology in the Fourth Gospel.* 3rd ed. The New Testament Library. Ed. C. C. Black, John T. Carrol, and B. Roberts Gaventa. Louisville: Westminster John Knox, 2003.

——. *Source Criticism and Religionsgeschichte in the Fourth Gospel.* Vol. 1 of *Jesus and Man's Hope.* Pittsburgh: Pittsburgh Theological Seminary, 1970. 247–73. Repr. in *The Interpretation of John.* 2nd ed. Ed. J. Ashton. Edinburgh: T&T Clark, 1997. 121–46.

Marxsen, W. *Mark the Evangelist. Studies on the Redaction History of the Gospel.* Trans. J. Boyce, D. Juel, W. Poehlmann, with R. A. Harrisville. Nashville: Abindgon, 1969.

Mastin, B. A. "A Neglected Feature of the Christology of the Fourth Gospel." *NTS* 22 (1975): 32–51.

Mattill, A. J. "Johannine Communities Behind the Fourth Gospel: George Richter's Analysis." *Theological Studies* 38 (1977): 294–315.

McFague, S. *Metaphorical Theology.* Philadelphia: Fortress, 1982.

——. *Models for God.* Philadelphia: Fortress, 1987

——. *Speaking in Parables.* Philadelphia: Fortress, 1975.

McKnight, E. V. *The Bible and the Reader. An Introduction to Literary Criticism.* Philadelphia: Fortress, 1985.

——. *Post-Modern Use of the Bible: The Emergence of Reader-Oriented Criticism.* Nashville: Abingdon, 1988.

——. *What Is Form Criticism.* GBS.NT. Ed. Dan O. Via, Jr. Philadelphia: Fortress, 1969.

McNamara, M. "The Ascension and the Exaltation of Christ in the Fourth Gospel." *Sc* 19 (1967): 65–73.

——. "Logos of the Fourth Gospel and Memra of the Palestinian Targum (Ex 12:42)." *ET* 79 (1968): 115–17.

——. *The New Testament and the Palestinian Targum to the Pentateuch.* AB 27. Rome: Biblical Institute, 1966.

——. *Targum and Testament.* Grand Rapids: Wm. B. Eerdmans, 1972.

McNeil, B. "The Quotation at John XII, 34." *NT* (1977): 22–33.

McPolin J. "Mission in the Fourth Gospel." *Irish Theological Quarterly* 36 (1969): 113–22.

Mead, L. *The Once and Future Church.* Herndon: Alban Institute, 1991.

Mealand, D. "The Language of Mystical Union in the Johannine Writings." *DR* 95 (1977): 19–34.

Meeks, W, A. *"Am I a Jew?"–Johannine Christianity and Judaism.* Vol. 1 of *Christianity, Judaism and Other Greco-Roman Cults. Studies for Morton Smith at Sixty.* Ed. J. Neusner. Leiden: Brill, 1975. 163–86.

——. "The Divine Agent and His Counterfeit in Philo and the Fourth Gospel." In *Aspects of Religious Propaganda in Judaism and Early Christianity.* Ed. E. S. Fiorenza. University of Notre Dame Center for the Study of Judaism and Christianity 2. Notre Dame: University of Notre Dame Press, 1976. 43–67.

——. "Galilee and Judea in the Fourth Gospel." *JBL* 85 (1966): 159–69.

——. "The Man From Heaven in Johannine Sectarianism." *JBL* 91 (1972): 44–72. Repr. in *The Interpretation of John.* 2nd ed. Ed. J. Ashton. Edinburgh: T&T Clark, 1997. 169–206.

——. "Moses as God and King." *RA.* 354–71.

——. *The Prophet-King: Moses Traditions and the Johannine Christology.* SNT 14. Leiden: Brill, 1967.

Meyer, P. W. "A Note on John 10:1-18." *JBL* 75 (1956): 232–35.

Michel, O. "Die Botenlehre des vierten Evangeliums." *Theologische Beiträge* 7 (1976): 56–60.

Minear, P. "The Beloved Disciple in the Gospel of John." *NT* 19 (1977): 105–23.

——. *John, the Martyr's Gospel.* New York: Pilgrim, 1984.

——. "'We Don't Know Where . . .' John 20:2." *Int* 30 (1976): 125–39.

Miranda, J. P. *Die Sendung Jesu im vierten Evangelium. Religions- und theologiegeschichtliche Untersuchungen zu den Sendungsformeln.* SB 87. Stuttgart: Katholisches Bibelwerk, 1977.

——. *Der Vater, der mich gesandt hat. Religionsgeschichtliche Untersuchungen zu den johanneischen Sendungsformeln. Zugleich ein Beitrag zur johanneischen Christologie und Ekklesiologie.* Europäische Hochschulschriften 23. R. Theologie 7. Frankfurt am Main: Lang, 1972.

Moeller, H. "Wisdom Motifs and John's Gospel." *Bulletin of the Evangelical Society* 6 (1963): 93–98.

Moloney, F. J. *Belief in the Word. Reading the Fourth Gospel: John 1–4.* Minneapolis: Fortress, 1992.

——. "The Fourth Gospel's Presentation of Jesus as 'the Christ' and J. A. T. Robinson's Redating." *DR* 95 (1977): 239–53.

——. *The Gospel of John.* Ed. D. J. Harrington, S.J. Sacra Pagina 4. Collegeville, Minn.: Liturgical, 1998.

——. "John 6 and the Celebration of the Eucharist." *DR* 93 (1975): 243–51.

——. *The Johannine Son of Man.* Biblioteca di Scienze Religiose 14. Rome: Libreria Ateneo Salesiano, 1976.

——. "The Johannine Son of Man." *BTB* 6 (1976): 177–89. Repr. in *Salesianum* 38 (1976): 71–86.

——. "Where Does One Look? Reflections on Some Recent Johannine Scholarship." *Salesianum: Periodicum internationale trimestre editum a professoribus Pontificiae Studiorum Universitatis Salesinane–Rome.* Annus 72 (2000): 223–51.

Moore, S. D. *Literary Criticism and the Gospels.* New Haven: Yale University Press, 1989.

——. *Mark and Method: New Approaches in Biblical Studies.* Ed. J. C. Anderson and S. D. Moore. Minneapolis: Fortress, 1992.

Morris, L. *The Gospel According to John.* The New International Commentary on the New Testament. Grand Rapids: Wm. B. Eerdmans, 1971.

——. *The New Testament and the Jewish Lectionaries.* London: Tyndale, 1964.

——. *Studies in the Fourth Gospel.* Grand Rapids: Wm. B. Eerdmans, 1969.

Moule, G. F. D. "The Individualism of the Fourth Gospel," *NT* 5 (1962): 171–74.

——. *The Origin of Christology.* Cambridge: Cambridge University Press, 1977.

Müller, U. "Die Bedeutung des Kreuzestodes Jesu im Johannesevangelium." *Kerygma und Dogma* 21 (1975): 49–71.

——. *Die Geschichte der Christologie in der johanneischen Gemeinde.* SB 77. Stuttgart: Katholisches Bibelwerk, 1975.

——. "Die Parakletenvorstellung im Johannesevangelium." *Zeitschrift für Theologie und Kirche* 71 (1974): 31–77.

Mussner, F. *The Historical Jesus in the Gospel of St. John.* Quaestiones Disputatae 19. London: Burns & Oates, 1967.

——. *Tractate on the Jews.* Philadelphia: Fortress, 1984.

Negoitsa, A., and C. Daniel. "L'Agneau de Dieu est le Verbe de Dieu." *NT* 13 (1971): 24–37.

Neirynck, F. "John and the Synoptics." *EJ.* 73–106.

Neugebauer, F. *Die Entstehung des Johannesevangeliums. Altes und Neues zur Frage eines historischen Ursprungs.* Aufsatx und Vortragen ur Theologie und Religionswissenschaft 43. Stuttgart: Calwer, 1968.

Neyrey, J. H. *An Ideology of Revolt: John's Christology in Social-Science Perspective.* Philadelphia: Fortress, 1988.

Nicholson, G. C. *Death as Departure: The Johannine Descent-Ascent Schema.* SBLD 63. Chico: Scholars, 1983.

Nicol, W. "The History of Johannine Research During the Past Century." *Neo* 6 (1972): 8-18.

——. *The Sēmeia in the Fourth Gospel.* SNT 32. Leiden: Brill, 1972.

Noack, B. *Zur johanneischen Tradition. Beiträge zur Kritik an der literarkritischen Analyse des vierten Evangeliums.* Publication de la Société et des Lettres d'Aarhus, Série théologique 3. Copenhagen: Rosenkilde, 1954.

O'Day, G. *The Gospel of John: Introduction, Commentary, and Reflections.* Vol. 9 of *The New Interpreter's Bible.* Ed. L. Keck. Nashville: Abingdon, 1995. 491-865.

——. *Revelation and Irony in the Fourth Gospel.* Philadelphia: Fortress, 1986.

Odeberg, H. *The Fourth Gospel Interpreted in its Relation to Contemporaneous Religious Currents in Palestine and the Hellenistic-Oriental World.* Uppsala: Almquist & Wiksells, 1929.

O'Grady, J. F. "Individualism and Johannine Ecclesiology." *BTB* 5 (1975): 227-61.

——. "Johannine Ecclesiology: A Critical Evaluation." *BTB* 7 (1977): 36-44.

Olbricht, T. H. "Its Works Are Evil (John 7:7)." *Restoration Quarterly* 7 (1963): 242-44.

Olsson, B. *Structure and Meaning in the Fourth Gospel. A Text-Linguistic Analysis of John 2:1-11 and 4:1-42.* Coniectanea Bibl. N.T., Series 6. Lund: Gleerup, 1974.

O' Rourke, J. "The Historic Present in the Gospel of John." *JBL* 93 (1974): 585-90.

——. "John's Fulfilment Texts." *Sciences Ecclesiastiques* 19 (1967): 433-43.

Ott, H. "Language and Understanding." In *New Theology.* No. 4. Ed. M. Marty and D. Peerman. New York: Macmillan, 1967. 124-46.

Painter, J. *John: Witness and Theologian.* London: SPCK, 1975.

——. *The Quest for the Messiah: The History, Literature and Theology of the Johannine Community.* 2nd ed. Nashville: Abingdon, 1993.

Pancaro, S. *The Law in the Fourth Gospel.* SNT 42. Leiden: Brill, 1975.

——. "'People of God' in St. John's Gospel." *NTS* 16 (1970): 114-29.

——. "The Relationship of the Church to Israel in the Gospel of John." *NTS* 21 (1975): 396-405.

Parker, P. "John the Son of Zebedee and the Fourth Gospel." *JBL* 81 (1962): 35-43.

——. "Two Editions of John." *JBL* 75 (1956): 303-14.

Parkes, J. *The Conflict of the Church and the Synagogue: A Study in the Origins of Anti-Semitism.* New York: World, 1961.

Patrick, G. "The Promise of the Paraclete." *Bibliotheca Sacra* 127 (1970): 333–45.

Patte, Daniel, ed. *Narrative and Discourse in Structural Exegesis. John 6 and 1 Thessalonians.* Semeia 26. Chico: Scholars, 1983.

Perrin, N. *Jesus and the Language of the Kingdom.* Philadelphia: Fortress, 1976.

——. *The New Testament: An Introduction.* New York: Harcourt Brace Jovanovich, 1974.

——. *What Is Redaction Criticism?* GBS.NT. Ed. Dan O. Via, Jr. Philadelphia: Fortress, 1969.

Pesch, R. "'Ihr müsset von oben geboren werden.' Eine Auslegung von Joh 3, 1-12." BL 7 (1966): 208–19.

Peterson, N. *The Gospel of John and the Sociology of Light: Language and Characterization in the Fourth Gospel.* Valley Forge, Penn.: Trinity International, 1993.

Phillips, G. A. "'This is a Hard Saying. Who Can Listen to It?' Creating a Reader in John 6." *Semeia* 26 (1983): 23–56. Ed. D. Patte. Chico: Scholars, 1983.

Plaskow, J. "Anti-Judaism in Feminist Interpretation." *Searching the Scriptures: A Feminist Introduction.* Ed. E. Schüssler Fiorenza. New York: Crossroad, 1997. 117–29.

Plummer, A. *The Gospel According to St. John.* Thornapple Commentaries. 1882. Grand Rapids: Baker, 1981.

Porsch, F. *Pneuma und Wort. Ein exegetischer Beitrag zur Pneumatologie des Johannesevangelium.* FTS 16. Frankfurt am Main: Knecht, 1974.

Porter, J. R. "Who Was the Beloved Disciple?" ET 77 (1966): 213–14.

Powell, M. A. *What Is Narrative Criticism?* GBS.NT. Ed. Dan O. Via, Jr. Minneapolis: Fortress, 1990.

Preiss, T. "Étude sur le chapitre 6 de l'évangile de Jean." *Études théologiques et religieuses* 46 (1971): 144–56.

Price, J. "Light from Qumran upon Some Aspects of Johannine Theology." JQ 9–37.

Proudman, C. L. J. "The Eucharist in the Fourth Gospel." *Canadian Journal of Theology* 12 (1966): 212–16.

Purvis, J. "The Fourth Gospel and the Samaritans." NT 17 (1975): 161–98.

——. *The Samaritan Pentateuch and the Origin of Samaritan Sect.* Harvard Semitic Monogr. 2. Cambridge: Harvard University Press, 1968.

Radermakers, J. "Mission et apostat dans l'évangile johannique." SE 2, pt. 1 (1961): 100–121.

Ramaroson, L. "La structure du prologue de Jean." *Science et Esprit* 28 (1976): 281–96.

Randall, J. F. "The Theme of Unity in John 17: 20–23." ETL 41 (1965): 373–94.

Reim, G. "John IV: 44. Crux or Clue?" NTS 22 (1976): 476–80.

——. "Probleme der Abschiedsreden." BZ 20 (1976): 117–22.

——. *Studien zum Alttestamentlichen Hintergrund des Johannesevangeliums.* SNTSM 22. Cambridge: Cambridge University Press, 1974.

Reinhartz, A. *Befriending the Beloved Disciple: A Jewish Reading of the Gospel of John.* New York: Continuum, 2001.

———. "'Jews' and Jews in the Fourth Gospel." In *Anti-Judaism and the Fourth Gospel: Papers of the Leuven Colloquium.* Ed. R. Bierlinger, D. Pollefeyt, and F. Vandecasteele-Vanneuville. Jewish and Christian Heritage. Series 1. Assen: Van Gorcum, 2001. 341–56.

———. "The Johannine Community and Its Jewish Neighbors: A Reappraisal." In *Literary and Social Readings of the Fourth Gospel.* Vol. 2 of *What Is John?* Ed. F. F. Segovia. SBLSS 7. Ed. G. R. O'Day. Atlanta: Scholars, 1998. 111–38.

———. *The Word in the World: The Cosmological Tale in the Fourth Gospel.* Atlanta: Scholars, 1992.

Ricca, P. *Die Eschatologie des vierten Evangeliums.* Zurich: Gotthelf, 1966.

Richard, E. "Expressions of Double Meaning and Their Function in the Gospel of John." *NTS* 31 (1985): 96–112.

Richter, G. "Die alttestamentlichen Zitate in der Rede vom Himmelsbrot, Joh. 6, 26-51a." *SJe.* 199–265.

———. "Bist du Elias? (Joh 1,21)." *BZ* 6 (1962): 79–92. *BZ* 7 (1963): 63–80. Repr. in *SJe.* 1–41.

———. "Blut und Wasser aus der durchbohrten Seite Jesu (Joh 19, 34b)." *Münchener Theologische Zeitschrift* 21 (1970): 1–21.

———. "Die Deutung des Kreuzestodes Jesu in der Leidensgeschichte des Johannesevangeliums (Jo 13-19)." *BL* 9 (1968): 21–36. Repr. in *SJe.* 58–73.

———. "Die Fleischwerdung des Logos im Johannesevangelium." *NT* 13 (1971): 81–126. *NT* 14 (1972): 257–76. Repr. in *SJe.* 159–98.

———. *Die Fusswaschung im Johannes-Evangelium. Geschichte ihrer Deutung.* Bibl. Untersuch. 1. Regensburg: Pustet, 1967.

———. "Die Fusswaschung Joh 13, 1-20." *Münchener Theologische Zeitschrift* 16 (1965): 13–26.

———. "Die Gefangennahme Jesu nach dem Johannesevangelium, 18, 1-12." *BL* 10 (1969): 26–39.

———. "Ist *en* ein strukturbildendes Element im Logoshymnus Joh 1,1ff?" *Bib* 51 (1970): 539–44. Repr. in *SJe.* 143–48.

———. "Präsentische und futurische Eschatologie im 4. Evangelium." *SJe.* 346–82.

———. "Zum gemeindebildenden Element in den johanneischen Schriften." *SJe.* 383–414.

———. "Zur sogenannten Semeia-Quelle des Johannesevangeliums." *SJe.* 281–87.

———. "Zum sogenannten Taufetext Joh 3,5." *SJe.* 327–45.

———. "Zur Formgeschichte und literarischen Einheit von Joh vi. 31-58." *ZNW* 60 (1969): 21–55.

———. "Zur Frage von Tradition und Redaktion in Joh 1, 19-34." *SJe.* 288–314.

Ricoeur, P. _Essays on Biblical Interpretation_. Ed. L. S. Mudge. Philadelphia: Fortress, 1980.

——. _Figuring the Sacred: Religion, Narrative, and Imagination_. Ed. M. I. Wallace. Trans. D. Pellauer. Minneapolis: Fortress, 1995.

——. _Interpretation Theory: Discourse and the Surplus of Meaning_. Fort Worth: Texas Christian University Press, 1976.

——. "Biblical Hermeneutics." _Semeia_ 4. "Paul Ricoeur on Biblical Hermeneutics" (1975). 29–145.

Riedl, J. _Das Heilswerk Jesu nach Johannes_. Freiburg, Theol. Stud. 93. Freiburg: Herder, 1973.

Riesenfeld, H. "A Probable Background to the Johannine Paraclete." _Ex Orbe Religionum_. Studia Geo Widengren. Numen Suppl. Stud, in the Hist. of Religions 21. Leiden: Brill, 1972. 266–74.

——. "Zu den johanneischen hina-Sätzen." _Studia Theologica_ 19 (1965): 213–20.

Riga, P. "Signs of Glory. The Use of 'Sēmeion' in St. John's Gospel." _Int_ 17 (1963): 402–24.

Rigaux, B. "Die Jünger Jesu in Johannes 17." _Theologische Quartalschrift_ 150 (1970): 202–13.

Ringgren, Helmer. _Israelite Religion_. Trans. D. E. Green. Philadelphia: Fortress, 1966.

Rissi, M. "Die Hochzeit in Kana (Joh 2, 1-11)." _Oik._ 76–92.

——. "Die Logoslieder im Prolog des vierten Evangeliums." _TZ_ 31 (1975): 321–36.

——. "John 1:1-18 (The Eternal Word)." _Int_ 31 (1977): 394–401.

Robinson, B. P. "Christ as a Northern Prophet in St. John." _Sc_ 17 (1965): 104–8.

Robinson, D. W. B. "Born of Water and Spirit. Does John 3:5 Refer to Baptism?" _Reformed Theological Review_ 25.1 (1966): 15–22.

Robinson , J. A. T. "The Destination and Purpose of St. John's Gospel." _NTS_ 6 (1959): 117–31. Repr. in his _Twelve New Testament Studies_. 107–25.

——. _The Human Face of God_. Philadelphia: Westminster, 1973.

——. "The Parable of the Shepherd (John 10:1-5)." Pages 67–75 in his _Twelve New Testament Studies_.

——. _The Priority of John_. London: SCM Press, 1962.

——. _Redating the New Testament_. Philadelphia: Westminster, 1976.

——. _Twelve New Testament Studies_. SBT 34, old series. Naperville: Alec R. Allenson, 1985. 107–25.

——. "The Use of the Fourth Gospel for Christology Today." _CS_. 68–76.

Robinson , J. A. T., and H. Koester. _Trajectories through Early Christianity_. Philadelphia: Fortress, 1971.

Robinson, J. M., ed. _The Nag Hammadi Library in English_. New York: Harper & Row, 1977.

———. "Recent Research in the Fourth Gospel." *JBL* 78 (1959): 242–52.

Rogers, D. G. "Who Was the Beloved Disciple?" *ET* 77 (1966): 214.

Roloff, J. "Der johanneische 'Lieblingsjünger' und der Lehrer der Gerechtigkeit." *NTS* 15 (1968): 129–51.

Ruckstuhl, E. *Chronology of the Last Supper.* New York: Desclee, 1965.

———. "Die johanneische Menschensohnforschung, 1957–1969." In *Theologische Berichte.* Vol. 1. Ed. J. Pfammatter and F. Furger. Zurich: Bensiger, 1972. 171–284.

———. "Johannine Language and Style. The Question of Their Unity." *EJ.* 171–284.

———. *Die literarische Einheit des Johannesevangeliums. Der gegenwärtige Stand der einschlägigen Forschungen.* Studia Friburgensia N.F. 3. Freiburg: Paulus, 1951.

Ruddick, C. T. "Feeding and Sacrifice. The Old Testament Background of the Fourth Gospel." *ET* 79 (1968): 340–41.

Sable, M. "The Arrest of Jesus in Jn 18,1–11 and Its Relation to the Synoptic Gospels. A Critical Evaluation of A. Dauer's Hypothesis." *EJ.* 203–34.

Sanders, J. N. "St. John on Patmos." *NTS* 9 (1963): 75–85.

Sanders, J. N., and B. A. Mastin. *A Commentary on the Gospel According to John.* Harper New Testament Commentary. New York: Harper & Row, 1968.

Sanders, J. T. *The New Testament Christological Hymns.* SNTSM 15. Cambridge: Cambridge University Press, 1971.

Sandmel, S. *Anti-Semitism in the New Testament?* Philadelphia: Fortress, 1978.

———. *A Jewish Understanding of the New Testament.* Cincinnati: Hebrew Union College, 1956.

Sandvik, B. "Joh. 15 als Abendmahlstext." *TZ* 23 (1967): 323–28.

Saunders, E. W. *John Celebrates the Gospel.* Nashville: Abingdon, 1968.

Schirmer, D. *Rechtsgeschichtliche Untersuchungen zum Johannes-Evangelium.* Berlin: Ragnit, 1964.

Schlatter, A. *Der Evangelist Johannes: Ein Kommentar zum vierten Evangelium.* Stuttgart: Calwer, 1960.

Schlier, H. "Glauben, Erkennen, Lieben nach dem Johannesevangelium." *BANT.* 279–93.

———. "Der Heilige Geist als Interpret nach dem Johannesevangelium." *Internationale Katholische Zeitschrift "Communio"* 2 (1974): 97–103.

———. "Johannes 6 und das johanneische Verständnis der Eucharistie." *Das Ende der Zeit.* Freiburg: Herder, 1971. 102–3.

———. "Meditationen über den Johanneischen Begriff der Wahrheit." *BANT.* 272–78.

———. "Der Offenbarer und sein Werk nach dem Johannesevangelium." *BANT.* 254–63.

———. "The Word and Man According to St. John's Gospel." In *The Relevance of the New Testament.* New York: Herder, 1968. 156–71. And *BANT.* 242–53.

Schlier, H. "Zum Begriff des Geistes nach dem Johannesevangelium." *BANT.* 264-71.

——. "Zur Christologie des Johannesevangeliums." In *Das Ende der Zeit: Exegetische Aufsätze und Vorträge.* Vol. 3. Freiburg: Herder, 1971. 85-101.

Schnackenburg, R. "Entwicklung und Stand der johanneischen Forschung seit 1955." *EJ.* 19-44.

——. *The Gospel According to St. John.* Trans. K. Smyth, C. Hastings, F. McDonagh, D. Smith, R. Foley, S.J., and G. A. Kon. 3 vols. New York: Crossroad, 1968, 1980, and 1982.

——. *Das Johannesevangelium.* 4 vols. Freiburg: Herder, 1992.

——. *The Johannine Epistles: Introduction and Commentary.* Trans. R. and I. Fuller. New York: Crossroad, 1992.

——. "Der Menschensohn im Johannesevangelium." *NTS* 11 (1965): 123-37.

——. "On the Origin of the Fourth Gospel." *JMH.* 223-46. And *BZ* 14 (1970): 1-23.

——. "Revelation and Faith in the Gospel of John." *Present and Future. Modern Aspects of New Testament Theology.* Notre Dame: University of Notre Dame Press, 1966. 122-42.

——. "Strukturanalyse von Joh 17." *BZ* 17 (1973): 67-78, 196-202.

——. "Das vierte Evangelium und die Johannesjünger." *Historisches Jahrbuch* 77 (1958): 21-38.

——. "Zur johanneischen Forschung." *BZ* 18 (1974): 272-78.

——. "Zur Rede vom Brot aus dem Himmel. Eine Beobachtung zu Joh 6,52." *BZ* 12 (1968): 248-52.

——. "Zur Traditionsgeschichte von Joh 4, 46-54." *BZ* 8 (1964): 58-88.

Schneider, H. "'The Word Was Made Flesh.' An Analysis of the Theology of Revelation in the Fourth Gospel." *CBQ* 31 (1969): 344-56.

Schneider, J. *Das Evangelium nach Johannes.* Theologischer Handkommentar zum Neuen Testament. Sonderband. Berlin: Evangelische Verlagsanstalt, 1976.

——. "Zur Komposition von Joh 10." *Coniectanea Biblica: New Testament Series* 11 (1947): 220-25.

Schneiders, S. M. *The Revelatory Text: Interpreting the New Testament as Sacred Literature.* San Francisco: HarperSanFrancisco, 1991.

Schnider F., and W. Stenger. *Johannes und die Synoptiker. Vergleich ihrer Parallelen.* Bibl. Handbibl. 9. Munich: Kösel, 1971.

Schottroff, L. *Der Glaubende und die feindliche Welt. Beobachtungen zum gnostischen Dualismus und seiner Bedeutung für Paulus und das Johannesevangelium.* Wissschaftlich Monographie zum Alt und Neun Testament 37. Neukirchen-Vluyn: Neukirchener Verlag, 1970.

———. "Heil als innerweltliche Entweltlichung. Der gnostische Hintergrund der johanneischen Vorstellung vom Zeitpunkt der Erlösung." *NT* 11 (1969): 294-317.

———. "Johannes 4:5-15 und die Konsequenzen des johanneischen Dualismus." *ZNW* 60 (1969): 199-214.

Schulz, S. *Das Evangelium nach Johannes.* Das Neue Testament Deutsch 4. Neues Göttingen Bibelwerk. Göttingen: Vandenhoeck & Ruprecht, 1972.

———. *Die Stunde der Botschaft. Einführung in die Theologie der vier Evangelisten.* Hamburg: Furche, 1976.

———. *Untersuchungen zur Menschensohn-Christologie im Johannesevangelium. Zugleich ein Beitrag zur Methodengeschichte der Auslegung des 4. Evangeliums.* Göttingen: Vandenhoeck & Ruprecht, 1957.

Schurmann, H. "Joh 6, 51c. Ein Schlüssel zur grossen johanneischen Brotrede." *BZ* 2 (1958): 244-62.

Schüssler Fiorenza, E. "The Ethics of Interpretation: De-Centering Biblical Scholarship." *JBL* 107 (1988): 3-17.

Schweizer, E. *Ego eimi. Die religionsgeschichtliche Herkunft und theologische Bedeutung der johanneischen Bildreden. Zugleich ein Beitrag zur Quellenfrage des vierten Evangeliums.* Diss. Basel. FRLANT N.F. 38. Göttingen: Vandenhoeck & Ruprecht, 1939.

———. "Jesus der Zeuge Gottes." *Stujn.* 161-86.

———. "Zum religionsgeschichtlichen Hintergrund der 'Sendungsformel.'" *ZNW* 57 (1966): 199-210.

Scobie, C. H. H. "The Origins and Development of Samaritan Christianity." *NTS* 19 (1973): 390-414.

Scott, B. B. "Essaying the Rock: The Authenticity of the Jesus Parable Tradition." *Foundations and Facets Forum* 2 (1986): 3-53.

———. *Hear Then the Parable: A Commentary on the Parables of Jesus.* Minneapolis: Fortress, 1989.

———. *Jesus, Symbol-Maker for the Kingdom.* Philadelphia: Fortress, 1981.

Segovia, F. F., and M. A. Tolbert, eds. *Social Location and Biblical Interpretation in the United States.* Vol. 1 of *Reading From This Place.* Minneapolis: Fortress, 1994.

———. *Social Location and Biblical Interpretation in Global Perspective.* Vol. 2 of *Reading From This Place.* Minneapolis: Fortress, 1995.

Shaw, A. "The Breakfast by the Shore and the Mary Magdalene Encounter as Eucharist Narratives." *JTS* 25 (1974): 12-26.

———. "Image and Symbol in John 21." *ET* 86 (1975): 12-26.

Shepherd, M. H. "The Jews in the Gospel of John. Another Level of Meaning." *ATR*, suppl. 3 (1974): 95-112.

Shulz, S. *Komposition und Herkunft der johanneischen Reden. Beiträge zur Wissenschaft vom Alten und Neuen Testament.* Stuttgart: Kohlhammer, 1960.

———. *Untersuchungen zur Menschensohn-Christologie im Johannesevangelium.* Göttingen: Vandenhoeck & Ruprecht, 1957.

Siegman, E. "St. John's Use of the Synoptic Material." CBQ 30 (1968): 182–98.

Simonis, A. J. *Die Hirtenrede im Johannes-Evangelium. Versuch einer Analyse von Johannes 10,1–18 nach Entstehung, Hintergrund und Inhalt.* Analecta Biblica 29. Rome: Päpstliches Bibelinstitut, 1967.

Smalley, S. "The Johannine Son of Man Sayings." NTS 15 (1969): 278–301.

———. "The Sign in John XXI." NTS 20 (1974): 275–88.

Smith, D. M., Jr. *The Composition and Order of the Fourth Gospel. Bultmann's Literary Theory.* New Haven: Yale University Press, 1965.

———. *Johannine Christianity: Essays on its Setting, Sources, and Theology.* Columbia: University of South Carolina Press, 1984.

———. *John among the Gospels: The Relationship in Twentieth-century Research.* Minneapolis: Fortress, 1992. 2nd ed. Columbia: University of South Carolina Press, 2001.

———. "Judaism and the Gospel of John." *Jews and Christians: Exploring the Past, Present, and Future* Ed. J. H. Charlesworth. New York: Crossroad, 1990. 76–99.

Smith, M. "Palestinian Judaism in the First Century." In *Israel: Its Role in Civilization.* Ed. M. David. New York: Jewish Theological Seminary, 1956. 67–81.

Smith, R. H. "Exodus Typology in the Fourth Gospel." JBL 81 (1962): 333–39.

Smith, T. C. "The Christology of the Fourth Gospel." *Review and Expositor* 71 (1974): 19–30.

———. *Jesus in the Gospel of John.* Nashville: Broadman, 1969.

Snyder, G. F. "John 13:16 and the Anti-Petrinism of the Johannine Tradition." *Biblical Research* 16 (1971): 5–15.

Spiro, A. "Stephen's Samaritan Background." In *The Acts of the Apostles.* AnB 31. Rev. W. F. Albright and C. S. Mann. New York: Doubleday, 1967. 285–300.

Spongheim, P. *Faith and the Other: A Relational Theology.* Minneapolis: Fortress, 1993.

Staley, J. L. *Reading with a Passion: Rhetoric, Autobiography, and the American West in the Gospel of John.* New York: Continuum, 1995.

———. *The Print's First Kiss: A Rhetorical Investigation of the Implied Reader in the Fourth Gospel.* SBLD 82. Atlanta: Scholars, 1988.

———. "Stumbling in the Dark, Reaching for the Light: Reading Character in John 5 and 9." *Semeia* 53 (1991): 55–80.

Stanton, Graham, ed. *The Interpretation of Matthew.* Issues in Religions and Theology 3. London: SPCK, 1983.

Stauffer, E. "*Agnostos Christos*: Joh. ii. 24 und die Eschatologie des vierten Evangeliums." In *The Background of the New Testament and Its Eschatology. In Honour of Charles Harold Dodd.* Ed. W. D. Davies and D. Daube. Cambridge:
Cambridge University Press, 1964. 281-99.

Stemberger, G. "'Er kam in sein Eigentum.' Das Johannesevangelium im Dialog
mit der Gnosis." *Wort und Wahrheit* 28 (1973): 435-52.

———. *La symbolique du bien et du mal selon Saint Jean.* Paris: Seuil, 1970.

Stendahl, Krister. *The School of Matthew and Its Use of the Old Testament.* Philadelphia: Fortress, 1968.

Stibbe, M. W. G. *John as Storyteller: Narrative Criticism and the Fourth Gospel.*
SNTSM 73. Cambridge: Cambridge University Press, 1992.

———. *John: Readings.* A New Biblical Commentary. Sheffield: JSOT, 1993.

———. *John's Gospel.* New York: Routledge, 1994.

Strand, K. A. "John as Quartodeciman. A Reappraisal." *JBL* 84 (1965): 251-58.

Sturch, R. L. "Jeremias and John: Parables in the Fourth Gospel," *ET* 89 (1978):
235-38.

Talbert, C. H. "The Myth of a Descending-Ascending Redeemer in Mediterra-
nean Antiquity." *NTS* 22 (1976): 418-39.

———. *Reading John: A Literary and Theological Commentary on the Fourth Gospel and
the Johannine Epistles.* New York: Crossroad, 1992.

———. *What Is a Gospel? The Genre of the Canonical Gospels.* Philadelphia: Fortress,
1977.

Teeple, H. *The Literary Origin of the Gospel of John.* Evanston: Religion and Ethics
Institute, 1974.

———. "The Oral Tradition that Never Existed," *JBL* 89 (1970): 56-61.

Temple, S. *The Core of the Fourth Gospel.* London: Mowbrays, 1975.

Theological Dictionary of the New Testament. Ed. G. Kittel and G. Friedrich. Ed. and
trans. G. W. Bromily. 10 vols. Grand Rapids: Wm. B. Eerdmans, 1968.

Thompson, J. M. "The Composition of the Fourth Gospel," *Expositor* 11 (1916):
34-36.

Thompson, M. M. *The Humanity of Jesus in the Fourth Gospel.* Philadelphia: Fortress, 1988.

Thussing, W. *Erhöhung und Verherrlichung Jesu im Johannesevangelium.* Münster:
Aschendorff, 1966.

Thyen, H. "Aus der Literatur zum Johannesevangelium." *Theologische Rundschau*
39 (1974): 222-52, 289-330. Repr. in *Theologische Rundschau* 42 (1977):
211-70.

———. "Entwicklungen innerhalb der johanneischen Theologie und Kirche im
Spiegel von Joh 21 und der Lieblingsjüngertexte des Evangeliums." *EJ.*
259-99.

Tillich, P. *Dynamics of Faith.* New York: Harper & Row, 1957.

Tillich, P. "Religious Symbols and Our Knowledge of God." *The Christian Scholar.* 38 (1955): 189–97.

——. *Systematic Theology.* 3 vols. Chicago: University of Chicago Press, 1951.

Traets, C. *Voir Jésus et le Père en lui selon l'Évangile de Saint Jean.* Rome: Pontificiae Universitatis Gregorianae, 1967.

Tragan, P.-R. *La parabole dur "Pasteur" et ses explications: Jean 10,1–18. La genèse, les milieux littéraires.* Studi Anselmiana 67. Rome: Editrice Anselmiana, 1980.

Tremel, Y.-B. "Le Fils l'homme selon Saint Jean." *LV* 12 (1963): 65–92.

Trudinger, P. "The Prologue of John's Gospel. Its Extent, Content, and Intent." *The Reformed Theological Review* 33 (1974): 11–17.

——. "The Seven Days of Creation in St. John's Gospel: Some Further Reflections." *The Evangelical Quarterly* 44 (1972): 154–58.

Turner, G. A. "The Date and Purpose of the Gospel of John." *Bulletin of the Evangelical Theological Society* 6 (1963): 82–85.

Untergassmair, F. G. *Im Namen Jesu. Der Namensbegriff im Johannesevangelium. Eine exegetisch-religionsgeschichtliche Studie zu der johanneischen Namensansage.* Forschungen zur Bibel 13. Stuttgart: Katholisches Bibelwerk, 1974.

Van Belle, G. *De Sèmeia-bron in het Vierde Evangelie.* Studiorum Novi Testamenti Auxilia 10. Leuven: Universitaire Pres, 1975.

Van Boxel, P. "Die präexistente Doxa Jesu im Johannesevangelium." *Bijdragen* 34 (1973): 268–81.

Van Hartingsveld, L. *Die Eschatologie des Johannesevangelium.* Assen: Van Gorcum, 1962.

Van der Horst, P. W. "The *Birkat Ha-Minin* in Recent Research." *ET* 105 (1994): 367–68.

Van Iersel. "Tradition und Redaktion in Joh 1:19-36." *NT* 5 (1962): 265–66.

Van Unnik, W. C. "The Purpose of St. John's Gospel." *SE* 1 (1959): 382–411.

Vanhoye, A. "Interrogation johannique et exégèse de Cana (Jn 2,4)." *Bib* 55 (1974): 157–67.

——. "Notre foi, oeuvre divine, d'après le quatrième évangile." *NRT* 86 (1964): 337–54.

Vawter, B. "Ezekiel and John." *CBQ* 26 (1964): 451–54.

Vellanickal, M. *The Divine Sonship of Christians in the Johannine Writings.* AB 72. Rome: Biblical Institute, 1977.

Venetz, H.-J. "Zeuge des Erhöhten. Ein Exegetischer Beitrag zu Joh 19, 31-37." *Freiburger Zeitschrift für Philosophie und Theologie* 23 (1976): 81–111.

Via, Dan O., Jr. *The Parables: Their Literary and Existential Dimension.* Philadelphia: Fortress, 1967.

Vincent, M. R. *The Epistles to the Philippians and to Philemon.* The International Critical Commentary on the Holy Scriptures of the Old and New Testaments. Ed. S. R. Driver, A. Plummer, and C. A. Briggs. Edinburgh: T&T Clark, 1897.

Vouga, F. *Le cadre historique et l'intention théeologique de Jean.* Beauchesne Religions. Paris, France: Beauchesne, 1977.

von Rad, Gerhard. *Old Testament Theology.* Trans. D. M. G. Stalker. 2 vols. New York: Harper & Row, 1962.

von Wahlde, U. C. *The Earliest Version of John's Gospel: Recovering the Gospel of Signs.* Wilmington: Glazier, 1989.

———. "The Johannine 'Jews': A Critical Survey." *NTS* 28 (1982): 33–60.

———. "A Redactional Technique in the Fourth Gospel." *CBQ* 38 (1976): 520–33.

Walker, R. "Jüngerwort und Herrenwort. Zur Auslegung von Joh 4:39-42." *ZNW* 57 (1966): 49–54.

Walter, L. *L'incroyance des croyants selon saint Jean.* Lire la Bible 43. Paris: Cerf, 1976.

Weise, M. "Passionswoche und Epiphaniewoche im Johannesevangelium. Ihre Bedeutung für Komposition und Konzeption des vierten Evangeliums." *Kerygma und Dogma* 12 (1966): 48–62.

Wengst, Klaus. *Bedrängte Gemeinde und verherrlichter Christus.* Biblisch Theologische Studien 5. Neukirchen-Vluyn: Neukirchener Verlag, 1981.

Wennemer, K. "Theologie des 'Wortes' im Johannesevangelium. Das innere Verhältnis des verkündigten Logos theou zum persönlichen Logos." *Scholastik* 38 (1963): 1–17.

Wheelwright, P. *Metaphor and Reality.* Bloomington: Indiana University Press, 1962.

Whitacre, R. A. *Johannine Polemic: The Role of Tradition and Theology.* SBLD 67. Chico: Scholars, 1982.

Whittaker, J. "A Hellenistic Context for John 10:29." *Vigiliae christianae* 24 (1970): 241–60.

Wilckens, U. "Der eucharistische Abschnitt der johanneischen Rede vom Lebensbrot (Joh 6,51c-58)." *NTK.* 220–48.

Wilcox, M. "The 'Prayer' of Jesus in John XI. 41b-42." *NTS* 24 (1977): 128–32.

Wilder, A. *Jesus' Parables and the War of Myths: Essays on Imagination in the Scriptures.* Philadelphia: Fortress, 1982.

———. *The Language of the Gospel: Early Christian Rhetoric.* New York: Harper, 1964.

Wilkens, W. "Das Abendmahlszeugnis im Johannesevangelium." *Evangelische Theologie* 18 (1958): 354–70.

———. *Die Entstehungsgeschichte des vierten Evangeliums.* Zollikon: Evangelischer Verlag, 1958.

Wilkens, W. "Die Erweckung des Lazarus." *TZ* 15 (1959): 22–39.

——. "Evangelist und Tradition im Johannesevangelium." *TZ* 16 (1960): 81–90.

Wilkens, W. *Zeichen und Werke. Ein Beitrag zur Theologie des 4. Evangeliums in Erzählungs- und Redestoff.* Abhandlungen zur Theologie des Alten und Neuen Testaments 55. Zurich: Zwingli, 1969.

Wilkinson, J. "The Incident of the Blood and Water in John 19.34." *SJT* 28 (1975): 149–72.

——. A Study of Healing in the Gospel of John. *SJT* 20 (1967): 442–61.

Williams, F. E. "The Fourth Gospel and Synoptic Tradition—Two Johannine Passages." *JBL* 86 (1967): 311–19.

Wind, A. "Destination and Purpose of the Gospel of John." *NT* 14 (1972): 26–69.

Wink, W. *The Bible in Human Transformation: Toward a New Paradigm for Biblical Study.* Philadelphia: Fortress, 1972.

Winter, S. C. "Little Flags. The Scope and Reconstruction of the Signs Gospel." In *Jesus in the Johannine Tradition.* Ed. R. T. Fortna and T. Thatcher. Louisville: Westminister John Knox, 2001. 219–35.

Woll, B. *Johannine Christianity in Conflict.* SBLD 60. Chico: Scholars, 1981.

Woodhouse, H. G. "The Paraclete as Interpreter." *Biblical Theology* 18 (1968): 51–53.

Worden, T. "The Holy Eucharist in St. John." *Sc* 15 (1963): 97–103. Repr. in *Sc* 16 (1964): 5–16.

Yamauchi, E. *Pre-Christian Gnosticism. A Survey of Proposed Evidences.* Grand Rapids: Wm. B. Eerdmans, 1973.

Yee, G. A. *Ideological Criticism.* Vol. 1 of *Dictionary of Biblical Interpretation.* Ed. J. H. Hayes. 2 vols. Nashville: Abingdon, 1999. 535–37.

Zimmermann, H. "Christushymnus und johanneischer Prolog." *NTK.* 249–65.

Index of Scripture References

8:58	84, 150	12:37-38	62
9:1-41	62, 168	12:37	61
9:13-17	156	12:42	93, 149 150, 153,
9:13-16	149		240, 241
9:18	149, 156	12:46	232
9:22-23	67	12:47-48	24
9:22	93, 148, 150, 152,	12:48	20, 113, 126
	240, 241	13:1-17	139, 140
9:39	19, 21, 113	13:2	229
9:40-41	149, 168, 173	13:19	84
9:40	149–74	13:27	229
10:1-42	85, 137	13:31f.	80
10:1-18	81, 145, 149,	14:1ff.	49, 115
	161–82, 197	14:2ff.	91
10:1-15	155	14:3	20
10:19-20	173	14:5	234
10:19	174	14:6	150
10:24	149	14:15-17	85
10:28	12	14:18	20
10:30	124	14:26	85
10:31-39	148	14:28	20
10:31	148	14:31	53
10:34	150	15:1-27	20, 85, 137
10:40-42	62, 67	15:12	222
11:1-44	62, 67, 241	15:18–16:15	115
11:5	105	15:26-27	85
11:8	148	16:1-33	20
11:19	149	16:1-4	47
11:31	149	16:2	93, 150, 153, 240,
11:36	149		241, 259 n.1
11:45	149	16:3	232
11:46-53	149	16:7-14	85
11:54	149	16:18-19	16:49
11:55	68, 148	17:1-26	90, 121, 127, 136,
11:57	149		154, 233
12:1-8	71	17:6	47
12:9	149	17:8	113
12:10-11	149, 241	17:24	12, 15, 122
12:13	156	18:3	149, 150
12:17	149	18:12	150
12:23f.	80	18:14	149
12:31	20, 24	18:19ff.	150
12:32	45, 215	18:31	150
12:34	39	18:37	132, 150
12:35	98	18:38-40	150

Index of Names